Strategic Marketing in Practice
2004–2005

The Chartered
Institute of Marketing

Strategic Marketing in Practice 2004–2005

ELSEVIER
BUTTERWORTH
HEINEMANN

AMSTERDAM BOSTON HEIDELBERG LONDON NEW YORK OXFORD
PARIS SAN DIEGO SAN FRANCISCO SINGAPORE SYDNEY TOKYO

Elsevier Butterworth-Heinemann
Linacre House, Jordan Hill, Oxford OX2 8DP
200 Wheeler Road, Burlington, MA 01803

First published 2004

British Library Cataloguing in Publication Data
A catalogue record for this book is available from the British Library

Library of Congress Cataloguing in Publication Data
A catalogue record for this book is available from the Library of Congress

ISBN 0 7506 6195 X

For information on all Elsevier Butterworth-Heinemann publications
visit our website at http://books.elsevier.com

Typeset by Integra Software Services Pvt. Ltd, Pondicherry, India
www.integra-india.com
Printed and bound in Italy

Contents

Preface
welcome to the
CIM coursebooks

The CIM has been working behind the scenes for several years to launch the new Professional Postgraduate Diploma in Marketing. As a result four new modules have been introduced (Marketing Analysis and Evaluation, Strategic Marketing Decisions, Marketing Performance and Strategic Marketing in Practice). The Strategic Marketing in Practice module is still based on a major case study. However, now this is a closed book examination and there is an allowance for pre-prepared analyses. This paper encompasses the multidisciplinary nature of marketing, drawing on a range of concepts studied at the Stage 1, Stage 2 and Stage 3 levels of the CIM qualifications. The paper is a test of the requisite skills in marketing as well as an in-depth and contemporary knowledge of marketing. The emphasis of this book is very much on developing a 'balanced' marketing individual who is both practically adept at marketing but one who can also interweave this skill with sound theory and innovative ideas.

Professor Ashok Ranchhod, BSc, MSc, MBA, PhD, FCIM, Chartered Marketer
Senior Assessor, Strategic Marketing in Practice

About the Author

Ashok Ranchhod is Faculty Professor in Marketing at Southampton Business School. Ashok has published extensively on e-marketing in Journals such as the *International Journal of Advertising* and the *Journal of Information Technology*.

He has undertaken consultancy work for major organisations and has written case studies on companies in several different sectors of industry for the Chartered Institute of Marketing. Prior to his work in academia, he was the managing director of a small biotechnology company based in Derbyshire.

In addition to the published papers he has received prizes for his papers at the Academy of Marketing and The British Academy of Management. Currently his research is into e-commerce and the marketing of biotechnology companies. He leads a team of research students. Ashok is a Senior Examiner for the Chartered Institute of Marketing (CIM) and is a Visiting Professor at the University of Angers in France. He is also a Fellow of the Chartered Institute of Marketing. He has generated substantial research funds for the Business School.

An introduction from the academic development advisor

In the last two years we have seen some significant changes to the CIM Professional Series initiated by the Chartered Institute of Marketing. The changes have been introduced on a year-on-year basis, with Stage 1 (Certificate) changes implemented in 2002, and the Stage 2 (Advanced Certificate in Marketing) being implemented last year in 2003, and in September of 2004 the Stage 3 (Postgraduate Diploma) changes will be implemented. These changes are very significant and focus much more on the strategic aspects of marketing management.

As a result the authoring team, Elsevier/Butterworth-Heinemann and I have all aimed to rigorously revise and update the coursebook series to make sure that every title is the best possible study aid and accurately reflects the latest CIM syllabus.

The revisions to the series this year include continued development at Stage 1 – Certificate in Marketing and Stage 2 – Advanced Certificate in Marketing, and complete rewrites at the Stage 3 – Postgraduate Diploma in Marketing level to align with the radical overhaul of the CIM syllabus. In particular we have aimed to develop the assessment support to include some additional support for the assignment route as well as the examination, so we hope you will find this helpful.

There are a number of new authors and indeed Senior Examiners in the series who have been commissioned for their CIM course teaching and examining experience, as well as their research into specific curriculum-related areas and their wide general knowledge of the latest thinking in marketing.

We are certain that you will find these coursebooks highly beneficial in terms of the content and assessment opportunities and a study tool that will prepare you for both CIM examinations and continuous/integrative assessment opportunities. They will guide you in a logical and structured way through the detail of the syllabus, providing you with the required underpinning knowledge, understanding and application of theory.

The editorial team and authors wish you every success as you embark upon your studies.

Karen Beamish
Academic Development Advisor

About MarketingOnline

Elsevier/Butterworth-Heinemann offers purchasers of the coursebooks free access to MarketingOnline (www.marketingonline.co.uk), our premier online support engine for the CIM marketing courses. On this site you can benefit from:

- o   Tutorials on key topics every two weeks during the term and every month during the holidays, provided by Marketing Knowledge, a global provider of online marketing and management qualifications.
- o   Fully customizable electronic versions of the coursebooks enabling you to annotate, cut and paste sections of text to create your own tailored learning notes.
- o   The capacity to search the coursebook online for instant access to definitions and key concepts.
- o   Useful links to e-marketing articles, provided by Dave Chaffey, Director of Marketing Insights Ltd and a leading UK e-marketing consultant, trainer and author.

○ A glossary providing a comprehensive dictionary of marketing terms.
○ A Frequently Asked Questions (FAQs) section providing guidance and advice on common problems or queries.

Using MarketingOnline

Logging on

Before you can access MarketingOnline you will first need to get a password. Please go to www.marketingonline.co.uk and click on the registration button where you will then find registration instructions for coursebook purchasers. Once you have got your password, you will need to log on using the onscreen instructions. This will give you access to the various functions of the site.

MarketingOnline provides a range of functions, as outlined in the previous section, that can easily be accessed from the site after you have logged on to the system. Please note the following guidelines detailing how to access the main features:

1. *The coursebooks* Buttons corresponding to the three levels of the CIM marketing qualification are situated on the home page. Select your level and you will be presented with the coursebook title for each module of that level. Click on the desired coursebook to access the full online text (divided up by chapter). On each page of text you have the option to add an electronic bookmark or annotation by following the onscreen instructions. You can also freely cut and paste text into a blank word document to create your own learning notes.

2. *The tutorials* To access the tutorials click on the link for any of the coursebook levels and underneath the coursebook titles you will see a list of the tutorials available from Marketing Knowledge. Simply click on the links provided to access each individual tutorial.

3. *E-marketing articles* To access the links to relevant e-marketing articles simply click on the link under the text 'E-marketing Essentials: useful links from Marketing Insights'.

4. *Glossary* A link to the glossary is provided in the top right hand corner of each page enabling access to this resource at any time.

If you have specific queries about using MarketingOnline then you should consult our fully searchable FAQs section, accessible through the appropriate link in the top right hand corner of any page of the site. Please also note that a **full user guide** can be downloaded by clicking on the link on the opening page of the website.

Change in CIM qualification titles from 2004

Please note that from 2004 CIM are changing the qualification titles, and there may be instances throughout the book where the old titles have been used. The old and new titles are therefore listed below for your information.

Old title	New title
Certificate in Marketing (Stage 1)	Professional Certificate in Marketing
Advanced Certificate in Marketing (Stage 2)	Professional Diploma in Marketing
Postgraduate Diploma in Marketing (Stage 3)	Professional Postgraduate Diploma in Marketing

unit 1

introduction

Introduction

The marketing strategy in practice is part of the new Stage 3 that has been developed at the Chartered Institute of Marketing. It replaces the old Analysis and Decision paper. It carries many of the same hallmarks, but the format is now slightly different and students are expected to prepare analyses before the examination. The examination will also now be a *Closed Book Examination*. It is likely that this will be the final paper that students studying for CIM qualifications undertake. It requires students to have a good knowledge of all the subjects covered at all levels. It is particularly important that candidates have a good knowledge of subject areas at Stage 1, Stage 2 and Stage 3. The assessment constitutes questions based on a major case study. For this reason, there is no specific syllabus for this paper and much of the rationale for this module lies in developing suitable outcomes for candidates considering a career in marketing. It is expected that candidates will have passed the other Stage 3 (Postgraduate Diploma) modules, marketing analysis and evaluation. strategic marketing decisions and managing marketing performance. Each of these modules covers a wide array of marketing topics that are important for a thorough understanding of marketing at higher levels. The paper requires the application of all or parts of the marketing knowledge and experience that students would have gained over several years.

As the title of the paper 'Strategic Marketing in Practice' suggests, candidates need to be able to *apply* their marketing knowledge and skills to a real-life case study. Also, as in real life, candidates are expected to analyse the case study prior to the examination and to utilize this analysis in their answers. For this reason, good analytical and implementation skills within a marketing context are required. Marketers always need to have good analytical capabilities in order to develop marketing strategies. Once these strategies have been developed, clear and sensible decisions need to be made. Candidates need to be conversant with all aspects of marketing, especially contemporary issues. Cases are by their very nature set in different sectors, have different contexts and require knowledge from different areas of marketing. Marketing problems are rarely neatly packaged. Candidates, therefore, have to have the capability to draw from their wealth of experience and knowledge and also to demonstrate flexibility and creativity by being able to tackle problems in a variety of contexts set in a variety of sectors in different areas of the globe. As we enter the new millennium, marketing is undergoing many changes and marketers need to be able to develop a range of skills. The module sits within the overall Stage 3 Scheme as outlined below:

	Entry modules	Research and analysis	Planning	Implementaion	Management of marketing
Stage 3	Entry module – Stage 3	Analysis and evaluation	Strategic marketing decisions	Managing marketing performance	Strategic marketing in practice
Stage 2	Entry module – Stage 2	Marketing research and information	Marketing planning	Marketing communications	Marketing management in practice
Stage 1		Marketing environment	Marketing fundamentals	Customer communications	Marketing in practice
Introductory Certificate	Supporting marketing processes (research and analysis, planning and implementation)				

Marketing drives the business agenda

Marketing is a set of activities concerned with creating value for shareholders and other stakeholders by creating and capturing exceptional value for customers. Marketers are the people, business as well as marketing professionals, who make decisions about marketing.

Research undertaken to support the development of this syllabus found that organizations expect professional marketers to take increasing ownership for the whole customer experience. This requires them to become more aware of the operational business agenda, more commercial, more strategic and more innovative. They have to develop an even deeper understanding of customers and take a more integrated approach to marketing, both internal and external. This syllabus is an early step in equipping strategic marketers of the future to fulfil these expectations. Professional marketers in publicly quoted or limited companies have to:

- o *Focus on the long term* The focus for marketing is the generation of economic profit (operating adjusted for the cost of capital invested in a business or activity), which is how shareholders measure value. While other business functions can maximize economic profit through efficiency, marketing is the only way to create value. Marketing typically creates three times more value than other functions.

- o *Create and capture value for customers* Marketers create value by increasing the value perceived by customers in an organization's products and services. The key is positioning which, in today's competitive markets, requires deeper insights (into customers' needs and behaviours) and innovation. By increasing perceived value, marketers create the opportunity for premium pricing through which economic profit is increased.

- o *Take charge of the business agenda* Marketing uses its activities and assets (such as brands and relationships) to create customer value. At the same time, these activities and the use of the marketing assets generate results which are consolidated with other financial results and reported. Shareholders measure the value that the business has created for them as the sum of dividends paid and the increase in price of the shares they own. Marketing has to take charge of investment in marketing assets and all the marketing activities that create value. In short, they must take charge of the business agenda.

'Models' of marketing

The type, or 'model', of marketing practised in any organization depends on a number of factors, not least of which are the nature of the business context and the organization's dominant orientation. Marketing activities in organizations can be grouped broadly into four models:

- ○ *Sales support*   The emphasis in this model is essentially reactive: marketing supports the direct sales force. It may include activities such as telesales or telemarketing, responding to inquiries, coordinating diaries, customer database management, organizing exhibitions or other sales promotions, and administering agents. These activities usually come under a sales and marketing director or manager. This form of marketing is common in SMEs and some organizations operating in a B2B context.

- ○ *Marketing communications*   The emphasis in this model is more proactive: marketing promotes the organization and its product/service at a tactical level, either to customers (pull) or to channel members (push). It typically includes activities such as providing brochures and catalogues to support the sales force. Some B2C organizations may use marketing to perform the 'selling' role using direct marketing techniques and to manage campaigns based on a mix of media to raise awareness, generate leads and even take orders. In B2B markets, larger organizations may have marketing communications departments and specialists to make efficient use of marketing expenditures and to coordinate communications between business units.

- ○ *Operational marketing*   The emphasis in this model is for marketing to support the organization with a coordinated range of marketing activities including market research, brand management, product development and management, corporate and marketing communications, and customer relationship management. Given this breadth of activities, planning is also a function usually performed in this role but at an operational or functional level. Typically part of FMCG or B2C organizations, the operational marketing role is increasingly used in B2B organizations.

- ○ *Strategic marketing*   The emphasis in this model is for marketing to contribute to the creation of value and competitive customer strategy. As such, it is practised in customer-focused and larger organizations. In a large or diversified organization, it may also be responsible for the coordination of marketing departments or activities in separate business units. Strategic marketing decisions, when not made by professional marketers, are taken by business leaders.

Professional marketers are likely to be responsible for strategic marketing only in those organizations with a strong market (note, not necessarily *marketing*), or customer, orientation or with separate marketing departments in business units that require coordination. In organizations with a weak customer orientation (typically those with a production, sales, product or technology orientation), the role of marketing is likely to be limited to one of sales support or marketing communications.

Marketing contexts

Organizations operating in a variety of contexts use different marketing activities. There is no 'one size fits all' approach. Organizations and their marketers have to select and use techniques appropriate to their specific context. Typically marketing contexts are summarized as:

Context	Characteristics
FMCG	Used in organizations with a strong market orientation, the 'standard' model of marketing is based on identification of customers' needs and techniques of segmentation, targeting and positioning supported by branding and customer communications
B2B	The model of marketing adopted depends on factors such as the importance of face-to-face selling, the dominant orientation and power of buyers. Markets are often less information-rich than FMCG markets, which constrains marketing decisions
Capital projects	A variant of the B2B model where opportunities for positioning are few and the value of any single order constitutes a significant proportion of turnover in a period
Not-for-profit	The organization is not driven by shareholder value and competition may not be a significant factor in strategy
SMEs	Operating in any of the above sectors, SMEs are characterized by their limited marketing resources and the limited use of marketing techniques

Not-for-profit organizations are driven not by shareholders but by other stakeholders, such as government (public sector), beneficiaries (charities) and volunteers (voluntary sector). The concept of shareholder value may not be relevant in these organizations where instead concepts such as 'best value' (public sector) and the level of disbursements to beneficiaries operate. The element of competition may not be explicit in the strategy of these organizations, whose strategies may be more collaborative. Such organizations may use a narrower and more tactical repertoire of marketing techniques than larger commercial organizations with a strong market orientation and driven by shareholder value. It is important, therefore, that students studying the SMIP paper can explore the application of marketing in a range of different contexts utilizing the syllabi from the various linked modules and also drawing from current Contemporary Issues in Marketing.

Strategic marketing activities

The full spectrum of strategic marketing activities is illustrated in the statements of marketing practice on which the syllabi of the three modules linked to the summative SMIP module. They include:

- o Research and analysis.
- o Strategy making and planning.
- o Brand management.
- o Implementing marketing programmes.
- o Measuring effectiveness.
- o Managing marketing teams.

It goes without saying that strategic marketing operates in a global context. This is not to say that the syllabus has nothing to offer the organization pursuing a domestic strategy or entering its first foreign market. Even if an organization is not operating across borders, it is likely to be working in a market in which competitors based in other countries are operating – in other words, a global context. Throughout this syllabus, the term 'global context' embraces domestic and international activities as well as true global activities of the largest organizations.

Plans and planning processes

The planning processes used in organizations are typically geared to the annual operating and financial reporting cycle. In those organizations in which annual or longer term plans are produced, these plans are usually at three levels:

- o Corporate level.
- o Business level.
- o Functional level.

Marketing contributes to corporate and business plans and develops its own functional plan at an operational level. In organizations with strong strategic management practices (often those with a strong customer orientation), plans are likely to contain the strategies of the organization or business. In organizations where plans are effectively 'budgets', strategy is unlikely to be explicit. It is therefore important to recognize that:

- o The terms 'strategy' and 'plan' may not be the same.
- o Strategy making and planning may be different processes in organizations.
- o Organizations approach strategy formulation in a range of formal and informal ways.

What is sometimes referred to as the 'strategic marketing plan' can take different forms in different organizations. For example:

- o It may be the name given to the plans that coordinate the marketing activities of the different businesses or units throughout an organization.
- o It may be synonymous with the term 'business plan' or 'corporate plan' in an organization with a strong customer focus or responsibility only for marketing products made elsewhere and bought in.
- o It may simply be the name given to the marketing plan, which specifies the objectives or targets, activities, resources and budgets of the marketing function.

However, it should be recognized that the majority of organizations do not produce a strategic marketing plan. The major plans that specify and control the organization's strategy are corporate or business plans, into which strategic marketing should have an input.

The role of strategic marketing

In organizations where strategic marketing does not exist as a function, the process or decisions are still undertaken by senior managers or business leaders. Where it is an explicit function, the strategic marketing role will usually be performed by a marketing function in a business unit and by a corporate level marketing function, which may also have responsibility for coordinating the activities of marketing departments in business units.

The primary role of strategic marketing is to identify and create value for the business through strongly differentiated positioning. It achieves this by influencing the strategy and culture of the organization in order to ensure that both have a strong customer focus. When this role is carried out by a marketing specialist, it is called 'marketing director' or 'strategic marketing manager', sometimes based in a department called 'marketing' rather than 'strategic marketing'. Strategic marketers should champion the customer experience and exert a strong influence on the organization to adopt a customer orientation, contribute along with other directors and senior managers to its competitive strategy, align the organization's activities to the customer, and manage the organization's marketing activities.

During strategy formulation, strategic marketing is about choices that customer-focused organizations make on where and how to compete and with what assets. It is also about developing a specific competitive position using tools from the marketing armoury including brands, innovation, customer relationships and service, alliances, channels and communications, and increasingly price. Strategic marketing does not own the business strategy but, like other departments and functions, should contribute to it and control the operational levers that make a strategy effective. However, marketing has an exceptional contribution to make in identifying opportunities and determining ways to create value for customers and shareholders.

During implementation, strategic marketing is the 'glue' that connects many aspects of the business. It will often manage one or a portfolio of brands. Increasingly, it works with HR to ensure that the culture and values in the organization are consistent with the brand and to ensure that marketing competencies are part of the overall framework for staff development across the business. Strategic marketing also has responsibility for directing the implementation of marketing activities needed to execute the organization's strategy. Other key tasks of strategic marketing in today's organizations are:

- o Contributing to strategic initiatives being undertaken by the organization, for example marketing input to a 'due diligence' evaluation of a prospective merger or acquisition. In some cases, strategic marketers will be managing multi-disciplinary teams.
- o Coordinating and managing customer information across the organization within the data protection and privacy legislation. This involves close relationships with the IT function.
- o Developing and driving the business case for investment in brands, new products and services.
- o Championing and developing innovation and entrepreneurship within the organization.
- o Ensuring that the marketing function is appropriately skilled and resourced.
- o Providing input with finance on the valuation of brands for reporting and disclosure.

This concept of strategic marketing draws heavily on the theory and practice of strategic management, not just of marketing. This is an important distinction since strategic marketing is as much a part of directing how the organization competes as it is a part of marketing itself. Professional marketers engage in relationships with most functions within the organization and are 'business people' rather than 'technical marketers'. This is particularly so at the strategic level. It requires participants at this level to embrace a wider range of management theory and practice than has been the case in the past. In addition to traditional marketing theory, strategic marketing also embraces:

- o Business and corporate strategy.
- o Investment decisions.
- o Culture and change management.

o   Quality management.
o   Programme and project management.

Marketers still have an essential role to play in contributing their specialist marketing skills to the formulation, implementation and control of strategy. These specialist marketing skills are of vital importance to organizations.

The syllabus at Stage 3 has been divided into four modules:

o   *Analysis and evaluation*   Covers the concepts, techniques and models involved in developing a detailed understanding of the market, customers and competitive environment externally and internally; the organization, its capabilities and assets, the opportunities available to it and its current performance.

o   *Strategic Marketing decisions*   Covers the concepts, techniques and models involved in formulating a customer-focused competitive business or corporate strategy and developing a specific and differentiated competitive position. It includes investment decisions affecting marketing assets.

o   *Managing marketing performance*   Covers the implementation stage of the strategy. This encompasses managing marketing teams, managing change, implementing strategy through marketing activities and working with other departments, and using measurement as the basis for improvement.

o   *Strategic marketing in practice*   Provides the opportunity to explore strategic marketing in a practical setting. It also incorporates the latest trends and innovations in marketing. This module will draw on all the preceding modules and their syllabi.

Figure 1.1 Strategic marketing in practice and links with the other modules at Stage 3

Aims and outcomes for strategic marketing in practice

In coming to understand the range of outcomes that are defined for SMIP it is useful to consider the range of skills that students will be expected to exhibit in this module. This is indicated in Table 1.1

Table 1.1

Key skill unit: personal skills development	Analysis and evaluation	Strategic marketing decisions	Managing marketing performance	Strategic marketing in practice
Communication				
Interpret and evaluate information	✓	✓		✓
Synthesize and structure information	✓	✓		✓
Present information	✓	✓		✓
Problem solving				
Select and use strategies to solve problems		✓		✓
Establish what is needed to get results		✓		✓
Monitor progress		✓	✓	✓
Working with others				
Gain commitment			✓	✓
Brief others			✓	✓
Lead implementation			✓	✓

Aim

Marketing has to be firmly rooted in both theory and practice. Practice informs theory and vice versa. The Strategic Marketing in Practice module is designed to allow participants to put strategic marketing into practice. As the final module at Stage 3, it not only builds on the knowledge and skills developed in all the preceding modules, but also looks for an overall competence in marketing that encompasses all the various subject areas covered in Stages 1 and 2. As marketing is constantly evolving, continuously informed by both academic and business research, one of the aims of this module is to explore the latest trends and innovations relevant to marketers who are operating at a strategic level within organizations. One of the other aims is to understand marketing as an activity, which is important in all contexts (profit, not-for-profit, societal, global). It is expected that participants undertaking this module will be able to add value to both their marketing experience and marketing knowledge. This module therefore does not have a specific syllabus and draws from all the preceding modules and syllabi.

Related statements of practice

Ad.1 Define intelligence requirements and lead the intelligence gathering process.
Ad.2 Develop a detailed understanding of the organization and its environment.
Bd.1 Promote a strong market orientation and influence/contribute to strategy formulation and investment decisions.
Bd.2 Specify and direct the marketing planning process.

Cd.1 Promote organization-wide innovation and cooperation in the development of brands.
Cd.2 Distil the essence of brands and direct/coordinate a portfolio of brands.
Dd.1 Develop and direct an integrated marketing communications strategy.
Dd.2 Lead the implementation of the integrated marketing communications strategy.
Ed.1 Promote corporate-wide innovation and cooperation in the development of products and services.
Ed.2 Direct and maintain competitive product/service portfolios.
Fd.1 Promote the strategic and creative use of pricing.
Fd.2 Lead the implementation of the strategic and creative use of pricing.
Gd.1 Select and monitor channel criteria to meet the organization's need in a changing environment.
Gd.2 Direct and control support to channel members.
Hd.1 Promote and create a customer orientation and infrastructure for customer relationships.
Hd.2 Direct and control information and activities that deliver customer relationships and service.
Jd.1 Establish and maintain a project management framework in line with strategic objectives.
Jd.2 Direct and control the delivery of programmes and projects.
Kd.1 Establish and promote the use of metrics to improve marketing effectiveness.
Kd.2 Create a system of critical review and appraisal to inform future marketing activity.
Ld.1 Provide professional leadership and develop a cooperative environment to enhance performance.
Ld.2 Promote effective cross-functional working linked to brands and the integration of marketing activities.
Ld.3 Promote and create an environment for career and self-development.
Ld.4 Contribute to organizational change and define and communicate the need for change within the department.

Learning outcomes

Participants will be able to:

9.64.1 Identify and critically evaluate marketing issues within various environments, utilising a wide variety of marketing techniques, concepts and models.
9.64.2 Assess the relevance of, and opportunities presented by, contemporary marketing issues within any given scenario including innovations in marketing.
9.64.3 Identify and critically evaluate various options available within given constraints and apply competitive positioning strategies, justifying any decisions taken.
9.64.4 Formulate and present a creative, customer-focused and innovative competitive strategy for any given context, incorporating relevant investment decisions, appropriate control aspects and contingency plans.
9.64.5 Demonstrate an understanding of the direction and management of marketing activities as part of the implementation of strategic direction, taking into account business intelligence requirements, marketing processes, resources, markets and the company vision.
9.64.6 Promote and facilitate the adoption and maintenance of a strong market and customer orientation with measurable marketing metrics.
9.64.7 Synthesize various strands of knowledge and skills from the different syllabus modules effectively in developing an effective solution for any given context.

9

Knowledge and skill requirements

There is no formal specification of knowledge and skills requirements for this module. Participants are required to demonstrate a full understanding of, and to satisfy the knowledge and skills requirements specified in, the syllabus modules at Stages 1, 2 and 3. The emphasis in this module is more on applying the knowledge and practical skills acquired in the previous modules. The essential skills assessed as part of this module are:

o Analysis, interpretation, evaluation and synthesis of information, including the ability to draw conclusions.
o Identification, exploration and evaluation of strategic options.
o Selection and justification of an appropriate option using decision criteria.
o Establishing the activities, resources and schedule needed to implement the chosen strategy.
o Working with others to implement and control the strategy.

Participants will be expected to demonstrate their awareness of current issues and an ability to make recommendations for a given context. From time to time CIM will publish a list of trends and innovations to guide tutors and participants in their preparation for assessment. Participants will be expected to read widely in the area of strategic marketing as part of their studies at this level.

The links with other syllabi

The syllabus aims of the three modules within Stage 3 are as shown below. They provide a link with key skills and show the linkage between the learning outcomes for each module and the Statements of Marketing Practice. All these are linked to the outcomes for SMIP as indicated.

1. Contribute research and insights to inform strategic marketing decisions. This encompasses:

   o Identifying the organization's business intelligence requirements.
   o Understanding organizational culture and its consequences for strategy.
   o Developing and synthesizing a detailed understanding of an organization's customers, internal and external environments and its current business performance from the relevant stakeholders' perspectives.

2. Influence strategic decisions in an organization to create value for customers and other stakeholders. This encompasses:

   o Contributing specialist marketing input to strategic decisions to achieve competitive advantage and customer preference.
   o Influencing decisions within the organization concerning priorities for marketing activities and investment in marketing assets.
   o Promoting a strong market orientation and consistency with the values of the brand.

3. Manage and measure marketing activities undertaken as part of the implementation of a customer-focused strategy. This encompasses:

   o Evaluating the techniques available to organizations for integrating teams and activities across the organization.
   o Identifying the barriers to effective implementation of strategies and plans and developing measures to prevent or overcome them and effect change.

○ Explaining techniques for managing a marketing team, including assessing the organization's need for marketing skills and resources and developing strategies for acquiring, developing and retaining them.
○ Initiating and critically evaluating systems for control of marketing activities.

4. Formulate, present and justify a creative, customer-focussed and innovative strategy for any given context. This encompasses:

○ Identifying and critically evaluating relevant marketing issues and opportunities, including trends and innovations in marketing and business.
○ Identifying and critically evaluating the various options available to achieve the desired goal(s).

Points to ponder

○ Marketing as a subject area is undergoing major changes. These changes are taking place as a result of dramatic shifts in technology demographics, globalization, systems of production, logistics and ecological issues. The papers, therefore are designed to reflect more of these contemporary issues in addition to the knowledge base mentioned above.

○ The case studies will also be designed to develop strategic marketing issues which can be operationalized and implemented within realistic constraints. It is often forgotten that marketing is not just about positioning and growth, but also about effectiveness within given constraints within most organizations. These constraints mean that strategies have to be sensibly evaluated and chosen with hard decisions being made. When particular strategies are chosen, it is clear that the constraints could be many and varied. Constraints, for instance, could be financial, organizational (both employee and culture related), marketing (image, size of markets, branding, distribution systems, networks) and if, the organization is a division of a larger entity, headquarter imposed constraints.

Globalization

○ The rapid changes in technology are far reaching as they are changing the normal paradigms of marketing. The four Ps cannot now be discussed with certainty. The nature and direction of marketing strategies necessarily have to take into account the massive computing power available and the new developments on the Web. Many multi-nationals have operated globally for decades, but technology is changing the patterns of production and consumption.

○ For instance, global brands are available anywhere and production facilities may be located in a myriad of different countries. For smaller companies, locked into local markets, the Internet holds the promises and pitfalls of operating in a global arena.

○ The introduction of the euro means that pan-European marketing strategies have to be thought through in a different manner. The changing nature and the growth of South Asian markets has an enormous impact on the marketing strategies of organizations. The nature and strength of the American market is often forgotten. The case studies will reflect these changes and will embrace many different sectors of industry.

Organizational issues

o When developing marketing strategies it is important that the culture and nature of the organization is taken into account. Marketing strategies often succeed and fail as a result of inappropriate personnel, inappropriate structures or climates within organizations. Success or failure of strategies can be defined by utilizing a number of different performance measures such as market share growth, return on investment, brand awareness and sales growth among others. Organizations are therefore always striving to create the appropriate structures and develop appropriate cultures to meet the demands of the market place.

o The customer is king and marketing strategists have to place the level of market orientation at the centre of their thinking.

Sustainability

o With the growing problems related to the general environmental deterioration and the increasing concern over climatic changes, the issues surrounding sustainability are of critical importance to marketers. Marketing literature has for long been concerned with growth and market share. It is important that issues surrounding the constraints imposed by the environment are taken into account. The world is facing an enormous challenge in terms of the availability of resources and the needs of the population.

Constraints

o In some respects a challenge posed to marketing strategists is the need to consider constraints and responsibility. Constraints can be financial (Biocatalysts case) or related to the human resource capabilities of an organization. In many instances constraints can be imposed by the external environment and these are particularly important for the growth of a company's markets (Acclaim case study).

Financial issues

o Financial issues will always play a key role in developing strategies. A good knowledge of basic financial statements such as P & L accounts, Balance Sheets and Cashflow statements is required.

Knowledge of contemporary marketing issues

o Each case is different and will therefore test some knowledge of contemporary issues. Students therefore need to be encouraged to read journal articles pertaining to the case study.

Application of previous knowledge

o The need to apply models for analysis will continue. However, a more critical approach in applying these techniques will be needed. The paper will reflect the need for both academic and practical knowledge, as true marketers need to have experience in both areas for developing sensible strategies.

Issues of implementation and control

o An awareness of the clear decision-making and implementation strategies will be tested. As will be strategic positioning, innovation and branding in the context of implementation and control.

o Formulating an appropriate strategy, incorporating investment decisions, control aspects and contingency plans.

Assessment methodology for the module

o Students will receive a case study – normally between 30–60 pages (including company/industry data) four weeks prior to the examination date.

o The examination on the case study will be a closed book examination, however, students will be allowed to bring in six pages of prepared analysis and a copy of their case study which may also be annotated. The examination questions will remain unseen until the start of the examination.

o The marking scheme will allocate 25 per cent of marks for the six pages of prepared analysis as follows:

   o 10 per cent awarded for originality and appropriateness of analysis in the context given.
   o 15 per cent awarded for appropriate application of analysis within the questions.

Guidelines for pre-prepared work

Candidates chosen for the pilot study should be given the following advice:

a. Write or print pre-prepared analysis on **six** pages. Examiners will be looking for tables, diagrams and key issues. Tables such as SWOT, though helpful, do not show deep analytical thought.
b. If candidates use the available sheets for writing 'crib' material, such as models or plans they will penalize themselves, as there will be less space for good analysis that counts towards the final marks.
c. The diagrams should be clearly visible and the writing should be clearly legible. Typing should be no less than font size 11.
d. Data given within the case should be analysed clearly and effectively.
e. All the work should be on CIM paper which will be issued two weeks before the examination.
f. Please note that it will be totally unacceptable for students to present standardized group analysis/appendices and they will therefore be penalized accordingly.

During the examination

a.   The answers should reflect the use of the pre-prepared material as necessary. When writing answers candidates should cross reference the work to guide the examiner to a particular table or chart or piece of analysis.

b.   Examiners do not expect students to use ALL the pre-prepared material to augment their answers. Obviously, they should only use whatever is necessary for answering the questions as set.

c.   Candidates should attach the pre-prepared work as an appendix. **All papers must be hole punched and include the student registration and centre number.**

d.   Please note that Fifteen marks are allocated **for the application** of the pre-prepared work.

e.   **Only the pre-prepared analysis can be taken into the examination room, therefore no textbooks, journals or other pre-prepared work will be allowed.**

Summary

This chapter gives you an idea of the marketing skills that SMIP module aims to develop and test. It also shows that learning outcomes are more important than specific syllabus regurgitation. In order to reach the desired outcomes, students need to be able to critically assess and absorb the key concepts in the other areas of the Postgraduate Diploma, Stage 3, and their applications to real marketing problems. When studying previous cases students should attempt to list the key outcomes that they have achieved, together with some of the key skills that they have used in order to reach a satisfactory level of competence.

unit 2
what is meant by case study analysis?

Outcomes

Relationship to outcomes

o Identify and critically evaluate marketing issues within various environments, utilizing a wide variety of marketing techniques, concepts and models.

o Identify and critically evaluate various options available within constraints and apply competitive positioning strategies, justifying any decisions taken.

Candidates should also be familiar with the Analysis and Evaluation module and the Strategic Marketing Decisions syllabi.

A brief overview

A case study is an account of the major events taking place in a business within an industry sector over a number of years. A case usually features many of the key events in that it chronicles the events that have been dealt with and have to be dealt with by marketing managers. Issues pertaining to the competitive environment, changes in the business definition and the main areas of the served market segments have to be dealt with by marketing managers.

Cases give students a chance to understand some of the problems faced by organizations and be able to analyse them in detail.

Cases allow students to utilize their understanding of key concepts. Their meaning is made clearer when applied to case studies. Theory and concepts help to analyse a company's situation. Analysing a case requires great powers of deduction. Facts and figures are often hidden in the different areas of the case. The conceptual tools help to probe the case and gather evidence of events. In the real world, it is important to understand that there are no right answers. For most companies strategic marketing management is difficult. Developing strategies is generally an uncertain game, making it more important to develop a careful diagnosis. All that managers can do is to make the best guess.

As different individuals have differing ideas, case studies provide students with the opportunity to participate in class and to learn from others. Tutors often act as facilitators in this process of enquiry and analysis. In actual businesses this is exactly the way decisions are made. It is important therefore, that students can analyse the situation and be confident of their solutions.

Analysing a case study

One of the purposes of the case study is to let you analyse the situation that the company finds itself in. In doing this you will need to apply many of the key concepts that you would have learnt in the other modules. A case study has to be read several times before a clear idea of the key issues can be established. This enables you to establish a picture of the environment in which the company is operating as well as the company's position within it. Eventually based on this analysis you will make a series of decisions to take the company forward into the future. A detailed and effective analysis of a case should include the following:

1. The key historical events that have contributed to the development of the company.
2. A PESTLE analysis, which looks at Political, Economic, Social, Technological, Legal and Environmental issues surrounding the case.
3. A SWOT analysis and its evaluation.
4. Product market analyses and the links to strategic marketing.
5. Any constraints that the company faces from a resource point of view. These could be human, financial, technical or environmental.
6. Any structural features or control systems.
7. A list of key issues that emanate from the above.

The analyses

The key historical events that have contributed to the development of the company

Cases often contain a history of the company. It is important to analyse this history and to list the key critical events that helped to shape the company's development. At the same time an analysis of the history will also offer insights into the evolution of a particular industry as in the case of Acclaim Incorporated. Historical analysis and charting can help in understanding product market decisions and any development and diversification decisions that have been made by the company.

A PESTLE analysis

A PESTLE analysis looks at Political, Economic, Social, Technological, Legal and Environmental issues surrounding the case. Cases will contain some or all of the key PESTLE factors. This type of analysis allows you to understand the macro environment facing the industry sector that the company is immersed in. The Porter five forces framework allows a structured analysis of the environment and the competitive pressures on companies within the industry sector. The PESTLE factors also help to highlight key trends within the markets. Amongst others, these could be

16

demographic profile trends (important in the Clerical Medical case), sociological issues (on GM Foods in Biocatalysts), branding trends in different markets (Philips case). Some of the technological factors may show up the lifecycle stages and any special factors affecting the model (Acclaim case). Analysing each of the factors gives some idea of the opportunities and threats facing a company.

A SWOT analysis and its evaluation

In addition to the PESTLE analysis, a review of the company strengths and weaknesses is required. This is an internal audit of the company allowing you to examine each function in which the company is currently strong or weak. Companies could have a weakness in their branding strategies or new product development, yet may have current products which are well positioned in the market. Is a company in an overall strong position? Can it operate profitably in its current market sectors? How can the company minimize the threats to its position and expand on its opportunities? Can the company turn its weaknesses into strengths? A good SWOT analysis helps you to understand, in a clear and succinct manner, how the company is positioned. As part of this analysis, you may want to use the Porter five forces framework (Figure 2.1).

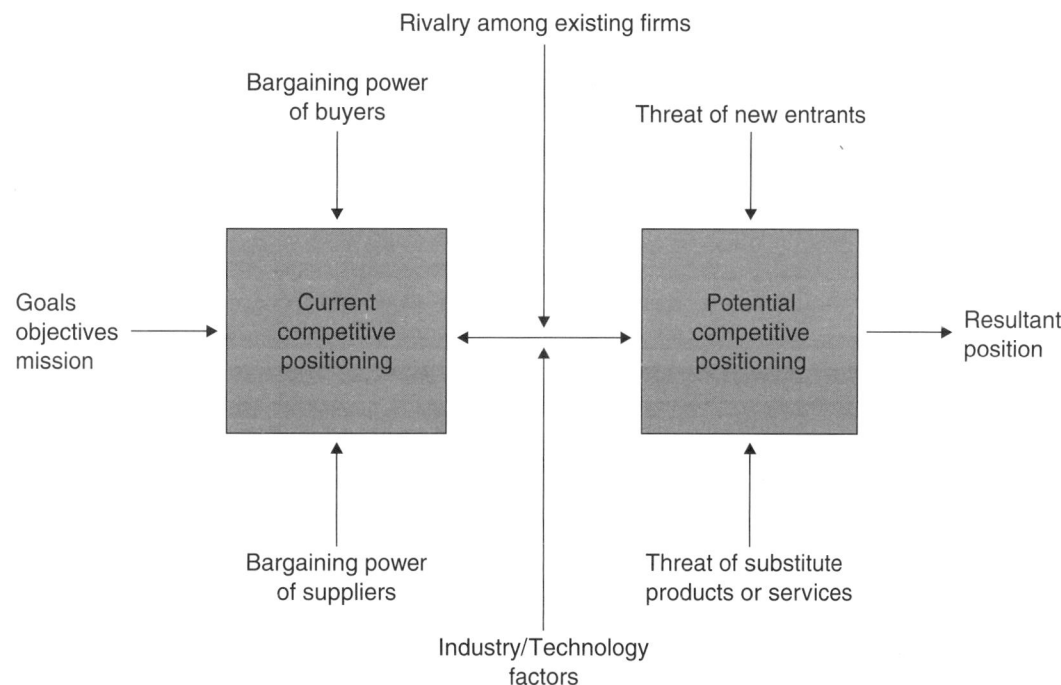

Figure 2.1 Porter framework

Product market analyses and the links to strategic marketing

Following on from the SWOT analysis, an analysis of the products and the markets within which the products and services are sold should be undertaken. This type of analysis will require you to be familiar with the various portfolio models such as the GE Matrix, the BCG matrix, the Ansoff matrix and various other relevant matrices. Below are examples of the expanded Ansoff Matrix (Figure 2.2) and Figure 2.3 shows the Directional Policy Matrix.

Product alternatives

	Present products	Improved products	New products
Existing market	Market penetration	Product variants imitations	Product line extension
Expanded market	Aggressive promotion	Market segmentation product	Vertical diversification
New market	Market development	Market extension	Conglomerate diversification

(left axis label: Options)

Figure 2.2 Growth vector analyses

Company capability			
High	Diversification	Market segmentation	Market leadership innovation
Medium	Saved withdrawal; merger	Maintenance of position; market penetration	Expansion product differentation
Low	Divestment	Imitation; phased withdrawal	Cash generation
	Unattractive	Average	Attractive

Market potential

Figure 2.3 Directional policy matrix

In addition to these you may wish to utilize perceptual maps and consider product positioning from a competitive point of view. Linked to the product/market analysis should be a review of any gaps that the organization faces. These gaps could be:

o **Product line gap** Closing this gap entails completion of a product line, either in width or in depth, by introducing new or improved products.
o **Distribution gap** This gap can be reduced by expanding the coverage, intensity, and exposure of distribution.
o **Usage gap** To increase usage a firm needs to induce current non-users to try the product and encourage current users to increase their usage.
o **Competitive gap** This gap can be closed by making inroads into the market position of direct competitors as well as those who market substitute products.
o **Internationalization gap** This gap can be shortened through exporting, joint venture arrangements and strategic alliances.
o **Communications gap** This gap can be shortened through advertising strategies, PR, or proactive use of the Web.

SPACE analysis

All these analyses can be tied together by using SPACE analysis as discussed by the BCG group. SPACE stands for Strategic Position and Action Evaluation. This analysis is based on the following:

1. The company's Financial Strength (FS).
2. The company's Competitive Advantage (CA).
3. The Industry strength (The strength of the industry sector in which the company operates [IS]).
4. The stability of the environment in which the company operates (ES).

This analysis is based on your ability to analyse key aspects of the case study, pertaining to the company. The analysis depends on answering a range of questions and then taking an average.

Financial strength (FS)

Factors determining financial strength

Return on investment	Low	0	1	2	3	4	5	6	High
Leverage (Debt to equity ratio)	Low	0	1	2	3	4	5	6	High
Liquidity (cash held)	Low	0	1	2	3	4	5	6	High
Capital required/capital available	High	0	1	2	3	4	5	6	Low
Cash flow	Weak	0	1	2	3	4	5	6	Strong
Ease of exit from the market	Difficult	0	1	2	3	4	5	6	Easy
Risk involved in the business	Low	0	1	2	3	4	5	6	High
Other (your own factor)	Low	0	1	2	3	4	5	6	High

Average:

Critical factors and your assessment of this area of the organization

Competitive advantage (CA)

Factors determining competitive advantage

Market share	Low	0	1	2	3	4	5	6	High
Product/Service quality (compared to competitors)	Low	0	1	2	3	4	5	6	High
Product life cycles stages (for range of products/services)	Similar	0	1	2	3	4	5	6	Different
Product/service replacement cycle	Variable	0	1	2	3	4	5	6	Fixed
Customer loyalty	Low	0	1	2	3	4	5	6	High
General utilization of capacity by the competition	Low	0	1	2	3	4	5	6	High
Technological knowledge and competence	Low	0	1	2	3	4	5	6	High
The degree of vertical integration of the company	Low	0	1	2	3	4	5	6	High
Other (your own factor)	Low	0	1	2	3	4	5	6	High

Average $- 6 =$

Suppose the total score comes to 36. This divided by 8 factors $= 4.5$ take away $6 = -1.5$ (So you will get a negative score for this factor)

Critical factors and your assessment of this area of the organization

Industry strength (IS)

Factors determining industry strength

Growth potential	Low	0	1	2	3	4	5	6	High
Profit potential	Low	0	1	2	3	4	5	6	High
Financial stability (within the sector)	Low	0	1	2	3	4	5	6	High
Technological know-how (needed to operate within the sector)	Simple	0	1	2	3	4	5	6	Complex
Resource utilization (generally within the sector)	Poor	0	1	2	3	4	5	6	Good
Capital intensity (requisite capital for operating in the sector)	High	0	1	2	3	4	5	6	Low
Ease of entry into the market	Easy	0	1	2	3	4	5	6	Difficult
Level of productivity and capacity utilization	Low	0	1	2	3	4	5	6	High
Other (your choice of factor)	Low	0	1	2	3	4	5	6	High

Average:

Critical factors determining industry strength:

Environmental stability (ES)

Factors determining environmental stability

Technological Changes	Many	0	1	2	3	4	5	6	Few
Rate of inflation	High	0	1	2	3	4	5	6	Low
Variability of demand	High	0	1	2	3	4	5	6	Low
Price range of competing products	Wide	0	1	2	3	4	5	6	Narrow
Barriers to entry into the market	Few	0	1	2	3	4	5	6	Many
Competitive pressure	High	0	1	2	3	4	5	6	Low
Price elasticity of demand	Elastic	0	1	2	3	4	5	6	Inelastic
Other (a factor of your own choice)									

Average $-6 =$

Again for this assessment, suppose the average is 40, this divided by $8 = 5$. Then $5 - 6 = -1$ (a negative figure)

The key critical factors that determine environmental stability.

Your analysis should then be plotted on the following axes in order to determine the strategic position of the company under question.

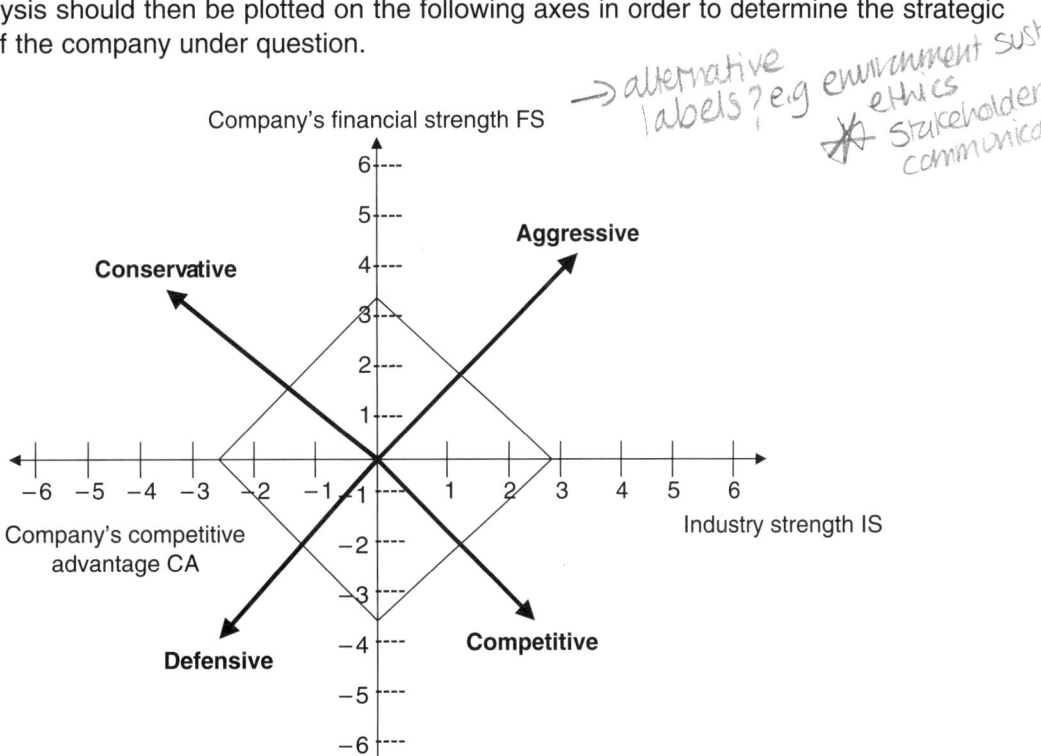

Figure 2.4 Strategic position and action evaluation space matrix

Once this analysis is done, you can plot the actual position of the company by just getting two points (one for the X axis and one for the Y axis). This can be easily obtained by adding CA and

IS (you will either get a negative point or a positive point) and adding FS and ES (you will either get a negative point or a positive point). These two points will then determine the overall quadrant in which the company will fall.

The implications for falling within particular sectors are these: (always remember that this exercise should be quite objective and be based on as much real information that you can obtain as possible. Like any other real life analysis you may also have to make certain assumptions).

(For all the examples it is assumed that the company positions are in the middle of each quadrant)

1. *Aggressive posture*   In this quadrant, a company is set within an attractive industry which faces little environmental turbulence. The company enjoys a good competitive advantage which it can protect with good financial strength. As this sector is attractive, it is likely to attract new entrants. The company needs to protect its position through acquisitions, by increasing market share or by extending its lead in specific products and services in which it is the market leader. Companies in this sector have the potential to be cost leaders if they are in an FMCG market.

2. *Competitive posture*   In this quadrant, the industry is attractive and the company enjoys competitive advantage within a turbulent environment. The company needs to acquire financial strength. It needs to do this in order to improve its marketing and improve its product lines. It may also need to reduce costs and protect competitive advantage in a declining market. In such a quadrant, a company may need to look for cash resources either through merger or through being acquired. Companies in this area need to differentiate their product offerings and utilize their marketing skills as much as possible.

3. *Conservative posture*   If a company is positioned within this quadrant, it has a focus on financial stability within a stable market. The chances are that the growth is fairly low. Under such circumstances, a company will need to become competitive in its product or service offering. It may also need to consider investing its cash in entering new attractive markets or offering new competitive products. It may also need to consider pruning its product lines. Companies located in this sector would benefit from a more focused product or service. They may be able to do well in niche markets, organized along geographic lines, product lines or along buyer groups.

4. *Defensive posture*   A company set within this quadrant lacks a competitive product or service. It also has low financial strength and is situated in an unattractive industry sector. Competitiveness is crucial and the company will have to consider retrenchment by pruning its product lines, reducing costs dramatically, cutting capacity and slowing down on any investment. Companies located within this sector are often ripe for turnaround strategies. They can also be relatively defenseless making them easy targets for takeovers. Product strategies probably need to consider 'harvesting' cash cows.

Note: It is important to realize that the SPACE analysis should be used *judiciously* as it may only be *appropriate* for many private sector companies. It may be *inappropriate* for public sector or non-profit sector analysis. Parts of the analysis could be modified for use in different sectors. This, however, will need sound knowledge, creativity and an ability to sensibly translate the basic premise of SPACE to a new sector.

Constraints faced by the company from a resource point of view

Companies face a variety of constraints when developing their strategies. These constraints could be market constraints (size and growth potential of a market), financial constraints (the ability to finance marketing campaigns, foster new product development, cashflow, ability to raise money, etc.), technical (the ability to develop new products, to market products, manage information systems, Web capability) and finally environmental (these could be pollution management capability, or public concerns as in the case of GM Foods in Biocatalysts).

Any structural features or control systems

Analyses should include an understanding of the present structural pattern of the organization and the way in which this contributes to or detracts from developing its marketing strategies. For instance, is there a defined marketing structure? Are there systems for monitoring marketing effectiveness or orientation? Are the systems rigid or flexible?

Key issues

As a result of these analyses, you should be able to list a number of key issues which are facing the company described in the case study. These key issues form a valuable resource when answering the questions set in the examination.

These types of analyses can then be linked to any *strategic plan* that you may have considered developing.

A generalized approach to formulating strategies would probably contain the following:

1. *Statement of the problem* This will contain a situation analysis of the company, its problem areas and its general capability.

2. *Analysis of data*

   o *Industry* This would cover an analysis of the growth potential, SWOT, market structure and competitive pressures.

   o *Product/Service analysis* This would consider areas such as market share, pricing, promotion, new product development, distribution, branding and level of market orientation of the company.

   o *Financial analysis* The financial performance of a company gives guidelines on its profitability, return on investment, shareholder value, liquidity, inventory levels and possible resource requirements for growth (see section on Financial Analysis).

   o *Management* If organization charts are available, any gaps in the marketing structure should be ascertained. Also, issues such as mission, values and objectives should be taken into account.

3. *Generation of options and an evaluation of these* In this section, the options regarding entry into different product/market sectors, strategic alliances, branding strategies, R & D development, internationalization, joint ventures, diversification, vertical or horizontal integration.

4. *Recommendations (Decisions) and strategies* This should be the crucial element of the plan, encompassing key decisions that may be taken, giving reasons for choosing these, understanding the possible reactions to these by competitors and the justifications for these. Resource implications also need to be considered. Clear and decisive objectives must be set.

5. *Implementation, contingency and control* This section should look at how easily the recommendations could be adopted, taking into account resource allocation, cost implications, budgets and timetables. This section should also envisage contingency requirements in case of difficulties regarding implementation strategies. When considering implementation, it is also important to develop monitoring systems for ascertaining the success of the recommended strategies.

Summary

When evaluating a case, it is important to be systematic. Analyse the case in a logical fashion, beginning with the identification of operating and financial strengths and weaknesses and environmental opportunities and threats. Move on to assess the value of a company's current strategies only when you are fully conversant with the SWOT analysis of the company. Ask yourself whether the company's current strategies make sense, given its SWOT analysis. If they do not, what changes need to be made? What are your recommendations? Above all, link any strategic recommendations you may make to the SWOT and GAP analyses. State explicitly how the strategies you identify take advantage of the company's strengths to exploit environmental opportunities, how they rectify the company's weaknesses, and how they counter any of the threats from the PESTLE factors. It is also important that you consider the strategic options that may be available to the organization. Some of the options may not be feasible, suitable or acceptable in the light of the points you will have covered above. Make sure that you outline the strategies that need to be adopted to implement any recommendations that you make. Many company strategies fail as a result of poor implementation or unrealistic expectations of market growth and demand. You therefore have to be aware that your recommendations are sensible and fit the existing resource base and capability of the firm. Remember that this chapter only gives you an indicative and not a comprehensive range of analytical tools. You need to read widely and use other new analytical tools that may be available, including your own ideas. You must also be familiar with all aspects of the syllabi in the other Stage 3 modules. Further ideas are given in Chapter 4. Finally remember that for the SMIP syllabus, you have to prepare analyses *before the examination* (as explained in Unit 1).

unit 3

understanding the direction and management of marketing activities

Outcomes

Demonstrate an understanding of the direction and management of marketing activities as part of the implementation of strategic direction, taking into account business intelligence requirements, marketing processes, resources, markets and the company vision.

Introduction

This outcome knits together a range of different areas of marketing. Marketing is a complex area of business and for successful implementation it is important for marketers to develop strategic direction for an organization, taking into account marketing intelligence in conjunction with company resources and processes. The importance of developing a vision is also very important when developing a strategic focus. This helps an organization to develop a clear direction. Strategy in marketing involves harnessing a company's resources to meet customer needs through market analysis, an understanding of competitor actions, governmental actions and globalization, together with consideration of technological and other environmental changes.

Business Intelligence

The development and organization of Marketing Intelligence Systems has always been an important aspect of marketing. Market Intelligence can be gathered in several ways. Companies can gather information from secondary sources and reports produced by companies such as Mintel and AC Neilson or undertake commission primary research. An example of primary research is provided by the following mini case (taken from a previous CIM Case Study – Titan).

Case study

Titan's Brand Image in India

Over the last five years, consumers have consistently regarded Titan as one of the top Brands in India. In 1998, Titan was regarded as the most admired consumer goods company, in a survey carried out by Advertising Marketing in India. Titan's history in the polls has been outstanding as Tables 3.1 and 3.2 indicate.

Table 3.1 Company rankings over six years in India 1993–1999

Company	1999	1998	1997	1996	1995	1994	1993
FMCG Companies							
HLL	1	1	1	1	1	1	1
Coca-Cola	2	7	9	11	13	16	–
Cadbury	3	8	3	3	6	7	6
Pepsi Foods	4	3	5	4	7	6	11
Colgate	5	9	6	5	4	5	5
Durables' Companies							
Titan	1	1	2	1	1	1	1
BPL	2	2	1	5	3	3	5
Maruti	3	4	5	2	–	–	–
Intel	–	–	–	–	–	–	–
LG Electronics	5	11	–	–	–	–	–

Source: Advertising, Marketing, eCommerce, India

Table 3.2 Most admired durable brands in India 1998/1999

Rank 1999	Rank 1998	Company	Score	Rank 1999	Rank 1998	Company	Score
1	1	Titan	7.96	19	26	Compaq	6.62
2	2	BPL	7.76	20	21	Eureka Forbes	6.6
3	4	Maruti	7.55	21	24	Carrier Aircon	6.51
4	–	Intel	7.47	22	9	Ericsson	6.5
5	11	LG Electronics	7.39	23	12	Philips	6.5
6	7	Godrej-GE	7.13	24	15	Modi Xerox	6.43
7	3	MRF	7.07	25	29	Videocon	6.41
8	13	Bajaj Auto	7.05	26	23	Chloride India (Exide)	6.38
9	13	Hero Honda	6.96	27	20	HCL Infosystems	6.22
10	5	Asian Paints	6.95	28	21	LML	6.16
11	24	Hewlett-Packard	6.9	29	27	Mahindra and Mahindra	6.1
12	18	Samsung	6.82	30	31	Hero Cycles	6.07
13	18	Whirlpool	6.81	31	33	Onida	5.93
14	15	TVS Suzuki	6.79	32	17	Bausch and Lomb	5.92
15	6	Nokia	6.78	33	30	Goodlass Nerolac	5.86
16	–	Telco	6.67	34	9	Motorola	5.85
17	–	Infosys	6.63	35	8	Baron International	5.82
17	28	Wipro Infotech	6.63	36	32	Blow Past	5.61

Source: Advertising, Marketing, eCommerce, India

In 1999, the Advertising and Marketing Survey was carried out by IMRB, along the same lines as the previous seven years, in order to maintain continuity and establish the survey's validity in enabling comparisons with previous years. The surveys were carried out exclusively among professional marketers in companies marketing fast moving consumer goods (FMCG) and durables. Respondents were drawn from all levels and conducted in the major cities of Delhi, Calcutta, Chennai and Bangalore. The company received top positions when the following questions were asked:

1. Products are designed to meet customer needs (7.88).
2. Products are different from competitors (7.25).
3. Better than average at new product launches (7.59).
4. Brands provide long-term stability (7.52).
5. Products are market leaders (7.91).
6. Products are innovative (number 2 slot) (7.32).
7. Products are consistently superior to competitors (7.51).
8. Products offer value for money (7.66).
9. Company's marketing personnel are of high calibre (7.20).
10. Company's advertising is consistently superior (number 2 slot) (7.53).
11. Company keeps in touch with market constantly (7.4).
12. Company has a superior distribution network (7.78).
13. Provides good after sales service (number 2 slot) (7.43) (figures in brackets are scores out of 10).

As can be seen, Titan retained its leadership position. Working in its favour was its product launches into new segments, including the Dash! Range for children. In 2000, an Economic Times survey of top Indian companies revealed that Titan was regarded as the top brand in India, ahead of all FMCG companies. A consumer brand is much more than a bundle of tangible and intangible benefits. For this particular survey, seven attributes were considered:

1. The quality of the brand.
2. Value for money.
3. The future of the brand.
4. Distinctiveness.
5. Uniqueness.
6. The feelings that the brand evokes amongst the consumer.
7. How inclined the consumers were to purchase the brand.

The target audience for the survey were, chief wage earners, housewives and young adults between the ages of 15–45 years belonging to the A/B/C households in urban India. In general, the brands are less well known in rural India. A ten-point scale was applied and a total of 3164 interviews were conducted, in the following locations – Mumbai (537), Delhi (520), Calcutta (423), Chennai (409), Rajkot (345), Allahabad (300), Cuttack (300) and Vijayavada (330). The brand received such success because it appeals to the youth segment and is aspirational. Titan in India is also known for its classy elegance, while being a popular mass-market brand with a strong presence at the lower end. The brand is regarded as 'mass with class' by brand consultants. It is a brand that is also equally popular with both men and women. The company is consistent in its brand expenditure and spends, on average, around Rs 25/30 crores on brand building. Although this is small compared to others within the top 10, the amount spent appears to be highly effective.

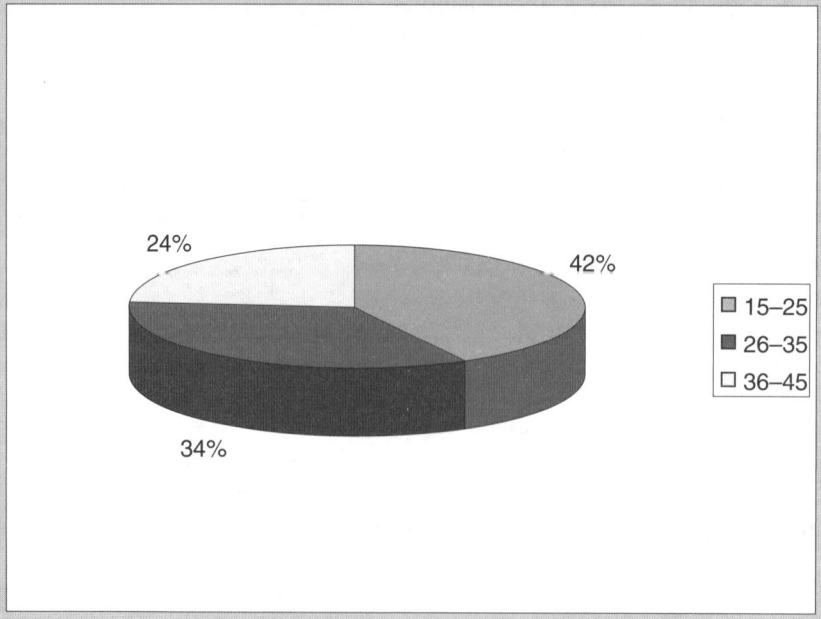

Figure 3.1 Respondent profile by age
Source: Economic Times, India

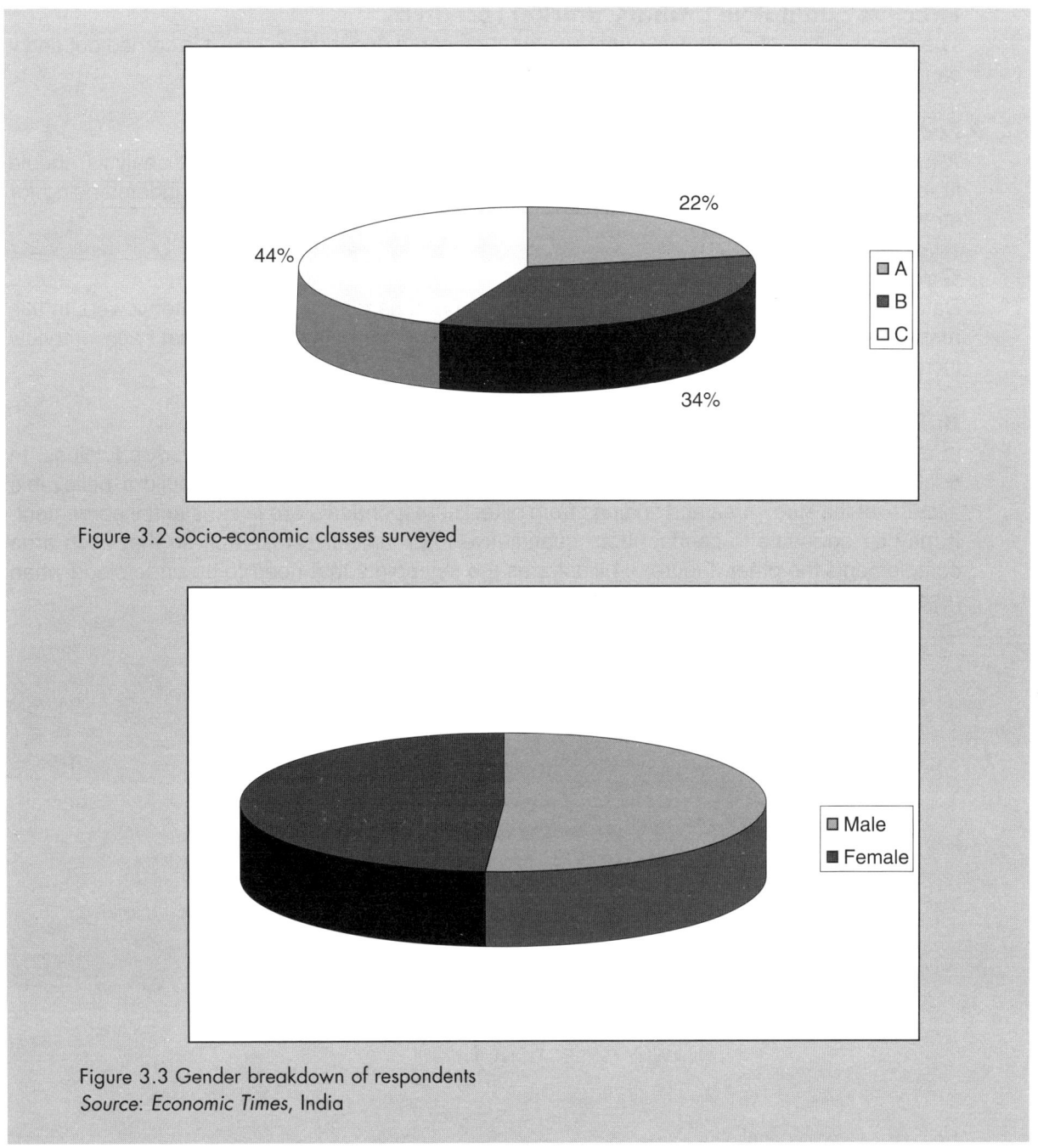

Figure 3.2 Socio-economic classes surveyed

Figure 3.3 Gender breakdown of respondents
Source: *Economic Times*, India

The above excerpt shows the usefulness of primary research carried out by various agencies to Titan. The company could also carry out its own primary research by commissioning agencies to carry out work on customer satisfaction or design of the watches.

Primary Research

Good market research provides a good foundation in formulating successful marketing strategy. Conducted carefully, qualitative primary market research studies can yleld insights on issues such as product usage patterns, unmet needs, product positioning, and pricing – all of which are central to strategy formulation and decision making.

Effective qualitative primary market research

The effectiveness of qualitative primary market research depends on how it is carried out and it can be improved by concentrating on the following issues:

Focus on strategic marketing decisions

All aspects of the research study, from questionnaire design to recruitment and analysis, should fit together and be focused clearly on developing information, insights and understanding for strategic decision making.

Quality of respondents

Data collected in any primary research is only as good as the respondents interviewed. In this respect, respondents should be identified and screened carefully to ensure that each interview increases confidence in the findings.

Building Confidence

In all market research studies it is important to develop confidence in the study's findings. In qualitative research such confidence is achieved as data accumulates to build a believable 'picture' of the study area and findings from different respondents are in substantial agreement. It may be advisable to conduct both quantitative and qualitative research so that each area complements the other. Figure 3.4 illustrates the key points that need to be understood when researching customers,

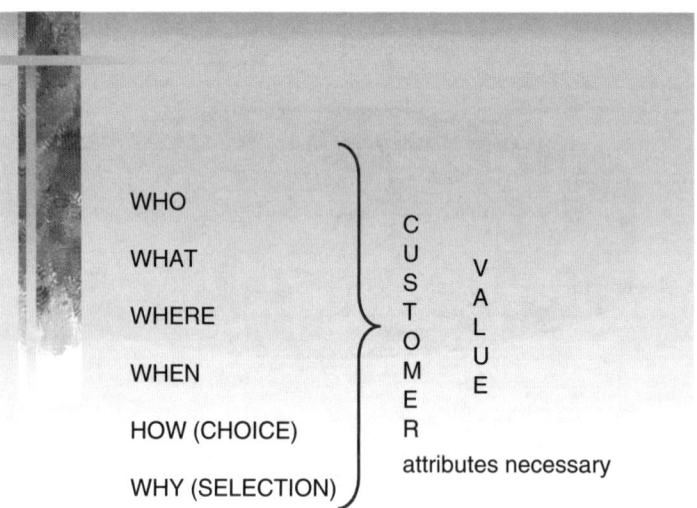

Figure 3.4 Customer analysis

At the same time an organization needs to take a comprehensive view of all its research areas. This is illustrated in Figure 3.5. This research is necessary to understand the market potential of products and services. Market research in conjunction with market intelligence helps an organization to develop effective marketing strategies. Success depends on information about a particular market segment, a geographic area or customer preferences, enabling better targeting.

Mini case

Marketing campaigns impact on consumer habits

Andy Farquarson looks at the way partnerships between business and charities leave their mark on the consumer.

Cause related marketing campaigns are having a significant impact on consumer habits and are bringing benefits to both businesses and the charities they link up with, according to new research. This latest study looks for the first time at how people respond to such campaigns – rather than how they think they would.

The key finding is surprisingly high public awareness of campaigns such as Tesco's donation of computers to schools, Avon's support for breast cancer research, or the Andrex puppy appeal in association with the National Canine Defence League. Almost 90 per cent of those surveyed had heard of at least one cause-related programme and almost half could spontaneously name a specific company or brand involved in a campaign. Two in three people believed more businesses should get involved. Against this, however, a small percentage felt cause related marketing was exploitative, or that it was inappropriate for business to become involved in social issues.

Until now, research into the effectiveness of cause related marketing campaigns has focused on consumers' attitudes, rather than their actions. The new study, Profitable Partnerships, was commissioned by Business in the Community (BITC) and is based on a survey of 2000 adults by the British Market Research Bureau. While previous work has established that a majority of people support the concept of cause-related marketing, and would probably express that support in their purchasing choices, the fresh research indicates that this broad approval is affecting consumers' choices.

More than 65 per cent of respondents said they had participated in a cause-related marketing campaign. Of them, three-quarters had either switched brand, tried out a product or increased their usage; and four in five had felt more positive about certain purchases, more loyal to a company or brand, and more inclined to look out for further cause related campaigns. Although 30 per cent of respondents were regular Internet users, comparatively few had found cause related marketing campaigns on the web. Old media predominated, with awareness of campaigns garnered through in-store promotion (23 per cent), television commercials (18 per cent) and advertisements in print media (11 per cent).

Cause related marketing is defined as any partnership between a business and charity which markets an image, product or service for mutual benefit. 'This is not about corporate philanthropy,' says Sue Adkins, BITC's director of marketing. 'It's about commercial benefit for both cause and company. Any business which tries to project this sort of campaign as strings-free giving is heading for a fall; the public is not gullible.' A good match between partners is also vital, says Adkins. Unless campaigns are properly managed, and based on integrity and transparency, they can be counter-productive.

The new report does not specify what constitutes a 'good' campaign. Among a wide variety of factors cited by those surveyed were schemes that supported local community activity, a high level of donation or support for the project or charity and clearly communicated, unambiguous benefits. Tesco's 'computers for schools' initiative is a good example of such clarity, argues Adkins. It has delivered more than £30m of computer equipment to schools, raised Tesco's profile (more than 40 per cent of adults know about the initiative), and bolstered public perception of the company as a good corporate citizen.

Unsurprisingly, Tim Mason, Tesco's marketing director, welcomes the BITC findings. 'Successful marketing is all about meeting customer needs and most consumers expect companies to be socially responsible,' he says. 'That's what is driving the rapid growth of cause related marketing and I am sure that growth will continue for the foreseeable future.' Marketing departments may formulate corporate strategies, but it is the advertising industry that gets the messages across to consumers. So it is hardly surprising that advertising agencies are establishing specialist teams to provide cause related marketing expertise to their clients.

One of the longest established is Saatchi & Saatchi's 'cause connection', set up in 1997 by Marjorie Thompson (who worked both in the public and voluntary sectors before joining Saatchis). 'There are huge opportunities to develop cause related marketing in the UK,' says Thompson. 'For instance, government could provide much more in the way of match-funding and tax breaks to encourage good corporate citizenship. That would help charities gain long-term funding and exploit the expertise of the communications profession to promote their missions and messages.'

Note: Profitable Partnerships is available at £75, or £50 to registered charities, from BITC, 44 Baker St, London W1M 1DH. Further information at www.bitc.org.uk.

Source: The Guardian, Wednesday, 15 November 2000

This article indicates the way in which market research can be utilized by companies to boost their corporate image.

Secondary research

This type of research is based on information gleaned from studies previously performed by government agencies, chambers of commerce, trade associations and other organizations. This includes Census Bureau information and Nielsen ratings. Such information is now readily available through the World Wide Web. In some instances detailed reports are produced for industry sectors by major agencies such as the Gartner group. However these are quite expensive to purchase.

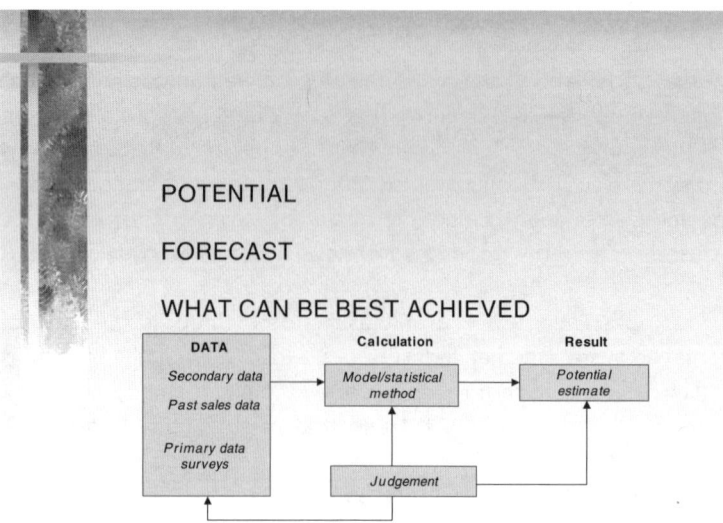

Figure 3.5 Market potential and forecasting

Although secondary research is less expensive than primary research, it is not as accurate, or as useful, as specific, customized research. For instance, secondary research may help a shoe manufacturer to understand the number of shoes sold within a country. However, pricing data, the impact of shoe design or how well the brand is accepted, may not be available. This is where primary research can be used to obtain more specific information. Organizations rely on information systems and this aspect is summarized in Figure 3.6. An organization, as it develops and grows has much historical information that it can draw from its archives. Often interesting information lies hidden until it is analysed. Market Intelligence is drawn from company sources, customers, salesforce, secondary information, commissioned research and the Internet. All the information has to be drawn together to form a Marketing decision Support System.

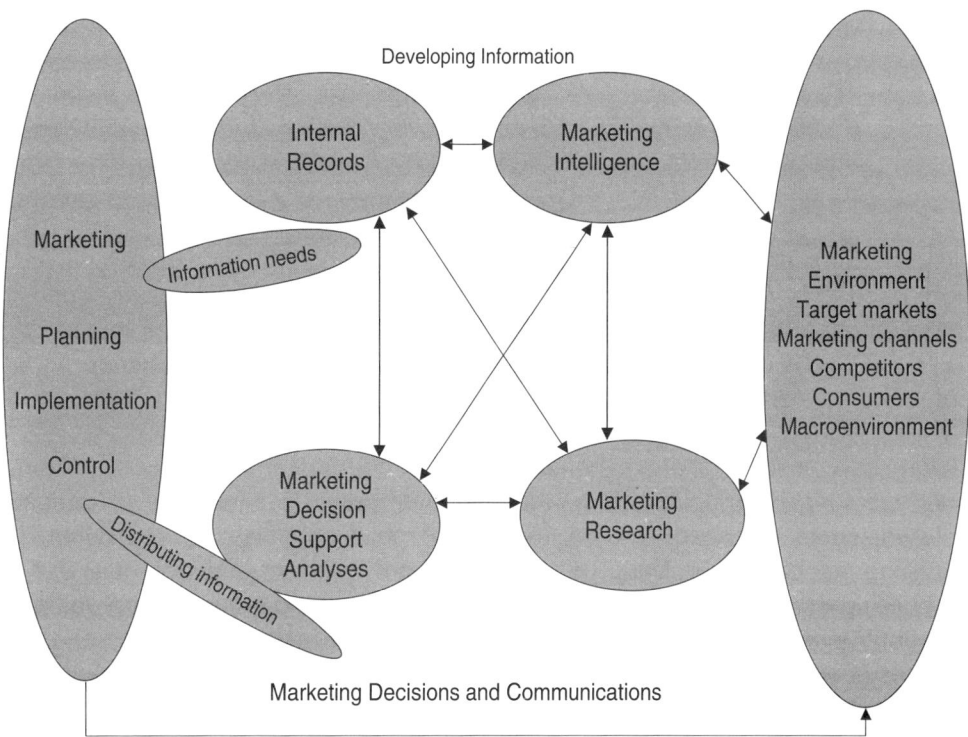

Figure 3.6 Marketing information system
Source: Adapted from Kotler, 1992

The role of information technology

In the last decade, information technology has become a very important part of a marketer's armoury. There is little in marketing that does not incorporate information technology. Market intelligence can therefore be gathered in many ways (Ranchhod, 2004):

a. Salesmen, on the road, can be updated on customer requirements as necessary. This information can be used for enhancing CRM and logistics.

b. As mobile devices become more sophisticated, customers will be able to access inventories of their suppliers. This means that they can place orders and specify delivery times. This can be done via links to an Intranet or the Internet. Well-organized companies can gather and store this information.

c. Individuals, apart from talking to others, will also be able to communicate with machines. This is already a reality with consumers being able to buy soft drinks, chocolates and car washes via mobile devices. Data on consumption patterns can be stored.

d. Consumers will be able to pay for restaurant meals via secure transactions through a mobile device.

e. The 'blue-tooth' devices can enable retailers to market special offers to customers on their mobile devices if they are within a twenty metre radius. This will also allow customers to undertake transactions with shops and restaurants.

f. Radio will become an integral part of the mobile device, allowing an individual access to a myriad of radio stations. This also has implications for advertising and branding.

g. The incorporation of GPS into mobile devices (Ground Positioning Systems, via satellite), means that individuals will be able to easily locate their positions and also the nearest outlets or services that they need.

As customers become fluid in the way they contact and interact with companies, companies in turn need to be fluid in their approach. Often the IT/Marketing link is not good. The marketing function often does not understand what happens in IT with regards to service provision and prices. There is often a cultural gap between marketing and IT and therefore there is a need to integrate data and for computer experts to work side by side with marketers.

There is a need to share experiences. It is important that for good customer relationship management, IT and Marketing work together, with IT being able to understand what the internal customer needs are. A change of philosophy is required, where IT shifts from 'building solutions' to defining requirements from the front end with business and customers in building the best solutions. The one-to-one relationship means that a customer is known to the enterprise and interacts with the enterprise, with the enterprise flexing and changing to meet his/her needs. The enterprise can then have a unified view of a single customer across the entire enterprise, linking other functional and geographical units together.

As the relationship develops across boundaries, it is clear that the organization truly becomes a learning organization, with the customer finding that he or she is investing in a continuing relationship with it. At every given opportunity the organization can 'tailor' and refit its behaviour to suit the customer. In the end the way the relationship is maintained, grown and nurtured means that a customer is less likely to invest time in building such a relationship with a competitor. This relationship building needs to be regarded as a business process rather than a technology suite. The technology needs to be able to support and enable this process.

The learning organization and market-based learning

The learning organization can 'learn' in different ways. An organization can be adaptive to its environment, thereby learning from the subtle changes taking place in the marketplace. In other instances an organization can become efficient in the way it utilizes information, developing information processing patterns that can enable it to 'read' the changes taking place in the marketplace and change its behaviour patterns accordingly. Authors such as Senge (1990) view a learning organization as a continuously creative, innovative organization, where each member is an active participant within the learning process. This allows for continuous learning and flexibility.

Learning is often constrained (single-loop learning) at a low level or it is of a higher, creative order where cognitive learning takes place (double-loop learning).

Single-loop learning

It is easy for organizations to be conditioned by single-loop learning. In many instances, companies have to adjust to specific demands in the market and often they will have well developed strategies to cope with this. Single-loop learning is also prevalent within functional areas of businesses as bureaucratic systems are in place to deal with orders and demands. These are routine patterns and are triggered by particular stimuli within the environment. The marketing function in a chocolate company, for instance, will respond to low demand by spending more on advertising. In general short-term tactical issues are dealt with efficiently. Single-loop learning does not stretch to questioning the phenomena that create the response (i.e. why are the chocolate sales low?), it merely sets in motion patterned responses to external pressures.

Single-loop learning is often constrained by a learning 'boundary' (Figure 3.7). This is not unusual or undesirable. In many instances, companies serve particular markets and they have to focus on these markets to deal with them efficiently and to give customers satisfaction. This efficiency in the marketplace can create rigid adherence to organized approaches and leave little to the imagination. The way in which the business is conceptualized guides core capabilities. However, in many instances these could become 'core rigidities' and can just concentrate on the served market, fostering quite a narrow perspective. Therefore an adaptive approach (single-loop) is usually sequential, incremental and focused on issues or opportunities within the traditional scope of the organization's activities. This leaves little room for imagination and for any moves towards more interesting and potentially lucrative areas of business.

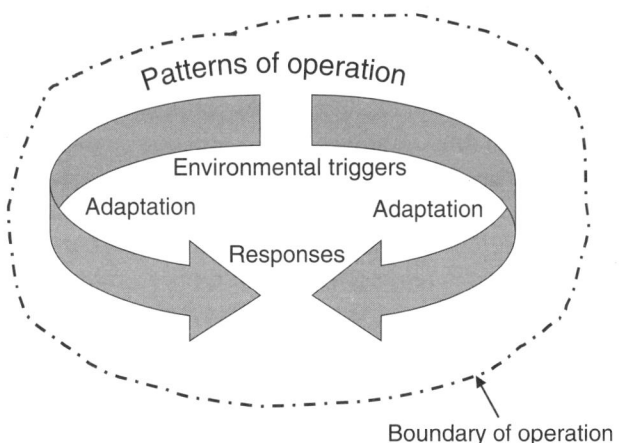

Figure 3.7 Single-loop learning

Double-loop learning

This higher level of learning affects the whole organization and is rarely contained within functional areas. It entails a deeper challenge to routine practices and rules. This type of generative learning shows a willingness to question long-held assumptions about mission, customers, capabilities or strategy. Often this is based on systems thinking and works through existing relationships, linking key issues and events. When an organization begins to embrace 'double-loop' learning, interrelationships and dynamic processes of change are important. Often a learning organization adept at double-loop learning can take advantage of 'windows' of opportunity that may be available to organizations. Often slower moving organizations that have 'fixed' views of markets and their role within them may fail to take advantage of these opportunities.

Higher-level learning usually occurs during some types of crisis, for example: new strategy, new leader, and significant changes in the market. It corresponds to the development of a new frame of reference(s). One of the consequences of a double-loop learning organization is the necessity to 'unlearn' an old process as old frames are no longer efficient in coping with the new reality.

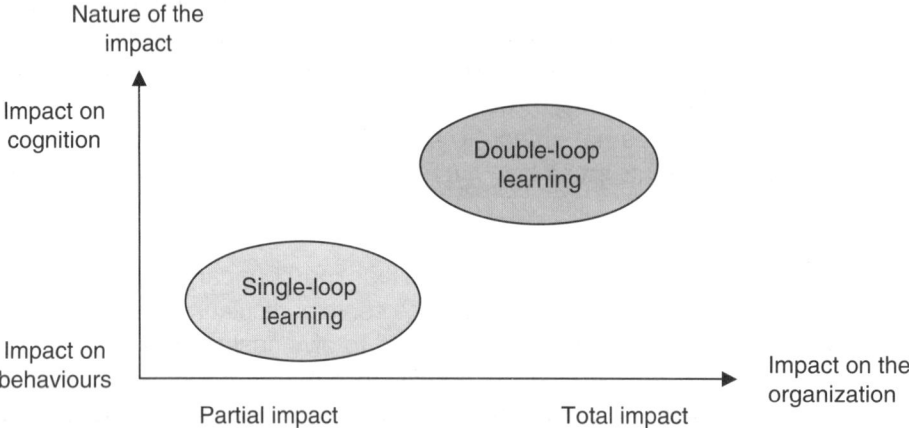

Figure 3.8 The impacts of single- and double-loop learning

For instance the advent of the Internet has profoundly changed the way in which music and entertainment are delivered. The record industry for instance was essentially stuck in its old paradigm of selling records or CDs through retailers. It generally failed to grasp the opportunities offered by the new medium. Records and movies are at the end of the day essentially bits of information. The Internet made it possible to transmit this information globally. Individuals began to freely exchange information and music. Although illegal, this still occurs regularly and vast amounts of pirated music changes hands on a daily basis. Artists now have their own websites and in some instances are distributing music through these sites. The music companies in general were very good at responding to fluctuating demands in the marketplace, but the single-loop response pattern created a situation where they failed to see the changes beyond their own self made 'boundaries'. No sensible Internet strategies were therefore developed. This has led to much heartache and refocusing within the sector. Music can now be stored on CD's, mobiles, Mpeg players, memory sticks and computer hard disks, making the one-dimensional approach to music sales obsolete. The same is true for television programmes and films.

A company's intelligence gathering system needs to be flexible and wide ranging so that old paradigms are constantly challenged. A true learning organization therefore will place great value on information transmission contributing to general learning. This will depend on the following:

○ *Knowledge acquisition* Converting data into knowledge that can be understood and assimilated.

○ *Information distribution* Distributing information and knowledge throughout the organization.

o *Information interpretation* Understanding the information and interpreting it so that sensible opinions can be formed.

o *Organizational memory* Understanding the new knowledge and embedding it in the organization's memory.

Organizations need to learn from the markets that they operate in so that the organizational memory consists of market-based learning. (Figure 3.8)

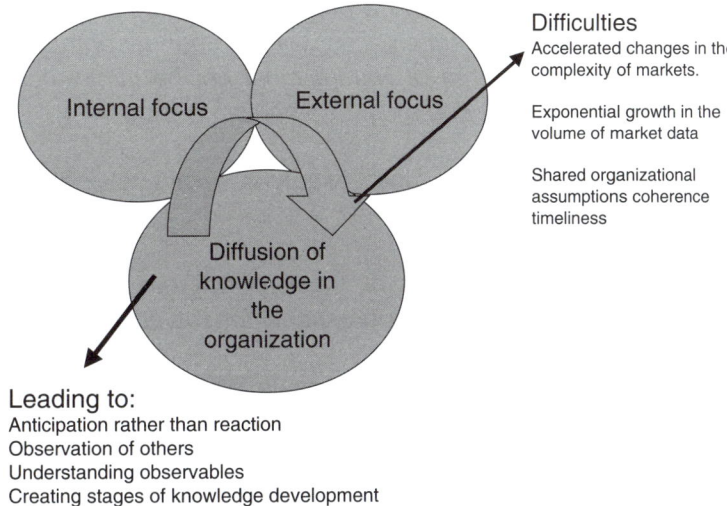

Difficulties
Accelerated changes in the complexity of markets.

Exponential growth in the volume of market data

Shared organizational assumptions coherence timeliness

Internal focus

External focus

Diffusion of knowledge in the organization

Leading to:
Anticipation rather than reaction
Observation of others
Understanding observables
Creating stages of knowledge development

Figure 3.9 Market-based learning

In order to achieve some sort of shared purpose so that organizations benefit from learning, a mission statement can be of benefit, provided its scope is not too narrow and constricting. Pearce and David (1987) suggested that a mission statement should contain the following aspects:

1. Customers (the target market).

2. Products/services (offerings and value provided to customers).

3. Geographic markets (where the firm seeks customers).

4. Technology (the technology used to produce and market products).

5. Concern for survival/Growth/Profits (the firm's concern for being financially sound).

6. Philosophy (the firm's values, ethics, beliefs).

7. Public image (contributions the firm makes to communities).

8. Employees (the importance of managers and employees).

9. Distinctive competence (how the firm is better or different compared to its competitors).

Each of these points covers aspects of the organization where information and learning are important. A broad encompassing statement can therefore be quite helpful to an organization.

Some examples of Mission statements:

The Co-operative Bank has this as their ecological statement:

> *However, we undertake to continually assess all our activities and implement a programme of ecological improvement based on the pursuit of the following four scientific principles:*
>
> o *Nature cannot withstand a progressive build-up of waste derived from the Earth's crust.*
> o *Nature cannot withstand a progressive build-up of society's waste, particularly artificial persistent substances which it cannot degrade into harmless materials.*
> o *The productive area of Nature must not be diminished in quality (diversity) or quantity (volume) and must be enabled to grow.*
>
> *Society must utilise energy and resources in a sustainable, equitable and efficient manner.*
>
> *We consider that the pursuit of these principles constitutes a path of ecological excellence and will secure future prosperity for society by sustainable economic activity.*
>
> *The Co-operative Bank will not only pursue the above path itself, but endeavour to help and encourage all its Partners to do likewise.*

From the Unilever company report we have this statement:

Our founders had strong values and a clear commitment to corporate social responsibility, (it wasn't called that then, but that is what it was). It was William Lever who famously built a 'garden village' for his workers at Port Sunlight near Liverpool. He introduced such pioneering initiatives as a shorter working week, sickness benefits, holiday pay and pensions. He felt so strongly about broadening the experience of his employees that he regularly took them all to London for the day to see exhibitions and even built them an art gallery.

William Lever was living at a time when the fabric of society and the forces in society were very different from today. When the Church and Christian values played a dominant role in people's lives, when there was little or no state-funded social provision and when businesses operated in often appalling conditions. He had clear moral views and believed he had a moral responsibility to help, both through business and his personal actions.

Indeed his very visionary mission statement was itself an expression of his values:

> 'To make cleanliness commonplace; to lessen work for women; to foster health and contribute to personal attractiveness, that life may be more enjoyable and rewarding for the people who use our products.'

From Cadburys we have the following:

o Promote social housing of good quality which enhances the environment.
o Manage all their housing and estates to the highest standards for all residents.

Encourage residents to share in decisions affecting their communities.

Each of the above examples are very good examples of mission statements where Corporate Social Responsibility is taken into account. Mission statements can be quite varied and address different issues. Often all the issues discussed by Pearce and Webb are rarely addressed.

Summary

This chapter considers the importance of having a mission for an organization and subsequently organizing for information acquisition and dissemination. It is clear that an organization with a well-developed sense of direction has the opportunity to create learning situations. Organizations have to learn and grow and base their learning on particular insights gained from the market. Technology also has an important role to play in the dissemination of knowledge and organizational learning.

unit 4
contemporary issues in marketing

Outcomes

○ Assess the relevance of opportunities presented by contemporary marketing issues within any given scenario including innovations in marketing.

In attempting to look at this outcome, this unit takes two pieces of contemporary issues, key account management (KAM) as used in relationship marketing management and sustainability in marketing. These issues have been taken from two books, *Relationship Marketing Management* by Little and Marandi and from *Marketing Strategies: A 21st Century Approach* by Ashok Ranchhod. Following each article, there is a short discussion on how these issues could be considered as contemporary, and how they could potentially be used when undertaking case study preparation.

KEY ACCOUNT MANAGEMENT

Source: Little, E. and Marandi, E. (2003) *Relationship Marketing Management*, Chapter 9, London: Thomson Learning, Reproduced with kind permission from Thomson Learning.

Introduction

Key account management (KAM) is a common manifestation of relationship marketing in business to business markets. With its roots in selling, the theory and practice of KAM is narrower in scope than that of relationship marketing – it can be seen as the application of 'external' RM principles in a business to business context, predominately from a supplier's perspective. Nevertheless, the subject offers valuable insights into the practical considerations of implementing RM, and hence can in turn inform the development of the broader theory.

This chapter begins by defining KAM, its costs and benefits, before looking at the nature of the business to business relationships and the key stages in their development. Decision-making frameworks for identifying key accounts and developing KAM programmes are then considered. After considering the subsidiary topic of global account management (GAM) the chapter ends with a discussion of the contribution that KAM can make to the wider theory of RM, and whether KAM practices in turn can be informed by more general work on RM.

What is key account management?

KAM defined

Key account management is a management practice aimed at optimizing the relationship between a supplying organization and a buying organization. As is usual in the marketing literature, there is some debate over the precise meaning of the term KAM. Further confusion is created by the fact that KAM is used interchangeably with national account management (NAM), strategic account management (SAM), and account management (AM), although there appear to be no significant distinctions between the meanings of the four terms. Nevertheless, there is general consensus that KAM consists of three elements. Kempeners and van der Hart (1999) represent these elements well by defining [key] account management as follows:

> *the process of building and maintaining relationships over an extended period, which cuts across multiple levels, functions and operating units in both the selling organisation and in carefully selected customers (accounts) that contribute to the company's objectives now or in the future. (Kempeners and van der Hart, 1999: 311)*

As reflected in this definition, the practice of KAM is characterized by:

- *The conscious selection of key accounts* The starting point of KAM is the identification of customers which will equate to strategic partners. All KAM programmes must therefore employ a mechanism for selecting these key accounts, based on the strategic objectives of the organization.

- *The development and maintenance of long-term relationships* Having identified the key customers, the organization must have strategies and systems in place to build and maintain a business relationship with that customer.

- *The establishment of cross-functional processes for servicing accounts* This is a common feature of all definitions and examples of KAM. In order to enable the other two features of the KAM programme, the organizational structure and systems must enable multifunctional processes based around individual accounts.

KAM activities

Homburg *et al.* (2002) identify KAM by the activities that the suppliers undertake in order to build and maintain relationships. These include:

- Special pricing.
- Customization of products and services.
- Development of special products or services.
- Joint coordination of workflow.
- Information sharing.
- Taking over the customer's business processes.

McDonald (2000) focuses on the communication ties between the two companies, which move from the 'bow-tie' formation shown in Figure 4.1 to a 'diamond' structure (Figure 4.2). Such a shift in structure can be both a response to and a stimulus for relationship development.

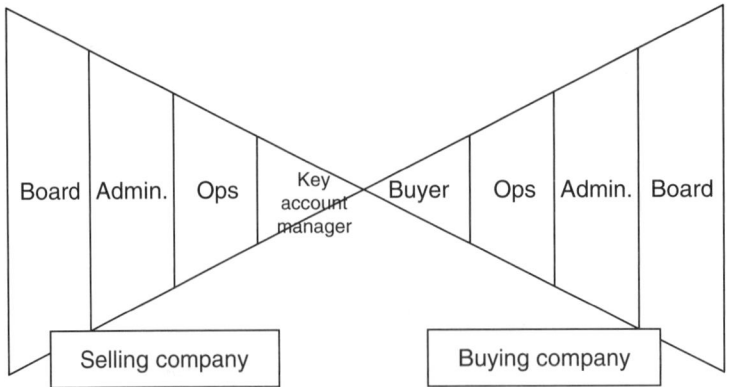

Figure 4.1 The bow-tie structure (evident early in KAM relationships)
Source: McDonald, M. (2000) 'Key account management – a domain review', *The Marketing Review*, 1, 15–34, Reprinted with permission of Westburn Publishers Ltd.

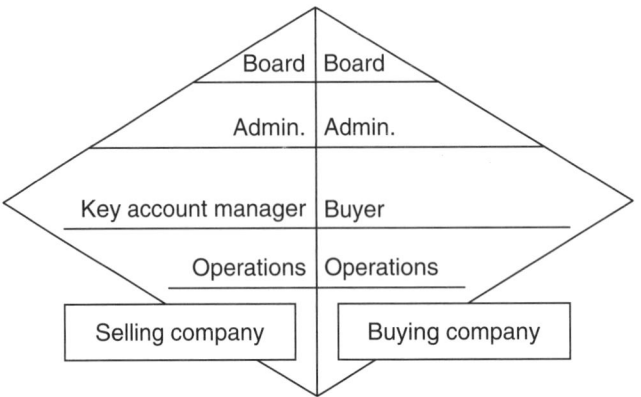

Figure 4.2
Source: McDonald, M. (2000) 'Key account Management – a domain review', *The Marketing Review*, 1, 15–34, Reprinted with permission of Westburn Publishers Ltd.

The rationale for KAM

Before examining the mechanics of KAM and its implementation, it is worth considering the advantages (and penalties) of the practice. These are summarized in Figure 4.3. The supplier benefits from increased turnover, since the proper selection and development of accounts implies, amongst other things, the cultivation of the high volume, high value customers. At the same time, costs associated with the winning of new customers, such as marketing research and communications, are reduced. Ellram (1991) further notes that the long-term relationships give the supplier the opportunity to plan its production and logistics with greater certainty, perfecting repetitive operations. Hence both production and transaction costs may be reduced. The buyer in turn benefits from products and services that are specifically tailored to its needs, whilst receiving some of the benefit of the supplier's cost reductions in the form of price discounts.

It is the mutual benefits, however, that bring the greatest strategic advantages to the parties involved. Both parties enjoy reduced risk, alleviating the threat of both short-term crises in supply and demand, and long-term planning uncertainty. By pooling their resources, the two companies not only make efficiency gains, but are able to explore business opportunities that might require a prohibitively high investment were they operating individually. Resources here refer to intangible assets, such as brand image, skills, information and organizational competences as well as to tangible assets. By sharing information, for example, the two parties may be able to develop products, process or strategies that could not have been developed individually. Similarly, one party may be able to capitalize on the brand image of its partner by association to gain access to new markets or buyers. Finally, Ojasalo (2001) notes that the benefits of KAM may occur at the individual as well the organizational level, through the enhanced social interaction arising from the bonds that inevitably form between individuals in the two companies. Given the effect this has on employee satisfaction and motivation, this would have indirect benefits at the organizational level.

It should be stressed, however, that these benefits arise from the successful implementation of KAM, and represent the greatest benefits which can accrue. It will be seen that the development of KAM infrastructure involves a significant investment in terms of management time, staffing and training, an investment that will probably not create a return during the early stages of the relationship. The proper selection of key accounts, and the proper development and maintenance of these relationships is critical to the long-term profitability of any KAM programme.

Figure 4.3 Benefits of key account management

The key account development cycle

Stages in the key account development cycle

As with all relationships, key account relationships develop over time and require different treatment at different stages in this development. The literature offers two competing models of key account development, though the differences between them are nominal. The explanation offered below is a synthesis of the two.

Pre- and early KAM

These stages are described by McDonald *et al.* (1997) as the 'scanning and attraction stages'. Here the supplier is concerned with the identification of potential key accounts, and gaining information by which the selection decision can be made. The move into early KAM is characterized by the willingness of the supplier to make adjustments to its standard offering. The types of information needed to select key accounts are discussed in the next section. Given the fact that customers in the pre- or early KAM stages of development are of relatively low importance to the organization, sales representatives play the central role in this process, with no special infrastructure or resources being devoted to the customer (Millman and Wilson 1995). The focus of the relationship remains on the product, and on a set of relatively discrete (albeit repetitive) transactions.

Mid-KAM

Here the focus of the relationship begins to shift to process, as trust and commitment develop between the two parties. Hence the range of value added services offered by the supplier assume as great an importance in the eyes of the buyer as the product and its price. Both begin

43

to view the relationship as long term, though the buyer will still maintain contact with alternative suppliers. The number of contact points between the two companies will increase, and the management of the account will tend to shift towards more senior levels of the organizations, as it takes on greater strategic importance.

Partnership and synergistic KAM (Mature KAM)

At this point in the relationship, the boundaries between the two companies reduce as the structural and social bonds between them strengthen. The sharing of sensitive information and joint problem solving will be common practice, and both formal and informal contacts will occur regularly at all levels of both the organizations. Synergistic KAM is described by McDonald *et al.* (1997) as 'quasi-integration' – a state in which the two organizations operate jointly.

Uncoupling KAM

Relationship disintegration may occur at any stage. McDonald *et al.* find that relationship breakdown is most frequently attributed to a breach of trust. Millman and Wilson stress however that relationship dissolution should not necessarily be viewed as a failure, since it may be in the interests of a party to end a relationship. Whether intentional or not, the uncoupling stage should be managed carefully to reduce the social and economic impact on the organization.

Implications of the key account development cycle

Clearly the different stages of the cycle bring differing levels of investment and varying returns. The early and mid-KAM stages are particularly demanding for the supplier, requiring investment in activities such as information gathering, communications and the developing of value added services in an attempt to gain the confidence of the buyer. The major benefits of KAM, however, occur in the later stages. The supplier must, therefore, ensure that the balance of its relationship portfolio is maintained, so that the superior returns from mature relationships can fund the development of those in the early or mid-KAM stages.

Identifying key accounts

The need for selection criteria

Given the cost/benefit implications of the key account development cycle, the need for the careful selection of potential key accounts is critical. Millman and Wilson (1995) describe the example of a business relationship between two multinational companies agreeing to develop jointly an advanced pigmentation system. Whilst the selling company saw the project as the start of a long-term, strategic relationship, the buyer viewed it as a one-off project. The buyer terminated the arrangement after two years, leaving the seller shocked and bitter, with no resulting sales gain to soften the blow. If a selling company is to profit from KAM, it must minimize the likelihood of such strategic failures. Although research in the field of KAM is limited, it has been found that companies that explicitly define and identify key accounts are more successful in targeting resources, and show a more sophisticated understanding of their customers (Millman and Wilson, 1999). The remainder of this section reviews various criteria for the selection of key accounts suggested by research into KAM.

Relationship history

Obviously, this criterion presumes that KAM is being implemented against a background of established accounts, and cannot be easily applied to new prospects. The literature commonly points to longevity as an indicator of the strategic importance of an account, constituting evidence of commitment and trust, both of which are important ingredients of strategic relationships (McDonald, 2000). Ojasalo (2001) points out, however, that longevity is no guarantee of profitability.

Volume

Theorists are virtually unanimous in identifying sales volume as a key determinant in the selection of key accounts (Krapfel *et al.*, 1991, McDonald *et al.*, 1997, Campbell and Cunningham, 1983). Research suggests that practitioners also find this criterion simple to apply, since it is easily quantified and readily accepted by key players within the organization. When 'selling' the importance of the account internally, key account managers found that sales turnover was well-recognized throughout the business (McDonald *et al.*, 1997). It should be stressed that potential sales volume is as important as current – the same research found that achieving links with fast growing companies or companies in developing markets was also a prime strategic consideration.

Profitability

Ojasalo (2001) points out that high sales volume does not always lead to profitability, and to be of value, the total revenue from an account must exceed its servicing costs within a given time-frame. The quantification of profitability, however, is not straightforward. The majority of costs associated with the servicing of key accounts involve services, management time and the resolution of day-to-day problems. Intangible activities such as this are difficult to cost, particularly in organizations where a single team or manager handles more than one account. Similarly the benefits accruing from a relationship may be equally nebulous and difficult to quantify – gains in areas such as innovation, learning and reputation are hard to assess in anything but qualitative terms. Hence Millman and Wilson (1999) found that the assessments of the net value of business relationships tended to rely on the subjective judgement of those involved in their operationalization.

Status

Ojalaso (2001) identifies the fact that organizations often derive benefit from association with a reputable partner. Research by McDonald *et al.* (1997) found that some selling companies actively targeted national or multinational or 'blue chip' companies, since the prestige associated with these organizations facilitated the winning of further customers. It was also noted that companies with a good reputation were more likely to focus on long-term value creating activities rather than short-term cost issues, and hence were more receptive to KAM initiatives.

Ease of replacement

This criterion is relevant to the decision to develop rather than to initiate a key account relationship, since it applies to existing customers only. Krapfel *et al.* (1991) recommend that by calculating the cost of replacing an exiting customer or supplier, an organization can obtain a useful quantitative measure of the relationships value.

Resources synergies

Campbell and Cunningham (1983) identify this as a separate criterion, whilst Millman and Wilson (1999) subsume it within broader considerations of 'strategic fit'. The selling organization will be able to service the account more effectively if it is able to leverage any resources or competences that distinguish it from its competitors. Hence it should look for partners amongst organizations that would benefit particularly from its unique strengths. Similarly, it should ensure that these partners command resources that may in turn benefit the selling organization.

Strategic compatibility

Millman and Wilson's (1999) notion of strategic fit also encompass the alignment of organizational goals, *modus operandi*, culture and relational norms. Similarly, McDonald *et al.* (1997) note that not all organizations seem willing or able to maintain long-term relationships, so receptivity to a KAM programme is an important consideration. More practical considerations such as compatibility between present and intended product and market arenas, and even such mundane issues as the physical location should not be ignored.

Criteria for selecting a key supplier

The literature tends to view KAM from the perspective of the supplier, and most of the criteria outlined above have been formulated with the supplier in mind. Many apply equally well to the buying company that is considering the development of strategic relationships with its supplier – the volume criterion, for example, becomes a question of whether the supplier can reliably fulfil current and future orders in the volume needed by the buyer. Similarly, issues of strategic compatibility or resource fit are mutual concerns. In addition, the research of McDonald *et al.* identified that the buying company is likely to weigh the following factors in its choice of strategic partner:

o *Product quality* Whether goods or service, the quality of the product and the relevance of value added service will be of prime importance to the buying organization.

o *Ease of doing business* Aggravation and problem solving are significant costs to the buying organization, and purchasing officers look very favourably on those suppliers that minimize these costs.

o *People quality* Purchasing officers took account of the personality and skills of key contacts in the selling company, valuing such qualities as *Honesty, integrity* and above all, *'a spirit of understanding'* (McDonald *et al.*, (1999: 748).

By understanding the criteria that the customer will apply in selecting suppliers, the supplier will be in a better position to design a KAM system that suits their needs.

Servicing key accounts: KAM activities

Adding value for key accounts

Having identified the key accounts, the next stage in the KAM process is to identify the means by which the relationship can be developed (Cann, 1998). This can in part be addressed by the installation of special resources dedicated to the servicing of the account, as discussed in the next section. However, before investing in such resources, the organization must have a clear idea of the activities to which they will be applied. There is a clear, though tacit, consensus in the literature that such activities involve adding value rather than cutting prices. Homburg *et al.* (2002) refer in passing to 'special pricing' and Ojasalo (2001) implies the use of discounting by listing cost savings as one of the benefits to buyers of key account relationships. Otherwise, the KAM literature is silent regarding the potential of pricing as a tactic in relationship development, focusing instead on the means by which added-value can be generated – McDonald *et al.* (1997) even found that suppliers actively targeted non-price-sensitive accounts so that the investment made in the account could be recouped through premium pricing.

Figure 4.4 summarizes the key activities or tactics that may be employed. These are arranged as a hierarchy of measures. Although the position of each element in the hierarchy is not definitive, it serves as a rough indicator of those elements that are basic pre-requisites of any strategic relationship, and those which characterize highly developed partnerships.

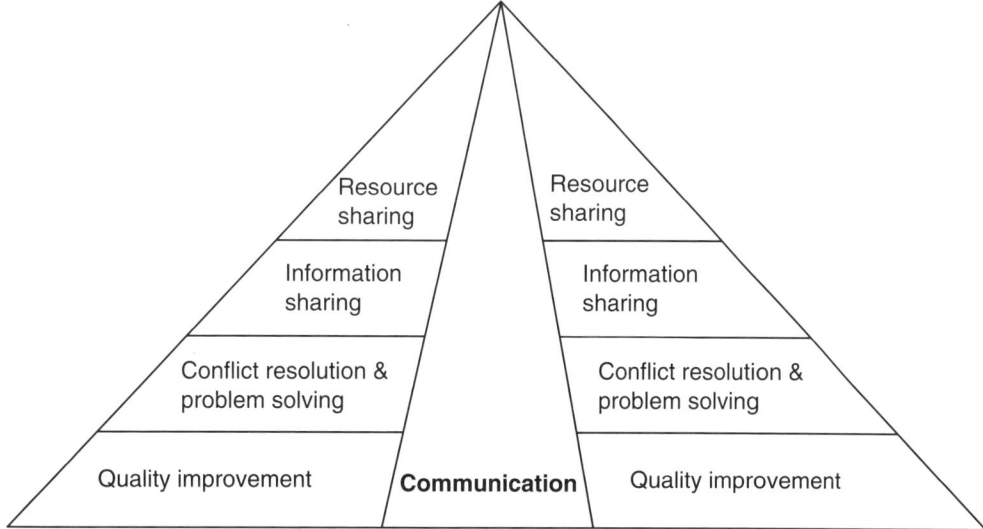

Figure 4.4 Adding value to key accounts

Quality improvement

This is perhaps the fundamental element of KAM, and the pre-requisite of a strategic relationship most commonly cited by buyers (McDonald *et al.*, 1997, Millman and Wilson, 1995). In the words of Millman and Wilson: 'The desire to serve key customers better must be matched by the capability to do so' (Millman and Wilson, 1999: 332). Given the long-term focus of strategic relationships, product excellence at any one moment is less important than the capability to continuously develop product offerings in response to market conditions, buyer requirements and competitor activity. Since, in all but the earliest stages of the relationship, the supplier's total offering is likely to involve a significant service element, even suppliers of manufactured goods must be able to reassure buyers of the quality of their processes and people, as well its manufacturing capability (McDonald *et al.* 1997). Hence the focus from the outset is on internal process quality rather than product quality.

Customization

Again, this can be seen as a pre-requisite of any relationship. In order to initiate any degree of exclusivity in the relationship, the supplier must be able to offer the buyer something that its competitors cannot. Customization may derive from the physical modification of tangible goods, or from the development of tailored services or transaction routines.

Conflict resolution and problem solving

Selnes (1998) found that the flexibility of the supplier in accepting responsibility for resolving the buyer's problems was a key determinant of a buyer's trust in their supplier, which in turn was a key antecedent of motivation to enhance the relationship. Responsiveness is often considered to be a dimension of service quality, since the ability of the supplier to resolve differences with, or the difficulties of the buyer will determine the latter's satisfaction with repeated transactions over time (Parasuraman, Zeithaml and Berry, 1988). It is listed separately here since it represents an important step away from a focus on specific, product-related transactions, and towards the development of a total offering based on joint processes.

47

Information sharing

Millman and Wilson (1995) found that mature relationships are characterized by the free exchange of commercially sensitive information between the two parties. Selnes (1998) states that the sharing of information can stimulate relationship enhancement in two ways. Firstly, information is a valuable resource which can greatly enhance the operations planning of the buyer. Secondly, willingness to yield potentially sensitive information is taken by the buyer as an expression of trust – an important antecedent of relationship development.

Resource sharing

Perhaps the pinnacle of key account relationship building is the ability of the two parties to share resources for mutual advantage. Whether through temporary joint ventures, or the development of permanent systems or structures, the sharing of resources is both a result of, and a stimulus for, very close bonds between organizations.

Communication

Communication occupies a special place in the servicing of key accounts, since it underpins all of the other tactics, and is universally cited as being of central importance to the initiation, development and maintenance of key accounts. The two major models of KAM development identify the various stages by the nature and extent of the communication channels existing between the two companies (McDonald, 2000). A key tactic for relationship development is therefore the development of communication channels between buyer and supplier.

Research by Schultz and Evans (2002) suggests that the nature of communication is important:

o *Informality* Customers are heavily concerned with interaction efficiency, and found informal methods less cumbersome than formal channels. Perhaps more important, informal communication is strongly linked to trust, suggesting that it is perceived to be more open and frank than carefully managed interaction.

o *Bi-directionality* In order to add value to the relationship, communication must be two-way, with suppliers both listening to and acting on feedback from the customer, and keeping them informed.

o *Frequency* In keeping with customers' preference for informal modes of communication, frequent, short episodes of interaction make customers feel they are being 'kept in touch with'.

o *Strategic content* the content of communication is just as important as the mode and frequency. Customers respond better to communication which they feel to be of strategic importance, reacting badly to being bombarded with trivial detail.

Servicing key accounts: developing a KAM infrastructure

Identifying the type of KAM system

Having identified the key accounts, the next stage in the development of KAM is the design of the system through which they will be serviced. Shapiro and Moriarty (1984) describe five major types of key account 'programme':

o No programme: no formal system or infrastructure is developed.
o Part-time programme: people with other roles take on the additional responsibility of managing the account.
o Full-time programme (unit level): the system is operated by fully dedicated staff, but decentralized at business unit or division level.
o Corporate-level programme: the system is run centrally by dedicated staff.
o National account division: a separate operating unit is dedicated to the account.

From a study of some 400 German and US suppliers, Homburg *et al.* (2002) identified eight distinct types of KAM system:

o *Top-management KAM* Involves highly formalized KAM programmes. As the label suggests, such programmes exhibit the highest degree of top management involvement, and are usually located at the organization's headquarters. Most have dedicated sales managers responsible for key accounts, and make extensive use of key account teams. Collaborative activities, such as the coordination of the manufacturing schedules are of high intensity, and the supplier is proactive in developing such activities. Despite this positive picture, access to functional resources is low.

o *Middle management KAM* Is also highly formalized, but attracts less involvement from senior management. The intensity of collaborative activities and the proactivity of the supplier are only of medium level. Key account managers tend to be locally based, and enjoy less prominent positions in the corporate hierarchy than their counterparts in top-management KAM systems. Access to functional resources is low.

o *Operating-level KAM* Is also relatively formalized, involving standardized procedures, and contributing significant value to the key accounts. Senior management involvement, however, is lower still, and a still greater proportion of account managers are based at local level. Access to functional resources is low.

o *Cross-functional, dominant KAM* Offers the most positive picture against all criteria. Access to resources is high, and senior management involvement is significant. Processes and structures are well developed, and key account managers enjoy a prominent role. Proactivity and intensity of collaboration are both high. Of all the organizations surveyed, those employing this form of KAM system key account managers spend the greatest proportion of their time on external activities.

o *Unstructured KAM* Systems are characterized by a lack of formality and standardization, and a reactive stance to collaborative activity. With little top-management involvement, account managers in this group spend the lowest proportion of their time on external activities.

o *Isolated KAM* Is a system in which KAM activities are instigated by local sales effort, but lacks support from the central business units. Although the involvement of senior

49

management is medium, access to functional resources is limited, and selling centre *esprit de corp* is low.

- o *Country-club KAM*   Systems exhibit a high degree of involvement from top management, but little else. Structures and processes are poorly developed, and teams are hardly ever formed. Special activities are neither intense nor proactive. The authors suggest that this form of KAM amounts to little more than representation by senior managers.

- o *No KAM*   Operators may pay lip service to a KAM system, often by awarding sales or general managers the title account coordinator or similar. However, no special activities of any significance are undertaken for their key customers.

Homburg *et al.* took a number of measures of the success of the various companies, both at the account level (i.e. how well the particular relationships were performing) and the organizational level (how well the business as a whole was performing). Perhaps predictably, the No KAM and isolated KAM approaches performed the worst, whilst cross-functional, dominant KAM companies performed particularly well against organization-level outcomes. Top-management KAM systems were found to be associated with the most profitable companies, suggesting that greater gains from other approaches are offset by higher costs.

This research offers valuable insights into the range of KAM systems that may be applied. It is also possible that the various systems, rather than being alternatives, are stages in the development of KAM systems. The key conclusion arising from the research is the desirability that senior management be actively involved in the design and implementation of KAM systems, rather than delegating the task to local sales managers.

The role of the account manager

The role of the key account manager will vary considerably depending on the nature of the organization, its environment and the KAM system in force. Millman and Wilson (1995), however, tentatively suggest a list of functions which are commonly associated with such posts:

- o Maintaining the sales/profitability of key accounts.
- o Customizing the seller's total offering to key accounts.
- o Facilitating inter-level or inter-functional processes that add value to the total offering.
- o Promoting the KAM concept within the organization.
- o Promoting the interests of the account within the organization.

Based on the research by Homburg *et al.* described above, and work by other authors (e.g. Millman and Wilson, 1996, McDonald *et al.*, 1997, Schultz and Evans, 2002), it is clear that the key account manager plays a crucial role in the implementation of KAM. Decisions on the responsibility, authority and resources allocated to key account managers will be critical in determining the effectiveness of the programme. Kempeners and van der Hart (1999) suggest the following checklist:

- o *Full or part-time system*   Should account managers be dedicated full time to the servicing of key accounts, or should they also have other responsibilities?

- o *The position of account managers in the system*   Should they be integrated into the sales department or should a new organizational layer be created? Should they be physically located at head office, or locally? Should different levels of key account management be created?

o   *Allocation of responsibility*   How many accounts should each manager control?

o   *Allocation of authority*   What resources should the account manager control? Should these be held centrally, or dedicated entirely to the account manager?

These questions have significant implications for the organization's structure, since the KAM framework will have to be integrated with existing structures and processes. The research of Homburg *et al.* indicates that, if medium term profitability is the chief focus, a centralized, highly developed key account executive function is not always the optimum solution, due to the cost of installing and maintaining such a system. It is possible, however, that the superior returns of such a system pays dividends in the longer term.

Skills of the key account manager

Given the importance of the key account manager, a significant amount of research has been conducted into the skills necessary to perform this function. According to Millman and Wilson, the demands of the role require:

> *High calibre people who are not only sufficiently 'rounded' to be able to diagnose/analyse complex commercial and technical situations; but also equipped to cope with highly politicized interaction, together with personal tensions and ambiguities inherent in the boundary-spanning role.* Millman and Wilson (1995: 17)

Shultz and Evans (2002) also single out communication skills as *the* key competence required of key account representatives, particularly the ability to share information of a strategic nature, rather than communicating predominantly on tactical issues. The research of McDonald *et al.* adds the following requirements:

o   Integrity.
o   Product service knowledge.
o   Understanding the buying company's business and business environment.
o   Selling/negotiating skills.

Possession of these skills and competences is understandably rare, and organizations seeking to implement KAM must be prepared to invest heavily in the selection, retention and development of suitable candidates.

The key account team

The use of key account teams to support the manager varies considerably between different examples of KAM systems, with account managers in some companies having no support from teams (Kempener and van der Hart, 1999, Homburg *et al.*, 2002). Homburg *et al.* (2002) found that the companies that performed best at the operational or account level made extensive use of teams. Shultz and Evans (2002) recommend the use of key account teams. Not only do they enable frequent contact with the customer, but they also help the flow of information in the selling organization, so that relevant information about the customer and the account is transferred to all points of customer contact.

According to Kempener and van der Hart, key account team decisions relate to the constitution and control of teams:

o   *Constitution of account teams*   The role of the account team is to support cross functional activities. To be of value, therefore, the teams should comprise members from all functions that have a hand in servicing the account. Team members may be full or part-time, and certain members (or indeed entire teams) may be involved only on an *ad hoc* basis, to solve a particular problem.

○ *Control of account teams* The most formalized control structure involves the key account manager with line-management responsibility for a dedicated, full time team. Where part-time or *ad hoc* members are involved, however, line management responsibility may be shared, or rest wholly with a manager in a functional department.

Clearly there are significant trade-offs here between efficiency and effectiveness, as demonstrated in the finding of Homburg *et al.* that the most formalized and 'successful' systems were not necessarily the most profitable. Moreover, the development of a permanent structure would be inappropriate in the early stages of a relationship – it is implicit in the notion of the account development cycle that supplier investments increase as trust develops between the two parties, and the chance of exit reduces (McDonald, 2000, Millman and Wilson, 1995). As with the various options for designing the role of the key account manager, so the different account team structures might be used by the same organization at different stages of the account's development.

The relevance of KAM to relationship marketing

A specific application of RM

Theories of KAM have been developed in high value, low volume, business to business markets, usually as an extension of theories of personal selling. This naturally sets limits on the applicability of KAM to RM practices in other types of market, particular to mass markets. Nevertheless, the KAM literature illustrates some important general principles of RM.

The need for senior management support

Both the empirical research and theoretical work provide strong evidence to suggest that KAM strategies will not work without the active support of senior management. This reinforces the general principle that RM requires a fundamental change in the values, goals and resource priorities of the organization, and will not be successful if viewed as a tactical issue. In the early stages at least, RM initiatives must be championed by influential members of the organization's management if they are to succeed.

The need for cross-functional coordination

KAM programmes appear to work better when they are supported by teams arranged around customers rather than functional areas. The development of KAM relationships involves a move away from the focus on rigid structures producing standardized offerings, and towards a more flexible network structure which can adapt to changing customer requirements, calling on new members and resources as circumstances require. This mirrors the consensus in the more general literature that RM is best supported by a network structure based on process rather than functional areas (see Chapter 5: Structure and Chapter 6: Internal marketing)

The importance of communication

Finally, the KAM literature underlines the central role of communication in building and maintaining the trust on which relationships depend. Whether dealing with customers, employees, channel members or referral markets, the management of relationships hinges on the development of open dialogue between the parties involved. This is as true for mass consumer markets as for business to business sectors.

References

Campbell, M. and Cunningham, M. (1983) 'Customer analysis for strategic developments in industrial markets', *Strategic management Journal*, 4, 4, 369–481.

Cann, C. (1998) 'Eight steps to building a business-to-business relationship', *Journal of Business and Industrial Marketing*, 13, 4/5, 395–405.

Ellram, L.E. (1991) 'Supply Chain Management', *International Journal of Physical Distribution and Logistics Management*, 21, 1, 13–22.

Homburg, C. Workman Jr., J. Jensen, O. (2002) 'A configurational perspective on key account management', *Journal of Marketing*, 66, 2, 38.

Kempeners, M. and van der Hart, H. (1999) 'Designing Account Management Organisations', *Journal of Business and Industrial Marketing*, 14 ,4, 310–355.

Krapfel, Jr. Salmond, D. and Spekman, R. (1991) 'A strategic approach to managing buyer-seller relationships', *European Journal of Marketing*, 25, 9, 22–48.

McDonald, M. (2000) 'Key account management – a domain review', *The Marketing Review*, 1, 15–34.

McDonald, M., Millman, T. and Rogers, G. (1997) 'Key account management: theory, practice and challenges', *Journal of Marketing Management*, 13, 737–757.

Millman, T. and Wilson, K. (1995) 'From key account selling to key account management', *Journal of Marketing Practice: Applied Marketing Science*, 1, 1, 9–21.

Millman, T. and Wilson, K. (1999) 'Processual issues in key account management: underpinning the customer-facing organization', *Journal of Business and Industrial Marketing*, 14, 4, 328–337.

Ojasalo, J. (2001) 'Key account management at company and individual levels in business-to-business relationships', *Journal of Business and Industrial Marketing*, 16, 3, 199–218.

Parasuraman, A., Zeithaml, V. and Berry, L. (1998) 'SERVQUAL: A multiple item scale for measuring consumer perceptions of service quality', *Journal of Retailing*, 64, 1, 12–40.

Schulz, R. and Evans, K. (2002) 'Strategic collaborative communication by key account representatives', *Journal of Personal Selling and Sales Management*, 22, 1, 23–32.

Selnes, F. (1998) 'Antecedents and consequences of trust and satisfaction in buyer-seller relationships', *European Journal of Marketing*, 32, 3, 305–322.

Shapiro, B.P. and Moriarty, R.T. (1984) 'Organising the National Account Force', working paper, Marketing Science Institute, MA.

Using the KAM Contemporary Issue within case studies

KAM has become increasingly important for many organizations as they attempt to develop effective strategies for dealing with the various segments that they operate in. For instance, in business to business marketing, KAM is highly relevant. In past cases such as WCI and Enzymes Ltd., growth was possible and sustainable through KAM. In business to consumer markets each account is an important account, especially in a case such as Reiss. In this instance some of the more tangible aspects of relationship marketing such as acquisition, retention and adaptation come into play. So a better understanding of KAM for the B2B markets can also help with trying to understand wider issues surrounding relationship marketing.

SUSTAINABILITY AND STRATEGY

Source: We are grateful to Pearson Education for granting us the permission to use Chapter 4 from *Marketing Strategies: A 21st Century Approach* by Ashok Ranchhod.

Sustainability: Limits to Growth

Introduction

As the world's population grows and some 90 million more individuals are added to the planet each year, many marketers are questioning some of the basic tenets of marketing. Is it right to expect continued growth? Should we be marketing goods that are likely to harm the planet? Should marketing concentrate on products that are 'green'? These and many other questions are being asked not just by marketers but by the general consumers themselves. In recent surveys, it has been shown that consumers are concerned about the products that they purchase; however cost may be a factor in purchasing products as well.

Nonetheless, in Germany, 88 per cent of consumers are ready to switch brands to greener products, the corresponding figures in Italy and Spain were 84 per cent and 82 per cent respectively (Wasik, 1996). In the US, the green market is estimated to include 52 million households (Ottman, 1993). In 1996, MORI categorized 36 per cent of its British poll respondents as 'green consumers' on the basis of their claim to have 'selected one product over another because of its environmentally friendly packaging, formulation or advertising' (Worcester, 1997). This compared with 19 per cent in 1988, (although it continued the steady decline from a peak of 50 per cent in 1990). This makes it important that marketers actually understand and respond to customer needs.

Furthermore, are the provisions of certain products and services sustainable? Sustainability is about understanding the interactions of the various stakeholders in an organization. Maximizing profits and looking for short-term gains in market share may in the long run be so harmful to certain groups of stakeholders that the company itself may suffer bad publicity. These stakeholders are the employees, the local community and government agencies. The main stakeholder is probably the planet itself and increasingly the public feels that business firms should take responsibility for environmental damage inflicted on parts of the earth in the pursuit of profit. An example of this is the cost to General Electric Company in the USA for removing two million cubic metres of contaminated sludge from the Hudson River (New Scientist, 2001). For 35 years the company poured some 500,000 kilogrammes of Polychlorinated biphenyls (PCBs) into the river, before they were banned in 1977. Residents living near the river bank claim to have suffered from a variety of PCB-related illnesses ranging from cancer to physical deformities. As a result of this, the US Environmental Protection Agency has decided to remove the sludge and have asked GEC to foot the $500 million bill.

In a situation like this, the factors are complex; however, the fact remains that the consumers of the period actually bought electrical equipment that was manufactured by GEC, generally unaware of the pollution problems. The onus, therefore remains on companies to ensure that their products and services are environmentally friendly or not and whether their practices are environmentally sustainable or not. This information also needs to filter through to the consumer. In this chapter, therefore we will explore various notions of sustainability, ranging from 'green' products to sustainable production. The aim of this chapter is to understand the implications of being environmentally friendly and how by taking such a stance, a company could create a sustainable competitive advantage in marketing.

Understanding environmental marketing

For many consumers, the term 'green' may evoke a range of different emotions and understanding. For some, it may mean products that do not harm the environment, for others it may mean products that have been made without harming the environment. Many may consider ethical and moral considerations such as fair trade with the developing nations. For some it could be charitable ventures such as Oxfam. From these examples, it can be seen that the term environmentally friendly encompasses a myriad of meanings for individuals, depending on their range of experiences and perspectives. The main issue here is the merging of the social concerns as well as ecological concerns. Many in marketing would argue that these are now inseparable (Peattie, 1995). Others argue that simply being green is not enough and that ethical issues also need to be taken into account. This is backed up by research into the notion of 'environmental justice' within the USA (Oyewole, 2001). The main contention is that many companies site chemical plants and dump toxic waste near poor or deprived communities. This is also part of a global concern where some products are cheaply made by communities who are too poor to complain about environmental issues, needing jobs and money to sustain themselves.

Hand in hand with this, crisis-ridden governments such as Indonesia, the Philippines, South Korea and Thailand cut back on environmental spend (French, 2000). For instance, in Russia, the budget for protected areas was cut by 40 per cent. The globalization of commerce is intensifying the environmental agenda, with many countries increasingly concerned about the effect of global consumption trends on the environment. This is shown in the diagrams below (Worldwatch Institute, 2000). The quotes are provided by the Institute.

Energy and climate

As our growing population increased its burning of coal and oil to produce power, the carbon locked in millions of years worth of ancient plant growth was released into the air, laying a heat-retaining blanket of carbon dioxide over the planet. Earth's temperature increased significantly. Climate scientists had predicted that this increase would disrupt weather. Indeed, annual damages from weather disasters have increased over 40-fold.

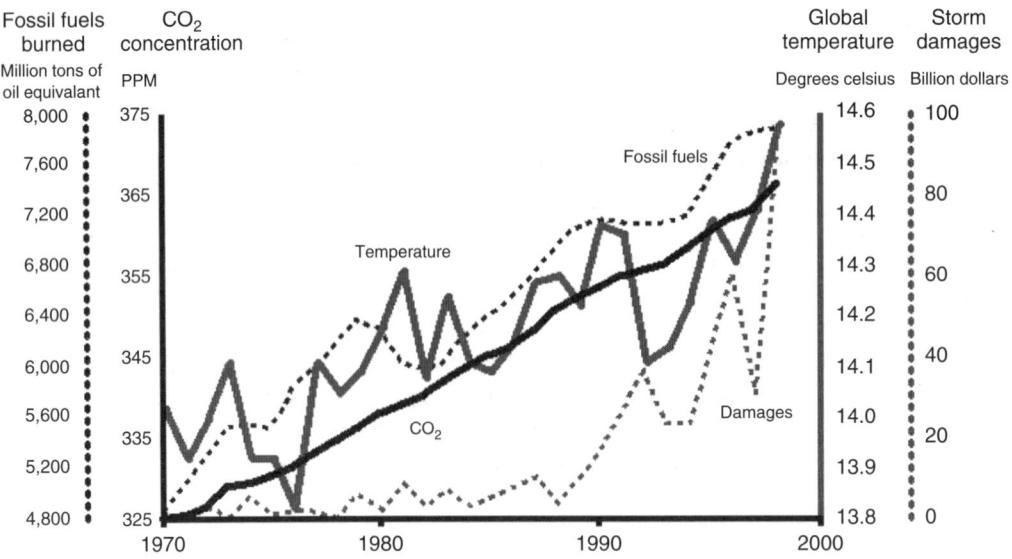

Figure 4.5 Energy and the climate

Chemicals and the biological boomerang

Our consumption of chemicals has exploded, with about three new synthetic chemicals introduced each day. Almost nothing is known about the long-term health and environmental effects of new synthetics, so we have been ambushed again and again by belated discoveries. One of the most ominous signs of this is the evolution of pesticide-resistant pests as the use of pesticides increases.

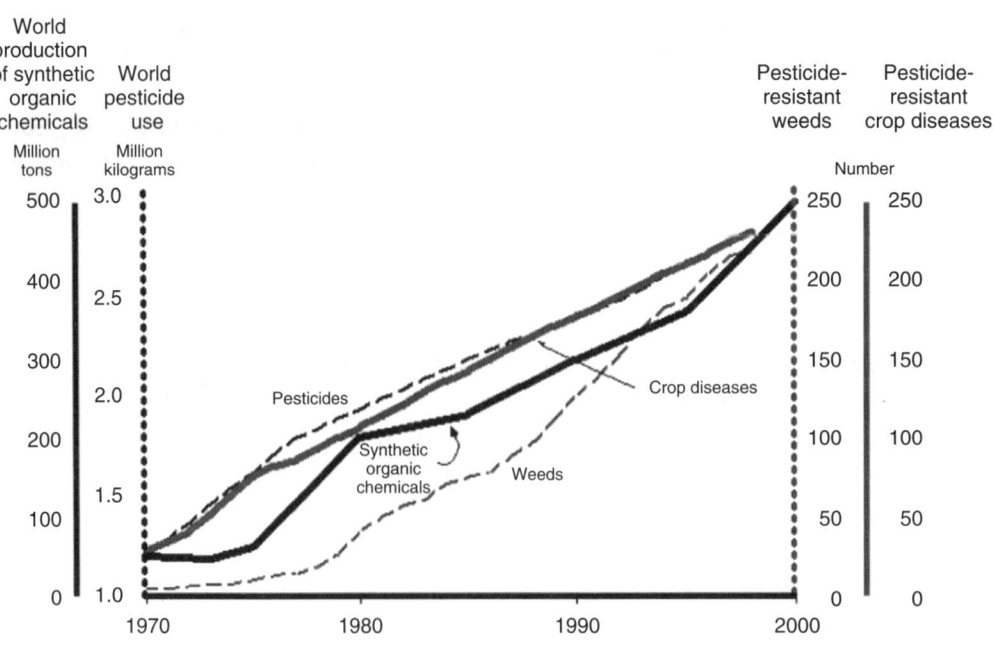

Figure 4.6 Chemicals and the biological boomerang

Commerce and the oceans

The global economy has more than doubled in the past 30 years, putting pressure on most countries to increase export income. Many have tried to increase revenues by selling more ocean fish – for which there is growing demand, since the increase in crop yields no longer keeps pace with population growth. Result: over fishing is decimating one stock after another, and the catch is getting thinner and thinner.

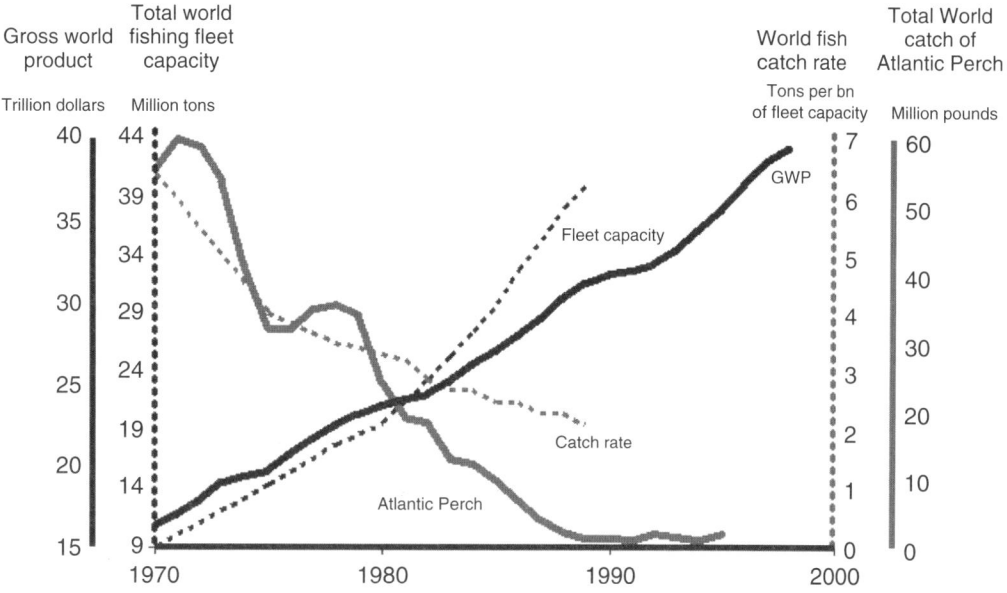

Figure 4.7 Commerce and the oceans

As production, marketing and consumption become increasingly global environmental issues affect every one of us. For marketers, who are often concerned with single products or brands, it is often difficult to disentangle the various interconnecting strands affecting the production of a single product. A complex piece of machinery such as a car may well have certain products which, have not been either ethically or environmentally produced. Some marketers would even say that the production and use of a car itself is environmentally unfriendly, as each car in use adds to local and global pollution. Given this range of views, we need to understand the different ways in which green marketing is perceived.

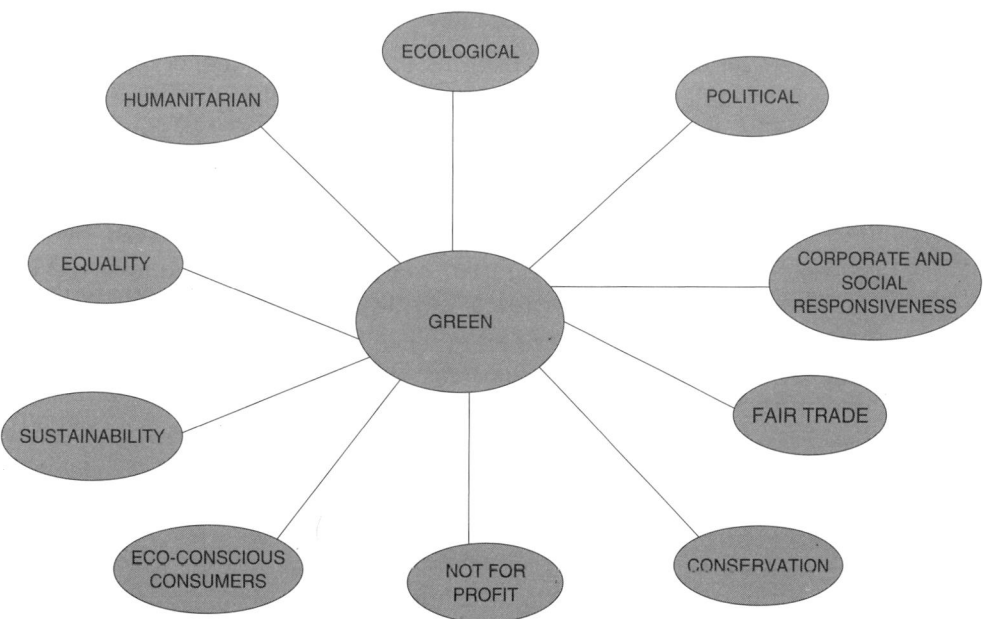

Figure 4.8 Green marketing
Source: Notions of GREEN from Peattie, 1995

In many ways, to be totally green means that the human population must eschew any luxuries beyond self-sufficiency. As the history of marketing shows, consumption has always played a large part in human existence. For this reason, many marketers feel that being totally green is unattainable, therefore the term 'greener' should be used (Charter and Polonsky, 1999). Figure 4.9 also shows the way in which many products are now global and the way in which consumption at the local level also has global implications.

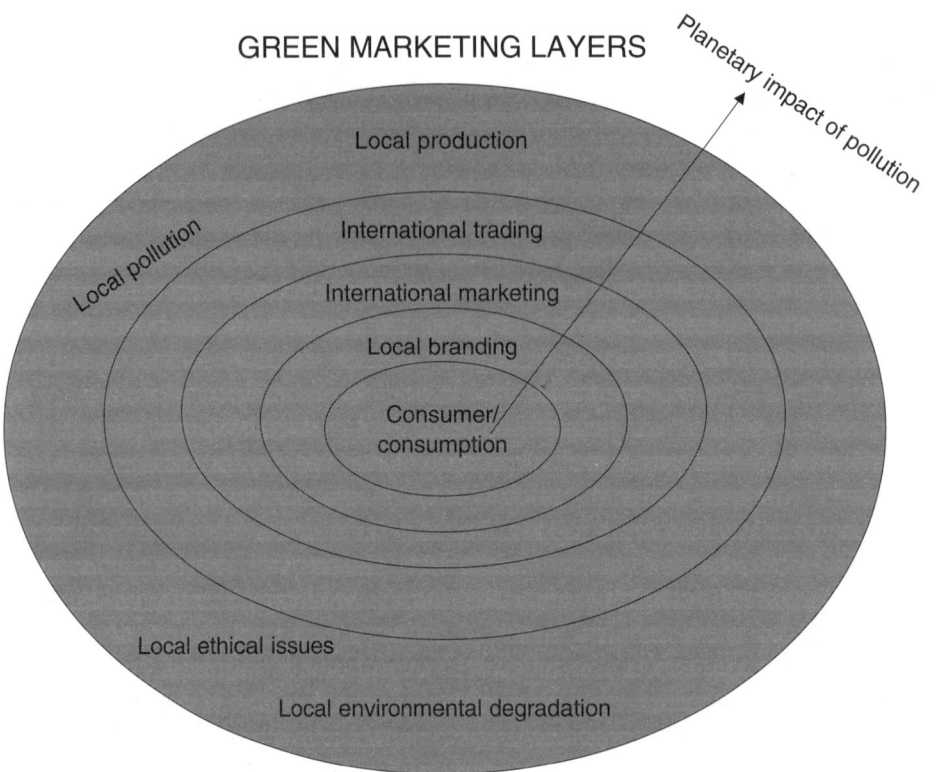

Figure 4.9 Global implications of Green marketing

In order to understand how products can be understood as being green, many complicated systems have evolved over the years and many multinationals are now taking the green issues more seriously. MacDonald's for instance has spent a great deal of money on improving their ability to recycle Its materials, but has been quiet on discussing the impact the company has on the environment as a result of the mass production of beef. McDonald's for instance have instituted the following programmes in order to combat energy wastage (Wasik, 1996):

a. *McRecycle USA programme* The company claims to purchase over $100 million of recycled packaging. Switching from white to brown bags has saved bleaching costs and prevented a greater degree of chemical pollution.

b. *Recycled materials in construction* The company sets aside 25 per cent of its construction budget for recycled materials for construction.

c. *Energy efficiency* In partnering with the US Environmental protection Agency, the company instituted a 'Green Lights' programme. Eco-efficient lighting was used in stores. The stores themselves were made more energy efficient. The energy saved has resulted in preventing over 30 tons of carbon dioxide being released into the air.

d. *Waste reduction action plan (WRAP)* The focus of this programme was to cut the amount of waste materials going to landfill sites by using recycled materials and paper.

Interestingly, the biggest failure of the many programmes instituted was in the recycling within the shop environment. Consumers were generally oblivious to this! So the final question is, is McDonald's a green product? This a difficult question to answer because the company has obviously tried hard to improve its products and services through the various ecologically efficient programmes. On the other hand the morality of mass-producing beef remains unresolved. Some would argue that even this brings necessary employment in poorer areas, others would argue that such farming is harmful to the environment. In the light of these fundamental questions, we can only argue for greener marketing.

Greener marketing may well colour different companies in different shades of green (see Figure 4.10). Again, it is important to note that both social and ecological issues are inextricably intertwined and a truly green company should address both issues simultaneously. Addressing both these issues are the correct routes to creating sustainable businesses and environments. The Nike case illustrates the particular problems faced by an organization caught exploiting workers and then as a result of public pressure, attempting to set things right.

Case example

Nike Corporation

Consider Nike, the $8 billion footwear and apparel company, which has become a lightning rod for activists, consumers, the media, and others, who have taken aim at the company's workplace, environmental and human rights practices. According to its critics, Nike has engaged in a variety of practices that have exploited Third World workers and the communities where they live. The images proffered by Nike's critics are vivid: women and young children toiling for long hours for low pay in squalid conditions, breathing fumes of toxic chemicals, unable to protest for fear of losing their jobs, manufacturing goods whose price tags exceed their monthly pay.

Nike acknowledges that in the past it was less than vigilant in monitoring the practices of its factories – although nearly all of which are contracted to independent manufacturers. It has now launched an aggressive and ambitious effort not only to correct such situations but to also set a shining example for its industry. The company has begun using sustainability as a design criterion to reduce the use of toxic materials and generation of waste in its manufacturing process. Nike cut the use of solvents in its adhesives by 800,000 gallons in one year and has a goal of reducing its use of volatile organic compounds per unit of production by 90 per cent by 2001. The company also supports organic cotton farming by providing incentives for farmers to switch to organic production.

None of this seems to have stemmed the tide of criticism. In recent years, Nike has been named among the ten 'worst' international corporations by Multinational Monitor magazine. It had an Indonesian factory looted and burned by protesters and suffered criticisms by US women's groups, who pilloried the company for commercials that call for empowering women while poorly paying its predominantly female overseas workers. Its hometown, Portland, Oregon adopted a resolution urging its troubled school district to 'respectfully decline' a $500,000 cash donation because of the company's alleged human rights abuses.

The experiences of Nike and other companies that have come under intense public scrutiny because of perceived wrongdoings suggest that consumers' expectations of brands are changing. It is no longer enough that a company delivers good-quality products. In the search for differentiation, the battleground shifts from the tangible – pounds of chemicals and other wastes released into the environment – to the intangible – ethics, values and corporate culture.

So ethics are part of understanding sustainable marketing strategies. The other part of understanding sustainability lies in taking a different view on the commonly quoted product life cycle.

The life cycle analysis (LCA) concept – life cycle thinking

One way of considering the creation and utilization of products and services which are environmentally friendly is the LCA concept. The LCA is recognized both as a concept and an analytical environmental management tool (SPOLD, 1995). This concept, sometimes termed life cycle thinking, helps everyone (consumers and producers alike) to understand the overall environmental implications of the services required by society. This promotes the consideration of the cradle-to-grave implications of any actions taken, forcing thinking to move beyond the narrow vestiges of supply chains and sector-based considerations of the environment and considers the wider implications of our activities.

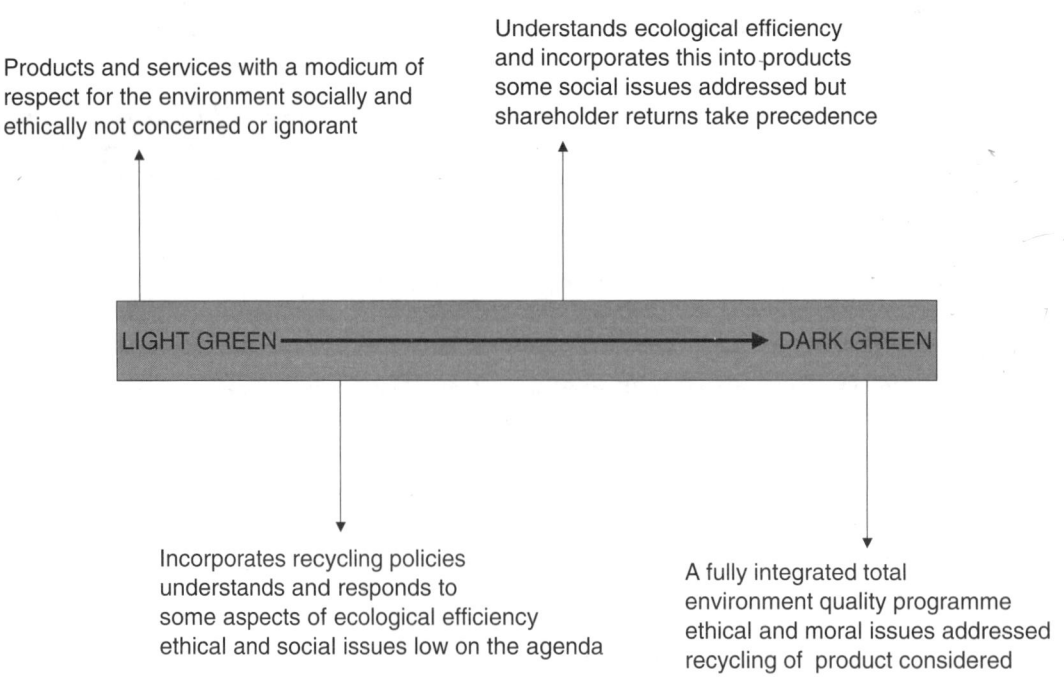

Products and services with a modicum of respect for the environment socially and ethically not concerned or ignorant

Understands ecological efficiency and incorporates this into products some social issues addressed but shareholder returns take precedence

LIGHT GREEN ————————————▶ DARK GREEN

Incorporates recycling policies understands and responds to some aspects of ecological efficiency ethical and social issues low on the agenda

A fully integrated total environment quality programme ethical and moral issues addressed recycling of product considered

How green is a company?

Figure 4.10 Measuring the green policy of organizations
Source: Ranchhod (2001)

Case study

MINI CASE

Asia is not renowned for being the most advanced region as far as environmental awareness goes. Just think of the car-clogged, highly polluted streets of many of Asia's big cities, the lack of paper recycling systems throughout much of the region or even the poor quality of drinking water in some places further off the beaten track.

But a mixed track record is no excuse for Asian industries today and many of the region's major pulp and paper manufacturers are facing up to the 'green challenge'. One such company is Indonesia's Riau Andalan Pulp and Paper (RAPP), part of the Asia Pacific Resources International (APRIL) group. On the environmental front, RAPP was arguably helped along by its cooperation, albeit short lived, with Finland's UPM-Kymmene. 'The presence of a European company helped raise environmental awareness and performance,' according to Canesio P Munoz, the company's environmental manager. But since the alliance broke down and RAPP was left standing on its own two feet, there has been no let-up in the company's momentum for greener and cleaner operations.

At present, RAPP is constructing a second pulp line at its Kerinci mill in the Riau province on the Indonesian island of Sumatra. As the company starts to expand towards a two million ton/yr pulp capacity target, the mill is becoming increasingly aware of the need to meet stringent environmental targets to satisfy both local and international demands. The company is targeting a first quarter 2001 startup date for the new line at the Riau mill.

As part of its environmental commitment, APRIL is working on its first annual environmental report. But it is not just a moral sense of concern for the mill's surroundings which is driving APRIL – pressure is coming from many quarters. Local people have lodged complaints about skin-related diseases and fish depletion in the nearby Kampar river. As a result of these allegations, non-governmental organizations (NGOs) have levelled criticisms at the pulp and paper mill. There have also been some critical voices from overseas, for example in Europe.

In an attempt to put these fears and accusations to rest, APRIL has appointed independent bodies to carry out research and help prove that the Indonesian mill operates in line with international standards, and in some cases, beats these targets (Table 4.1).

Outside approval

One independent body that RAPP selected was the Finnish Environmental Research Group which carried out an environmental impact assessment at the mill. The report was published last September and concluded that RAPP's industrial complex contained low levels of pollutants and that the external treatment seemed to work efficiently, although improvements of nutrient dosage could be carried out. The Finnish group also came to the conclusion that the risk for humans coming into contact with the Kampar river water was 'negligible or non-existent'. As for the river's fish life, investigations suggested that the level of pulp mill-effluent contaminants was low enough not to have any serious effect on the animals.

Soon after the Finnish report, RAPP launched a one-year programme with local NGOs to carry out further studies into the effects of the pulp and paper operations on the quality of the local river. The gist of these investigations is to sample biodata from the Kampar river every three months and compare examples taken from upstream, downstream and at the point of effluent discharge from the pulp mill.

Table 4.1 RAPP-effluent load as compared to international standards (kg/ton)

Parameter Cluster Rules	Indonesian		Canada			Sweden
	RAPP (Early 2000)	(BC)				Existing Mills
New mills	(Oct 1999)					
BOD5	8.5	4.5	8.7	8.05	5.5	2.93
COD	29.75	No Spec	31	No Spec	No Spec	11.22
TSS	8.5	7.0	4.0	16.4	9.5	4.41
pH	6–9	5–9	5–9	5–9	5–9	7.1–8.2
AOX	No spec	1.5	0.23	0.623	0.272	0.12

No Spec = No Specification

The research is a three-pronged effort, with local NGO Riau Mandiri assessing the water quality, the Fisheries department of the University of Riau in charge of the river biology/ecology and the University of Singapore investigating health-related matters.

The preliminary results are good news for RAPP, with no strong condemnations being thrown in its direction. The water quality is described as 'generally good', although Riau Mandiri is looking further into the COD (chemical oxygen demand) and BOD (biological oxygen demand) readings which have recently started to rise. The University of Riau has not noticed any significant difference to the natural river life either. In fact, fish stocks actually increased due to higher nitrogen and phosphorous levels in the effluent treatment. The university team continues to assess the quality of the fish stocks as it seems that sulphur levels are slightly higher than normal, though.

On top of that, the reports from local people about skin irritations are not being blamed on RAPP and it is thought that plants may be the problem. The findings of one Riau University study suggest that it is 'unlikely' that river water is a cause of inflammatory skin problems among villagers. Monitoring will continue, though, until a more conclusive verdict is reached.

It is certainly in RAPP's interests to cooperate with the NGOs and prove the mill's case wherever possible, as the NGOs can act as a powerful lobbyist. As Riau Mandiri spokesperson, Anny Hardiyanti, says, 'After a year's monitoring, if we find negative results, we will urge the company to address the problem. And if the problem is not addressed, we will launch a campaign against the company responsible.' Added to that, the NGO is not afraid of carrying out threats of action. It has already launched several campaigns against other companies, which were found to be polluting another nearby river in the region.

Forest sustenance

A key tenet of APRIL's environmental policy is striving towards fully sustainable forest management. The Indonesian mill's long-term goal is to achieve sustainable forest management certification. But as an interim step, the mill is focusing on an ISO 14001 certificate for its forestry operations, which it hopes to receive by the end of this year. If the company sticks to the timetable, certification would come just a few months after RAPP was awarded ISO 9002 for its pulp and paper operations.

ISO 14001 is an environmental management system, which provides criteria for assessing a company's use of air, water, soil and resources. The drive towards this certification comes from RAPP's customers around the globe, and particularly from European consumers.

Part of the company's efforts towards full sustainability is the development of its acacia plantations. Planting started back in 1993 and some of the plantations are already mature, but the company is waiting until next year before harvesting the area for strategic reasons. RAPP aims to make a full switch from mixed tropical hardwood to acacia plantations by 2008.

The company has also carried out extensive tests on the plantations and is extremely pleased with the yield and quality results. The plantations are expected to yield 210 m^3/ha at harvest and achieve a wood to pulp conversion rate of 4.5 m^3/ton/ib. As a result, RAPP hopes to gain the double advantage of higher yields and limiting any adverse effects on the environment.

By RAPP's calculations, the mill will need 127,500 ha of plantations to supply pulp line #1 which has an 850,000 ton/yr capacity (Table 4.2). Pulp line #2A is due to come on line by the first quarter of 2001, bringing total capacity up to 1.3 million tons/year. RAPP calculates that it will need 195,000 ha/yr of acacia plantations to meet this pulp capacity, and it is no surprise perhaps that the company happens to have exactly this amount available. Originally the government allocated 280,000 ha of land to RAPP for conversion into plantations. The area chosen by the government was so-called 'non-productive land' – in other words the land had already been logged over and exploited. Some of this area must be maintained as a greenbelt area to protect wildlife and ensure biodiversity in the area, leaving the company with the magic number of 195,000 ha/yr for converting into plantations.

Indonesia's social scene

On paper, the land transfer sounds like a relatively simple procedure – the government allocates land and the company decides to convert the area into plantations. In practice, though, there are many more hurdles to be cleared. For example, some of the allocated land is next to local settlements and the communities claim that the ground is theirs in accordance with 'community rights'. Companies such as RAPP are only able to operate effectively by avoiding conflicts with these local communities. This involves talking with the people, suggesting alternative sources of income and convincing them that they will not lose out. As environmental manager, Munoz, says, 'We don't drive people out. Resolutions are always reached by consensus.'

Of the total area allocated to RAPP, some 60,000 ha of land were termed so-called 'problem areas'. So far, the company has resolved approximately half of the issues. RAPP is all too aware of the need to work with the local people to avoid potentially serious problems. For example, last December the Kerinci mill was brought to a standstill as demonstrators took to the streets in protest over a labour dispute. And in the new era of 'reformation' which is flourishing in Indonesia, local communities are becoming increasingly aware of their rights, and companies such as RAPP clearly want to avoid conflicts wherever possible.

To date, RAPP has employed a host of community development (CD) projects to try and keep the peace with the locals. The CD programs have existed since 1993, although the initiative was significantly expanded in 1998. Last year alone, the company implemented programs in six local villages. RAPP has carried out initiatives such as building a mosque, providing drinking water, building bridges to overcome transportation difficulties and training the villagers to cultivate unused land for productive and profitable uses.

RAPP's budget for CD programs in 2000 is $2 million and the company's management believes that it is money well spent. Not only does it benefit the local people, but it also promotes good relations with neighbouring communities and improves the skills of potential employees for the pulp and paper mill.

One village called Gunung Sahilan chose to develop oil palm plantations with the company's CD program funds. As a result, APRIL teamed up with an associated company, Asian Agri, which is active in the oil palm industry. The alliance has worked well and the villagers seem extremely pleased with the project's success. But when asked if he was satisfied, the village chief replied, 'We don't need more, but we want more.' A note of warning to RAPP, perhaps, that it cannot sit back and relax. The company must constantly remain attentive to the demands of the local people just as much as, if not more than, those of the international community.

Table 4.2 Plantation supplies at RAPP

		Line 1	Line 1+2A	Line 1+2A+ 2B
Pulp mill capacity		850,000	1,300,000	2,000,000
Acacia growth rate				
Mean annual increment	M3/ha/a	30	30	30
Rotation	Yr	7	7	7
Yield at harvest	M3/ha	210	210	210
Wood to pulp conversion				
Acacia species	M3/t/ib	4.5	4.5	4.5
Wood and HTI requirement				
Annual acacia input	M3/yr	3,825,0-00	5,850,000	9,000,000
Total net HTI area required	ha	127,500	195,000	300,000
Land resources for tree				
Plantation development				
RAPP HTI concessions area	ha	195,000	195,000	195,000
Associated companies/jvs	ha	0	0	85,000
Tree farms	ha	0	0	20,000
Total area	ha	195,000	195,000	300,000

HTI = hutan tanaman industry

The case illustrates the various factors involved in a company striving to be green. The chain to the final consumer however, can be quite long.

Paper/Pulp production ──────▸ Packaging ──────────────▸ Consumer
                                       Printing(newspapers/books)   │
                                       Paper products   ▼
                                                                    Disposal/Recycling

Consider the life cycle of the products taking into account the various stages of responsibilities.

According to SPOLD, life cycle thinking reflects the acceptance that key company stakeholders cannot strictly limit their responsibilities to those phases of the life cycle of a product, process or activity in which they are actively involved. It expands the scope of their responsibility to include environmental implications along the entire life cycle of the product, process or activity. The implication of this type of thinking is that all processors, manufacturers, distributors, retailers, users and waste managers in the life cycle share responsibility.

The individual share of responsibility for each of them will be greatest in the parts of the life cycle under their direct control and least in the other stages of the cycle. Life cycle thinking has been applied to much of the legislation emanating from the European Commission, especially with regards to product and waste policy. The concept of producer responsibility is at the heart of waste strategy, and it follows life cycle thinking. An example of this is given in Figure 4.11.

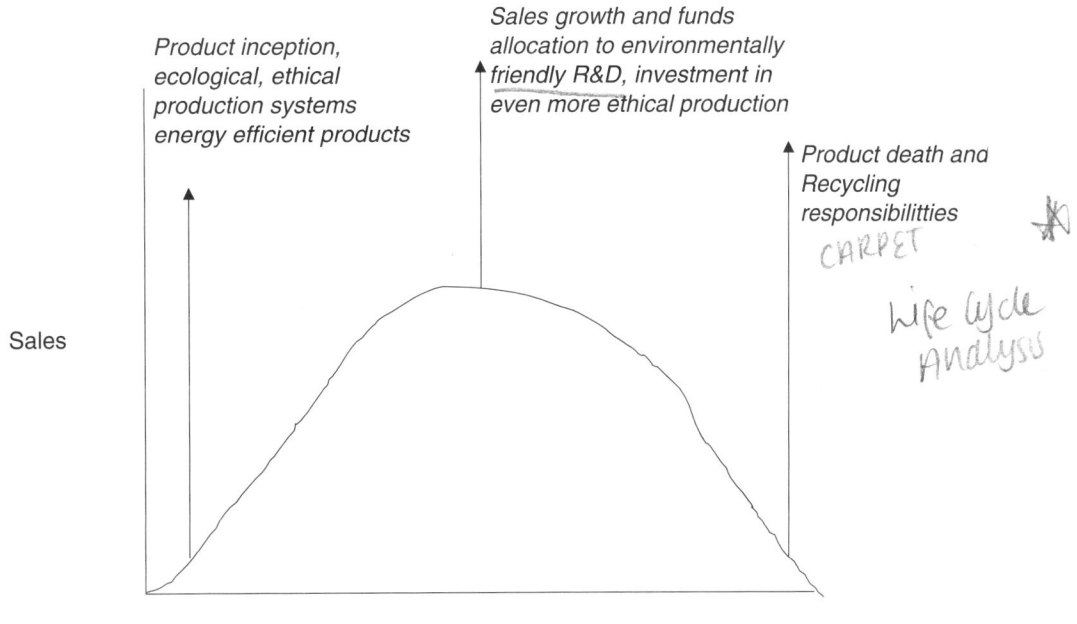

Figure 4.11 Green life cycle analysis
Source: Ranchhod (2001)

Currently there are various different concepts that are related to developing ecologically sound products. Some of these are as follows:

a.   *Design for the environment*   There are many initiatives for reducing the various environmental impacts that a product may unleash. These could be at the production stage, the usage stage, or the disposal stage. In designing for the environment, technologists are concerned with reducing energy consumption (both in the production of an item as well as when it is in use) and generally conserving resources. The main trends are:

   1.   The incorporation of information from LCA into design.
   2.   The definition of environmental objectives.
   3.   A focus on the relationship between the product and the consumer and how the design can encourage environmentally responsible behaviour in the consumer.

According to the US EPA (1992) Life Cycle Design is

   A systems-oriented approach for designing more ecologically and economically sustainable product systems which integrates environmental requirements into the earliest stages of design. In LCD, environmental performance, cost, cultural and legal requirements are balanced

b. *Clean technology*   A definition of Clean Technology is that it is the means of providing a human benefit which, overall, uses less resources and causes less environmental damage than alternative means with which it is economically competitive (Clift, 1995).

c. *Industrial ecology*   This is generally concerned with the evolution of technology and economic systems in such a way that human activities mimic mature biological systems with regard to being self-contained in their material and resource use (Allenby, 1994). Governments and non-governmental organizations often use this idea when they assess industrial processes.

d. *Total quality environment management*   This concept synthesizes environmental management and total quality management (TQM) (GEMI, 1993). TQEM relies on the following basic parts:

   1. *Identify customers*   The definition of quality dependent on what the customers want (a broader definition of customers is taken and they include consumers, legislators, environmental groups and society at large).

   2. *Continuous improvement*   A systematic approach at continuously improving processes all the time.

   3. *Do the job right the first time*   In terms of the environment, eliminate problems at the outset. Quality failures may be detrimental to the environment and also incur financial costs, without providing benefits to the consumer

   4. *Take a systems approach*   Each part of environmental management is considered to be a 'system'. This includes people, equipment and processes. Weak links in the system are addressed.

In general the Plan-Do-Check-Act (PDCA) cycle is followed in common with typical TQM programmes.

All these concepts are interlinked and there is now a concerted approach to take a more holistic view and incorporate each of these concepts into a general framework for sustainable development (SETAC, 1998).

Implications for organizations

For organizations it is becoming increasingly important to incorporate green thinking into their processes and products. Organizations need to consider very carefully how much their activities impact on the planet. Any improvement creates a net benefit for both the consumer and the planet. There are charges against companies that they embrace a green attitude at a superficial level and are generally engaged in 'greenwashing' the public through clever advertising and public relations activities. In fact even companies like Body Shop have been criticized for exaggerating their claims with regards to promoting sustainable development and the purity of their ingredients (Stauber and Rampton, 1995) In many cases, companies even pursuing a modicum of green policies are not rewarded in the marketplace (Wong, Turner and

Stoneman, 1996). Such criticisms could be levelled at almost every corporation. Nonetheless, it is important to realize that corporations can, even by implementing *some* of the concepts discussed above, have a major impact on the environment. For instance:

o Anheuser-Busch has developed an aluminium can that is 33 per cent lighter. This reduced use of aluminium combined with an overall recycling plan saves the company $200 million a year.

o Ford Motor Company used more than 60 million two-litre plastic soda bottles in the manufacturing of grille reinforcements, window frames, engine covers and trunk carpets. In 1999, this effort accounted for 7.5 million pounds of plastic.

o Kellogg's plant in Bremen, Germany, employs a wastewater recycling operation that reduces water consumption and wastewater effluent. In India, a Kellogg vapour absorption system is used to provide plant air conditioning, eliminating the use of ozone-depleting substances. Fluorescent bulbs at the Kellogg plant in New Jersey are sent for recycling, removing potentially hazardous materials from landfills (Rand Corporation, 2000).

In spite of cynical views, these efforts not only save the companies concerned millions, but also save resources. These types of savings are not easily obtainable through individual customers. It is important that companies pursue such strategies. This is especially important when you consider that a study showed that of the 100 largest economies in the world, 51 were global corporations – only 49 were countries (Anderson and Cavanagh, 1996). Mitsubishi was larger than the fourth most populous nation on Earth, Indonesia. General Motors was bigger than Denmark, and Toyota bigger than Norway. Often large chunks of world trade are actually transactions between different parts of organizations. Companies therefore, have to be proactive in pursuing ecologically friendly processes and also in producing such products. In addition to this, they are also under pressure from consumers and non-governmental organizations (NGOs such as Greenpeace). Companies have become much more sensitive to such pressures because of (Bennet and James, 1999) :

o The growing economic value of a good corporate reputation and a strong positively regarded brand. These can be put at risk by adverse criticism of environmental and social performance (Fomburn, 1996).

o The growing number of customers who are becoming more 'green conscious' (this is discussed later), taking social and environmental criteria into account when purchasing goods or services.

o The tremendous flow of information, at unprecedented levels, through satellite TV stations such as CNN and the Internet. In the future, it is likely that information will also be transferred 'on the move' through mobile communication devices such as WAP phones. This flow of information increases the visibility of any enterprise.

o Companies are also dependent on workforces who are highly educated and are often more environmentally literate than their older counterparts.

Interestingly, a recent survey of ethical funds shows that they have performed strongly over the past three years. Many funds have shown growth ranging from 73 to 50 per cent (Bien, 2001). These are early days, but the current results bode well for ethical and green investments. What then, should companies strive to achieve? Some of the key questions that companies should be addressing are given at the end of the chapter. In many ways, companies have to strive to get into a virtual circle and constantly look forward to the future with their R&D (Figure 4.12).

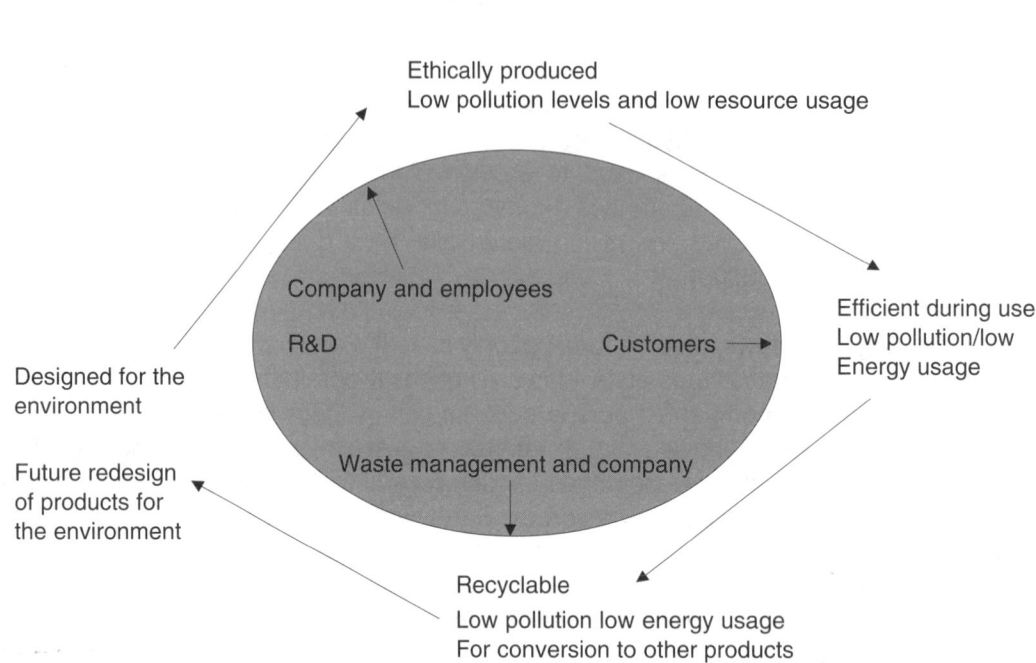

Figure 4.12 Assessing green credentials

Given this type of virtual way in which companies could operate, the competitive advantages that could be gained are considerable. Various authors have tried different types of categorizations, for instance Hart (2000) has developed the sustainability strategy where companies can rate themselves on the following scale for each quadrant (1 – nonexistent; 2 – emerging; 3 – established; or 4 – institutionalized). Based on this assessment each individual organization can look for gaps and attempt to understand their sustainability credentials and begin to plan both internal and external strategies for the future.

Another way of assessing the total commitment of a company to sustainability and ethical consideration is to utilize the matrix shown below (Figure 4.13). The questions help in understanding the box in which a company falls.

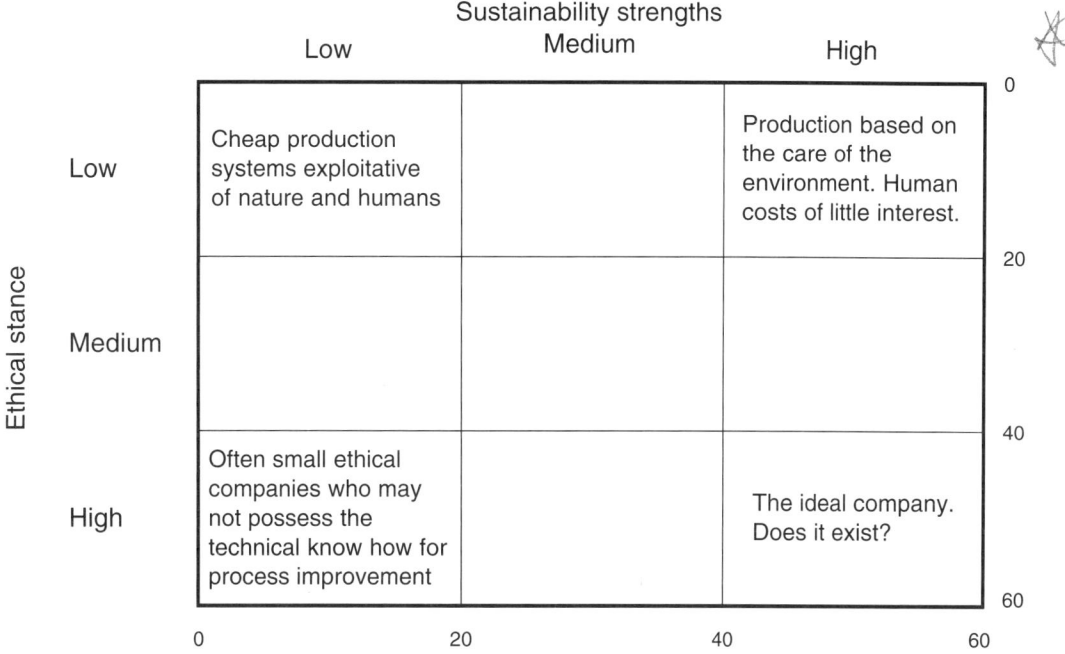

Figure 4.13 Sustainability and ethical matrix

The following questions were formulated by understanding the various cases for greener organizations (Peattie and Charter, 1997, Piasecki, Fletcher and Mendelson, 1999, Crosbie and Knight, 1995). Look at the questions set. Companies scoring 12 points in both sets of questions fall into the top left-hand quadrant. Companies scoring 60 in both sets of questions fall into the bottom right hand quadrant. The set of questions is designed to show the quadrant in which a company falls (Figure 4.14). It also then points the way for future improvement and the opportunities that may be available.

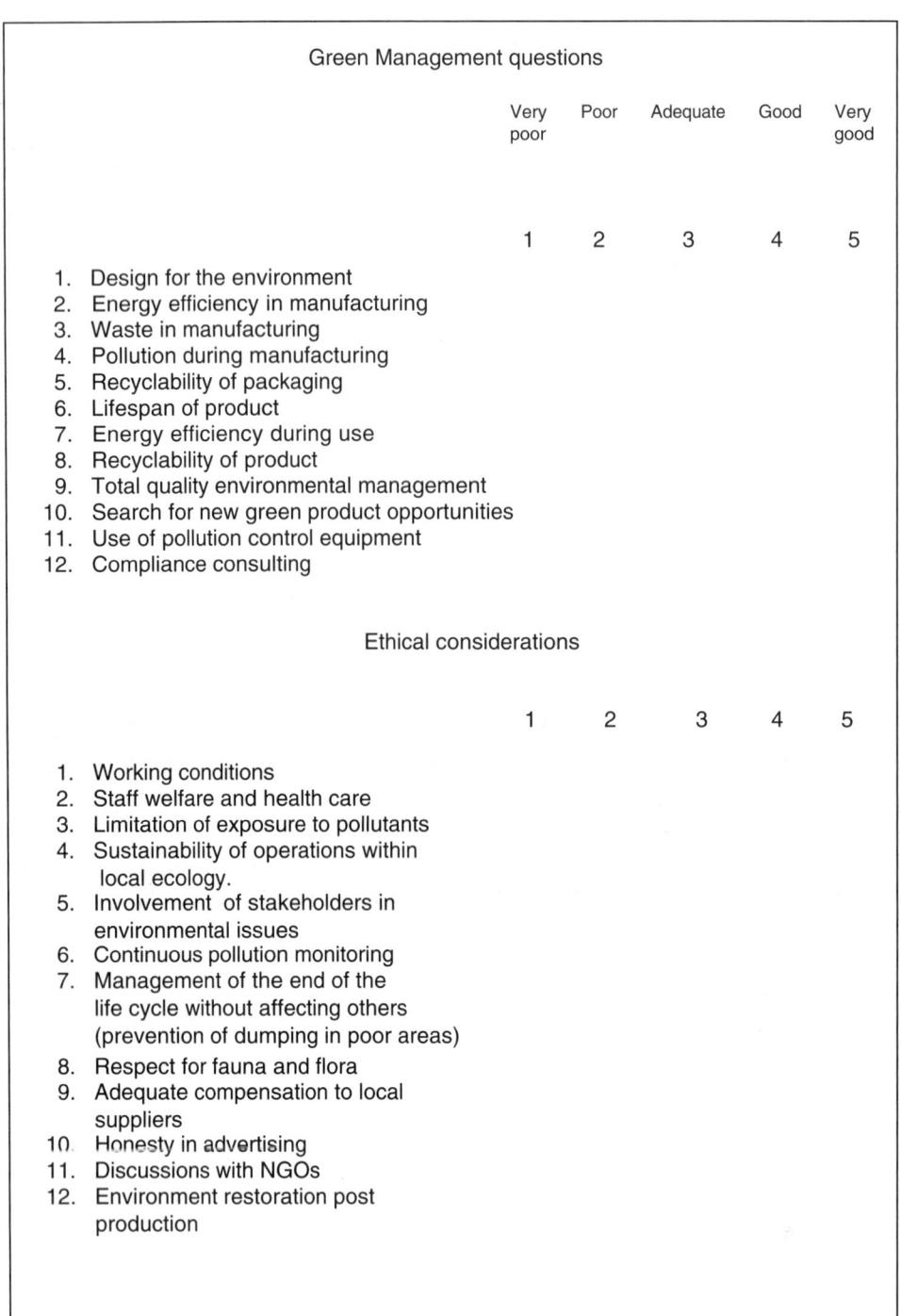

Green Management questions

	Very poor	Poor	Adequate	Good	Very good
	1	2	3	4	5

1. Design for the environment
2. Energy efficiency in manufacturing
3. Waste in manufacturing
4. Pollution during manufacturing
5. Recyclability of packaging
6. Lifespan of product
7. Energy efficiency during use
8. Recyclability of product
9. Total quality environmental management
10. Search for new green product opportunities
11. Use of pollution control equipment
12. Compliance consulting

Ethical considerations

	1	2	3	4	5

1. Working conditions
2. Staff welfare and health care
3. Limitation of exposure to pollutants
4. Sustainability of operations within local ecology.
5. Involvement of stakeholders in environmental issues
6. Continuous pollution monitoring
7. Management of the end of the life cycle without affecting others (prevention of dumping in poor areas)
8. Respect for fauna and flora
9. Adequate compensation to local suppliers
10. Honesty in advertising
11. Discussions with NGOs
12. Environment restoration post production

Figure 4.14 Green management questions

Companies scoring in the medium/medium range (middle of the matrix) can be prone to resorting to strong advertising campaigns and PR in order to 'greenwash' the public. Consumers often have to rely on specialist journals or articles in newspapers for a true indication of a company's policy. There is a great danger for companies to pay lip service to green strategies and not necessarily address the key issues involved. These issues are explored in detail in the hard-hitting book by Stauber and Rampton (1995). As discussed before, a company that is truly following sustainable principles has to be both ethically and environmentally sound. Customers too are realizing that we do not live in a world with infinite resources. In fact the new-world paradigm reflects the fact that we are *a part* of nature and not *apart* from it (Wasik, 1996). The Postmodern consumer is more concerned about nature and is likely to look at issues holistically, Table 4.3 illustrates this.

Table 4.3 Old versus new paradigms

Old World View	New World View
Continuous unbridled growth	Sustainable, green economics
Conquer nature, reap resources	Biophilia (affinity for nature)
Environmental compliance	Eco-auditing
Marketing to fill needs	Marketing to sustain life
Materialism	Personalism
Industrial production	Industrial ecology
Design for obsolescence, disposal	Design for environment
Cost accounting (profit/loss statements)	Full cost accounting
Departmentalism, reductionism	Holism

Green consumer behaviour

According to a survey carried out by the Wirthlin Group (Wirthlin Worldwide, 2000), two-thirds of American consumers agreed that 'environmental standards cannot be too high and continuing improvements must be made regardless of the costs.' In 1999, a Gallup poll survey found that 68 per cent of Americans worried a great deal about the pollution of drinking water and 53 per cent about the contamination of soil and water by toxic waste. Understanding the complexity of the human/ecological interface requires a degree of scientific understanding. Yet surveys conducted by the National Science Foundation suggest that, even using lenient standards, only about 11 per cent of citizens understand enough of the vocabulary and concepts of science in general, in order to be considered scientifically literate (National Science Foundation, 1998).

This is an especially important issue when companies are advertising the green benefits of their products. How many consumers will actually understand the claims made? Are they likely to understand the scientific reasoning behind particular policies or are they likely to be emotively manipulated by the press in a simplistic manner? Quite often, people are very likely to understand simple cause-and-effect relationships. According to Coyle the NEETF president (NEETF/Roper, 2000):

'…[People] understand that cars pollute, or that species become extinct when habitat is destroyed. But when there are two or more steps involved…such as energy production from fossil-fuelled power stations contributing to climate change, thereby warming ocean waters sufficiently to inhibit the production of plankton for fish, thus impairing the survival of marine life…public understanding drops precipitously.' Each year, The National Environmental Education & Training Foundation (NEETF) issues a 10-question survey on environmental awareness; in a typical year, Americans averaged fewer than 25 per cent correct answers to basic environmental literacy questions. Furthermore, myths and misconceptions persist. Surveys indicate that many Americans still believe that trash bags can be made to biodegrade in landfills (virtually nothing degrades in landfills). Many people still believe aerosol cans contain ozone-destroying ingredients (chlorofluorocarbons were banned from aerosols in 1978) and that landfills are brimming with plastic (plastic accounts for just 9 per cent of municipal solid waste, paper and cardboard four times as much).

This can be illustrated by an Energy and Environmental Profile Analysis of Children's Single-Use and Reusable cloth diapers carried out by Franklin Associates in 1992 and explained in Fuller (1999). For many consumers, the intuitive understanding is that plastic/paper diapers are vastly energy consuming and polluting. The comparative scientific analysis however shows that the environmental answers are not clear cut. The results show that:

- o Home cloth diapers consume 33 per cent more energy than single-use diapers and 12 per cent more energy than commercial cloth diapers.
- o Single-use diapers produce about twice the total solid waste by volume of home or commercial cloth diapers.
- o Home cloth diapers produce nearly twice the total atmospheric emissions of single-use diapers or commercial cloth diapers.
- o Home or commercial diapers produce about seven times the total water-borne waste of single-use diapers.
- o Home or commercial cloth diapers consume more than twice the water volume of single-use diapers.

Many criticisms can be levelled at such an analysis and indeed, some authors argue that single use diapers also contribute to air pollution, via incineration. They may also be the cause of allergic skin reactions. Nonetheless the case illustrates the complexity of issues involved when undertaking some sort of life cycle analysis for products. Consumers, too, need to be able to follow complex arguments in order to make valid judgements.

Roper Starch (Rand Corporation, 2000) who produce the Green Gauge Report on the environment and environmentally conscious purchase decisions, showed how consumer attitudes broke down in the 2000 survey:

11 per cent True-Blue Greens   The recyclers, composters, letter-writers, and volunteers of the world, the ones most likely to go out of their way to buy organic foods, recycled paper products, rechargeable batteries, less toxic paints and other goods with environmentally preferable attributes.

5 per cent Greenback Greens   Those who will contribute to environmental organizations or spend more for green products, but not consider changes in lifestyles or housekeeping due to environmental concerns.

33 per cent Sprouts   Those who care about the environment, but who will only spend slightly more for environmentally sensitive products.

18 per cent Grousers   These are people who care about the environment but view it as someone else's problem; Grousers don't seek environmentally sensitive goods or consider green-minded lifestyle changes.

33 per cent Basic Browns   People who are essentially unconcerned about the environment. There is another way of slicing the consumers and that is the traditional method of classifying consumers as:

a. *Traditionalists* Those who believe in the nostalgic image of small towns and conservative churches.

b. *Moderns* These are individuals who are more materialistic and consumer oriented. They are generally individuals who see life through the same filters as Time magazine.

c. *The cultural creatives* This is a new category, discussed by Dr Paul Ray (Rand Corporation, 2000) as a result of market research studies in consumer behaviour. The cultural creatives (CCs) have often been involved in or care about three to six social movements. These are:

- ◦ Very strong environmentalism.
- ◦ The condition of the whole planet.
- ◦ Civil rights.
- ◦ Peace.
- ◦ Social justice.
- ◦ New spiritualities.
- ◦ Organic food.
- ◦ Holistic health.

Many follow personal paths and spiritual goals. These individuals account for a high proportion of people using alternative healthcare and every other Lifestyle of Health and Sustainability (LOHAS) product and service. The individuals are very good at putting their own big picture together from a diverse range of sources of information. They compare and contrast and are adept at understanding the real issues. They are the least likely to be 'greenwashed'. In addition to this, to fully appreciate the sustainable lifestyle, the Natural Business Communications and the Natural Marketing Institute believe that the greater paradigm of such existence is LOHAS. The LOHAS market comprises five core market segments – sustainable economy, healthy lifestyles, personal development, alternative healthcare and ecological lifestyles. The five segments combined represented a $226.8 billion US market and an estimated $546 billion global market in 2000. Within each of these five segments are many specific categories of products and services across a vast array of businesses and industries. The chart below shows the total size for the five key LOHAS segments and the associated industry categories:

Table 4.4 Key LOHAS Segments and Industries

LOHAS market segment	Total in $ millions
Sustainable economy	$76,470
Healthy lifestyles	$27,811
Alternative healthcare	$30,698
Personal development (mind, body, spirit)	$10,628
Ecological lifestyles	$81,178
TOTAL US LOHAS MARKET	$226.8 billion

Source: Rand Corporation, 2000

The 'Ecological Lifestyles' and 'Sustainable Economy' segments represent nearly 75 per cent of the global market, if the US breakdown is emulated around the world. In the light of this complexity of what exactly is a green consumer, several interrelated factors have to be taken into account as shown in Figure 4.15. The complexities surrounding the definition of a green consumer are indeed great. However, the examples above and the discussions show that a new breed of consumer is indeed emerging. This new consumer is influenced by many factors. These factors are generally concerned for a need to protect the environment and to lead ethically correct lifestyles. The market trends show that these consumers are growing in numbers. Companies wishing to understand this growing band of potential customers' need to address their marketing offer in a sensible and honest manner. They also need to consider the way in which markets may move in the future.

Green marketing strategies

options: *FOR*

In many cases, companies often take reactive stances to green issues. These reactive stances often damage the credibility of a company and the products that are sold. It is therefore important for companies that are seriously concerned about green issues to be more proactive and pursue a market orientation that is green in its design. In order to gain competitive advantage, companies have to exhibit the following characteristics:

value chain a. Offering products that address the ethical, moral and sustainability issues described above.

value chain b. Producing goods which are not only commercially viable, but which also meet consumer needs.

c. Using some of the profits for environmental and social improvement at the source of production.

SEG d. Segmenting the markets effectively, so that the complexity of the niche markets and the 'new' consumer are understood and targeted accordingly.

comms e. Communicating honest and credible messages to the customers. These messages should be transparent and should be understood by internal stakeholders, external stakeholders and the consumers.

value chain f. The transportation and logistics systems should mirror the company's aims and objectives of lessening pollution, being environmentally friendly, etc.

g. Developing a marketing perspective that takes a cradle-to-grave approach for products.

comms h. In cases where products are complex, offering certain levels of educational marketing literature.

value chain i. Presenting advertising in a clear and concise manner.

j. Understanding the *future* needs of the customers and stakeholders.

customer analysis

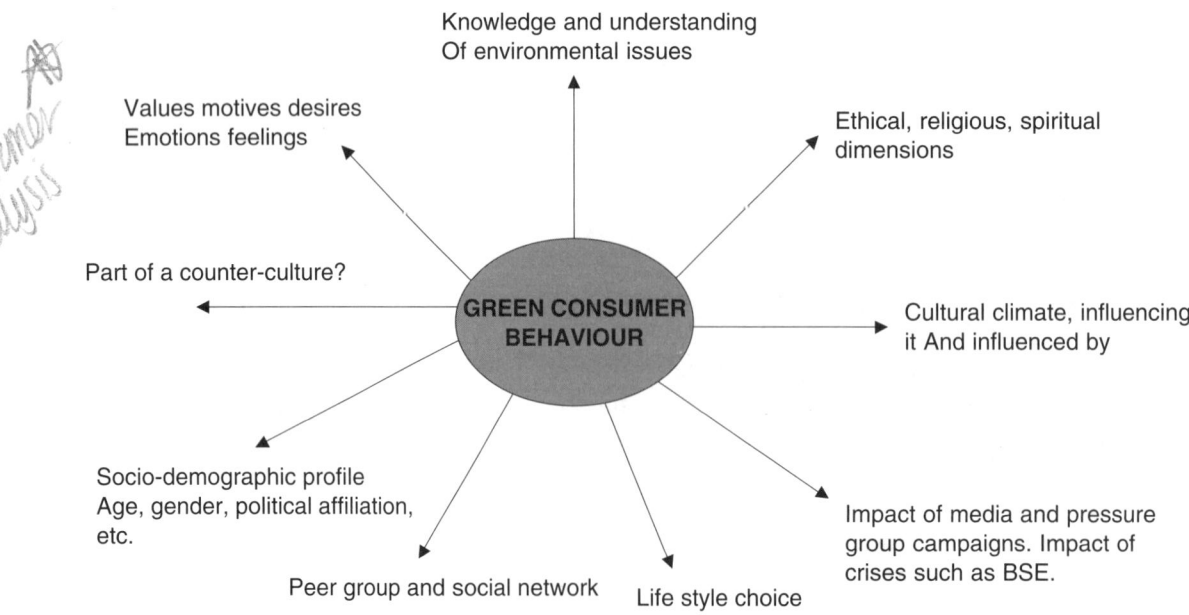

Figure 4.15 Interrelated green consumer factors
Source: Adapted from Wagner (1997)

Anticipating the *future needs* of consumers are of vital importance as the 21st century dawns. Future technological and biotechnological advances could spell either triumphs or disasters for the environment. Already there is considerable disquiet over the introduction of GM foods. The way in which foods are produced, distributed, commercialized and perceived has been radically changed in the last 20 years by the advent of new technologies such as Genetic Engineering.

The creation of genetically modified foods and organisms has increased the general public awareness about the elements and the quality of foods. The main concern over GM foods centres on the fact that they have not conclusively been tested in people's diets using rigorous standards (Cottrill, 1998). The negative perceptions surrounding GM foods lie deep in the myths and fears of the modern civilization (the expression Frankenstein Foods is a good example) (MacMillan, 2000). Given these negative and in many cases serious concerns about the possible consequences of the environmental spread of 'rogue' genes via cross-pollination, the public are concerned about clarity of messages and clear labelling. As a reaction against GM foods and continuing health scares, organic food sales have grown rapidly. The growing and consumption of organic foods, by many, is seen as ecologically friendly and sustainable.

According to Datamonitor, organic sales in the US reached $5.4 billion in 1998 and were estimated at $6.4 billion in 1999. Datamonitor (1999) projects sales will continue to grow at approximately 20 per cent per year, reaching $7.76 billion in the year 2000, $9.35 billion in 2001, slightly more than $11 billion in 2002, and slightly more than $13 billion in 2003. Sales during the 1990s grew by 20–24 per cent per year. Organic produce still remains the leading category, although such categories as organic frozen foods, organic dairy, organic bakery items/cereals, organic baby food, and organic ready meals are growing at a faster rate. Another aspect of future consumer trends may be the need for convenience, access to product use and a desire to be free from material possessions.

It is quite possible that in the future, companies may have to design products that can be shared amongst different individuals. For instance cars could be pooled within cities, and individuals could subscribe to leasing and using cars as and when necessary, pick them up and drop them at their destination. Many other items including recreation products such as surfboards could be leased in such a manner. This type of consumption points the way towards a shared existence, away from the individualistic pursuit of gathering material goods.

Summary

This chapter outlines the major environmental threats to the planet through the consumption patterns of organizations and consumers. It also shows the way in which companies can look at what being green means and how they can translate this into effective action and competitive advantage. It is clear that consumption patterns and consumer actions are going to change as we move further into the 21st century. Also, marketing has a key role to play in the greening of companies and the environment and in developing consumer tastes that benefit the planet as stressed in this chapter. At the same time it offers a chance to improve the social status of poorer and less well-endowed sections of the developing world. Sustainability issues and ethics go hand in hand and the opportunities that exist are immense for companies that can think and act holistically in meeting the growing demand for greener products.

References

Allenby, B. (1994) *Industrial Ecology gets down to Earth*, IEEE Circuits and Devices, 10, 1, 20–24.

Anderson, S. and Cavanagh, J. (1996) 'Top 200: The Rise of Global Corporate Power', Institute for Policy Studies, Washington DC.

Anonymous (2000) *The State of the World*, Worldwatch Institute.

Anonymous (2001) 'Clean me a river', *New Scientist*, 171, 2303, 17.

Bennet, M. and James, P. *1999. Sustainable Measures: Evaluating and Reporting of Environment and Social Performance*, Sheffield, UK: Greenleaf Publishing.

Bien, M. (2001). Ethical Investing, Even a Blue Chip Share Can be Green, *The Independent*, February 25 (Foreign Edition). UK.

Charter, M. and Polonsky, M.J. (1999) Greener Marketing: A Global Perspective on Greening Marketing Practice, Sheffield, UK: Greenleaf.

Clift, R. (1995) Clean technology: an Introduction, *Journal of Chemical Technology and Biotechnology*, 62, 321–326.

Cottrill, K. (1998) Out of the lab and onto the table, *Journal of Business Strategy*, 19, 2, 38–39.

Crosbie, L. and Knight, K. (1995) *Strategy for sustainable business: environmental opportunity and strategic choice*, Maidenhead, UK: McGraw-Hill Book Company Europe.

Datamonitor (1999) Organic Trade Association and Datamonitor (Datamonitor's 1999 US Organics Report).

EPA (1992) Life Cycle Design Guidance Manual. Environmental Protection Agency (EPA), EPA 600 1R-92/226, Cincinnati, USA. http://www.epa.gov/.

Fomburn, C. (1996) *Reputation, Realising Value from the Corporate Image*, Cambridge, MA: Harvard Business School Press.

French, H. (2000) Coping with Ecological Globalization. *The State of the World*. W. Institute, New York and London: W.W. Norton and Company, 184–211.

Fuller, D.A. (1999) Sustainable marketing: managerial-ecological issues, *Industrial Examples*, Sage Publications Ltd.

GEMI (Global Environmental Management Initiative) (1993) Total Quality Environmental Management, GEMI, Washington.

Hannis, M. (1998) *The Myth of Green Consumerism; Consumption, Community and Free Markets*, Lancaster University Mave Programme.

Hart, S.L. (2000) Beyond Greening: Strategies for a Sustainable World. *Business and the Environment*, Boston, MA: Harvard Business School Publishing.

Jenkinson, A. (2001) 'APRIL Takes a leaf out of the green book', *Pulp and Paper International*, 42, 8, 19–21.

MacMillan, A. (2000) Genetically Modified Foods: the British Debate, http://cbc.ca/news/viewpoint/correspondents/macmillan_gmf.html.

Makower, J. (1994) Beyond the bottom line: putting social responsibility to work for your business and the world. Simon and Schuster.

National Science Foundation (1998) Science and Engineering Indicators (1998) http://www.nsf.gov/sbe/srs/seind98/frames.htm.

NEETF/Roper (2000) The Ninth Annual National Report Card on Environmental Attitudes, Knowledge and Behaviours, NEETF/Roper.

Ottman, J. (1993) Green Marketing: Challenges & Opportunities for the New Marketing Age. Lincolnwood, IL, NTC Books.

Oyewole, P. (2001) 'Social Costs of Environmental Justice Associated with the Practice of Green Marketing', *Journal of Business Ethics*, 29, 239–251.

Peattie, K. (1995) Environmental Marketing Management, London: Pitman.

Peattie, K. and Charter, M. (1997) 'Green marketing', in McDonagh, P. and Prothero, A. (eds), *Green Management: A Reader*, London: Dryden Press, 388–412.

Piasecki, W.B., Fletcher, K.A. and Mendelson, F.J. (1999) Environmental Management and Business Management: *Leadership Skills for the 21st Century*, John Wiley and Sons.

Rand Corporation (2000) Consumer Power and Green Consumption. http://www.rand.org/scitech/stpi/ourfuture/Consumer/Section6.html.

SETAC (1998) Evolution and development of the conceptual framework and methodology of life-cycle impact assessment. http://setac.org/files/addendum.pdf.

SPOLD (1995) 'Synthesis Report on the Social Value of LCA Workshop', SPOLD/IMSA (obtainable from Proctor and Gamble Services Company, Temsalaan 100, 1853 Strombeek-Bever, Belgium, (Fax +32 2 568 4812) Spold terminated its activities at the end of 2001. Its history may be obtained on http://www.spold.org/whatis.html.

Stauber, J. and Rampton, S. (1995) *Toxic Sludge is Good for You: Lies, Damn Lies and the Public Relations Industry*, Monore, ME: Common Courage Press.

Wagner, S.A. (2001) *Understanding Green Consumer Behaviour*. London and New York: Routledge.

Wasik, J.F. (1996) *Green Marketing and Management: A Global Perspective*, Cambridge, MA: Blackwell.

Wirthlin Institute (2000) Environmental Update, 10, 8, http://209.204.197.52/publicns/Twr1100.pdf.

Wong, V., Turner, W. and Stoneman, P. (1996) Marketing Strategies and Market Prospects for Environmentally-Friendly Consumer Products, *British Journal of Management*, 7, 3, 263–281.

Worcester, R. (1997) 'Public Opinion and the Environment', in Jacobs, Michael (ed.), *Greening the Millennium? The New Politics of the Environment*, Oxford: Blackwell.

Contemporary issues in the context of the case study

This chapter highlights some of the major issues surrounding company organization and development in an ever diminishing energy base in the world. At the same time, issues of sustainability and corporate responsibility are becoming extremely important for developing marketing strategies. These topics are now at the forefront of many company decisions and students can use some of these ideas in the context of cases such as Enzymes Ltd., Titan Watches (ethical issues). Within the correct context, the chapter offers a rich array of analytical tools and concepts and tools that can be used for case analysis.

Questions for discussion

    a.   How difficult is it for companies to embrace green marketing strategies?
    b.   How is consumer behaviour likely to change in the future?
    c.   How can companies develop strategies for implementing green consumer behaviour?

unit 5
effective customer orientation

Outcomes

° Formulate and present a creative, customer-focused and innovative competitive customer strategy for any given context, incorporating relevant investment decisions, appropriate control aspects and contingency plans.

° Promote and facilitate the adoption and maintenance of a strong market and customer orientation with measurable marketing metrics.

This chapter will consider

a. Customer relationship management.

b. Market orientation and customer orientation.

c. Details of financial analysis and marketing metrics as control mechanisms.

d. Discussion and formulation of contingency plans.

Introduction

Being customer-focused is becoming an important plank of many organizations' marketing strategies. Being customer focused largely results from a well developed customer relationship marketing strategy. At the same time companies need to understand whether strategies are working or not. For this reason metrics need to be developed to measure the effectiveness of customer orientation or market orientation.

Relationship marketing

In recent years, Relationship Marketing (RM) has gained enormous popularity amongst academics and practitioners of marketing. This popularity has been gained at the expense of, so called, traditional or transactional marketing which has been taught and practised for the past fifty years or so, and is based primarily on the management of the 4Ps. RM attempts to gain customer loyalty by focusing on building long-term relationships with customers, placing importance on a customer's life-time value to the company rather than the profit achieved in a single transaction. Furthermore, RM emphasizes share of customer rather than market share, which is often a yardstick for success in transactional marketing.

Various researchers have found that it is cheaper to keep existing customers than to acquire new ones, and that normally the longer a relationship lasts the more profitable it is for a company. Technological developments make it possible, more than ever before, to build accurate and up to date databases on customers, and make it possible to determine their purchase requirements and profile accurately. As a result customized offerings could be made to each customer, and in the process added value is created.

Relationship marketing, if successful, creates a confidence by the customer in the supplier (and vice versa) helping to build trust and, hence, loyalty particularly in situations where there is customer perceived risk in the purchase. Successful RM requires an integrated approach, involving all the stakeholders of a company, change of organizational culture in favour of RM and adherence to TQM. The latter goes hand in hand with RM and is essential to a customer and quality orientated marketing operation.

Christopher, Payne and Ballantyne distinguish RM and transactional marketing in the following manner:

Transaction marketing	Relationship marketing
o Focus on single sale.	o Focus on customer retention.
o Orientation on product features.	o Orientation on product benefits.
o Short time-scale.	o Long time-scale.
o Little emphasis on customer service.	o High customer service emphasis.
o Limited customer commitment.	o High customer commitment.
o Moderate customer contact.	o High customer contact.
o Quality is primarily a concern of production.	o Quality is the concern of all.

Source: Christopher, M., Payne, A. and Ballantyne, D. (1991) *Relationship Marketing – Bringing quality, Customer Service, and Marketing Together.*

Payne *et al.*, suggest that the process of RM involves attempts at moving customers up *the relationship marketing ladder of loyalty*, illustrated below:

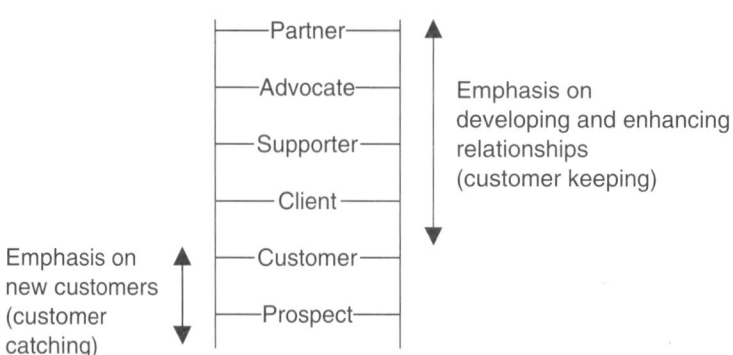

Figure 5.1 The relationship marketing ladder of loyalty
Source: Payne, A., Christopher, M., Clark, M. and Peck, H. (1997) *Relationship Marketing for Competitive Advantage-Winning and Keeping Customers.*

Kotler proposes that there are three levels of benefits that a company can offer to its customers in attempting to build a relationship with them:

Financial These are based on financial benefits offered by companies in the form of frequency-marketing programmes and club-marketing programmes. These benefits are usually in the form of reward or incentives to frequent buyers.

Social These are benefits that customers are offered by the company through individualized and customized relations and treating customers as clients.

Structural These are benefits offered by the existence of structural ties between the supplier and the customer where the supplier offers equipment, computer linkages and advice to help customers manage their orders, inventory, etc.

Source: Based on Kotler, P. (2000) *Marketing Management – The Millennium Edition.*

Obviously, the existence of social and structural ties and a genuine belief in relationship marketing as a philosophy of business are more likely to help create mutually profitable long-term relationships.

In addition to this, technology is rapidly changing the way in which relationships are managed. Customers are able to contact companies through various channels and these need to be understood and managed by an organization. These are shown in the figure below.

Creating a relationship web

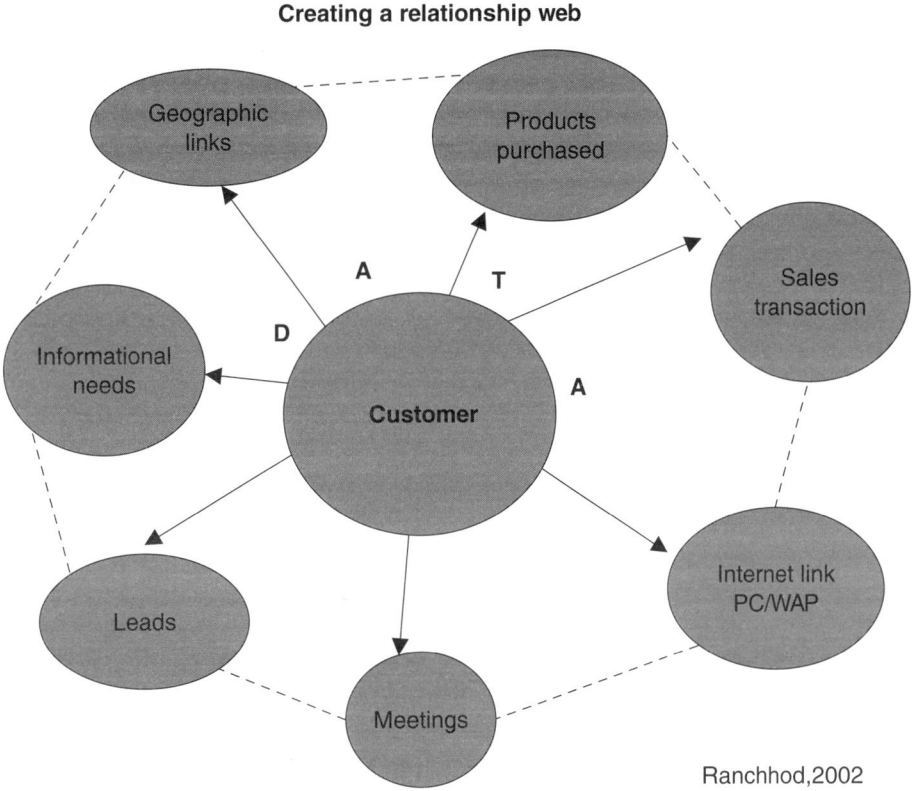

Ranchhod,2002

Figure 5.2

Valuing customers

In calculating customer profitability, most methods start from the Customer Lifetime Value. Customer Lifetime Value is a controversial concept among the business specialists (Ranchhod and Gurau, 2003). Some consider it as 'an elaborate fiction of presumed precision' (Jackson, 1992), while other analysts declare that companies should abandon lifetime value theories and take care of the customers now (Ambler, 2001).

In mathematical terms, the CLV consists in taking into account the total financial contribution – that is, revenues minus costs – of a customer over his or her entire life of a business relationship with the company. Despite its simplicity, the measurement of CLV requires great care. All cash flows involved in the process have to be identified and measured on a very detailed level, and allocated precisely to each customer or type of customer. The diagram in Figure 5.3 represents a concise seven-step approach to measure CLV (Bacuvier et al., 2001).

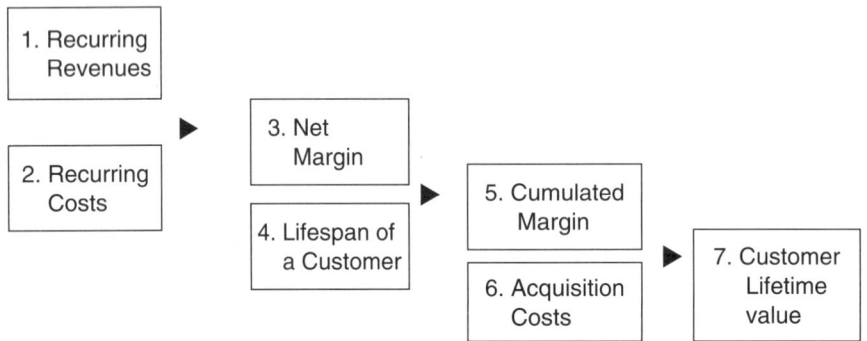

Figure 5.3 Seven step process to measure Customer Lifetime Value

Translating Figure 1 into mathematical formulas, we obtain:

CLTV – Customer Lifetime Value (Profitability)
RR   – Recurring Revenues
RC   – Recurring Costs
Y   – Lifespan of a customer, or number of transactions
AC   – Acquisition costs
P   – Total Profits
C   – Number of customers

$$CLTV = (RR - RC)\ Y - AC \qquad\qquad (5.1)$$

$$P = CLTV \times C \qquad\qquad (5.2)$$

$$P = [(RR - RC) \times Y - AC] \times C \qquad\qquad (5.3)$$

The mathematical expression of the Customer Lifetime Value can represent a sound basis for analysing the existing situation, and for identifying the possible strategies to increase customer profitability. Analysing formula (5.3), five levers of customer value creation can be identified (Bacuvier et al., 2001). These strategies represent only the starting point of a company-wide operational effort. Table 5.1 shows the complexity of implementing customer-oriented strategies based on the analysis of the Customer Lifetime Value.

Table 5.1 The operational requirements for implementing customer-oriented strategies based on Customer Lifetime Value analysis

Strategy	Tactics	Operation	Requirements
Conquer – increase C – the number of customers	o Improve the existing offer in order to attract the potential customers close to the existing customer segments	o Improve: o Product o Price o Distribution o Promotion	Research Segmentation Investment
	o Diversify the offer in order to attract new segments of customers	o Increase the product/service portfolio	Research Segmentation Investment
Increase RR – recurring revenues	o Increase the volume of sales	o Diversification o Stimulate the demand	Research Segmentation Investment
	o Increase the value of sales	o Upgrade the offer	Research Segmentation Investment
	o Increase both the volume and the value of sales	o Diversification o Stimulate the demand o Upgrade the offer	Research Segmentation Investment
Reduce RC – recurring costs	o Reduce general costs (administration, maintenance, etc.)	o Increased efficiency	Research Segmentation Investment
	o Reduce cost of: o product/service o distribution o communication	o Cheaper supplies o Cheaper outsourcing o Increased efficiency	Research Segmentation Investment
Retain – increase Y	o Increase customers' loyalty maintaining and/or increasing customer satisfaction	o Improve present offer o Better targeting o Score better than competition	Research Segmentation Investment
Reduce AC – acquisition costs	o Better targeting of potential customers	o Improve offer o Improve targeting o Use the same resources more efficiently	Research Segmentation Investment

Problems in calculating the Customer Lifetime Value

The calculation of the Customer Lifetime Value is not problem-free. However, most of these problems can be successfully solved taking into consideration two main issues:

1. the company applying this method has to clearly define from the beginning the purpose of using Customer Lifetime Value analysis and the expected benefits;
2. the problems raised by the Customer Lifetime Value analysis are often industry and company specific, as a result the company has to select the most appropriate way to apply this concept in its particular situation.

Defining a 'customer'

The first challenge is to define the customer unit (Ness *et al.*, 2001). Is it an individual, an account, a household or a business address? A second challenge is linking customer information into a single customer record when they leave and return multiple times during their lifetime.

The answer to these questions is industry specific. The business organization has to identify the characteristics of its customer relationship, and, on this basis, to define the customer unit and the customer lifetime cycle. In the present marketplace, a company can be confronted with the following situations:

Table 5.2 The characteristics of customer relationships in different industrial markets

Number of customers	Number of transactions	Level of involvement
Large	Large	high
Medium	Medium	medium
Small	Small	low

Table 5.2 shows the possible combinations of customer relationships characteristics, different among industrial sectors and even among companies within the same industry. For example, a company with a small number of customers, which makes a small number of transactions that require a high level of company-customer involvement, will probably define the customer unit as being single customers (individuals or organizations), and the customer lifecycle depending on the business cycles specific for the industry (production cycle, investment cycles, consumption cycles). On the other hand, for a company dealing with a large number of clients, with large number of transactions and low involvement, it might be more appropriate to aggregate the individual customers into particular segments with homogeneous profiles and behaviour. This type of segmentation helps a company to become more customer focused in a sensible profitable manner, (Figure 5.4) illustrates this. It also helps a company to develop feedback loops and a chance to develop contingency plans in case a given situation does not materialize.

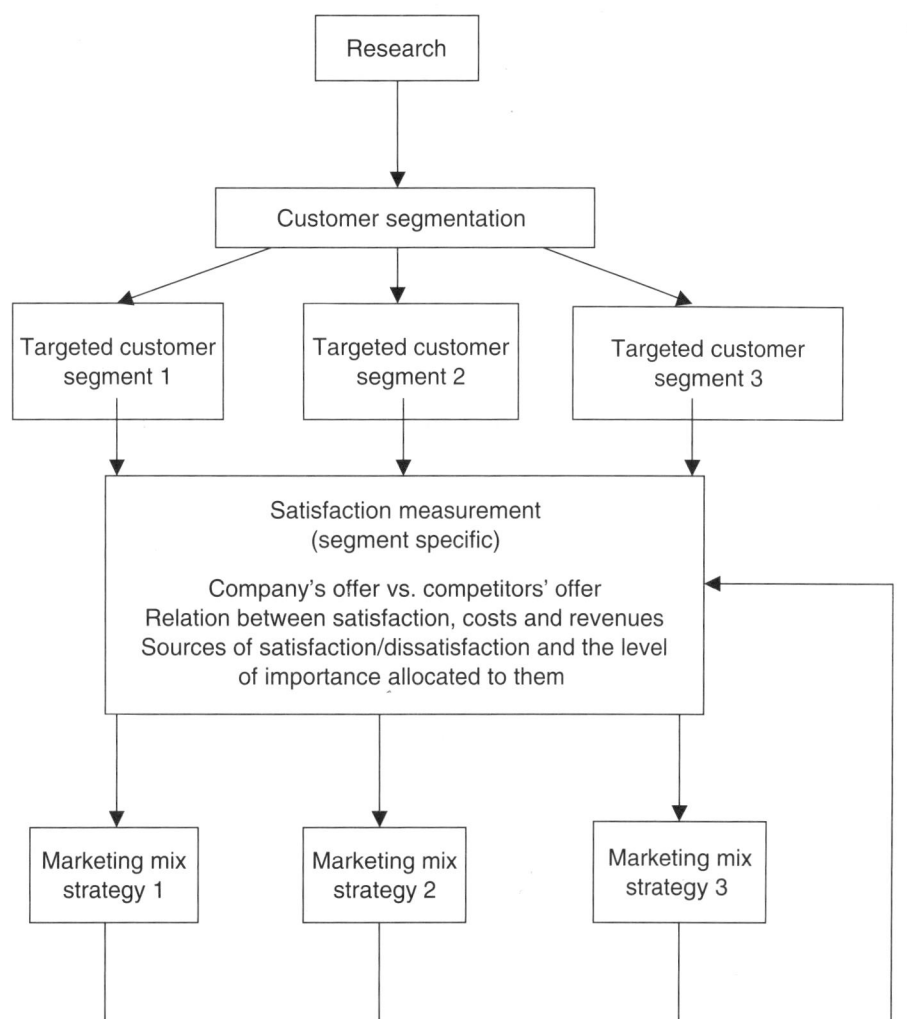

Figure 5.4 The use of customer segmentation and customer satisfaction measurement for designing and implementing targeted marketing mix strategies

Financial analysis and marketing measures

Introduction

Cases are based on real companies which have financial reporting systems. Usually, for the purposes of disseminating information to shareholders and stakeholders, companies produce annual accounts explaining financial flows, profits and losses and balance sheets. Many accounts also contain information on market shares, geographical segmentation and regional segmentation. Recently there has been considerable interest generated in understanding the use of particular sets of data pertaining to marketing. These can be measurement of brand equity, customer satisfaction, loyalty/retention, share of voice and marketing spend. Some of these measures are shown in the table below. Interestingly not many companies actually utilize the full range of marketing metrics for measuring their marketing performance. Often we are only left with the age-old financial measures. These measures do help in understanding the position of a company. Quite often they are used by senior managers to gauge trends, especially if data for previous years is available in the same format. In most cases, the analyses are based on financial ratios. These accounting ratios are used in the interpretation of financial statements. Usually, these ratios are at their most useful when compared to ratios for different time periods. This can be helpful in identifying trends and understanding strengths and weaknesses. If for instance, inventory levels are high in a balance sheet, does it imply that there is a peak, where the company is anticipating a surge in demand for products, or does it imply falling sales? The section below outlines the key ratios that are useful for analysing company performance. In addition to this, companies have to be able to understand measures that are about marketing performance. Some of these measures may link up to financial performance and indeed may be key to the success or failure of a company's marketing strategy. Such measures could be customer satisfaction, information dissemination capability within an organization, IT sophistication, market share, customer retention, amongst others.

Profit ratios

Profit ratios measure the management's overall effectiveness in generating profits from the available resources. If a company is highly efficient in its markets, then it should exhibit a high level of profitability. It is useful to compare a company's profitability against that of its major competitors in its industry. Such a comparison tells whether the company is operating more or less efficiently than its rivals. Over a period of time any changes in profit ratios will indicate whether a company is improving its performance or not.

1. *Gross profit margin* The gross profit margin is obtained by deducting variable production expenses from the general sales. The amount remaining can then be allocated to cover general and administrative expenses and

2. *Other operating costs* It is defined as follows:

$$\text{Gross profit margin} = \frac{\text{Sales revenue} - \text{Cost of goods sold}}{\text{Sales revenue}}$$

3. *Net profit margin* This is based on the net profits obtained after taxes, loan interest and administration expenses have been paid. This net income is then divided by the sales revenue to obtain the net profit margin. Net profits are important because companies need to make profits to survive and also invest in the future to develop and grow markets.

$$\text{Net profit margin} = \frac{\text{Net income}}{\text{Sales revenue}}$$

4. *Return on total asset* This ratio measures the profit earned on the employment of assets. It is defined as follows:

$$\text{Return on total assets} = \frac{\text{Net income}}{\text{Total assets}}$$

5. *Net income* Is the profit after preferred dividends (those set by contract) have been paid. Total assets include both current and fixed assets.

6. *Return on shareholders' equity* This ratio measures the percentage of profit earned on the shares held within the company. Companies attractive to shareholders are those that can maximize this ratio. The greater the return, the greater the amount of money that can be distributed to individual shareholders. It is defined as follows:

$$\text{Return on shareholders' equity} = \frac{\text{Profits after taxes}}{\text{Total equity}}$$

7. *Liquidity* The amount of liquidity refers to ready cash that may be available to a company, for immediate use. The lower the liquidity, the greater the danger of a company not being able to meet its immediate cash commitments or tactical marketing requirements.

    a. $$\text{Current ratio} = \frac{\text{Current assets}}{\text{Current liabillities}}$$

    b. $$\text{Quick ratio} = \frac{\text{Total assets}}{\text{Total liabilities}}$$

    c. $$\text{Inventory to net working captial} = \frac{\text{Inventory}}{\text{Current assets} - \text{current liabilities}}$$

8. *Leverage* If a company has borrowed little money, then it is possible for it to increase the amount of money it can raise in the marketplace, either through loans or share issues. The money can enable further investments in marketing or new product development.

    a. $$\text{Debt to assets ratio} = \frac{\text{Total debt}}{\text{Total assets}}$$

    b. $$\text{Debt to equity ratio} = \frac{\text{Total debt}}{\text{Total equity}}$$

    c. $$\text{Long term debt to equity ratio} = \frac{\text{Long term debt}}{\text{Total equity}}$$

9. *Activity* This reflects the efficiency with which the company is dealing in the market place. High inventory levels could signify flagging sales, indicating poor distribution, lack of advertising or sales efforts.

    a. $$\text{Inventory turnover} = \frac{\text{Sales}}{\text{Inventory}}$$

    b. $$\text{Fixed asset turnover} = \frac{\text{Sales}}{\text{Fixed assets}}$$

    c. $$\text{Average collection period} = \frac{\text{Accounts receivable}}{\text{Average daily sales}}$$

Marketing metrics

These will vary from one company to another. The key points to consider are: 'Who are the main users of company reports, and how important are they as data sources?' Shareholders will be interested in profitability and long-term growth. On the other hand directors and employees will be interested in issues such as market share, growth in the client base, profitability per customer, distribution costs, customer satisfaction, etc. Thus information usage is very dependent on the functions within an organization.

Marketing metrics have become a point for serious consideration for many organizations that are looking for the best ways in which performance can be measured. Performance varies according to company characteristics and according to the sector in which it operates. Having standard metrics for all organizations is difficult, so it is useful to consider how metrics models can be developed for each organization. Figure 5.5 offers an idea of how some general marketing measures could be developed for an organization. However there are many other issues to consider such as:

a. Brand equity measures.
b. Environmental measures.
c. Customer satisfaction measures.
d. Customer loyalty measures.
e. Customer profitability measures.
f. New product success measures.

amongst a range of others. In all cases, it is useful to categorize the measures according to their acceptability, suitability or feasibility for adoption by a particular organization (Ranchhod, 2004): Table 5.3 indicates the types of metrics that could be considered by companies.

Table 5.3 Marketing metrics for possible use in company reporting

Market data	Market size	Market trend
Relative market performance	o Unit volume trend o Market share (volume) o Market share by mix by major market segment (value)	Relative price levels and trends sales by major brand (value) major brand trends (value) channel (value)
Customer performance	o Number of customers o Customer loyalty o Customer complaints o Relative quality o Relative value	o Customer service levels o Customer satisfaction o Consumption per capita (value) o Would recommend company or brands to friend
Innovation	o Activity calendar (past year) o New product/service review o New products/services launched in past 5 years as percentage of this year's sales	o Statement of future opportunities and objectives o Partnerships, acquisitions, licenses
Efficiency	o Capacity utilization o R & D productivity	o Awards
People and Competency	o Percentage employee turnover o Percentage employees participating in share purchase or profit sharing	o Training activities, and training spend o Spend as percentage of sales o Employee satisfaction o Intellectual property
Investment	o R&D priorities and spend as percentage of sales o Capital expenditure activity and spend as percentage of sales o Advertising spend as percentage of sales	o Total marketing spend as percentage of sales o Technical support to customers
Branding	o Preference o Purchase intent o Brand value o Brand strength	o Awareness o Image o Perceived differential o Brand positioning
Distribution	o Level o Trend	o Channel mix o Channel trend

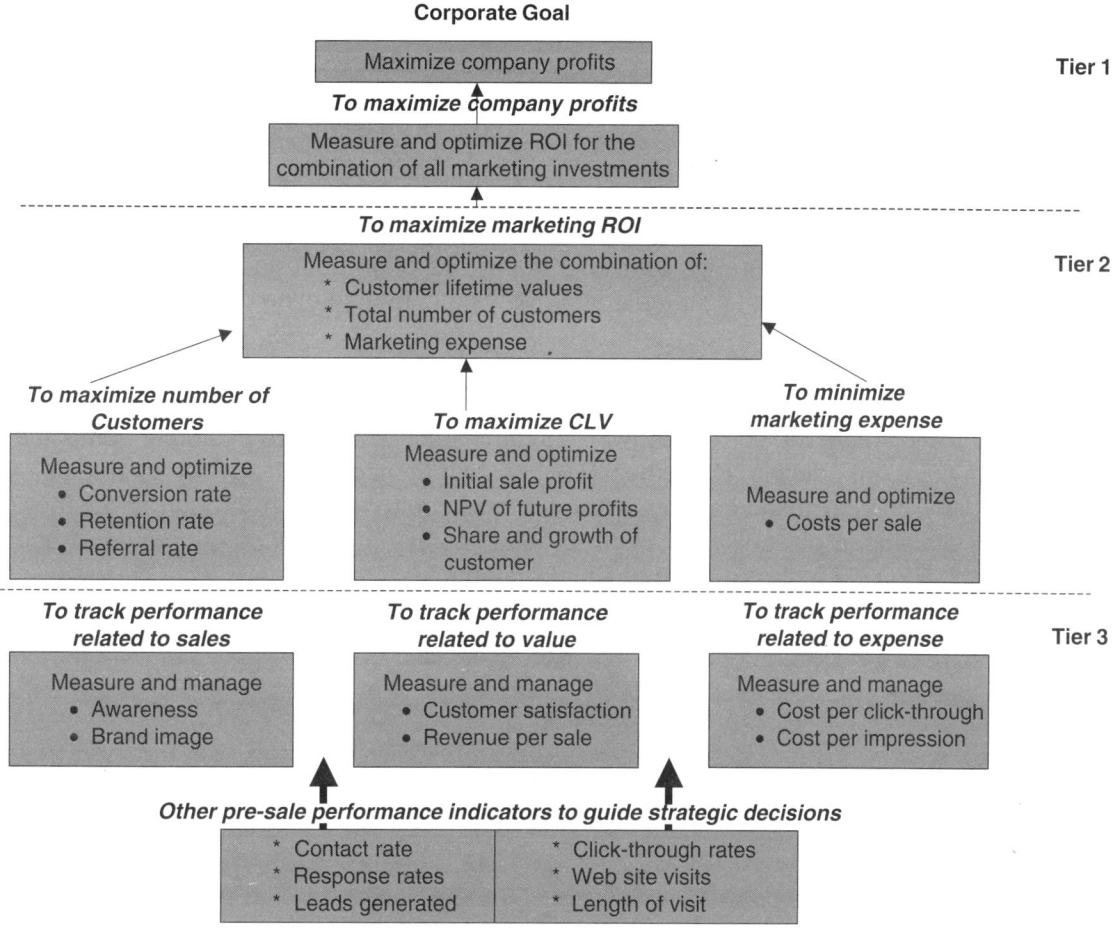

Corporate Goal

Maximize company profits — Tier 1

To maximize company profits

Measure and optimize ROI for the combination of all marketing investments

To maximize marketing ROI — Tier 2

Measure and optimize the combination of:
* Customer lifetime values
* Total number of customers
* Marketing expense

To maximize number of Customers

Measure and optimize
• Conversion rate
• Retention rate
• Referral rate

To maximize CLV

Measure and optimize
• Initial sale profit
• NPV of future profits
• Share and growth of customer

To minimize marketing expense

Measure and optimize
• Costs per sale

To track performance related to sales — Tier 3

Measure and manage
• Awareness
• Brand image

To track performance related to value

Measure and manage
• Customer satisfaction
• Revenue per sale

To track performance related to expense

Measure and manage
• Cost per click-through
• Cost per impression

Other pre-sale performance indicators to guide strategic decisions

* Contact rate
* Response rates
* Leads generated

* Click-through rates
* Web site visits
* Length of visit

Figure 5.5

Suitability

This provides an assessment of the most suitable measures that could be adopted for a particular company. This is likely to depend on the following:

a. Industry sector.
b. Service or product orientation of the organization.
c. Not-for-profit or a non-governmental organization (NGOs).
d. The level of technology used for automatic measurement. For instance on the Internet, transactions can be recorded automatically. When loyalty cards are used, the customer transactions are recorded in a database. These records can then be subsequently used for datamining.
e. The strategic vision of the company. For some companies there may be an emphasis on rates of return on others such as NGOs, the emphasis could be on the rates of consumer awareness or the level of funds generated.
f. Is the measure chosen likely to be valuable in the long run and can trends be ascertained?
g. Can the measures chosen be used to benchmark against competitors?

These measures can then be screened by considering the following criteria:

Acceptability

Are these measures acceptable to the various stakeholders? Do they make sense and do they actually measure the right areas/issues? There are instances where measures have been adopted, but have really not been acceptable to the individuals developing the strategies. This then results in fudged or anomalous results. The measures would also have to demonstrate something tangible to the various stakeholders and be in line with their expectations. Measures such as brand equity are often undertaken by advertising agencies and as such need to be acceptable and meaningful to marketing personnel.

Feasibility

This tests whether the chosen measures can be usefully adopted. For instance, does the organization have the correct software to automatically measure customer contact, especially if they are introducing Customer Relationship Management (CRM) strategies? Has the company enough resources to carry out brand equity research through an agency? Does it have systems in place with retailers to obtain details of revenues generated at point of sale through EPOS (Electronic Point of Sale) systems?

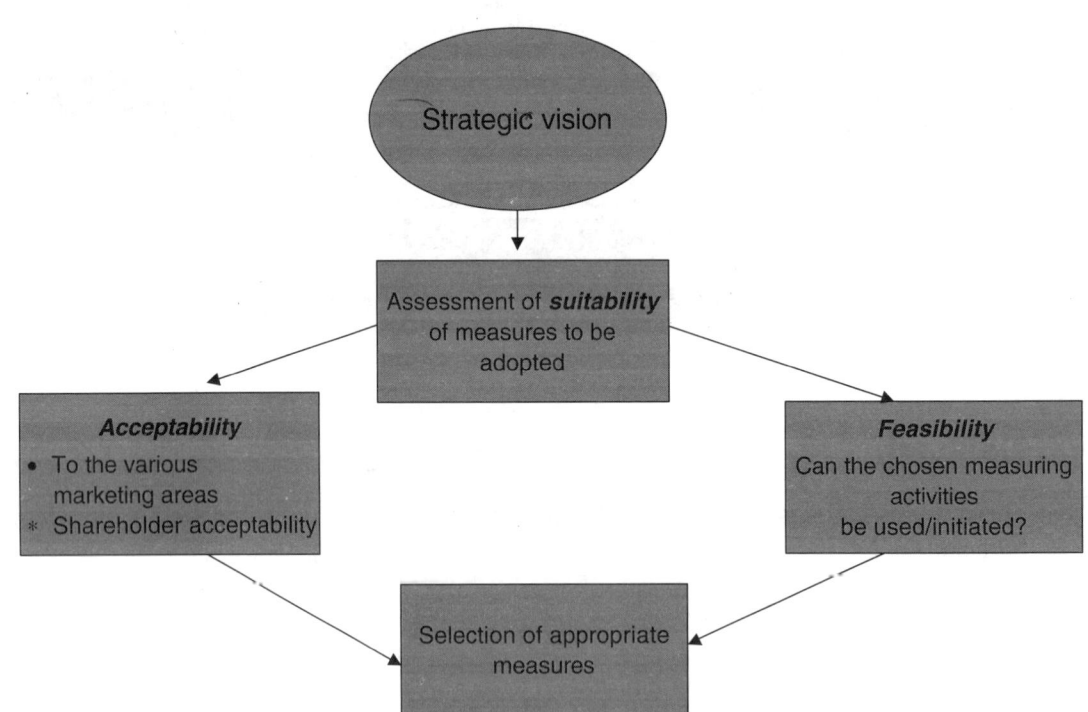

Figure 5.6 A framework for selecting marketing measures
Source: Ranchhod, 2004.

Some common measures

Usually in marketing, there are some measures which are used commonly by organizations. These measures are:

a. *Customer satisfaction* Measurement can be complex and depend on attributes measured-internal barriers to measurement.
b. *Customer loyalty* A measure of good marketing?? Brand purchase measures? financial performance also affects the situation/ 'lifetime value' of customers in the base.
c. *Brand equity* Many academics and managers believe that a powerful brand is probably among the greatest marketing assets a firm can have.

d. Allow firms to charge price premiums over unbranded or poorly branded products.

e. Can be used to extend the company's business into other product categories.

f. Reduce perceived risk to customers (and investors?)

The measures could be behavioural, looking at perceptions or purchase patterns. They could also indicate knowledge of the brand and show the effectiveness of brand marketing within a complex portfolio. Another important measure could be the financial value of the brand to a company's investors. Such measures may be long term rather than short term in nature.

Understanding online metrics
Online companies spent £150m on advertising last year. Did it work?

Oliver Rowe reports on the business of getting your dot com company recognized in the real world.

It is one of the most important questions you have to face. You are setting up an Internet business. Everybody tells you that marketing and advertising the site will make or break you. There is no point having a good idea if nobody hears about it. So you siphon off a large part of your launch budget for the purposes of building your brand. Domination of your market is what you seek. And to achieve that you pay advertising companies lots of money to tell the world that you have arrived. But does it work? Advertising and media agencies up and down the country have certainly enjoyed a windfall over the past few months. But new figures revealed here show that many companies, whatever they spend on advertising their wares, are not getting the immediate brand recognition they crave. As we all know, brand is king. 'The only effective barrier to entry in e-commerce is branding,' says Simon Murdoch of Amazon. David Taylor, head of digital branding at the Added-Value Company, a leading brand consultancy, concurs. 'Dot com companies have a real need to develop a clear positioning and identity to survive and prosper in the long run.' Data from ACNielsen MMS, which records advertising expenditure, shows that online companies spent in excess of £150m on advertising in 1999 – not including direct mail, sponsorship or promotions. This has all been spent advertising online brands in the real world of traditional media. It represents a threefold increase in what was spent in 1998. However the issue now is whether these companies are getting value for money.

This should cause some alarm for online companies because what naturally preoccupies all advertisers is how effective their advertising spend actually is. One key measure of advertising effectiveness is awareness of the brand amongst the public. Research undertaken in the last two weeks by CIA MediaLab as part of its Sensor study has analysed what the UK's major online companies spend on advertisers and compared it to people's awareness of the brand. What is clear from this analysis is that the public's awareness of your brand and the amount you actually spend on advertising are certainly related. But, more worryingly for those spending precious resources telling the public 'We're here!', some brands have got more recognition bang for their advertising buck.

Let's look at the figures. Four major brands, AOL, Yahoo!, Freeserve and BT, all achieve awareness of over 40 per cent amongst the UK adult population. The amount each has spent on advertising differs hugely, raising the question: who has the most effective advertising? Of course the level of recognition also reflects other factors such as the time since each launched and the amount of press coverage they have received. Looking specifically at Internet Service Providers (ISPs) we find that AOL has only been outspent by Freeserve. The two have very similar awareness levels despite the fact that AOL has been around much longer than Freeserve. AOL's recent merger with Time Warner will certainly have helped general awareness levels. What is clear is that Freeserve has been more aggressively going after market share, but AOL has decided to fight back with a spend of around £1.4m in the past two months.

It should be made clear that advertising needs to play a different role in the marketing mix as the brand moves through its cycle from an initial launch, to growth to maturity. These ISPs are still growing but are using advertising to help attract both existing and new Internet users. The fascinating part of all this is not only trying to work out why differing levels of advertising spend have delivered different results, but also why so many companies are spending so much on advertising. The perception is that there is currently an opportunity to build online brands, and thus market share, more quickly and easily (and cheaply) than in a year or two's time when the Internet will be a bigger place. When a market is being launched it is cheaper to buy a share while it is still small than try and steal it off competitors once the market has matured. It is for this reason that venture capitalists are keen to give promising young Internet start-ups large sums of money to spend advertising their brand before someone else gets into that sector of the market.

A prime example of the advantage of being first to market can be seen in the differences in awareness levels and advertising spend between Amazon and BOL. Despite spending nearly £3.7m on advertising in the last 12 months BOL only has an awareness of 27 per cent amongst people who used the internet in the past month. This compares to a significantly higher awareness of 75 per cent for Amazon from a slightly smaller spend. Maintaining awareness is an easier job than gaining it in the first place. Also, the amount BOL has spent on advertising does not compare favourably to other online brands such as Lastminute which has a 29 per cent awareness from a £1m spend. Meanwhile, online retailer Boo has spent more than £750,000 in the past two months and has failed to show any significant change in awareness amongst CIA's sample.

To be fair, asking people whether they are aware of a brand at a particular moment in time is a relatively crude measure of advertising effectiveness. However, doing it amongst a pre-defined target audience that has been agreed by the brand owners and the media agency is a good place to start, but media agencies do get judged by the awareness they deliver. Even so, as for AOL and Freeserve, achieving awareness may only be the first part of the advertising process. As well as achieving awareness, advertising needs to communicate some brand values which should help drive share and loyalty. The temptation for brands is to launch with a fanfare to the world, but without any budget left they cannot follow it up. The result is that brand awareness will quickly decay. It could be argued that some brands should use their advertising budget more wisely.

Media agencies could more accurately target the right consumers, possibly using other media and over a longer period of time, thus satisfying the joint media requirements of frequency of advertising exposure and recency. But does this excite investors, or the MD, as much as blowing the annual budget on a few weeks of high-profile TV advertising?

One sector that is moving wholeheartedly online is banking, and its experience with advertising and brand building holds some important lessons. As yet unreleased research by CIA shows that amongst those that have already opened an online bank account or who intend to open one in the next year, 89 per cent of those aware of Egg say it appeals to them as a brand. This compares to only 60 per cent for the parent brand Prudential. The Smile brand appeals to 70 per cent of those aware of it in this target audience compared to 58 per cent for parent Co-operative Bank. Smile has shown impressive awareness growth in the last two months on the back of a £1.2m advertising budget.

Advertising is clearly establishing new values for a new brand while trying not to cannibalize the existing customer base of the parent. As the Internet audience grows, then so the amount brands will be encouraged to spend on advertising will increase until those that can't afford to play the spend game drop out or get bought up. Make sure your brand works. Spend money on advertising. But make sure it works.

Note: Oliver Rowe is operations manager at CIA MediaLab, ORowe@cia-group.com.

The above article demonstrates the use of marketing metrics within the context of the Internet and the difficulties of determining the effectiveness of online advertising.

Source: The Guardian, Monday, 6 March 2000.

Contingencies

With an increasingly uncertain and risky environment, the need for developing contingency plans is becoming increasingly important. Unfortunately, often companies develop budgets for marketing plans, with little thought given to 'what if' scenarios. Sometimes subjective assessments of potential growth in market share are made and risks are discounted. Contingency is described as an allowance for unforeseen expenditures or revenues. Contingency, if not applied reasonably, might destroy an otherwise good plan, and if not applied adequately, might create financial problems.

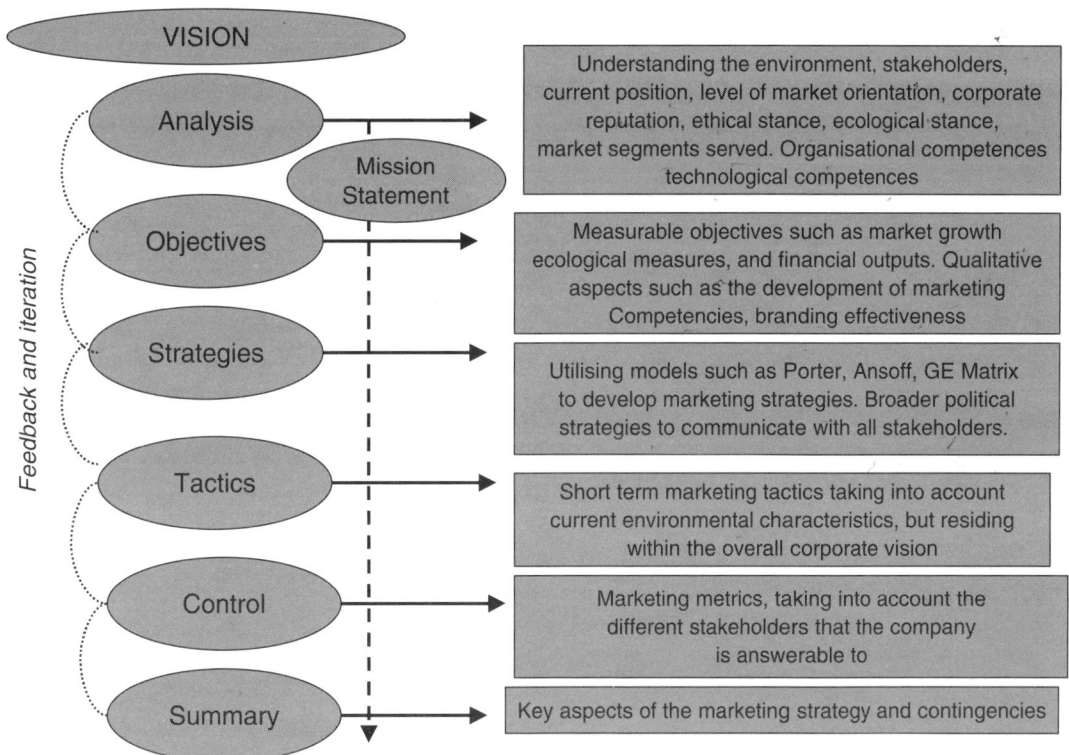

Figure 5.7 Strategic marketing model for the 21st century
Source: Ranchhod, 2004.

As Figure 5.7 shows, the control aspects are important and contingency plans can be taken into account in Figure 5.8. Metrics can help to understand the deviations from given plans and situations. However, when the strategies do not go according to plan, the contingencies come into play. These contingencies can be quite variable in nature:

 a. Greater than expected growth in sales or vice versa.
 b. Greater expenditure on advertising due to failure of set campaigns.
 c. Supply chain cost variations.
 d. Price pressures resulting from customer actions.

    e. Variations in product quality/quality recall.
    f. Poor or good publicity for the company affecting sales.
    g. Changes in economic conditions, for example, rise in interest rates.
    h. Changes in technology rendering the current product range obsolete.
    i. Internal production delays, affecting sales.

And many others, depending on the nature of the business and the sector in which it operates.

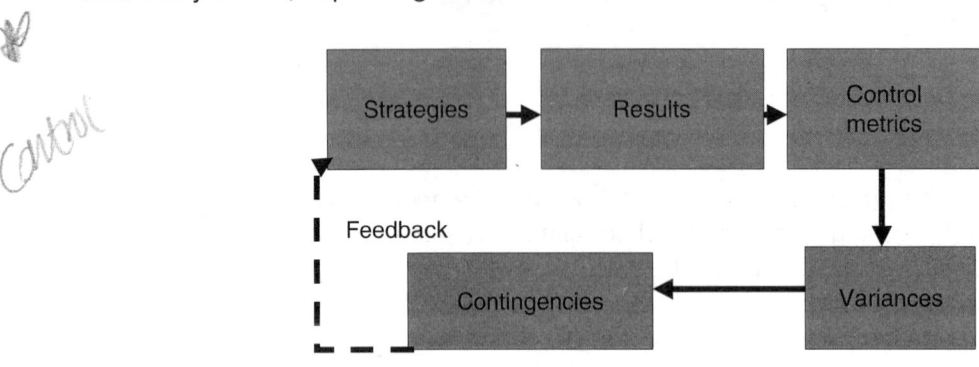

Figure 5.8 Contingencies and control

Summary

This chapter demonstrates the usefulness of understanding customer related issues when developing marketing strategies. It also shows the importance of developing strategies that take into account measures which are useful and meaningful within the context of the company under consideration. Every organization, in every sector, has its own key issues that it needs to take into account. These key issues then translate into effective control measures based on their suitability, acceptability and feasibility for adoption. Finally every plan needs to incorporate contingencies that come into play as a result of the detection of variances within the determined control metrics.

References

Ambler, T. (2001) Abandon lifetime value theories and take care of customers now, *Marketing*, July 12, p.18.

Bacuvier, G., Peladeau, P., Trichet, A. and Zerbib, P. (2001) Customer Lifetime Value: powerful insights into a Company's Business and Activities, http://www.bah.com/viewpoints/insights/cmt_clv_2.html.

Jackson, D.R. (1992) In quest of the grail: breaking the barriers to customer valuation, *Direct Marketing*, 54, 11, 44–48.

Ness, J.A., Schroeck, M.J., Letendre, R.A. and Douglas, W.J. (2001) The role of ABM in measuring customer value, www.mamag.com/strategicfinance/2001/03f.htm.

Ranchhod (2004) Marketing Strategies: A 21st Century Approach.

unit 6
the examination

o Putting everything together

   a. How to analyse case studies and formulate good analyses in line with the new requirements of SMIP.

   b. How to apply and use analyses in the closed book examination.

   c. What the examiners will be looking for.

The examination

Examination approaches

The examiners, when looking at answers to examination questions based on the case study, look for:

Analytical and critical thinking

The case study is based on real organizations and we expect candidates to critically analyse it utilizing a range of techniques. The case study is sent to students four weeks before the date of the examination. As this is a closed book examination and we are looking for pre-prepared analyses, it is important that in the weeks before the examination, time is spent on understanding and analysing the case. The purpose of a case is to develop the following:

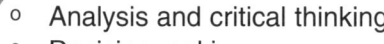
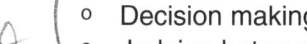

o Analysis and critical thinking.
o Decision making.
o Judging between courses of action.
o Handling assumptions and inferences.
o Presenting a point of view.
o Listening to and understanding others.
o Relating theory to practice.

Candidates should be able to analyse each case and comprehend the other areas of the Stage 3 syllabi from where they may need to draw their underpinning knowledge. Although candidates need to demonstrate their underpinning knowledge in the context of the case study, it is important that they show some creative flair and innovation in their answers. Candidates will also be expected to show an understanding of contemporary marketing issues. Examples of this are given in Chapter 4.

95

The examiners are looking for the candidates to demonstrate analytical ability, interpretive skills, insight, innovation and creativity in answering questions. They are also looking for candidates to take clear and sensible decisions within the context of the case study. A critical awareness of the specific issues involved, relevant theoretical underpinning, attention to detail, coherence and justification of strategies (within the context of the questions set) adopted will also be assessed.

Answering questions within the set context

The SMIP paper asks for special understanding of the case within the context of the questions set. As this is a closed book examination, the only material allowed in the examination will be the pre-prepared analysis. The title of the paper Strategic Marketing in Practice (SMIP), means that we are looking for an understanding of strategic issues involved in developing specific strategies within a company. The candidates need to be competent enough to analyse problems within a marketing context and subsequently take appropriate decisions to implement marketing strategies for an organization. In order to achieve competence in this area, prospective candidates will need to be conversant with all aspects of marketing, as strategic marketing problems do not come in neat packages. A comprehensive grasp of the basic subjects at the Certificate and Advanced Certificate level together with the syllabi for the Stage 3 modules is needed. Decisions made have to reflect the fact that candidates have thoroughly understood the key marketing issues impinging on the case. They have to make decisions which are realistic and justifiable and above all actionable within the given constraints.

Judging between courses of action

When analysing a case study, it would be surprising if only one course of action was possible. Often there are several alternatives to a problem and a company has to weigh up the chances of success and pursue a particular course of action. As an examination candidate, you are expected to pursue courses of action which are possible, realistic and sustainable. The examiners are not looking for right or wrong answers, they are searching for solutions that will work within the given scenario of the case study.

Handling assumptions and inferences

All cases are based on real life information that may have gaps within it. No company works in a perfect environment or with perfect information. This would not only be impossible, but would be outside the capability of any human being. The result is that we all create an image of the way in which a company is operating. In creating that image and understanding it, there may be gaps that need filling. These can be done by the projection of trends or by making certain assumptions about market demand or product suitability. In most cases students will need to make certain assumptions. As long as these are not wildly off the mark and help to augment the case and your arguments, they are perfectly acceptable. In some cases candidates may wish to point out that further market research is necessary.

Presenting a point of view

All cases are about presenting a point of view. Examiners expect student answers to vary. It is therefore important, when preparing for the case, that you do not get hung up on thinking that your friend or colleague has the right answer. If you have analysed the case thoroughly and you feel that you have a clear view of the strategies that should be adopted by the company then you should put these forward. At all times you should consider the detail, coherence and strategic aspects of arguments, justifying them fully.

Relating theory to practice and vice versa

In order to be a good practising marketing manager, you need to be able to seamlessly knit marketing theory to practical solutions. I see this as a symbiotic process. Too often we see managers who only emphasize the practical aspects and by doing that, deny their companies the benefit of marketing frameworks and any new knowledge that may be available. By the same token, simply propounding theoretical frameworks, with little or no thought given to the practical application of these frameworks to real problems is also unacceptable. In order to formulate sensible solutions to cases you will need to be knowledgeable about both practical marketing aspects and theoretical issues and contemporary marketing thinking.

How to pass the case study paper

In general, candidates are expected to allocate some study time at a centre in order to prepare for the case study. The notional study time is 45 hours over a period of ten to twelve weeks. Roughly half of this time should be allocated for work on previous cases and the rest for developing analyses and scenarios for the new case and preparing for the examination that candidates will be sitting.

The paper

The SMIP paper is the culmination of all the marketing subjects covered at all levels, but especially the Diploma and the Advanced Diploma. For this reason, there is no specific syllabus for this paper. This type of expertise will be needed to tackle the case study paper. It is also clear that it will not be possible to tackle the case study without a clear grasp of the fundamentals of Analysis and Evaluation, Strategic Marketing Decisions and Managing Marketing Performance. In this sense, for all students the case study is a culmination of the application of all the marketing knowledge that you have gained over several years.

Closed book examination

For all the students, the SMIP paper is a **closed** book examination. This means that candidates are only allowed to take their per-prepared analyses into the examination. Used judiciously, this material can be useful for referencing when answering questions. Fifteen marks are also allocated for the *application* of the analyses to the question set. Many candidates think that excellent analyses with poor answers will enable a pass. This is misguided as no matter how good the analyses are, they have to be applied within the context of the case. Skimpy answers relying on analyses will almost certainly fail. It is therefore important for candidates to spend time developing good answers and using the analyses to augment these answers.

It is highly important, therefore, that a considerable amount of time is spent on developing tables, undertaking detailed analyses, producing diagrams and assembling this information on six A4 papers. This is helpful for quick referencing during the examination. It also leaves candidates free to think about which bits of information may be useful to use in framing answers.

Allocation of marks

Owing to the closed book nature of the examination, the marks will be allocated in the following manner:

Marks for analysis: 10

Marks for the application of the analysis: 15

(On the day of the examination)

This methodology:

1.   Rewards students for work done in the four weeks between the release of the case and the day of the examination.
2.   Enables students to concentrate on the case and utilize the analyses effectively in their answers.

Candidates should undertake the following advice (repeated from Unit 1):

a. Write or print pre-prepared analysis on six pages. Examiners will be looking for tables, diagrams and key issues. Tables such as SWOT, though helpful, do not show deep analytical thought.

b. If candidates use the available sheets for writing 'crib' material, such as models or plans, they will penalize themselves as there will be less space for good analysis that counts towards the final marks.

c. The diagrams should be clearly visible and the writing should be clearly legible. Typing should be no less than font size 11.

d. Data given within the case should be analysed clearly and effectively.

e. All the work should be on CIM paper which will be issued two weeks before the examination.

f. Please note that it will be totally unacceptable for students to present standardized group analysis/appendices and they will therefore be penalized accordingly.

(During the Examination)

a. The answers should reflect the use of the pre-prepared material as necessary. When writing answers, candidates should cross reference the work to guide the examiner to a particular table or chart or piece of analysis.

b. Examiners do not expect students to use all the pre-prepared material to augment their answers. Obviously, they should only use whatever is necessary for answering the questions as set.

c. Candidates should attach the pre-prepared work as an appendix. All papers must be hole punched and include the student registration and centre number.

d. Please note that Fifteen marks are allocated for the application of the pre-prepared work.

e. Only the pre-prepared analysis can be taken into the examination room, therefore no text books, journals or other pre-prepared work will be allowed.

f. You will be allowed to bring an annotated copy of the case study into the examination.

Notes to candidates

These notes are modified from time to time, depending on the context within which the cases are set. The following is an example of what was used in the June 2003 case study.

Extended knowledge

Notes to candidates, June 2003. The examiners will be marking your scripts on the basis of questions put to you in the examination room. Candidates are advised to pay particular attention to the *mark allocation on the examination paper and budget their time accordingly.*

Your role is outlined in the candidates' brief and you will be required to recommend clear courses of action.

You will be awarded marks for analysis, but poor application may mean the difference between a pass and a failure. The analyses should have been undertaken before the examination day in preparation for meeting the tasks which will be specified in the examination paper.

Candidates are advised not to waste valuable time collecting unnecessary data. The cases are based upon real world situations. No useful purpose will therefore be served by contacting companies in this industry and candidates are *strictly instructed not to do so* as it would simply cause unnecessary confusion.

As in real life, anomalies will be found in this case situation. Please simply state assumptions where necessary when answering questions. The CIM is not in a position to answer queries on case data. Candidates are tested on their overall understanding of the case and in key issues, not on minor details. There are no catch questions or hidden agendas. In addition, for this particular case, the CIM is not prepared to answer any financial queries.

Additional information will be introduced in the examination paper itself which candidates must take into account when answering the questions set.

Acquaint yourself thoroughly with the case study and be prepared to follow closely the instructions given to you on the examination day. To answer examination questions effectively, candidates must adopt a report format.

The copying of pre-prepared 'group' analyses written by consultants/tutors is strictly forbidden and will be penalized. The questions will demand analysis in the examination itself and individually composed answers are required to pass.

From case to case, there may be minor modifications to the candidates' notes depending on the type and style of case.

The candidate's brief

This brief is an integral part of the case study. It gives some idea of the role you are expected to play in solving the case study. The candidate's brief gives individuals a position either as an external consultant or an internal manager. On the day of the examination they are expected to answer the questions set from the point of view of the role that has been allocated. The brief is likely to contain the following:

- o   A brief analysis of the company situation.
- o   Some idea of the deliberations within the company.
- o   An attempt to place you at the centre of the action, asking you to prepare reports on some critical strategic issues/problems facing the organization.
- o   Some statement on incorporating any contemporary issues of your choice into the answers that you propose.

The use of additional information

Cases will vary in nature and from time to time additional information may be provided. It is important therefore for you to incorporate this material in your answers, as and when it is needed.

The additional information is something that you should take into consideration when answering the questions set, as it is likely to have some bearing on the market conditions or on some areas of the case. The additional information will not invalidate all the work that has been undertaken over the four weeks. The additional information is introduced to test the ability of candidates to be flexible in their thinking and to test the ability to assimilate and effectively incorporate new material into the development of their strategies.

Gauging performance

To perform well on the paper, candidates will have to exhibit the following:

○ A need to concentrate on the strategic aspects of marketing underpinned by the necessary detail.
○ The ability to identify 'gaps' in the case study and to outline the assumptions made.
○ The ability to critically apply relevant models for case analysis.
○ The ability to draw and synthesize from any of the diploma subject areas as relevant.
○ Concentration on the question set rather than just the pre-prepared analysis.
○ The ability to answer in the report format with comprehensive sentences rather than providing simplistic lists.
○ The judicious use of diagrams for illustrative purposes.
○ The ability to draw disparate links together and give coherent answers.
○ The use of interesting and useful articles from journals in their answers.
○ Developing strategic ideas, centred around contemporary marketing issues.
○ Innovation and creativity in answering the questions.
○ Demonstration of practical applications of marketing knowledge.
○ Sensible use of time and an ability to plan the answers within the set time.
○ A good understanding of the case study set.

The best way to prepare for the case would entail the following considerations:

○ Practice on previous examination papers.
○ Reading and digesting the senior examiner's report.
○ Reading books, newspapers, relevant marketing and academic journals.
○ For each examination case ascertaining the relevant knowledge base that will be required.
○ Being flexible and critical when using analytical models instead of being prescriptive.
○ Depending on the case study, utilizing a range of different analytical models and tools appropriate to the context of the case (see Figure 6.1 for an illustrative schedule for preparing for the examination).

In addition to the above, candidates should also be prepared to undertake the following:

○ The use of relevant models for the sector in which the case study is based.
○ The use of each candidate's practical and business experience using any illustrative examples.
○ The use of diagrams.
○ A thorough marketing and financial analysis of each case study within the given context of the case study.
○ An awareness and application of strategic marketing ideas and solutions.
○ Revisiting relevant syllabi from the Diploma and Advanced Diploma within the given context of the case study.

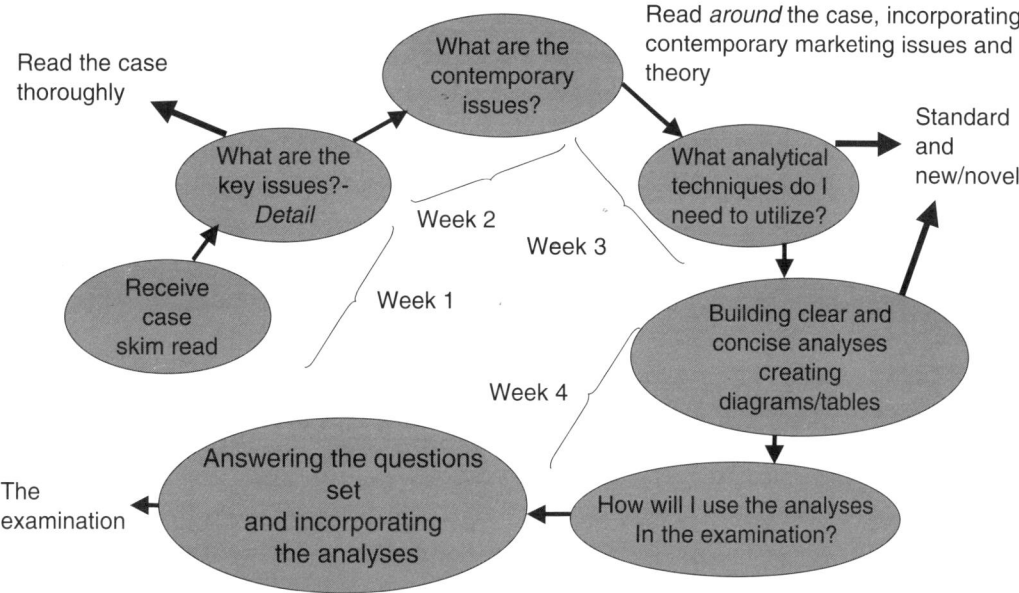

Figure 6.1 Approaching the SMIP case

Summary

When working on the case and in the examination, do not repeat in summary form large pieces of factual information from the case. The examiners are fully aware of the case. It is better to use the information in the case to illustrate your statements, to defend your arguments, or to make salient points. Beyond the brief introduction to the company, you must avoid being descriptive; instead, you must be analytical. *Why? So what?*

You will need to ensure that the sections and subsections of your discussion flow logically and smoothly from one to the next. Try to build on what has gone before so that each analysis builds on the previous one. A piecemeal approach to analysis results in fragmented writing lacking coherence. This is because the parts do not flow from one to the next, and this becomes apparent to the examiners. Sometimes this happens when intensive group and individual approaches are put together.

It is important to write in a report format using clear English, avoiding grammatical and spelling errors. Clarity of approach and the judicious use of diagrams help examiners to follow your arguments easily.

Finally:

- Practice on previous cases to see how you would have approached the case differently from the specimen answers given.

- Read and digest senior examiner's reports.

- Read books, newspapers and relevant marketing and academic journals.

Be flexible and critical when utilizing analytical models and steer away from being prescriptive in your approach. More practice will result in better insights and help you with being creative and innovative when framing your answers.

The units that follow give you an indication of the way that students have approached examinations. This has been done through the usage of specimen questions for this NEW module with a general examination brief for answering the set questions by the Senior Examiner. As the first examination for this paper is in December 2004, you have been provided with ILLUSTRATIVE QUESTIONS AND ANSWER BRIEFS, together with ILLUSTRATIVE sets of Analyses.

Unit 7
case study

The Chartered
Institute of Marketing

Case Study
June 2003

Strategic Marketing Management: Analysis & Decision

Titan Industries Limited

Case Study – June 2003

Strategic Marketing Management: Analysis & Decision

Important Notes for Candidates

The examiners will be marking your scripts on the basis of questions put to you in the examination room. Candidates are advised to pay particular attention to the *mark allocation on the examination paper and budget their time accordingly.*

Your role is outlined in the candidates' brief and you will be required to recommend clear courses of action.

You WILL NOT be awarded marks merely for analysis. This should have been undertaken before the examination day in preparation for meeting the tasks which will be specified in the examination paper.

Candidates are advised not to waste valuable time collecting unnecessary data. The cases are based upon real world situations. No useful purpose will therefore be served by contacting companies in this industry and candidates are **strictly instructed not to do so as it may cause unnecessary confusion.**

As in real life, anomalies will be found in the information provided within this Case. Please simply state your assumptions where necessary when answering questions. The CIM is not in a position to answer queries on Case data. Candidates are tested on their overall understanding of the Case and its key issues, not on minor details. There are no catch questions or hidden agendas.

Additional information will be introduced in the examination paper itself which candidates must take into account when answering the questions set.

Acquaint yourself thoroughly with the Case Study and be prepared to follow closely the instructions given to you on the examination day. To answer examination questions effectively, candidates must adopt a report format.

The copying of pre-prepared 'group' answers including those written by consultants/tutors is strictly forbidden and will be penalized by failure. The questions will demand analysis in the examination itself and individually composed answers are required to pass.

Candidate's Brief

You have been appointed as a Marketing Consultant to the Board of Titan Industries Limited. Titan Industries Limited, an Indian company, is a relatively new entrant to the watch industry, but has performed well over the last ten years. The company saw the potential for gaining a large market share in the Indian market and took full advantage of the prospering economy. At the same time it has invested heavily in new product development. As part of its global ambitions, the company has established companies in various centres around the world. The world's watch industry is a very difficult and diverse market, which is dominated by two countries – Switzerland and Japan. The Swiss are renowned for their brands and quality. The Japanese on the other hand are present in the middle-of-the-range market. The biggest challenge facing Titan Industries Limited is in establishing a substantial and unique brand presence outside India. At the same time it has to protect its strong image in India from the growing influence of Swiss and Japanese imports. In order to help the company develop a market focus for the next decade, you have been hired to work closely with the Board and the marketing team. Your name is Jane Marandi and you have previously worked in the electronics sector. Based on an initial request, you have prepared the following report on the state of the company and the recent trends in the sector. At a later meeting scheduled for 13 June 2003, you will be asked to elaborate on this report to the Board of Directors, who will pose specific questions to you based on your current findings.

© The Chartered Institute of Marketing

Titan Industries Limited

Introduction

This case is about an Indian company called Titan Industries Limited that specializes in producing wristwatches for the general consumer. Titan Industries Limited is a joint venture between the Tata Group and the Tamil Nadu Industrial Development Corporation (TIDCO). The company commenced operations in 1987 under the name of Titan Industries Limited. The company diversified into the jewellery market in 1994. Currently the company is India's leading watch producer, with a domestic market share greater than 50 per cent. The company strives to cater for a vast range of consumers and places an emphasis on innovation in design, quality and reliability.

A short history of the watch industry

The watch industry has a long and fascinating history. Although it is possible for many different inventors to claim that they invented the first portable time device, it was really Peter Henlein who created the first portable time keeping device (Nürnberg Egg) in 1509 in Nürnberg, Germany. In 1485, Leonardo da Vinci had sketched a fusee clock and this system was later used in watches, especially in England. Religion, and in particular Martin Luther's influence, had a great impact on the industry, especially when his Protestant reformation took over Geneva in 1535. The city had no watchmaking industry, but it was well-known for its jewellery. When John Calvin moved to Geneva, he made it the centre for reformation. There were many strict laws enacted, such as the banning of theatre, dancing and many other forms of entertainment. The wearing of jewellery and fashionable clothing was also forbidden. However, watches were exempted as they were regarded as practical items. There was also an emphasis on hard work and time keeping. This loophole attracted the finest watchmakers from France and Germany, who collaborated with the jewellers to make intricate watches with jewels, enamels and engravings. This spawned the luxury watch industry in Geneva. The fashion in watches continued to grow and many different shapes, sizes and covers were developed.

In the late 17th century there was a breakthrough in technology, pioneered by Christian Huygens in Holland, who invented the 'Remontoire'. The spiral hairspring and the balance wheel were also invented. Watches were now accurate to within a few minutes and also had minute hands. Technology moved on with the use of rubies in watch movements in order to lessen friction. The use of drums and cylinders made watches slim compared to earlier versions. Later enamelling on watch faces was also introduced. In the 17th century much of the new technology in watches was developed. At the same time, watches to determine longitude at sea were developed in Britain. Britain was at the forefront of watch technology until the self-winding watch was developed by Bruguet in France. In the 19th century watches became even more complicated and elaborate. The Americans went into mass manufacturing, as did the Swiss and British. Markets in Turkey and China generally tended to import from Britain and Switzerland. Automatic winding became normal in the 20th century. Watches were also made to be shockproof, waterproof and able to perform in extreme conditions of pressure or vacuum. The battery-powered watch became available in 1952 as an alternative to the automatic. The electronic watch, which replaced the escapement with the electronic vibrations of a tuning fork (quartz digital), was a completely new concept. This changed the beat of the watch from about 2.5 beats per second for a mechanical watch to nearly 2.5 million beats per second for an electronic watch. This new technology was embraced and enhanced by the Asian watch industry, particularly Japan. This system allowed cheap and very accurate watches to be mass produced in the millions. These watches were so successful that the mechanical watches were nearly lost forever. However, the Swiss watch industry fought back with quality, developing marketing and branding strategies to combat the inroads made by Japanese watches. The Swiss watch industry now employs around 30,000 workers, only a third of the number employed in 1960. Manufacturers such as Blancpain, Rolex, Patek Philippe, Audemars Piguet, Jaeger LeCoultre, A. Lange & Söhne and Vacheron Constantin still make high-quality mechanical watches in Switzerland. The industry has evolved to such an extent that mechanical and electronic watches sit side by side.

Branding is becoming more important and large amounts are spent in advertising watches such as Rolex, Cartier, Omega, etc. Different watches appeal to different segments of the population. There are watches for children, men, women, and a vast range of segments of populations around the world. Watches have always fascinated the public, and as the miniaturization of electronic parts continues unabated, many new and novel types of watches are beginning to emerge. Consumers are also buying several types of watches for different occasions. In most countries, individuals possess multiple watches. Titan, which entered the market in 1987, embraced the new technologies and decided to build its image as an indigenous watchmaker in India. It now has global ambitions for the watches and its new venture into jewellery through the Tanishq brand.

Titan products

Titan is the umbrella brand name for a range of sub-brands that are designed to focus on specific consumer segments. These are shown in Table 7.1.

Table 7.1

Titan sub-brands	Market segment
Insignia	High-end offering for the consumer who seeks international styling.
Nebula	Jewellery watches for men and women, fashioned in gold and precious stones.
Fastrack	Targeted at the young, fashion-conscious customer.
Classique	A collection for the workplace.
Regalia and Royale	Designed for a flamboyant look.
Raga	Designed as a tribute to Indian women.
Sonata	Introduced in 1999 for the budget-conscious market – this has become the largest watch brand in India.
Ovations 2000	Designer type watches, especially for the Middle Eastern market.
Titan Steel Collection	Launched in 2001 to meet the growing demand for the contemporary 'steel' look in watches – targeted at the 25–35 age group.

Source: Compiled from information supplied by Titan Industries Limited

Examples of these watches can be seen in Appendix 5.

'Ovations 2000' was launched in the United Arab Emirates (UAE), especially to cater for individuals who desire exclusive watches to fit in with their fashion-conscious image. There are 150 faces of 'Ovations 2000', comprising of dress watches, pair watches (for men and women), and sporty watches for outdoor enthusiasts. All the watches are water-resistant and have clear, finely etched dials. The 'dress' watches are very ornamental, with bracelets made of solid metal links. The 'His & Hers' collection makes an ideal gift, with bracelets made in steel, steel/gold plated, or gold.

The 'Fastrack' collection is designed to meet the changing needs of the modern young consumer. It has an original and fresh identity. These watches come in a frosted finish that is popular throughout the world. This collection of watches emphasizes an informal and sporty look, as the casings are fabricated in steel or black. The body is crafted from tough stainless steel and a range of straps is available. It is these straps (leather, sporty in nature, or made of metal mesh), which give the watch an unusual look. The different variants of straps, combined with the styles of the watches, create a 'trendy' and 'cool' look. The collection's design signatures are its special crown, date display at 4 o'clock, hands with coloured tips, and an exclusive back cover marking which is either acid etched or laser engraved. Within the range are multifunction chronographs, dual-time models, with water-resistance up to 100 m. The straps are also designed to be water-resistant. Currently there are 50 different variants of 'Fastrack' for both men and women.

In addition to the above, the company has also launched Euro-watches that are targeted at the European market. Renowned designers in Europe design the watches for this market. These watches match the very best designs on offer from the Swiss watchmakers.

In 2001, the company launched a new range of watches in steel, a metal that is currently all the rage in younger circles. The Titan Steel Collection has a range of bracelet and leather strap watches to suit all tastes and budgets (the price range being between Rs 1,250 [£17][1] and Rs 6,000 [£82]). According to Bijou Kurien, Chief Operating Officer of Titan's Watch Division:

---

[1]Currently the Exchange Rate varies between 73 and 78 Rupees to the £, so all figures given in £ are approximate.

'Steel is very much in vogue and we are offering consumers an opportunity to move towards a more individualistic and bolder look.' The Steel Collection is targeted at urban men and women in the 25–35 age group, who are not just conscious of style and fashion, but who take great interest in co-ordinating their clothes and adding image enhancing accessories. The Collection was created by Titan's in-house design team and manufactured at Titan's own hi-tech plant. The geometric forms and straight lines characterize the collection and give the watches a fresh bold look. Blue, black and white dials with prominent markings make them ideal for formal occasions. The idea behind the Steel Collection is the concept of multiple occasions for wearing them. According to Prateek Srivastava, Vice President of Ogily & Mather in Bangalore: 'The idea is that just as you change your clothes to get ready for an evening out, you also need to change your watch.' This has so far worked well in India, although initially watches were not regarded as fashion accessories in the country. In order to sell more watches, the company has spent Rs 2.5 crore[2] on advertising. However, there was a debate on whether the company should have launched very high priced watches, which compete against the Swiss labels. Titan is regarded as a relative newcomer to the watch industry compared to the Swiss labels that are regarded as 'heritage' brands in the eyes of the consumer. As the regulations on imports have been eased in the Indian market, more foreign brands have been made available to consumers. Many of these brands start at Rs 6,000, and consumers are often willing to pay a little more for foreign brands. Some commentators felt that Titan was diluting its brand equity by bringing out watches that were not in gold. However, the sceptics were proved wrong as the Steel Collection has sold well (Appendix 4 has figures for current sales).

Recent research and development

In 2002, the company launched Titan Edge, the slimmest watch in the world. This was produced after four years of intensive research and development. The watch is just 3.5 mm thick and its movement is a wafer thin 1.15 mm. The watch was produced through close collaboration between Titan's Design Studio, the Production Department and the R&D team. The Titan Edge has a fully jewelled quartz analogue movement and is water-resistant up to 30 m. This is unheard of in slim watches, which are usually around 5 mm thick. The watch has a state-of-the-art silicon chip that conserves power and doubles the life of the battery. The movement of Titan Edge was tested and certified by M/s Chronofiable, a world-renowned horological testing agency in Switzerland.

> 'Even in terms of design, the issues we faced were in designing the functional parts of the watch to fit the slimness of the movement,' said Michael Foley, Head of the Design Studio at Titan Industries Limited. He went on to say, 'From the wedge profile of the case to the finely etched ceramic dials, the uniquely crafted skeletal hands, the elongated markings and the specially designed fine leather strap and buckle, the Titan Edge speaks of elegance and sophistication with a defined slimness.'

The Titan Edge currently boasts 13 variants – eight in stainless steel and five in the gold-plated version. The watches are priced between Rs 4,495 (£61) and Rs 4,995 (£68). The watch carries a two-year comprehensive guarantee and is available at all the World of Titan showrooms and major cities in India and selected locations around the world. In India, the watch is supported by a TV campaign, backed by red and black visuals in the shops and on billboards.

Titan's brand image in India

Over the last five years, consumers have consistently regarded Titan as one of the top brands in India. In 1998, Titan was regarded as the most admired consumer goods company, in a survey

---

[2] A crore equals 10,000,000 and one lakh equals 100,000.

carried out by Advertising and Marketing (*A&M Magazine*) in India. Titan's history in the polls has been outstanding as Tables 7.2 and 7.3 indicate.

Table 7.2

Company	Company rankings over six years						
	1999	1998	1997	1996	1995	1994	1993
FMCG companies							
HLL	1	1	1	1	1	1	1
Coca-Cola	2	7	9	11	13	16	–
Cadbury	3	8	3	3	6	7	6
Pepsi Foods	4	3	5	4	7	6	11
Colgate	5	9	6	5	4	5	5
Durables Companies							
Titan	1	1	2	1	1	1	1
BPL	2	2	1	5	3	3	5
Maruti	3	4	5	2	–	–	–
Intel	4	–	–	–	–	–	–
LG Electronics	5	11	–	–	–	–	–

Source: Advertising, Marketing, e-Commerce, India

Table 7.3 Most admired durable brands in India 1998/1999

Rank 1999	Rank 1998	Company	Score	Rank 1999	Rank 1998	Company	Score
1	1	Titan	7.96	19	26	Compaq	6.62
2	2	BPL	7.76	20	21	Eureka Forbes	6.6
3	4	Maruti	7.55	21	24	Carrier Aircon	6.51
4	–	Intel	7.47	22	9	Ericsson	6.5
5	11	LG Electronics	7.39	23	12	Philips	6.5
6	7	Godrej-GE	7.13	24	15	Modi Xerox	6.43
7	3	MRF	7.07	25	29	Videocon	6.41
8	13	Bajaj Auto	7.05	26	23	Chloride India (Exide)	6.38
9	13	Hero Honda	6.96	27	20	HCL Infosystems	6.22
10	5	Asian Paints	6.95	28	21	LML	6.16
11	24	Hewlett-Packard	6.9	29	27	Mahindra and Mahindra	6.1
12	18	Samsung	6.82	30	31	Hero Cycles	6.07
13	18	Whirlpool	6.81	31	33	Onida	5.93
14	15	TVS Suzuki	6.79	32	17	Bausch and Lomb	5.92
15	6	Nokia	6.78	33	30	Goodlass Nerolac	5.86
16	–	Telco	6.67	34	9	Motorola	5.85
17	–	Infosys	6.63	35	8	Baron International	5.82
17	28	Wipro Infotech	6.63	36	32	Blow Plast	5.61

Source: Advertising, Marketing, e-Commerce, India

In 1999, the Advertising and Marketing Survey was carried out by IMRB, along the same lines as the previous seven years. In order to maintain continuity and establish the survey's validity in enabling comparisons with previous years, the surveys were carried out exclusively among professional marketers in companies marketing fast moving consumer goods (FMCG) and durables. Respondents were drawn from all levels and the research was conducted in the major cities of Delhi, Calcutta, Chennai and Bangalore. The company received top positions when the following questions were asked:

1. Products are designed to meet customer needs (7.88).
2. Products are different from competitors (7.25).
3. Better than average at new product launches (7.59).
4. Brands provide long-term stability (7.52).
5. Products are market leaders (7.91).
6. Products are innovative (number 2 slot) (7.32).
7. Products are consistently superior to competitors (7.51).
8. Products offer value for money (7.66).
9. Company's marketing personnel are of high calibre (7.20).
10. Company's advertising is consistently superior (number 2 slot) (7.53).
11. Company keeps in touch with the market constantly (7.4).
12. Company has a superior distribution network (7.78).
13. Provides good after-sales service (number 2 slot) (7.43).

Note: Figures in brackets are scores out of 10.

As can be seen, Titan retained its leadership position. Working in its favour was its product launches into new segments, including the Dash! range for children.

In 2000, an *Economic Times* survey of top Indian companies revealed that Titan was regarded as the top brand in India, ahead of all FMCG companies. A consumer brand is much more than a bundle of tangible and intangible benefits. For this particular survey, seven attributes were considered:

1. The quality of the brand.
2. Value for money.
3. The future of the brand.
4. Distinctiveness.
5. Uniqueness.
6. The feelings that the brand evokes amongst the consumer.
7. How inclined the consumers were to purchase the brand.

The target audience for the survey were chief wage earners, housewives and adults between the ages of 15–45 years belonging to A/B/C households in urban India. A ten-point scale was applied and a total of 3,164 interviews conducted in the following locations – Mumbai (537), Delhi (520), Calcutta (423), Chennai (409), Rajkot (345), Allahabad (300), Cuttack (300) and Vijayawada (330). The Titan brand received such success because it appeals to the youth segment and is aspirational. In India Titan is known for its classy elegance, whilst being a popular mass-market brand with a strong presence at the lower end. The Titan brand is regarded as 'mass with class' by brand consultants. It is a brand that is also equally popular with both men and women. The company is consistent in its brand expenditure and spends, on average, around Rs 25/30 crore on brand building. Although this is small compared to others within the top 10, the amount spent appears to be highly effective.

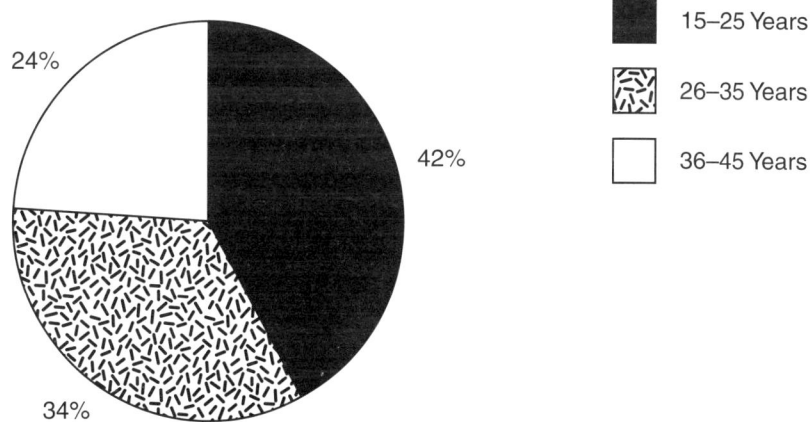

Figure 7.1 Respondent profile by age
Source: Economic Times, India

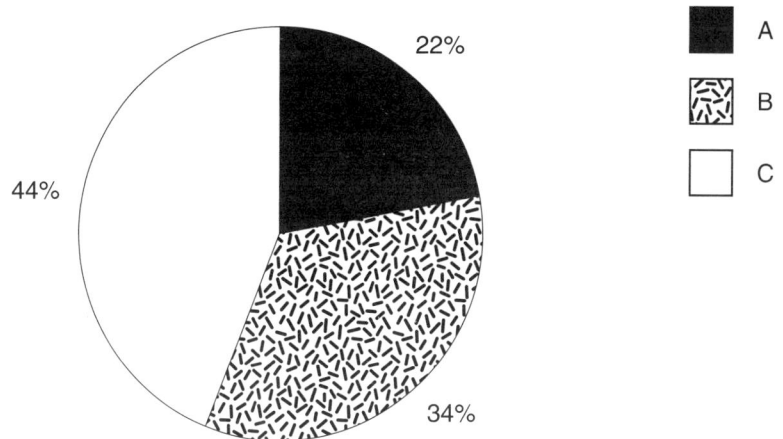

Figure 7.2 Socio–economic classes surveyed
Source: Economic Times, India

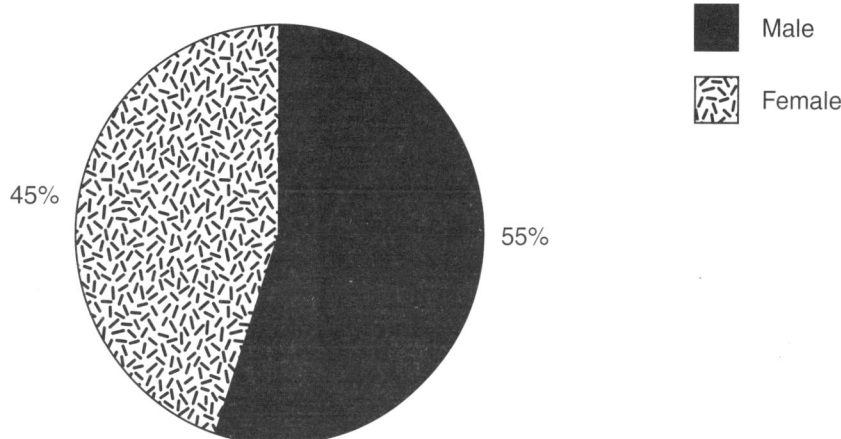

Figure 7.3 Gender breakdown of respondents
Source: Economic Times, India

In a September 2001 *Business World (India)* survey of companies in different sectors, such as FMCG/Durables, Information Technology, Auto Ancillaries, Financial Services, Infrastructure, Media/Entertainment, Pharma/Biotech, Ready-made garments and Services, Titan was ranked third out of 23 companies surveyed for a range of factors. The people surveyed were marketing managers of companies within the sector. These factors were:

a. Number of times a company was chosen (29).
b. Overall quality (7.52).
c. Top management leadership (7.48).
d. Top management relationship (7.14).
e. Depth and quality of talent (6.93).
f. Ability to attract/manage/retain talent (6.83).
g. Believes in transparency (7.00).
h. Ethical organization (6.59).
i. Environmentally conscious organization (6.55).
j. Quality of product/services provided (7.45).
k. Believes in customer satisfaction (7.52).
l. Record of product corporate brand management (7.45).
m. Is a dynamic organization (7.21).
n. Responds quickly to business scene changes (7.10).
o. Believes in continuous innovation (7.24).
p. Has global competitiveness (6.83).
q. Has a record of steady corporate performance (7.14).
r. Gives good returns to shareholders (6.59).
s. Ability to create value for stakeholders (6.63).

Note: Figures in brackets are scores out of 10 (except for a.).

Table 7.4 FMCG/durables sector

Company	Rank
HLL	1
Pepsi	2
Titan	3
Cadbury India	4
ITC	4

Source: *Business India*

The company is now concerned that it should translate its brand advantage into profits. Titan's domestic watch business, according to Mr Xerxes Desai (Vice Chairman and Managing Director), is very profitable in India, returning 25 per cent on the capital employed (ROCE). This is because of the strong brand equity. However, the company's exposure in Europe and the venture into jewellery have conspired to erode profitability. The challenge for the company is to improve its brand performance in international markets.

Branding

To achieve high brand equity in any market sector requires consistency of approach, and the promise of a relationship with the customer that fulfils the promises of the brand image.

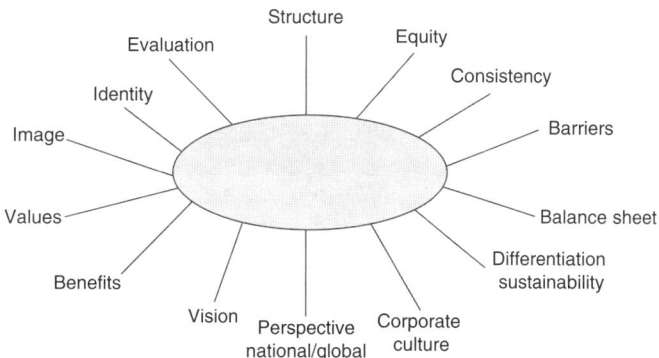

Figure 7.4 Brand structure
Source: From *Communicating Globally: An Integrated Marketing Approach,* by Don Schultz and Philip J Kitchen; published by McGraw-Hill. USA

The brand structure is complicated and has to encompass a range of factors as shown in Figure 7.4. A brand has both assets and liabilities associated with it (Aaker, 1991). These aspects are shown below:

1. *Brand loyalty* Encourages customers to buy a particular brand time after time and remain unresponsive to competitors' offerings.
2. *Brand awareness* Brand names attract attention and convey images of familiarity. This can be translated into how large a percentage of the customers know the brand name.
3. *Perceived quality* 'Perceived' means that the customers decide upon the level of quality, not the company.
4. *Brand associations* The values and the personality linked to the brand.
5. *Other proprietary brand assets* Including trademarks, patents and market channel relationships.

In addition to this, in order to succeed in the marketplace a brand has to build on a range of different factors before it is universally accepted, known and desired. These factors are shown in Figure 7.5.

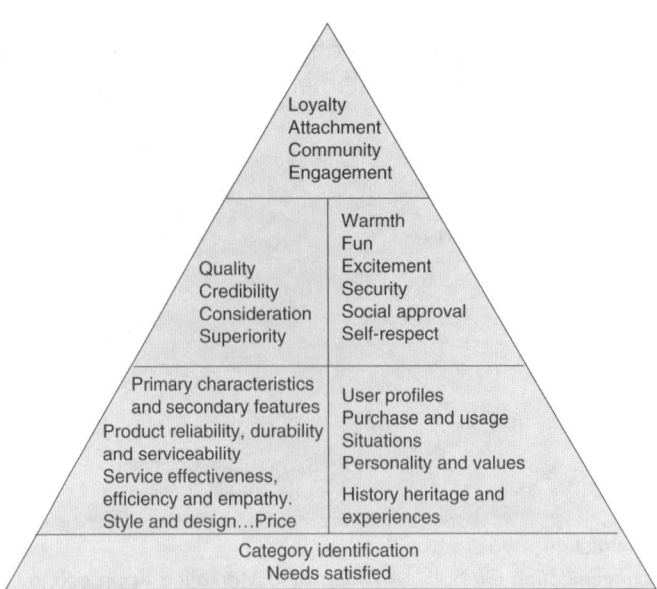

Figure 7.5 Sub-dimensions of brand-building blocks
Source: Reprinted with permission from *Marketing Management*, by Kevin Lane Keller, July/August 2001 edn, Vol.10(2), p.14; published by the American Marketing Association

In addition to the factors shown in Figure 7.5, it is increasingly clear that branding is very much affected by a company's reputation. Reputation management is intricately associated with brand management. The way a company manages its reputation with a range of stakeholders such as customers, suppliers, trade partners and employees affects its brands. At the same time a company has to exhibit an exemplary history, including environmental, ethical, work and economic policies. With the advent of the Internet, reputations can either be enhanced or destroyed very quickly. A company has to show integrity and honesty in its day-to-day management. The customer interface is also very important in managing brands. To this end, Titan have attempted to develop good customer relationships through selling a large volume of its watches through their own retail shops named 'The World of Titan'. Titan's products are sold in over 1,800 cities in India through 7,000 outlets. Of these, 136 outlets are exclusive 'World of Titan' stores, and another 136 are TimeZone outlets, a chain of high-profile multi-brand outlets with a significant Titan presence. In addition to this Titan has an extensive Customer Service Network. The World of Titan showroom network is arguably the largest network of exclusive watch showrooms in the world. Internationally the Titan brand is now available in over 31 countries, supported by associate companies in London, Dubai, Singapore, Amsterdam and an extensive distribution network.

The Indian watch market

The volume of watch sales in India is estimated to be around 25 million units per annum. This results in approximately 25 sales per thousand consumers, compared to 60 per thousand in China and 400 per thousand in the USA. The key players in the market are HMT, TIMEX and a large number of small operators. With the abolition of import restrictions, many of the famous international brands have now entered the Indian market. Currently in India, Titan enjoys an estimated 80 per cent of the premium segment, with almost 100 per cent brand recall among consumers intending to purchase a watch. Titan is held in great esteem and has a high regard amongst the Indian public, as it was one of the first Indian companies to provide the Indian consumer with a wide range of internationally styled products of consistent high quality which are sold and serviced through a high quality retail and after-sales service network. However, luxury Swiss watches are now competing at the high end of the market, with prices in excess of Rs 10,000. Japanese watchmakers are offering products retailing between Rs 1,000 and Rs 10,000. The bottom end of the market (watches selling at less than Rs 1,000) is being threatened by grey market operators and cheap watches imported from China.

At the same time the retailing of watches is also undergoing significant change, especially in the major cities, with the growth of department stores. These stores see watches as providing a growing and profitable business opportunity. Many of the top Swiss, European and Japanese brands have also opened exclusive watch stores in the major cities. The traditional watch dealers therefore face increasing challenges as a result of these developments. Increasingly, the after-sales service provided by the manufacturer is viewed as a significant differentiating factor for the retailer and for the brand in the eyes of the consumer. With the market becoming increasingly crowded and competitive this is an important factor.

Competitive strategies

The company has built on its existing strengths and skills and is beginning to capitalize on a more global approach to business in India by expanding internationally. The process works both ways, with the company able to access international suppliers as well as selling watches and jewellery internationally. The strategy of segmenting the market and catering to every different segment with a particular brand has created a dominant brand position, together with a leading market share in India. The growth and development of a retail chain with dedicated as well as multi-brand outlets controlled by the company, has posed a considerable barrier to the growth of brands from other parts of the world. Part of the company strategy is to extend these outlets. The company constantly strives to improve its efficiency through cost reduction strategies and better supply chain management. Titan has also ventured into jewellery through the Tanishq brand, setting new standards for luxury jewellery. The Tanishq brand has grown rapidly in India. The biggest challenge that the company faces is in consolidating its position in the international arena.

The global market for watches and jewellery

Globalization is becoming an increasingly important consideration for branded goods. There appears to be a globalization of styles, trends and cultures. More and more retailers now have the experience to adapt their own formats to foreign markets – as well as learning from the local norms and styles. The situation in Asia and the weakness of currencies post-1997 has increased the buying power of Western brands, creating one-off opportunities to invest in retail infrastructure and regional distribution. In India itself, the MTV culture and the westernization of Bollywood have led to a convergence of tastes amongst women and men. More traditional dress and accessories are either westernised or discarded. The Japanese and the Swiss dominate the world watch industry. The overall production of watches is estimated to be around 1,240 million units (Figure 7.6). Japan is by far the largest producer of watches, as indicated in Figure 7.7.

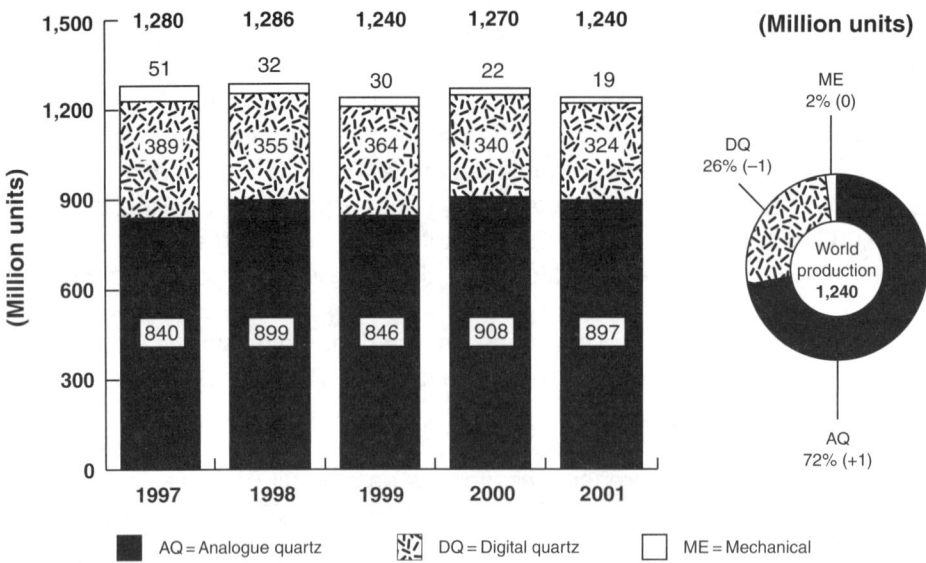

Figure 7.6 Global watch production
Source: The Japan Watch and Clock Industry

Mechanical Watches Derive their running power by means of a mainspring that is either wound up manually, or in an automatic watch, by the rotor constantly actuated by the motion of the wearer's arm.

Quartz Analogue Have 12-hour faces, are operated by a quartz mechanism, and the majority are powered by a battery.

Quartz Digital Are similarly powered but display the time in numeric form by means of a Liquid Crystal Diode (LCD).

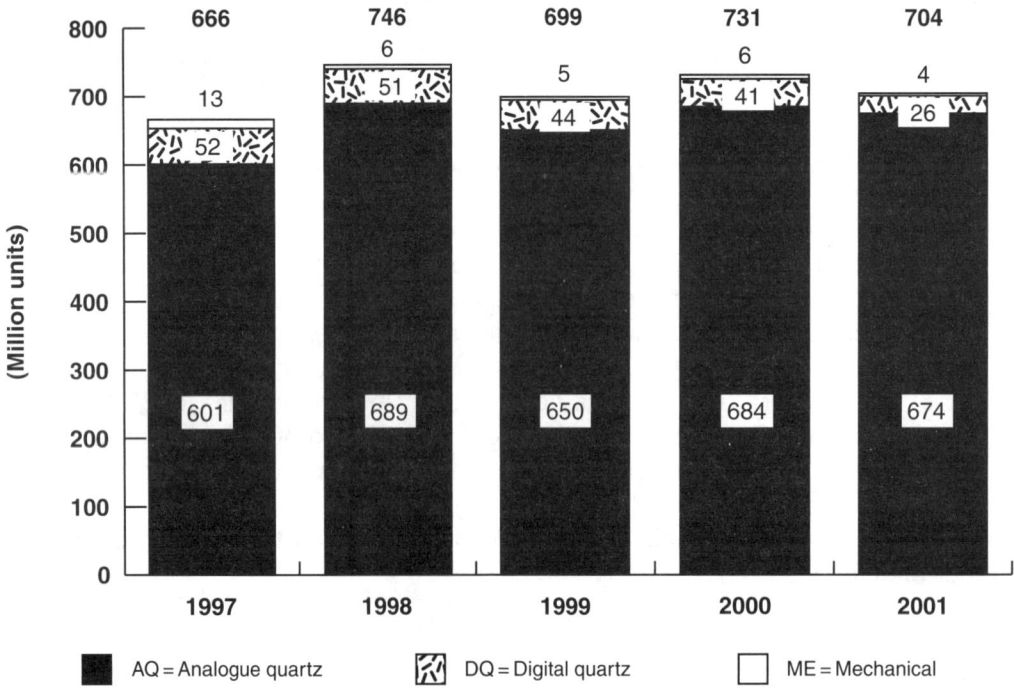

Figure 7.7 Development of Japanese watch production: by type (complete watches and movements)
Source: Japan Watch and Clock Industry
Note: Often surveys show watches and movements, creating difficulty in interpreting actual watch production. According to sources at Titan, the world watch production is around 750 million pieces.

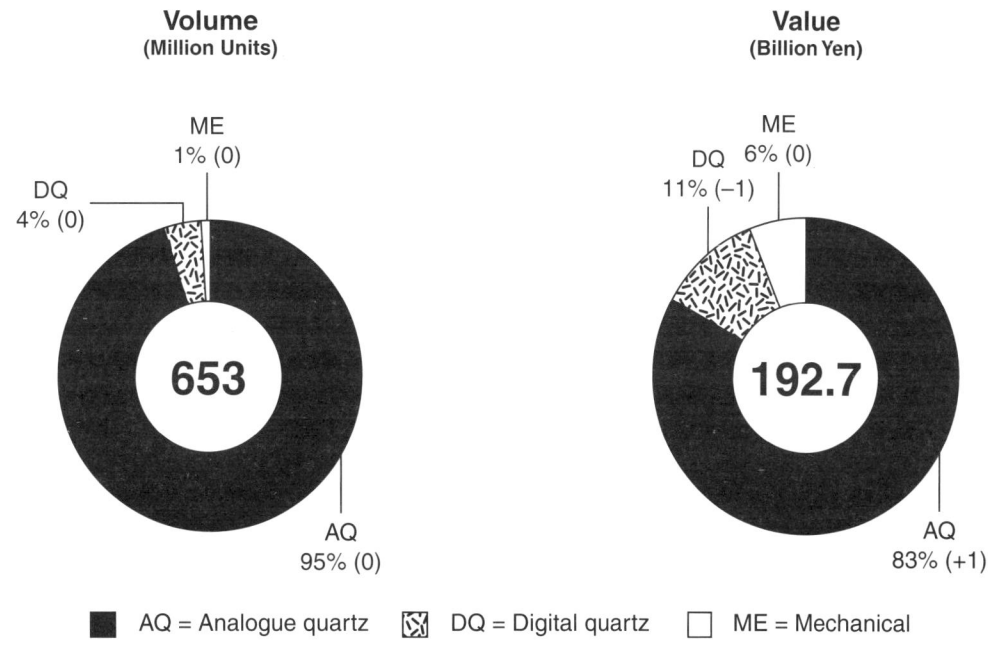

Volume
(Million Units)

ME
1% (0)

DQ
4% (0)

653

AQ
95% (0)

Value
(Billion Yen)

ME 6% (0)

DQ
11% (−1)

192.7

AQ
83% (+1)

■ AQ = Analogue quartz   ⊠ DQ = Digital quartz   ☐ ME = Mechanical

Figure 7.8 2001 world distribution of Japanese watch exports (complete watches)
Source: Japanese Watch and Clock Exports

Japanese total watch production for 2001 (consisting of complete watches and movements), including overseas production, was estimated to account for 57 per cent of the world total watch production, showing a decrease of 1 per cent point in relation to 2000. In the analogue quartz business, Japanese watches are estimated to account for 75 per cent of the world total, keeping the same level as the previous year.

In 2001, 27.8 million finished timepieces were manufactured in Switzerland, 3.6 million pieces fewer then in 2000. This drop in volume was accompanied by a rise in value to 10.517 billion Swiss Francs (+3.7 per cent).

Table 7.5

	2001	2000
Units (in millions)		
Mechanical	2.7	*2.7*
Quartz Analogue	24.5	*27.9*
Quartz Digital	0.6	*0.8*
Total	**27.8**	*31.4*
Value (in millions of Swiss Francs)		
Mechanical	5,468	*4,826*
Quartz Analogue	4,994	*5,248*
Quartz Digital	0,055	*0,064*
Total	**10,517**	*10,138*

Source: Swiss Watch Federation

Table 7.6 Watch Exports of Main Watch Producing Countries in the World

Country	Export Value in US$ million
Switzerland	6,500
Germany	400
France	239
United Kingdom	203
Japan	141
Hong Kong	75.5

Source: Swiss Watch Federation

Table 7.7 Average Price per Watch when Exported

Country	Price US$
Switzerland	247.60
Germany	75
France	52.60
United Kingdom	55.30
Japan	27.70
Hong Kong	5.30

Source: Swiss Watch Federation

Some companies manufacture some of their watches in the UK.

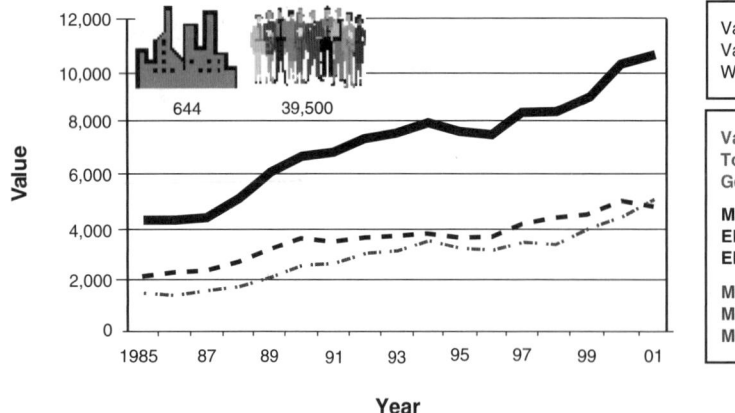

Figure 7.9
Source: Swiss Watch Federation

Table 7.8 Swiss watch exports

Pays Countries Länder	Valeur Value Wert (SFr million) 2001	Valeur Value Wert (SFr million) 2000	Variation Change Änderung (%)	Part Au Total Share Anteil (%)
1. United States	1,585.7	1,847.0	−14.1	14.9
2. Hong Kong	1,508.1	1,423.2	+6.0	14.2
3. Japan	1,052.3	928.4	+13.3	9.9
4. Italy	840.0	883.3	−4.9	7.9
5. Germany	783.2	716.2	+9.4	7.3
6. France	720.3	652.9	+10.3	6.7
7. Great Britain	509.8	429.4	+18.7	4.8
8. Singapore	438.4	422.5	+3.8	4.1
9. Spain	342.3	329.3	+3.9	3.2
10. Taiwan	195.6	185.8	+5.3	1.8
11. United Arab Emirates	189.2	180.5	+4.8	1.8
12. Thailand	177.6	192.7	−7.8	1.7
13. Saudi Arabia	172.8	142.0	+21.7	1.6
14. Austria	126.5	108.7	+16.4	1.2
15. Netherlands	116.5	114.5	+1.7	1.1
Total 15 Countries	**8,758.3**	**8,556.4**	**+2.4**	**82.2**
Other Countries	**1,895.2**	**1,740.8**	**+8.9**	**17.8**
World Total	**10,653.5**	**10,297.2**	**+3.5**	**100.0**

Source: Swiss Watch Federation

The details shown in Tables 7.5 and 7.8 indicate the depth and strength of the Swiss watch industry, based on heritage, quality and image. Although the country is a much smaller volume producer than Japan, it is significantly more profitable and valuable as an export industry. This indicates the value of brand equity in the global watch industry. In value terms, within the Swiss watch exports, steel watches account for 43 per cent of value, and precious metal watches take a 48 per cent share. A company such as Titan has to develop its brand equity globally in order to emulate the 'mass with class' success that it has enjoyed in India.

Common to all luxury products is a set of characteristics including:

- ○ Strong brand image.
- ○ Premium pricing.
- ○ Exceptional design quality and craftsmanship.
- ○ Controlled, exclusive or selective distribution.

Table 7.9 The Global watch industry

Country	Units (million)	Value (SFr million)	Units (%)	Value (%)
China/Hong Kong	400	1,500	80	10
Switzerland	33	8,888	7	59
Japan	20	991	4	7
France	7	312	1	2
Other Countries	40	3,309	8	22
Total	**500**	**15,000**	**100**	**100**

Source: FHS, from Mintel

More than 90 per cent of Swiss production is exported and virtually all luxury watch making is carried out in the major production centres of Switzerland. The FHS segments the watch industry by price level into three categories:

Luxury Priced ex-factory at SFr 500 or above (equivalent to US$ 1,120 at retail), with annual production of about 3.3 million units and dominated by Swiss manufacturers.

Medium Range Priced between SFr 200 and SFr 500 (equivalent to the US$ 390 to US$ 1,120 range at retail). More widely distributed through watch retailers and department stores rather than jewellers and brand boutiques.

Mass Market Priced below SFr 200 (US$ 390 at retail) and dominated by Japanese producers Citizen, Casio, Seiko, as well as the Swiss Swatch Group.

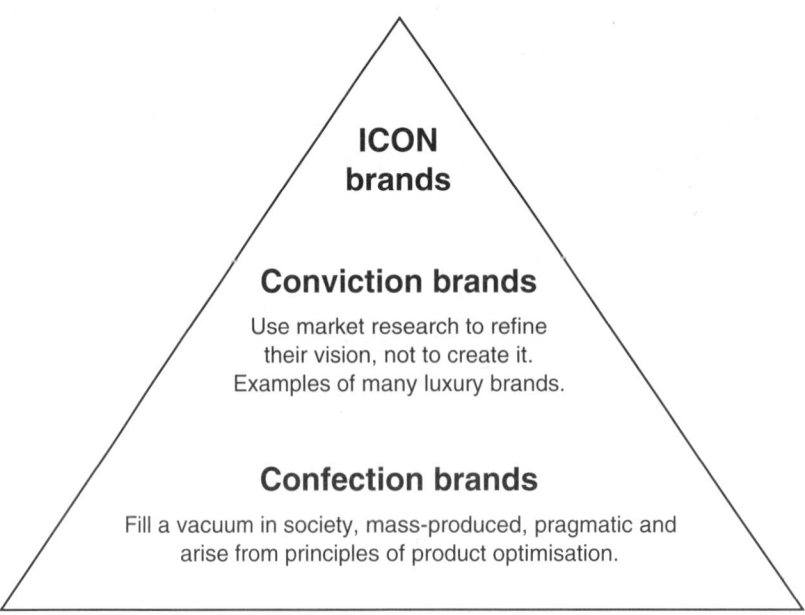

Figure 7.10
Source: Retail Intelligence/Mintel

As Figure 7.10 shows, brands can be divided into ICON, Conviction and Confection brands on a global basis. Most of the Swiss watches are ICON brands, fetching high prices. The average price per watch indicates how far ahead the Swiss are compared to other countries in terms of developing desirable brands. The Japanese watchmakers have well-known brands such as Sekonda and Seiko, which are strong in the middle priced range.

Within the trade there has been a polarization of watch and jewellery demand during the last few years. Products are becoming more varied, with consumers prepared to invest in high-priced lines such as Rolex and 18-carat gold jewellery as status symbols. At the same time there is increased interest in a variety of niche products, from sports watches to the likes of Camel Trophy and Original Swiss Army brands, and TAG Heuer who have pioneered a large fashion-oriented market. Growth potential is exemplified in the popularity of both Rolex and Flik Flak by Swatch at both ends of the scale. Market insiders comment that consumers nowadays are showing a tendency to wait longer to purchase a piece of jewellery, but will then spend more money on a valuable piece of high quality. As in other luxury market segments there is a tendency to purchase a number of different items for different social occasions.

According to Mintel (certainly in the UK, and also reflected in other developed markets), the competition in all price bands is increasing. The interesting feature of the market is that although more watch specialists have entered the market, they are beginning to be outnumbered by the growing number of non-specialists – notably the fashion and sports brands (such as Calvin Klein, Storm, Kahuna, etc.). In response to this, many of the dedicated watchmakers have attempted to move upmarket with higher quality watches at higher prices, supported by technical innovation and the use of costly materials and finishes. This influences the customers to bear an upward shift in prices. Another interesting development is that a growing number of watchmakers are also becoming involved in jewellery (counterbalancing to some extent the jewellers and accessory specialists who are moving into watches). This development will probably increase familiarity amongst women. It would also help to maximize the brand values to a related product (Bulgari, Cartier, Chaumet, Chanel, Chopard and Piaget). Titan has followed this route with the establishment of the Tanishq brand of jewellery. The current developments have created a very fragmented and highly competitive market, making it quite difficult for Titan to get established in European and American markets.

New developments in watches and watch designs

Innovation in watch design has increased over the last few years as a result of the world of fashion intruding into the industry domain. This has encouraged wearers to think of watches as fashion accessories, promoting sales and accelerating the product purchase cycle. Some of the more recent style developments include the following:

a. A limited return to gold and other yellow metal.
b. A continuing preference for bracelets over straps, with a growth in the use of mesh straps.
c. Growing attention to the shape of the dial, with square, elongated rectangle and tonneau shapes all in evidence, as well as a very streamlined round shape.
d. More streamlined and elegant shapes for chronographs and sports watches.
e. A growing use of diamonds and other expensive stones. Concurrently there is also a growing use of less costly substitute stones.

As fashion changes dictate watch designs, so does technology. Technological developments not only affect the design of watches, they also allow new features to be incorporated. For instance some manufacturers such as Casio and Timex have made this the cornerstone of their marketing efforts. Watches can now incorporate:

a. Cameras.
b. Ground Positioning Systems (GPS).
c. MP3 players.
d. Navigation and PC links.
e. Mini personal organizers.

121

f.   Heart monitors.
g.   Data storage for numbers and records.
h.   Video remote controls.
i.   Light power.

As the electronic world becomes increasingly miniaturized, more facilities can be incorporated into watches, making them more versatile. Titan has embraced the use of new technology by developing the Edge, the Slimmest Watch in the Universe. These types of watches are increasingly popular with the youth market. Casio, for instance, with its G-Shock watch, sponsors the Pro Surfing World Tour. Technologically driven (see Appendix 3) watches fall into the following segments:

o   Marine.
o   Health and fitness.
o   Leisure.
o   Business and communications.
o   Outdoor sports.
o   Pro-Trek.
o   Wrist networks.

It is only a matter of time before these watches also start doubling as mobile communication devices.

It is interesting to note that the watch market is growing and fragmenting at the same time. More people are happy to purchase watches as accessories. In a world where individuals have a range of interests and hobbies, it may not be uncommon for them to buy different watches for these different pursuits.

The growing impact of Indian culture

Recently in the United Kingdom and the USA there has been a growing interest in Indian culture, fuelled by the success of Bollywood films such as Monsoon Wedding and Ashoka. In London, Andrew Lloyd Webber's musical Bombay Dreams has been a runaway success. These films and musicals not only appeal to the local Indian population, but also permeate the general population within the USA and the UK especially. India is extremely dynamic, with various layers to its entertainment industry. The most prominent layer of India's entertainment business is not assimilated content but rather a blend of local and international content, or hybridization. American culture is mixed with local Indian culture to give an Indian cultural hybrid. This is most evident in the industry of Bollywood. Bollywood today has refashioned Hollywood ideals to fit Indian values and ideals. Bollywood retains the glamour, ritz, wealth and epic nature of Hollywood, but strongly infuses this with Indian tradition. Bollywood has drawn mass audiences all over the world. The 25 million South Asians of today comprise a ready-made audience, for they are passionate about keeping their culture alive. They popularize Bollywood culture in countries around the world. This market accounts for about 55 per cent of international Bollywood ticket sales *(Pax Indianna*, The Globalist). The audiences are a mix of second generation Indians who have settled around the world and indigenous audiences in most of the Middle East, parts of Africa, much of South East Asia and China.

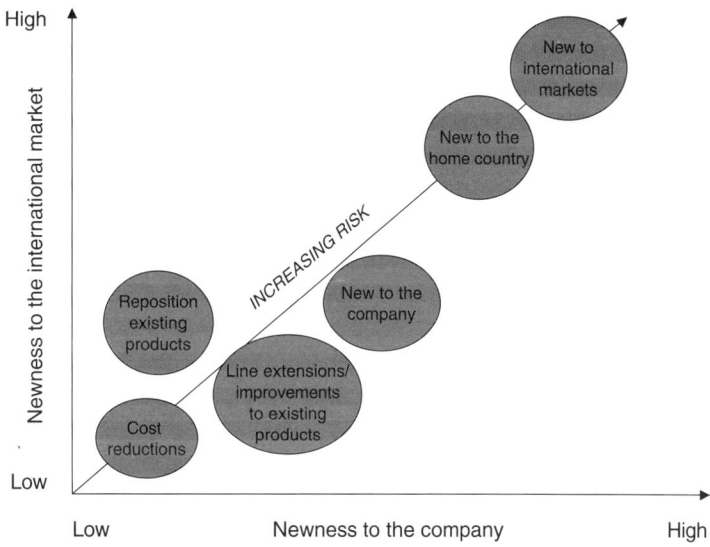

Figure 7.11 Different degrees of product newness
Source: Adaptation of the Ansoff Matrix

In Arab countries, fans opt for Hindi movies over Hollywood ones. India has shown that glocalization (global localization), enables nations to preserve their own cultures, and exert influence over the American content received. Most importantly, glocalization allows the voices of smaller nations to be amplified globally. In the Middle East, United States, Canada, Africa, United Kingdom, and all over the world, Bollywood's influence and uniqueness is being felt strongly. In terms of niche markets therefore, the Indian diaspora represents a market niche for producers such as Titan, both for watches and jewellery. Figure 7.11. illustrates how the risks increase as a company such as Titan extends its reach into new markets. Details of consumption within the UK and USA markets are presented in Appendix 1, as are details of the ethnic mix in the USA and India. The appendix also includes an article on the types of brands that Indians who live abroad buy.

Titan industries limited performance

Titan's watch and clock business showed a sales turnover of Rs 457.12 crores. As the economy was slowing down, this represented a decline of 7 per cent. The decline was slightly more pronounced in some of the local channels and sales to its international companies. The operating profit before interest and depreciation was Rs 87.7 crores (further details are contained in Appendix 4). Export sales of watches totalled US$6.25 million. The showroom channel continues to grow in significance. At the end of the year, the company had 136 exclusive 'The World of Titan' showrooms across 86 towns and cities, together with a chain of 136 Time Zone multibrand outlets across 85 towns. In addition to this, Titan was also present in over 7,000 dealer outlets across 1,800 towns and cities. The addition of outlets continues and the stores are continuing to be revamped with the new look found in the Mumbai store which opened in September 2001. This revamp is continuing throughout the major outlets. All the retail outlets are supported by a SAP system of supply chain management, with 35 stock points and 60 distributors. The company prides itself on its after-sales service, in terms of geographical coverage, speed of response and service, costs and handling of customers. The service levels have set industry standards and benchmarks. The service network comprises of more than 340 authorized service centres, 63 watch care centres, four authorized service workshops and 213 service points. The use of IT is central in the continuing development of its service levels, with B2B systems being installed in the major outlets, and the automation of order processes by staff in the field. However, the biggest asset (though not recorded in the balance sheet) continues to be the Titan brand. It is the only national jewellery brand in India. The company has a chain of dedicated stores and registered a turnover of Rs 267.66 crores and an operating profit before interest and depreciation of Rs 14.74 crores. Jewellery worth US$5.20 million was exported in 2001.

Ethical performance

The company also manages to maintain an ethical stance in its approach to the community at large. It has the highest paid employees in the region in which it has factories (Hosur). Titan has consciously helped disabled people by offering them employment. Among its staff, which number 2,500, there are 202 disabled people, approximately 8 per cent of the workforce. This is higher than the national recommended average of 3.4 per cent sought by the National Disability Act. The company also employs a large number of rurally located women, generating much needed income in these locations. Disabled employees are engaged in tasks such as housekeeping, polishing of cases and strapping (putting leather straps on watches). Titan recruits disabled individuals from sign language schools in Tamil Nadu and Andhra Pradesh, as no verbal training is required to perform these tasks. The company trains them. This has meant that many of them have a regular source of income and that they can marry and own property. The women in the Dharmapuri district are engaged in metal strap making. As part of its work with the community, the company also gives out 40 annual scholarships, ranging from Rs 2,000 to Rs 10,000, to help the very poor undertake Industrial Training Institute (ITI) courses. As a result of these efforts, Titan won a national award for its efforts in a survey carried out by Businessworld (in 2002).

Summary

The company is extremely successful in India (see Appendix 2) and has also launched a successful range of jewellery. The foray into international markets is not yielding the necessary profits, but it has helped to establish the Titan brand in many centres in Europe, Asia Pacific and the Middle East. The challenge is to develop lucrative niches in markets such as the UK and USA. The growing interest in Indian culture should help in this respect. It is clear that fashion brands such as Gucci and Christian Dior, to name but two, continue to use their reputation in fashion and design to leverage strong positions in the personal wear category. This creates a growing threat to traditional watchmakers. As a result of rapid technological changes, there is a convergence of a range of technologies in products such as mobile phones, posing a global threat to watches as timekeeping devices. The watch and jewellery business in general is a good indicator of the general well-being of an economy. In recessions consumers have less disposable income and are more likely to cut back on watches and jewellery. In many markets throughout the world there is a growing threat from smuggling and the influx of cheap watches from China. The Indian market is now also eyed as a good business opportunity by the major Swiss and Japanese brands. The company's entrance into European markets has entailed large investments. While the company has been successful in creating a physical presence in several countries and is now being perceived as a global player, the losses need to be slowly turned around. The company is well-positioned in its home markets but needs to develop strategies to gain a strong foothold in overseas markets. The company has over the years acquired technology and developed technical expertise to produce contemporary watches. It has a talented in-house Design Studio which asimilates the latest fashion trends and creates cutting-edge products. The company also has a well-developed system for capturing market information and tracking the competition. The company is therefore well-poised for future development and is at an exciting stage in its own development.

Appendix 1

Market Data

Percentage of the population, by race and Hispanic origin: 1990, 2000, 2025, and 2050 (Middle-series Projections)

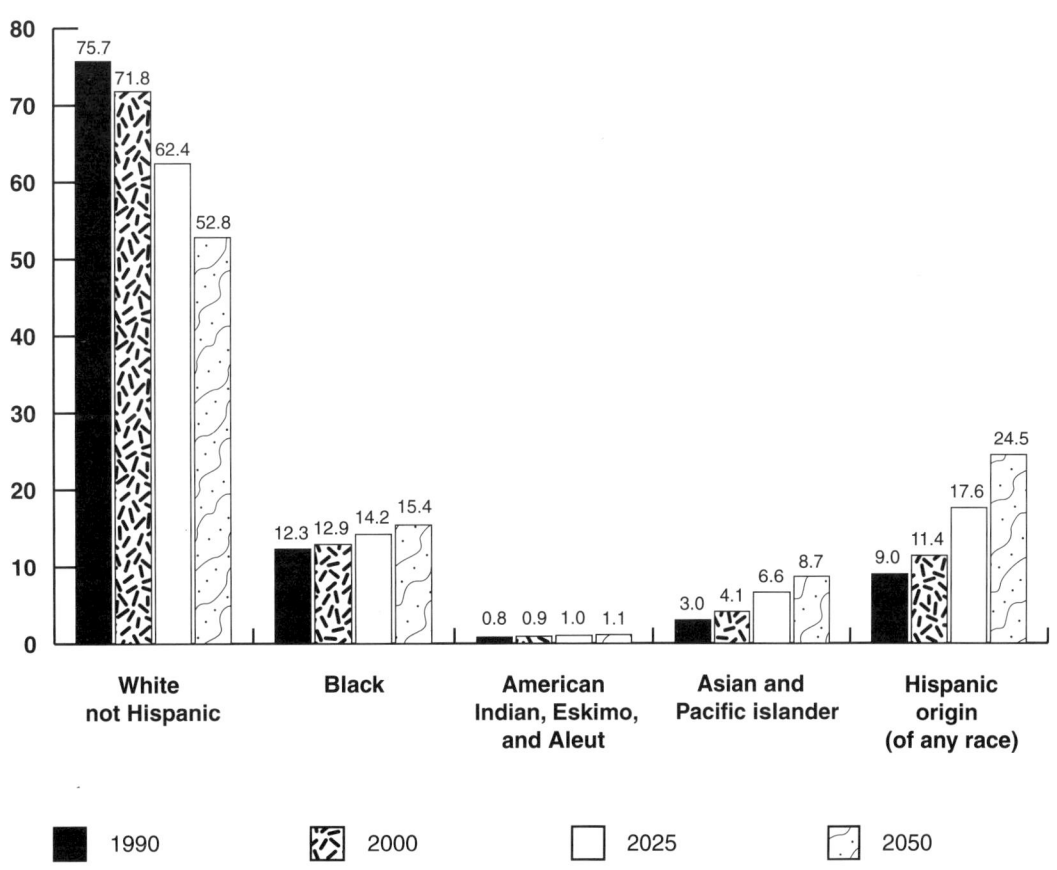

Source: US Bureau of the Census, decennial census and population projections

Markets

Keith W. Strandberg

16 March 2002 – Geneva   Despite a 13.7 per cent dip in exports in December 2001, Swiss manufacturers exported horological products worth $12,155 billion, a 3.5 per cent increase over 2000, according to the Federation of the Swiss Watch Industry.

In the last two months of 2001, Hong Kong held first place in the exports ranking, but the United States nevertheless remains the leading market for the Swiss watchmaking industry. However, the American market is adversely affected by its economic situation and has been falling since March 2001. For the year 2001 as a whole, this fall in value represents a drop of 14.1 per cent.

Less expensive watches are experiencing greater difficulties and sales are down; for example, there was a 23.3 per cent drop in value terms for aluminium watches. These cheaper watches still accounted for one in five watches exported at the end of 2000, but one year later the proportion fell to one in six. The average price of exported watches confirms this trend with a 17.4 per cent increase from US$355 to US$418 between 2000 and 2001. This reflects a concentration on up-market products on the one hand and an increase in the real price on the other.

US watch imports by type	2000	1999	% Change
	(Millions of US$)		
Quartz Analogue	1,804	1,687	+7
Digital	286	263	+9
Anadigi	80	73	+9
Mechanical (automatic)	441	391	+13
Mechanical (manual)	85	69	+23
Pocket watches, stop watches, other	64	71	−11

US watch exports by country	2000	1999	% Change
	(Millions of US$)		
Switzerland	1,134	1,001	+13
Japan	796	705	+13
China	327	300	+9
Philippines	138	147	−6
Hong Kong	135	193	−30
Rest of World	231	208	+11

Source: Europa Star

United Kingdom

Population approximately 60 million.

Ethnic groups: English 81.5 per cent, Scottish 9.6 per cent, Irish 2.4 per cent, Welsh 1.9 per cent, Ulster 1.8 per cent, West Indian, Indian, Pakistani, and other 2.8 per cent.

UK consumer data
The consumer

In November 2001, Mintel commissioned research through BMRB among 980 adults to ascertain their views of the most important aspects of a watch and where they would buy one. Resultant data were weighted to conform with national demographic profiles. Respondents were first asked: 'If you were buying a wristwatch either for yourself or someone else, which if any of these aspects would be important to you?' This question replicates one asked in December 1999. However, earlier results are not shown since there has been no significant shift in attitudes.

Table 7.10 shows topline findings for 2001 and the responses by gender where there are significant differences in a number of instances.

Base: Adults Aged 15+

Table 7.10 Importance of different aspects in buying a watch, November 2001

	Total 980 %	Men 477 %	Women 503 %
In my price range	53	49	57
For everyday use	40	33	46
Water-resistant	39	45	34
Quartz movement (incl. battery)	38	40	37
Traditional 12-hour face	35	35	34
Well-known brand name	29	25	33
Day/date display	24	31	18
Fashionable design	22	18	26
Bracelet strap	20	15	24
Leather strap	19	18	19
Suitable for sportswear	12	14	10
For special occasions	8	6	11
Digital display (LCD)	8	12	4
Swiss made	8	8	7
Extra functions, e.g. alarm	6	7	5
Mechanical movement	6	7	5
Exclusive/prestige make, e.g. Rolex	5	6	5
Don't know/none of these	2	3	2

Source: BMRB/Mintel

Table 7.11 shows five particular aspects of watches in further demographic detail.

Base: 980 Adults Aged 15+

Table 7.11 Selected aspects considered important, by demographic sub-group, November 2001

	Water-resistant %	12-hour face %	Brand name %	Fashionable design %	Suitable for sports %
Total	**39**	**35**	**29**	**22**	**12**
Men	45	35	25	18	14
Women	34	34	33	26	10
15-24	38	29	29	49	19
25-34	41	27	32	26	21
35-44	46	35	28	22	10
45-54	44	45	31	11	7
55-64	39	35	25	15	6
65+	27	36	27	10	5
AB	40	40	26	24	11
C1	42	35	32	23	12
C2	35	33	27	24	13
D	41	33	35	14	9
E	35	32	22	23	14
London	38	32	23	24	11
South	35	39	32	24	13
Anglia/Midlands	42	32	34	20	13
South West/Wales	31	39	24	17	6
Yorks/North East	43	33	37	20	15
North West	46	37	29	28	12
Scotland	28	34	33	18	5
Lifestage:					
Pre-/no family	44	30	30	38	18
Families	42	33	30	22	15
Third age	41	40	28	14	6
Retired	27	36	27	10	5
Special groups:					
ABC1 pre-/no family	44	29	29	41	19
ABC1 families	45	32	32	21	14
ABC1 third age	41	46	26	17	5
ABC1 retired	30	46	32	6	5
Two full-time earners	43	33	34	25	11
One-person households under 65	34	37	30	16	11
Internet users	44	32	30	29	15
Broadsheet users	40	36	27	22	13
Mid-market tabloid readers	42	35	29	19	10
Popular tabloid readers	36	32	31	25	14

Source: BMRB/Mintel

Table 7.12 shows a cross-analysis of responses.

Base: Adults Aged 15+

Table 7.12 Cross-analysis of selected aspects in buying a watch, November 2001

	Total 980	Water-resistant 384	12-hour face 340	Brand name 284	Fashionable design 215	Suitable for sports 114
	%	%	%	%	%	%
In my price range	53	56	54	51	50	52
For everyday use	40	44	46	36	31	41
Water-resistant	39	100	39	35	37	58
Quartz movement	38	41	46	41	27	31
Traditional 12-hour face	35	35	100	38	20	22
Well-known brand name	29	26	31	100	26	25
Day/date display	24	36	22	22	22	34
Fashionable design	22	21	13	20	100	20
Bracelet strap	20	20	22	23	24	8
Leather strap	19	17	21	16	10	11
Suitable for sportswear	12	17	7	10	11	100
For special occasions	8	7	7	7	18	5
Digital display	8	8	3	9	6	15
Swiss made	8	6	7	7	4	5
Extra functions	6	9	3	6	6	12
Mechanical movement	6	5	7	7	2	3
Prestige make	5	4	4	6	10	3

Source: BMRB/Mintel

Respondents were next asked: 'If you were looking to buy a watch, either for yourself or as a gift, where would you go to buy it?'

Base: Adults Aged 15+

Table 7.13 Choice of retail outlets for buying a watch, November 2001

	Total 980 %	Men 477 %	Women 503 %
Specialist jewellers chain, e.g. H. Samuel	42	39	43
Specialist independent jeweller	34	29	39
Catalogue showroom, e.g. Argos	27	27	27
Department store	22	25	19
Airport shop/abroad	9	9	9
Clothing store, e.g. M&S, Next	6	4	7
Mail order	4	3	5
Manufacturer's branded store, e.g. Swatch	4	4	3
Sportswear shop	4	5	2
Specialist designer store, e.g. Paul Smith	3	3	4
Market stall	3	4	3
Other outlet	4	5	3
Don't know	2	2	1

Source: BMRB/Mintel

Forecast

Consumer expenditure on watches will show steady year-on-year growth over the forecast period 2001–2006. Mintel forecasts that at current prices the total market will grow by 27 per cent, which when the effects of inflation are taken into consideration represents 12 per cent growth in the 2001–2006 period.

Table 7.14 Forecast of the UK Market for Watches, By Value, 2001–2006

	Mainstream		Luxury		Total	
	£m	Index	£m	Index	£m	Index
At Current Prices						
2001	300	100	360	100	660	100
2002	313	104	378	105	691	105
2003	326	109	400	111	726	110
2004	339	113	422	117	761	115
2005	353	118	445	124	798	121
2006	367	122	473	131	840	127
At Constant 2001 Prices						
2001	300	100	360	100	660	100
2002	304	101	367	102	671	102
2003	309	103	379	105	688	104
2004	314	105	391	109	705	107
2005	320	107	404	112	724	110
2006	324	108	418	116	742	112

Source: Mintel

Luxury watches to drive growth

Growth will primarily be driven by increasing expenditure on luxury watches, with sales in this sector increasing by 31 per cent at current prices, compared to the 22 per cent in the mainstream sector. This is very much a reflection of the shift towards upmarket and premium products in consumer goods markets, which is indicative of relatively high consumer confidence.

By volume, the total number of watches sold in 2006 compared to 2001 will rise by 23 per cent to reach some 22.6 million units sold. The average price paid per watch will increase by 3 per cent to a little over £37 in 2006.

Market in focus: Asian Indians

By Christine Lee
Asian Diversity Web Site

The statistics don't lie – Asian Indians are on the move in America. According to the Census Bureau, they have the highest per capita income and spending power of any Asian ethnic group.

So why do advertisers continue to ignore this demographic cash cow?

The most cited answer is a higher rate of assimilation. Because English is widely used in India, Asian Indians have the highest English fluency of the various Asian ethnic groups in the United States. This often leads marketing and advertising agencies to assume Asian Indians can't be targeted separately from the mass American audience.

'This can be a big mistake on the part of corporations,' said Neeta Bhasin, President of ASB Communications, an advertising, marketing and public relations company in New York City serving the South Asian market. *'Many Indians know the brands they used in India, and will buy it simply because it's familiar. If an effort is made to educate them about their options, they may switch.'*

Bhasin points out that Colgate is a popular toothpaste brand among Asian Indians in America as a result of the brand's prevalence in India.

'When you go to the store and there are so many brands to choose from, you just go with what you know,' Bhasin said. *'Even when people mean Crest, they'll say Colgate because that is the brand that is stuck in their mind.'*

Another mental hurdle for marketers is the misconception that Asian Indians are too fragmented to target as a group because of the complicated caste system, religions and languages surrounding Asian Indian culture. However, many of these differences diminish in the United States.

'Indian is Indian in this country,' Bhasin said. *'As a whole, we don't like what is happening back home with the caste system, so why would they want to recreate that here in the States?'*

131

This doesn't necessarily mean blanketing Asian Indians with a single ad campaign will work. Like any group, Asian Indian individuals in the United States cover a broad spectrum of incomes, industries and assimilation levels.

Contrary to the perception that Asian Indians exclusively hold jobs in computer programming, Bhasin points out that the choice of profession for Asian Indians, and immigrants in general, stem from American economic trends rather than personal choice.

'In the late sixties, there was a shortage of professionals in the medical industry, so that was how many Asian Indians were able to immigrate to the United States,' she said. 'In those days, if you met any Indian, you would ask, "are you a doctor or a nurse?" Then in the eighties, when these professionals in turn sponsored their relatives, the question was "are you a taxidriver or a construction man?" Now, the trend has changed again.'

Today, Asian Indians in the United States cover a broad spectrum of income levels, industries and assimilation. That said, there are a few overarching consumer habits worth noting.

In general, Asian Indians tend to be very price conscious, rating price as a stronger incentive to brand name, according to Kang & Lee, an Asian ad agency based in New York City.

Television advertising is the most effective marketing medium, in contrast to the popularity of print advertising for most Asian ethnic groups. In-language ads are not always effective either.

'Instead of having the whole ad in-language, it is more effective to just have some words in-language, especially common words that are used every day,' Bhasin said. 'By having it partially in English and partially in-language, it creates an act of inclusion, of reaching out, while also giving them something to connect with and recognise.'

What Bhasin says makes sense. Remaining sensitive to their native culture while making them feel part of the whole may just be the key to unlocking Asian Indian wealth in America.

Source: From www.AsianDiversity.com. Reprinted with permission

Brands and Groups Featured in Europa star Web Site Daily News Section

Tiger Woods Joins TAG Heuer as Global Ambassador

TAG Heuer, the worldwide leader in luxury sports watches and chronographs since 1860, is proud to announce that the number one ranking golfer, Tiger Woods, has signed a long term ambassador agreement with the Swiss luxury watches company, covering product development, advertising, public relations and merchandising.

Tiger Woods comments *'It is an honour to be associated with a company like TAG Heuer. To me, TAG Heuer is known for understated luxury and style, prestige, and exceptional quality. I look forward to working with TAG Heuer in the coming years.'*

The TAG Heuer agreement with Tiger Woods also marks a milestone in the brand's historical involvement in sports combining prestige and performance. Indeed, alongside Formula 1 where TAG Heuer is the FIA world championship official timekeeper, as well as partner of the McLaren-Mercedes Team, golf will become with Tiger Woods the second pillar of TAG Heuer product and communication inspiration. Like Formula 1, golf epitomises the utmost in human talent and precision, as well as in prestige and technology, several values that have made TAG Heuer significantly different from other luxury watches brands for the past 142 years. Moreover, TAG Heuer is partner of Oracle BMW Racing for the Louis Vuitton Cup 2002/2003 (Auckland, New Zealand) and Official Timekeeper to the FIS alpine skiing world championship in February 2003 at St. Moritz (Switzerland).

The contract between TAG Heuer and Tiger Woods will begin 1st January 2003, and Tiger Woods will soon be seen in the TAG Heuer corporate campaign 'What are you made of?', launched on the international market in January 2003.

TAG Heuer SA is part of LVMH (Moët Hennessy Louis Vuitton) the world's leading luxury goods group. The Group is represented in Wines and Spirits by a portfolio of brands that includes Moët & Chandon, Dom Perignon, Veuve Clicquot Ponsardin, Krug, Chateau d'Yquem, Hennessy. Its Fashion and Leather Goods division includes Louis Vuitton, the world's leading luxury brand, as well as Celine, Loewe, Kenzo, Givenchy, Christian Lacroix, Thomas Pink, Fendi and Donna Karan... In the Perfumes and Cosmetics sector LVMH owns brands such as Parfums Christian Dior, Guerlain, Givenchy, Kenzo. LVMH is active in selective retailing through DFS, Miami Cruiseline, Sephora, Le Bon Marche and La Samaritaine.

LVMH's Watch and Jewellery division comprises TAG Heuer, Ebel, Chaumet, Zenith, Fred, as well as Omas and the Joint Venture De Beers LV.

Source: TAG Heuer Press Release, October 2002

133

Appendix 2

Articles on Titan

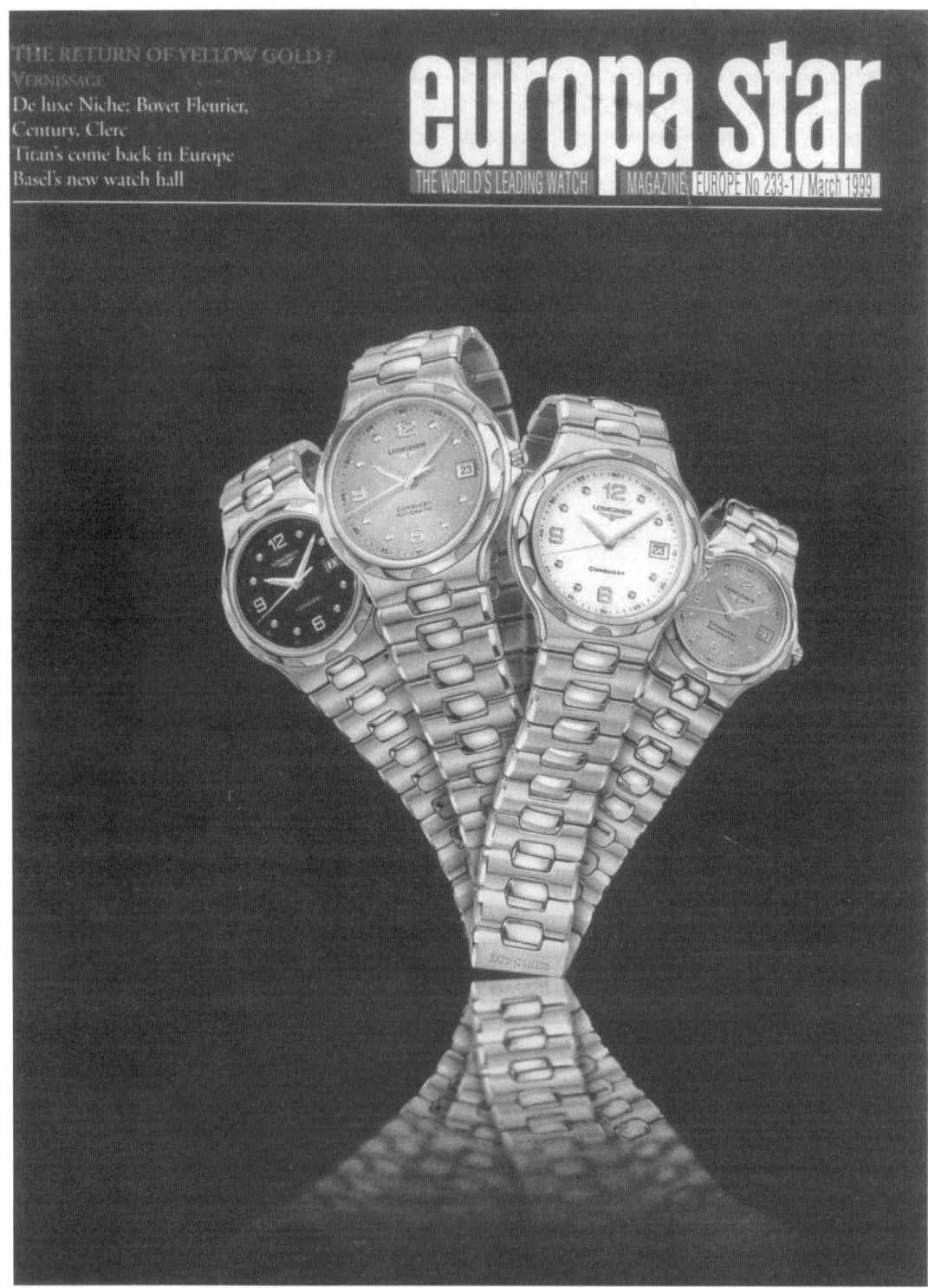

Source: Europa star, The World's Leading Watch Magazine, Europe No. 233-1/March 1999

TITAN STRIKES BACK

During a recent trip to India, Europa Star's Editor-in-Chief, Pierre Maillard, traveled to Bangalore, home turf of the Titan group, to talk with the watch company's President, Xerxès Desai. The discussion focused essentially on Titan's intentions in Europe, where after a strong start, the brand has become noticeably quiet.

Europa Star: *We have the impression that the arrival of Titan on European markets was a little like a soufflé: after an initial onslaught, it suddenly sank.*

Xerxès Desai: This image is not correct, if you don't mind me saying, because once a soufflé sinks, it cannot rise up again.

ES: *And Titan has the intention of rising up again?*

XD: We intend to establish a permanent presence in Europe. We are going to strengthen our current position and establish new bases of operation there.

CRITERION COLLECTION by Titan: stainless steel, water resistant to 50m and sapphire crystal.

The elegant Titan Watch Division building with its landscaped gardens.

ES: *Could you summarize your activity in European markets?*

XD: Our first real move into Europe was in 1995. It was a good year for us and was followed by a positive 1996. However, by 1997, our competition got its act together and started regaining territory, much to our detriment. This happened for several reasons. Despite the fact that our product was good and its price positioning was good, the Indian origin caused certain problems. Unfortunately and I might add, unjustly, Indian products are not perceived as high quality goods. This is totally false, of course, but nonetheless this situation does exist.

ES: *So your expansion slowed down?*

XD: Yes, but it is also true that we had help in this respect. The other large watch groups put all sorts of spokes in our wheel and have even exercised pressure on distributors.

Source: Europa star, The World's Leading Watch Magazine, Europe No. 233-1/March 1999

BUSINESS & MARKETING

FIVE-STAR FACTORIES

Titan's magnificent Jewelry Division building.

Workbenches in the jewelry workshops.

The Tata group, which owns Titan, has adopted the concept of excellence as its principal motivating force. There is no disputing this large group's ideas of excellence, which can be seen at all levels of the enterprise's activities, including the social management of its personnel.

Two years ago, during a first visit, we were already very impressed by the size as well as the excellent condition of Titan's factories. The cleanliness and hygiene are worthy of a hospital. The sophisticated production procedures use state-of-the-art tools and equipment and are totally computerized.

It is no exaggeration to say that Titan's factories are among the best watchmaking installations in the world. They are totally integrated, capable of creating all the elements of a watch, from quartz movements to cases, bracelets and dials, right down to the smallest elements such as hands.

Over the last two years, the firm has doubled its capacity and now has a new totally automated workshop for making step motors. An impressive automatic assembly line for movements has been developed near Bangalore where nearly 5 million finished movements, 3 million cases, 5 million assembled watches and 1.5 million bracelets are created annually.

In addition, Titan owns a jewelry factory located just five minutes from its watch production center. Its annual production of gold and gold and diamond watches is around 20,000 pieces. It also produces more than 150,000 individual pieces of jewelry. Like its sister watch factory, it is also totally integrated. Its activities include gold refining (2 tonnes per year), alloy production, highly developed artisanal techniques, basic operations (tubes, cables, wires, spheres, grains, etc.) and the specialized trades of the wax model makers, casting, assembling, stone setting and polishing.

ES: *Isn't this precisely what you are reproached for in India?*

XD: I have always stood firm against these accusations, which arise because Titan is the predominant player in India. Actually, the contrary is true. We have intervened on a number of occasions to request that the government lower its customs duties for imported watches. In fact, we have greatly contributed to opening the Indian market for prestige foreign time-pieces. However, we do not set Indian policy. I would like to add, too, that all restrictions on imported watches will be abolished from 2002 onwards.

ES: *Let's return to Titan's problems in Europe ...*

XD: In 1997, we were also confronted with another problem. This time it was an internal one. You see, we are sometimes negatively affected by Indian policy as well. From 1997, we experienced serious administrative difficulties in taking money that was required for investment abroad, out of

The clinically-clean watch assembly workshop.

Source: Europa star, The World's Leading Watch Magazine, Europe No. 233-1/March 1999

—— BUSINESS & MARKETING ——

'Worldly Possessions'
Titan's advertising for its
Criterion Collection.

Titan window
display material.

India. To make matters worse, foreign currencies fell against the rupee, thus hurting our competitiveness and we also had interest rate problems. Combined with all these factors were the profound changes in European taste and style. Taken together, these various elements had a very serious negative impact on our position in Europe.

ES: *Do you intend to launch a new offensive?*

XD: Yes, and it will be based on a whole new strategy for our long-term ambitions. More precisely, it will mean a new product line, a new look, lower prices, new advertising campaigns, an improved media plan and a new approach to sales material and window displays. We have examined and modified everything down to the smallest detail.

ES: *What are your concrete objectives?*

XD: I'll repeat what I've already said. Our first goal is to have a permanent presence in Europe. Our second objective is to make a profit. For those who think that we are doing this only for the sake of image, they are badly mistaken. What I said earlier must also be seen in the perspective of the whole picture. Despite our problems, we still sold 120,000 watches in Europe in 1998. Our objective for 1999 is 175,000. In the medium term, we would like to reach 350,000 pieces.

TITAN IS A TITAN

Over the last few years, Titan has become synonymous with the watch in India. Under the enlightened, sophisticated and wise management of Xerxès Desai, the brand, belonging to the giant Tata group (electronics, automobiles, financial services, luxury hotels, cement, communications, tea, real estate, etc.), totally dominates the Indian watch market.
Currently, Titan sells six million timepieces annually on the Indian market, offering a com-

plete range of products. Marketing studies have shown that its brand awareness is an amazing 100%!
Distributed at various levels of quality, the brand possesses 108 of its own stores called Titan World (selling only Titan products) and 120 Time Zone stores (carrying other brands but mainly Titan). In addition, the brand is distributed in about 5000 independent stores, giving it nearly total coverage of the vast Indian territory.

Titan also boasts having, "the best after-sales service organization in all of India for all products". At the end of 1998, the brand had 472 service centers located in 225 cities, covering 84% of the geographical locations of its clients. The remaining 16% is handled by technicians trained by Titan. About 95% of repairs are executed within four days, with a large percentage having same-day service. These centers operate on a very original concept.

Comparing the watch repairer to a 'doctor' and understanding that it is never pleasant to go to the doctor, a particular emphasis has been placed on the client's reception and on the brand's facilities, as we were able to observe firsthand in Bangalore. "When someone brings in a watch, there are three things to repair: the watch, the customer and our reputation," says company President, Xerxès Desai. In that respect, repair prices have been deliberately kept very low.

Source: Europa star, The World's Leading Watch Magazine, Europe No. 233-1/March 1999

—— BUSINESS & MARKETING ——

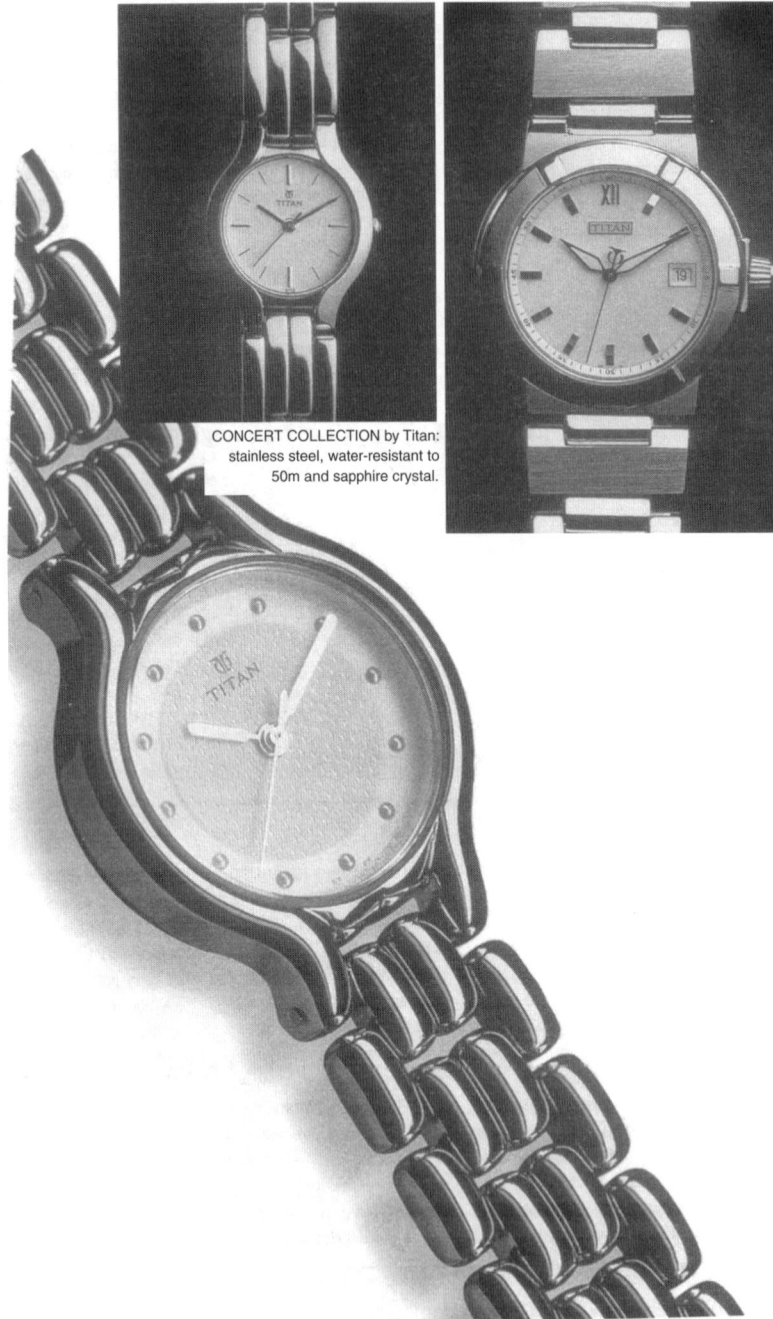

CONCERT COLLECTION by Titan:
stainless steel, water-resistant to
50m and sapphire crystal.

ES: *More than ever though, the sinews of war are in the distribution...*

XD: From what we are now seeing, retailers understand that Titan, despite its temporary difficulties, is here to stay. And to support this, we are offering new products. Look at them. Examine them. Take them in your hand and feel their weight. Stylistically, they are perfect and in tune with the demands of the marketplace. From a quality standpoint, our products are irreproachable. When you add the ultra-competitive price factor, you'll understand why we are optimistic. Just this last November, we shipped 40,000 watches.

ES: *Rumors abound that you intend to make a "Swiss Made" product.*

XD: In our opinion, "Swiss Made" only makes sense for collections of mechanical and automatic timepieces. This is not for tomorrow, but is not to be excluded. One option is that we might manufacture Titan in Switzerland. Another possibility would be to buy another brand. I see this as a part of our global strategy for watches. ∎

Source: Europa star, The World's Leading Watch Magazine, Europe No. 233-1/March 1999

BUSINESS | TITAN

MITU JAYASHANKAR

L AST month, Titan Indus-
tries unveiled a new range
of white-finished steel
watches. It was a departure
of sorts. Titan's been tradi-
tionally associated with gold-
plated, quartz watches, never
shiny steel ones. Marketers would
even say that this shift would create confusion in the minds of consumers. But the Bangalore-based
Tata outfit is willing to embrace such
criticism and argue out a case for Titan
Steel, the name the new range goes by.
Says Titan sales and marketing vice-
president Bijou Kurien: "We are deliberately creating this dissonance." Why?

At the core of this strategy is an effort
by Titan to look contemporary and up-
scale. And, Titan insiders will tell you,
much rides on that. Begin with the fact
that the company has discovered, to its
alarm, that the bulk of Titan's sales today
comes from the 30-35 age group, while
the 18-30 age group doesn't find the
brand exciting anymore. "Today, of the
1.5 million customers who walk into
Titan's exclusive showrooms each year,

THE WHITE KNIGHTS

Titan hopes its steel watch range will shore up its premium brand image

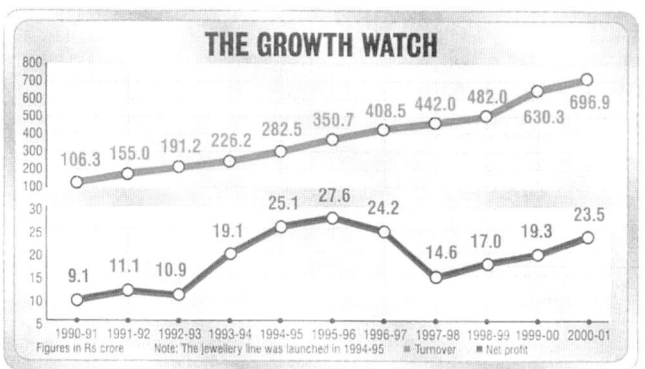

THE GROWTH WATCH

106.3 155.0 191.2 226.2 282.5 350.7 408.5 442.0 482.0 630.3 696.9

9.1 11.1 10.9 19.1 25.1 27.6 24.2 14.6 17.0 19.3 23.5

1990-91 1991-92 1992-93 1993-94 1994-95 1995-96 1996-97 1997-98 1998-99 1999-00 2000-01
Figures in Rs crore   Note: The jewellery line was launched in 1994-95   ■ Turnover   ■ Net profit

gins (including its jewellery business
that accounts for 28% of sales) are under
severe pressure. It has fallen from 18.7%
in 1998-99 to 14.4% in 1999-00 to 13.3%
in 2000-01.

Enter Titan Steel.

The move seems sensible enough.
The white look, as Lakshmi Seth, vice-
president, Quantum Market Research,
will tell you, is the preferred one. "Globally, there is a shift in consumer preferences towards white metals, be it jewellery or watches," says Seth.

This global shift is visible here as
well. All overseas labels, like Swatch, Esprit and Rado, retailing in India — since
April 1999 the government's allowed the
import of complete watches — are white
metal led. Even Timex is going easy on
gold-plated watches (BW, 28 May 2001).
Now, even though the new MNC brands
collectively sell barely 5% of Titan's volumes, their presence puts pressure on
Titan to offer the latest global styles, if it
has to maintain its premium image.

not many are young; if this set goes out
of the Titan family today, tomorrow it
will be difficult to sell to him again," ad-
mits Kurien.

Then, though Titan controls a whop-
ping 50% of the watch market in the organised sector, in the last two years most
of Titan's growth has come from the
Sonata range of watches. Sonata was
launched in 1998 to wean away consumers from the unorganised sector.
Priced below Rs 1,000, Sonata has grown
by almost 30% compounded annually in
the last two years. Over the same period,
the watches costing slightly more, be-

tween Rs 1,000 and Rs 4,000, grew by
barely 4%. In fact, in fiscal 2000-01, half
of Titan's volumes of 6.68 million units
came from the Sonata.

Paradoxically, the success of the
Sonata range could harm Titan in two
ways. One, it could take the sheen off the
Titan label, till now seen as premium.
Two, it could also put pressure on Titan's
overall cost structure, as it is not suited to
churning out a budget brand.

The average price of a Titan (2001-01
turnover: Rs 696.9 crore) watch has declined from Rs 794 in 1999-00, to Rs 728
in 2000-01. Also, Titan's operating mar-

Source: Mitu Jayashankar, *Businessworld*, 22 October 2001, p.26. Reprinted with permission of *Business World online Inc.*

Timex corners 22% market share

NEW DELHI, Feb. 27. TIMEX Watches Ltd. has recorded a market share of 22 per cent in 2002, compared with 15 per cent the previous year, according to a study conducted by KSA-Technopak.

The survey titled 'KSA Technopak Retail Study' involved random retail telephonic interviews with 50 key retailers across four zones, which was a representative sample of a total of 300 retailers across the country.

In a press release issued by the company, Mr Kapil Kapoor, Managing Director, Timex Watches said, 'This survey by KSA-Technopak, an authority on trends in the Indian retail industry, has once again reaffirmed the liking and appeal for brand Timex amongst the Indian youth. This increase in our market share indicates that we are edging towards achieving our target of capturing 33 per cent of the Indian watch market by the year 2004.'

As part of the company's growth strategy in the current year, Timex plans to differentiate the brand at key retail outlets by creating a retail experience at 100 key stores in India called Club Timex.

'This concept is designed to be used flexibly in a range of options based on the space available at the best retail locations all over the country. Club Timex could be an exclusive showroom, or a designer space within a retail outlet,' said Mr Kapoor.

Source: *Business Line, India*; 28 February 2003. Reprinted with the kind permission of *The Hindu Business Line*, India

Appendix 3

Developments in the watch industry
Timepieces designed for every dangerous occasion
By Gill Plimmer
Published: 9 May 2002 11:07 / Last Updated: 9 May 2002 11:07

Ellen MacArthur's watch does not just help her keep track of the time when she is sailing around the world. It can help to save her life.

Ms MacArthur's watch contains a small radio transmitter that sends a signal to the nearest receiver when it is activated – either manually or by falling in the water.

The signal triggers an alarm telling crew members someone has fallen overboard and this is picked up by any ship, helicopter or rescue service within five miles. Rescuers can then use direction-finding equipment to find the person. Crucially, the watch is waterproof to a depth of 50 metres, so it is not set off by the usual splash of sea spray.

Produced by McMurdo, a UK manufacturer, the Guardian Man-Over-Board (MOB) watch was developed for use on oil rigs and is currently used by BP. However, it is also used by divers who can switch off the automatic device. After receiving a message, rescuers can locate a diver who has become separated from the boat, even in poor light or bad weather and sea conditions.

The MOB is typical of a new generation of sports watches available to those with a taste for adventure.

Blurring the line between watches and computers is the Stinger, made by Suunto, which provides divers with information on the current and maximum depths, water temperature, dive time and dive number.

Most importantly, it has audible and visual alarms that warn divers when they are reaching their oxygen limits or are surfacing too quickly. It also has a memory function that tracks dive information – data that can later be downloaded to a personal computer.

Anyone thinking about climbing Everest can buy any of a range of watches that include altimeters, barometers and digital compasses. Nike adds a thermometer, too, so you can be the equivalent of a walking weather station.

GPS-enabled handheld devices are now available, such as those made by Garmin, which allow you to pinpoint your position to within 15 metres or less in a matter of seconds by using up to 12 satellites.

However, those prone to getting lost should consider Breitling's Emergency watch. It contains a miniature distress beacon that transmits a signal to rescue services.

To prevent misuse, the beacon can be used only once and the company warns that if it is activated accidentally, the climber may be liable for a fine. If it is a genuine emergency, however, Breitling will replace the watch for free.

For those in need of a personal trainer, there is a range of more modest sports watches that will help to monitor performance. Most include a stopwatch or chronograph, with some including 'split-time' chronographs, which can time two or more runners. But beyond these basic functions there is a range of specialist products tailored to your chosen sport.

The Polar S410 enables runners to key in their age, height and weight so it can calculate the target heart rate for an efficient cardiovascular work-out.

Runners can also track energy expenditure and programme work-outs and download a record of their activities on to their PCs, where it can be reproduced in graph form to monitor long-term performance.

Golf players can buy the lightweight Dunlop Caddy Golf Score Keeper watch, which will allow them to record golf scores.

For those concerned with sun-burn, Apa Optics has produced the SunUV watch, which tells outdoor types how long they can stay safely in the sun. The wearer keys in skin type and the protection factor of the sunscreen used and the watch monitors the ultra-violet index and informs users when to head for the shade.

Adventurous types starved for modern entertainment in the wilderness my be tempted by Timex's new Internet Messenger watch. This combines speed, distance and pace-tracking mechanisms with the ability to receive text messages, web pages, internet email and Yahoo updates on stocks, weather, news and sports all on the wrist.

Of course, this could also appeal to armchair sportsmen, who can be found monitoring their heart-beat from the comfort of their armchairs.

Source: *Financial Times*, 9 May 2002. Reprinted with permission

Makers turn to jewels to enhance brands
By Susan Rossi
Published: 9 May 2002 11:07 / Last Updated: 9 May 2002 11:07

The cost of a watch that combines prestige watchmaking with luxury jewellery is beyond the means of most. Yet, an increasing number of companies are producing watches at the highest end, with solid results.

Gracing the wrist of pop singer Elton John is a Chopard jewelled watch elaborately decorated with diamonds and coloured gemstones set in white gold that begs the question: is it a watch or is it a jewel?

This is a question asked increasingly in Geneva and Basle, as the line between watches and jewellery becomes blurred in response to increased competition in the luxury market.

Following recent acquisitions among the luxury groups of long-established watch brands, we are entering a period whereby companies vie for the top end of the market, using their quality names to diversify into jewellery production as well as create the highest value product imaginable.

'Haute Horlogerie watches that combine technical prestige and luxury jewellery are more and more appealing to wise and well-advised customers from all over the world, only, however, if tradition matches creativity, as well as a strongly mastered craftsmanship,' says Claude-Daniel Proellochs, Chief Executive Officer of Vacheron Constantin.

'Today's high-end customers are looking first for legitimacy and long-standing values. Vacheron Constantin will never be out of fashion, because it never courted fashion.'

This long-established Swiss watchmaker recently won the first Geneva Watchmaking Grand Prix for its Lady Kalla watch in white gold encrusted with more than 120 diamonds and with a manually-wound mechanical movement. It costs SFr 492,000.

A single sale of a watch like this would significantly improve the bottom-line for a small manufacturer, and have an impact even on the larger luxury groups, which are increasingly moving to the high end.

Results for luxury groups such as LVMH and Richemont demonstrate that, while watches were not their strongest luxury product in 2001, it is the cheaper end of the market that is dragging down sales, while they have held firm at the high end.

Figures for watch exports in 2001 show that while the number of platinum watches exported from Switzerland increased by less than 4 per cent, the value of platinum watches increased by 64 per cent. No doubt the reason for this is due to more platinum pieces being set with jewels and thus being of higher value.

The number of timepieces exported was in decline, yet the value of exports was higher for the year, due to 'a greater concentration on upmarket products on the one hand and an increase in the real price on the other', according to the Federation of the Swiss Watch Industry.

'The demand for jewelled watches is increasingly important. Accordingly, this year at the Basle fair, most of the watches presented are jewelled watches. The world just came out of a long recession period . . . that is why women favour the purchase of luxury and high-quality goods, which goes along with a return to deep values to the detriment of minimalist purchases,' says

Caroline Gruosi Scheufele, Vice President and Creative Director for Chopard, the company that produces the Elton John watch, which is now available in 14 styles.

Likewise, the Swatch Group remarks that, in the top-of-the-range segment, Breguet made remarkable progress and Longines posted solid growth in last year's difficult environment, with the negative impact on the group being at the lower end of the market.

Following the drop in watch sales for LVMH in 2001, the brands in the luxury watch group have 'improved their product portfolios to concentrate on higher-end products and more profitable lines', culminating later this year in the debut of a Louis Vuitton watch collection and new jewelled watch models from Ebel, Chaumet and Fred at this week's Basle show.

According to LVMH, luxury watch brands continue to increase their market share in all countries where they are sold.

'The Middle East and Asia have always been the target markets but today the demand for jewelled watches is more and more important in Europe and in the US,' says Ms Gruosi Scheufele.

Fred, the jewellery and watch retailer with a long tradition of adorning Hollywood film stars, is exemplary of the type of brand that luxury watchmakers want to emulate.

The company, acquired by LVMH in 1995, recently expanded its European operations by opening its first British shop, in London's New Bond Street, in addition to another outlet in Paris. These additions, plus another shop in Tokyo, bring the total number of Fred boutiques worldwide to 10. So-called trends in watches at this level focus on classic, retro styles and use the strap to demonstrate contemporary fashion.

Piaget, Chaumet, Harry Winston, all offer feminine, curved jewelled watches that hark back to the 1920s. Longines, in celebration of its 170th anniversary this year, has brought out three replicas of watches from the 1920s, called Les Elegantes, each in 18 carat white gold, set with diamonds and sapphires in a limited edition.

A lower quality strap, or one that is diminutive in value compared to the watch, graces jewelled watches at trade events this spring. A satin strap features on Harry Winston's Golden Aurora watch set with yellow and white diamonds – it costs US Dollars 19,800, – while a new watch from Chopard's Happy Diamonds collection, called Happy Beach, comes on a rubber strap.

A bright blue strap surrounds one of the most bejewelled watches of the year. The watch, called Stardust, is adorned with no less than 2,036 diamonds covering two sides of the movement, the case, the crown and the clasp, on offer from Antoine Preziuso, an independent watchmaker.

Ironically, the watch celebrates the 200th anniversary of the Tourbillon's invention by Abraham-Louis Breguet.

Source: *Financial Times*, 9 May 2002. Reprinted with permission

Appendix 4

Company information

Organisation chart

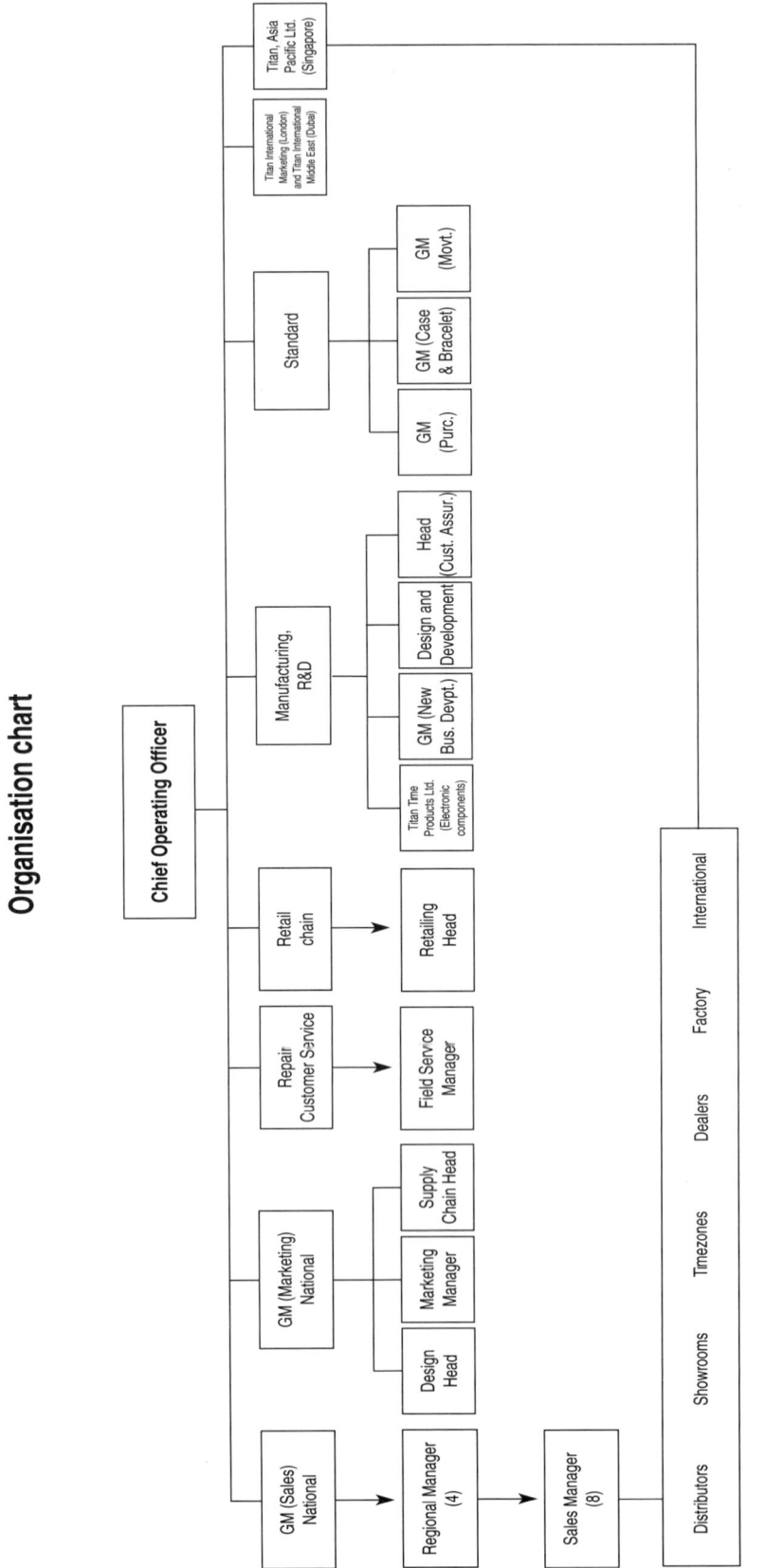

Chief Operating Officer

GM (Sales) National	GM (Marketing) National	Repair Customer Service	Retail chain	Manufacturing, R&D	Standard	Titan International Marketing (London) and Titan International Middle East (Dubai)	Titan, Asia Pacific Ltd. (Singapore)

- Regional Manager (4)
- Design Head
- Marketing Manager
- Supply Chain Head
- Field Service Manager
- Retailing Head
- Titan Time Products Ltd. (Electronic components)
- GM (New Bus. Devpt.)
- Design and Development
- Head (Cust. Assur.)
- GM (Purc.)
- GM (Case & Bracelet)
- GM (Movt.)

- Sales Manager (8)

- Distributors
- Showrooms
- Timezones
- Dealers
- Factory
- International

GM = General Manager
VP = Vice President

Source: Company Resources

Sales figures – last four years

Year	Domestic			International	
	Brand	Volume (%)	Value (%)	Volume (in 000s)	Value (in Rs mn)
1998–1999	Titan	49.6	66.4	347.00	195.70
	Sonata	50.4	33.6		
	Total	100.0	100.0	347.00	195.70
1999–2000	Titan	57.3	73.9	506.53	411.20
	Sonata	42.7	26.1		
	Total	100.0	100.0	506.53	411.20
2000–2001	Titan	48.7	67.9	573.58	329.60
	Sonata	51.3	32.1		
	Total	100.0	100.0	573.58	329.60
2001–2002	Titan	45.9	65.9	503.86	262.90
	Sonata	54.1	34.1		
	Total	100.0	100.0	503.86	262.90
Ytd Oct	Titan	42.8	64.5	321.63	177.50
2002	Sonata	57.2	35.5		
	Total	100.0	100.0	321.63	177.50

All years are from April–March.
Source: Company Sources

The revenue generated by the two divisions in the 2001–2002 financial year is indicated below:

Division	Sales Revenue 2001–2002 (Rs Crore)	Growth Over Previous Year
Time Products	457.12	−7%
Jewellery	267.66	31%
Total	724.78	4%

Source: Company Sources

Performance of Titan share price in comparison with BSE Sensex

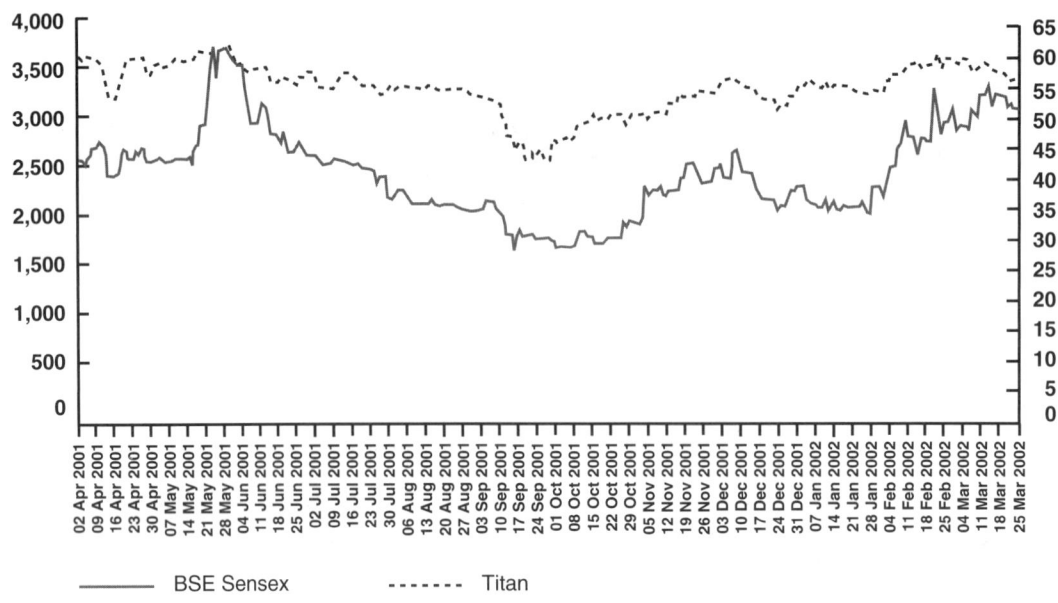

-------- BSE Sensex   ------- Titan

Source: Titan Industries Limited, 18th Annual Report, 2001–2002

Balance Sheet as at 31st March 2002

	Rupees in Lakhs	
Sources of Funds	**31-03-2002**	31-03-2001
Shareholders' funds		
Share capital	**8,227.63**	8,227.63
Reserves and surplus	**8,241.54**	12,508.87
	16,469.17	20,736.50
Deferred tax liability	**4,457.66**	-
Loan funds		
Secured loans	**21,008.32**	23,548.83
Unsecured loans	**23,320.99**	18,652.28
	44,329.31	42,201.11
Total	**65,256.14**	62,937.61
Application of Funds		
Fixed assets		
Gross block, at cost	**37,813.75**	36,622.92
Less: Depreciation	**18,049.72**	15,868.11
Net block	**19,764.03**	20,754.81
Advances on capital account and		
capital work in progress, at cost	**326.34**	360.71
	20,090.37	21,115.52

Investments

Current assets, loans and advances		**2,462.43**	2,308.51
Inventories	**12,481.90**		14,622.75
Sundry debtors	**20,774.99**		15,903.74
Cash and bank balances	**1,732.98**		2,751.69
Loans and advances	**19,740.42**		15,066.83
	54,730.29		48,345.01
Less:			
Current liabilities and provisions			
Current liabilities	**11,436.92**		7,579.09
Provisions	**1,207.86**		1,572.24
	12,644.78		9,151.33
Net current assets		**42,085.51**	39,193.68
Miscellaneous expenditure			
(To the extent not written off or adjusted)			
Deferred revenue expenditure		**617.83**	319.90
Total		**65,256.14**	62,937.61
Notes			

Source: Titan Industries Limited, 18th Annual Report, 2001–2002

Profit and Loss Account for the Year Ended 31st March 2002

	Schedule	Rupees in Lakhs	
		Current Year	Previous Year
Income			
Sales		**72,478.36**	69,690.26
Other income		**224.34**	197.20
Total		**72,702.70**	69,887.46
Expenditure			
Operating and other expenses		**58,048.62**	55,607.23
Excise duty		**5,883.63**	5,812.65
Depreciation		**2,327.99**	2,092.80
Interest		**4,626.64**	4,784.02
Total		**70,886.88**	
Operating Profit for the Year		**1,815.82**	
Profit on sale of investments		–	
Profit Before Taxes		**1,815.82**	
Income taxes – Current	**612.00**		
– Deferred	**(105.54)**		
		506.46	
Profit After Taxes		**1,309.36**	

147

Profit brought forward	**4,230.74**		
Less: Deferred tax liability of earlier years	**2,500.00**		
		1,730.74	
Amount available for appropriation		**3,040.10**	
Appropriations			
Dividend paid on preference shares	**256.90**		
Proposed dividend on equity shares	**634.14**		
Proposed dividend on preference shares	**96.06**		
Tax on dividends	**26.39**		200.27
Transfer to general reserve	**65.47**		234.76
		1,078.96	1,930.04
Balance carried to balance sheet		**1,961.14**	4,230.74
Notes			
Earnings per share – Basic and diluted (Rs)		**2.20**	4.41

Source: Titan Industries Limited, 18th Annual Report, 2001–2002

Schedule Forming Part of the Accounts

	Rupees in Lakhs	
	Current Year	Previous Year
"J" Operating and other expenses		
Raw materials and components consumed	**36,182.15**	32,142.99
Loose tools, stores and spare parts consumed	**1,531.99**	1,839.61
Purchase of finished goods	**208.81**	136.70
Payments to and provisions for employees		
Salaries and wages	**6,263.12**	6,165.18
Company's contribution to provident and other funds	**416.93**	408.25
Welfare expenses	**730.90**	672.21
Gratuity	**220.60**	160.87
	7,631.55	7,406.51

Other expenses			
Power and fuel	**785.22**		854.55
Repairs to buildings	**81.31**		87.75
Repairs to plant and machinery	**185.08**		210.51
Advertising	**3,654.84**		4,009.51
Selling and distribution expenses	**1,303.10**		1,193.86
Insurance	**250.19**		331.51
Rent	**467.50**		412.28
Rates and taxes	**1,114.06**		1,089.81
Travel	**347.37**		418.27
Deferred revenue expenditure written off	**511.20**		106.64
Provision for doubtful debts	**40.00**		94.57
General expenses	**1,909.88**		2,496.27
		10,649.75	11,305.53
Auditors' remuneration			
Audit fees	**18.00**		15.00
Fees for taxation matters	**3.86**		3.86
Fees for other services	**8.55**		5.04
Reimbursement of expenses and levies	**1.83**		1.99
		32.24	25.89
Directors' fees		**2.35**	1.64
Decrease/(Increase) in work progress and finished goods			
Closing stocks			
Work in progress	**3,617.37**		3,852.87
Finished goods	**4,750.64**		6,398.76
		8,368.01	10,251.63
Opening stocks			
Work in progress	**3,852.87**		4,348.71
Finished goods	**6,398.76**		8,729.69
		10,251.63	13,078.40
		1,883.62	2,826.77
		58,122.46	55,685.64
Less: Expenses capitalised		**73.84**	78.41
		58,048.62	55,607.23

Source: Titan Industries Limited, 18th Annual Report, 2001–2002

Segment Information for the Year Ended 31st March 2002

a. Primary Business Segments

	Watch & Clocks	Jewellery	Corporate (Unallocated)	Rupees in Lakhs Total
Revenue	46,390	26,649	–	73,039
Net sales/income from segments (There is no inter-segment revenue)				
Result				
Profit/(Loss) from segments before interest, other income and taxes	5,268	1,287	(433)	6,122
Add: Other Income	595	6	52	653
Profit/(Loss) from segments before interest and taxes	5,863	1,293	(381)	6,775
Less: Interest				4,978
Profit before taxes				1,797
Taxes				526
Profit after taxes				1,271
Other Information				
Segment Assets	55,992	17,285	2,444	75,721
Segment Liabilities	10,017	3,943	360	14,320
Capital expenditure during the year (including capital Work-in-progress)	1,131	28	–	1,159
Depreciation/Amortisation	2,891	214		3,105

Source: Titan Industries Limited, 18th Annual Report, 2001–2002

b. Secondary Geographical Segments

	India	Others	Rupees in Lakhs Total
Revenue	67,137	5,902	73,039
Segment Assets	61,367	14,354	75,721
Capital expenditure during the year (including capital Work-in-progress)	1,159	–	1,159

Source: Titan Industries Limited, 18th Annual Report, 2001–2002

Managing Director:

Curaçao Corporation Company N.V. (A Titan Industries Limited subsidiary)

De Ruyterkade 62
Curaçao
Netherlands Antilles

Balance Sheet at 31st March 2002

		(Expressed in Euros)	
		03-31-2002	03-31-2001
Assets			
Fixed Assets			
Trademarks		**8,304,178**	8,304,178
Current Assets			
Royalty receivable	–		13,322
Prepaid expenses	**1,377**		1,367
Cash at bank	**1,528**		172
		2,905	14,862
		8,307,083	8,319,040
Shareholders' Equity and Liabilities			
Shareholders' Equity			
Share capital paid up	**12,500**		11,345
Deficit	**(105,511)**		(9,542)
			1,803
		(93,011)	
Loans payable		**4,903,604**	4,900,826
Other payables		**3,403,352**	3,403,352
Current Liabilities			
Netherlands Antilles profit tax	**5,774**		5,569
Interest payable	**63,657**		–
Intercompany account	**7,186**		3,186
Accounts payable and accrued expenses	**16,524**		4,304
		93,138	13,059
		8,307,083	8,319,040

30th July 2002

Source: Titan Industries Limited, 18th Annual Report, 2001–2002

Curaçao Corporation Company N. V.

Statement of Income and Expenses for the Year Ended 31st March 2002

		(Expressed in Euros)	
		03-31-2002	03-31-2001
Income			
Royalty income		262,622	344,405
Expenses			
Interest expenses	327,481		323,368
Bank account expenses	27		51
Notarial expenses	784		725
Accounting fees	4,521		5,242
Audit fees	1,343		3,187
Domiciliary and administrative expenses	6,781		4,875
General expenses	1,377		2,545
		342,314	339,993
Income before realised gains/(losses)		(79,692)	4,412
Realise currency exchange gain/(loss)		(14,332)	(1,075)
Net result before taxes		(94,024)	3,337
Netherlands Antilles profit tax		(1,945)	(3,024)
Net result for the period		(95,969)	313

30th July 2002

Source: Titan Industries Limited, 18th Annual Report, 2001–2002

Curaçao Corporation Company N.V.
Notes to the Financial Statements for the Year Ended 31st March 2002

	(Expressed in Euros)

General:

The Company was incorporated under the laws of the Netherlands Antilles by Deed of a Civil-Law Notary dated 24th December 1998.

The Ministerial Decree of No-Objection was issued on 22nd December 1998 by the Minister of Justice of the Netherlands Antilles, under number 2669/N.V.

The authorised share capita of the Company amounts to EUR 50,000.- divided into 10,000 shares of EUR 5.- each. At balance sheet date 2,500 shares are issued and paid for.

The Company is a wholly-owned subsidiary of Titan International Holdings B.V., Amsterdam, The Netherlands.

1. The purpose of the Company is:

   a. To invest its assets in securities, including shares and other certificates of participation and bonds, as well as other claims for interestbearing debts however denominated and in any and all forms, as well as the borrowing and lending of monies;

   b. To acquire:

      i) Revenues, derived from the alienation or leasing of the right to use copyrights, patents, designs, secret processes or formulae, trademarks and other analogous property;

      ii) Royalties, including rentals, in respect of motion picture films or for the use of industrial, commercial or scientific equipment, as well as relating to the operation of a mine or a quarry or of other extraction of natural resources and other immovable properties;

      iii) Considerations paid for technical assistance;

   c. To invest its assets directly or indirectly in real property, to acquire, own, hire, let, lease, rent, divide, drain, reclaim, develop, improve, cultivate, build on, sell or otherwise alienate, mortgage or otherwise encumber real property and to construct infrastructural works like roads, pipes and similar works on real estate;

   d. To guarantee or otherwise secure, and to transfer in ownership, to mortgage, to pledge or otherwise to encumber assets as security for the obligations of the company and for the obligations of the company and for the obligations of third parties.

2. The Company is entitled to do all that may be useful or necessary for the attainment of its object or that is connected therewith in the widest sense, including the participation in any other venture or company.

Exchange Rates:	Closing	Average
US Dollars	1.14718	1.13020
Neth. Antillean Guilders	1.55163	1.57495
Pound Sterling	1.63531	1.61978
Dutch Guilder	2.20371	2.20371

Balance Sheet:

1. **Trademarks** — 8,304,178

   Represents:
   The full and exclusive rights to and beneficial ownership of the Titan Industries Limited trademark and certain other trademarks in various countries as specified in the sale and purchase agreement dated 31st March 1999 together with beneficial ownership of the applications for registration pending in other countries.

   The value of the trademarks has not been amortised as amortisation of trademarks is not compulsory under existing Netherlands Antilles regulations, and the management is of the view that the book value of the trademarks represents the current fair value.

2. **Cash at Bank:** — 1,528

   Represent the balance on the current account held at Citco Banking Corporation N.V., Curaçao.

3. **Share capital paid up:** — 12,500

Authorised Share Capital	
– 10,000 common shares @ EUR 5.-	50,000
Unissued Shares – 7,500 common shares @ EUR 5.-	(37,500)
	12,500

4. **Deficit:** — (108,104)

Balance as at 1st April 2001	(9,542)
Gain/(Loss) for the period	(98,563)
Balance as at 31st March 2002	(108,104)

5. **Loans payable:** — 4,903,604

   Represents the following:

– Loan payable to the shareholder interest rate of 6% p.a.	NLG	750,000	340,335
– Loan payable to Titan Industries Limited, at variable interest rates, which are linked to the Bank rate of the Reserve Bank of India	NLG	5,000,000	2,268,901
– Loan payable to Titan Industries Limited, at variable interest rates, which are linked to the Bank rate of the Reserve Bank of India	USD	2,000,000	2,294,367
			4,903,604

6. **Other payables:** — 3,403,352

   Amount payable to Titan Industries Limited of NLG 7,500,000.00

7. **Interest payable:** — 63,656

   Represents the net interest payable after the deduction of: royalty receivable from trademarks

8. **Intercompany account:** — 7,186

   Represents the balance due to:

– Titan Industries Limited	3,186
– Titan International Holdings B.V.	4,000
	7,186

9. **Accounts payable and accrued expenses** — 19,145

– CITCO invoice 98068197	USD	777	891
– CITCO invoice 98070729	USD	11,912	13,665
– Accrued audit expenses			247
– Accrued accounting fees	USD	1,500	1,721
			16,524

Source: Titan Industries Limited, 18th Annual Report, 2001-2002

153

Titan Watches and Jewellery International (Asia Pacific) PTE LTD

Profit and Loss Account for the Period from 1st July 2001 to 31st March 2002

		1.7.2001 to 31.3.2002 S$*	1.7.2000 to 30.6.2001 S$*
Auditors' Report to the Members of	**Revenues**		
Titan Watches and	Sales of goods	**7,078,205**	4,054,015
Jewellery	Fixed deposit Interest Income	**473**	461
International	Loan Interest Income	**6,672**	–
(Asia Pacific) PTE LTD	Other Income	**–**	4,115
(Incorporated in the Public of Singapore)	Total Revenues	**7,085,350**	4,058,591
	Costs and Expenses		
	Cost of sales	**6,222,379**	3,418,060
	Audit fee		
	– Statutory	**4,000**	3,700
	– Non-Statutory	**–**	1,175
	– Prior Year's Underprovision	**300**	200
	Depreciation	**422**	1,299
	Amortisation of deferred trademark royalty	**18,938**	16,871
	Foreign currency fluctuation	**21,116**	149,799
	Salaries and employee benefits	**56,518**	121,045
	Other operating expenses	**565,284**	591,519
	Total costs and expenses	**6,888,957**	4,303,668
	Profit/(Loss) from Operating Activities	**196,393**	(245,077)
	Finance Cost		
	Interest on loan	**(92,680)**	(49,796)
	Profit/(Loss) Before Taxation	**103,713**	(294,873)
	Taxation	**–**	–
	Net Profit/(Loss)	**103,713**	(294,873)

*Singapore Dollars

Source: Titan Industries Limited, 18th Annual Report, 2001–2002

Titan Watches and Jewellery International (Asia Pacific) PTE LTD

Balance Sheet as at 31st March 2002

	2002 S$	2001 S$
Share Capital	**100,000**	100,000
Accumulated (Losses)	**(235,554)**	(339,267)
	(135,554)	(239,267)
Represented by:		
Fixed Assets	**703**	1,125
Deferred Expenditure	**–**	24,969
Deferred Trademark Royalty		
Expenditure	**787,704**	806,642
Current Assets		
Stocks	**2,191,368**	1,974,702
Trade debtors	**2,130,354**	893,780
Other debtors	**31,757**	127,962
Loan to holding company	**1,111,272**	–
Fixed deposit	**19,654**	17,181
Cash and bank balances	**395,896**	106,006
	5,880,301	3,119,631
Less: Current Liabilities		
Trade creditors and accruals	**4,841,692**	1,858,227
Amount due to related company	**–**	460,411
Loan repayable within 12 months	**489,770**	414,596
	5,331,462	2,733,234
Net Current Assets	**548,839**	386,397
Non-Current Liabilities		
Loan repayable after 12 months	**(1,472,800)**	(1,458,400)
	(135,554)	(239,267)

Source: Titan Industries Limited, 18th Annual Report, 2001–2002

Appendix 5

Products

SONATA

Very reliable and durable, this is a complete collection in all respects. These watches range from smart plastics to elegant gold-plated ones and from hardy steel to all-weather gold and leather looks. Sonata also features stylish dials in a variety of colours. In short the perfect value-for-money watch.

Source: Titan Industries Limited Promotional Literature

2120YL01 SP103
2120YL02 SP104
2120YL03 SP105

2121YL01 SP112
2121YL02 SP113
2121YL03 SP114

141YL62 SP145
599YL27 SP321
599YL28 SP322

1014YL19 SP337
1014YL20 SP338
1014YL21 SP339

Source: Titan Industries Limited Promotional Literature

Nebula

Nebula, a range of watches crafted from solid gold
embellished with precious stones, available with both
leather straps and intricately designed bracelets. With
Nebula, Titan turns watches into precious jewellery.
The finishing touch to this exquisite collection is the
sapphire crystal that crowns each of the watches.

Source: Titan Industries Limited Promotional Literature

INSIGNIA

Insignia is the perfect fusion of design, craftsmanship and precision engineering. With European designs incorporating high-grade anti-allergenic steel, scratch-resistant sapphire crystal and special hard gold plating the Insignia is as sophisticated a watch as you'll get.

Source: Titan Industries Limited Promotional Literature

Source: Titan Industries Limited Promotional Literature

REGALIA

Magic in gold and unique futuristic material. Finely crafted sleek cases and patterned dials with special appliqué flowing into intricately designed bracelets. A unique combination of an all-gold and bicolour look, the 'Regalia' range represents the essence of dress-wear.

Source: Titan Industries Limited Promotional Literature

‖ RAGA ‖ *Exclusive watches for women. An exciting collection that includes decorative motifs, 'kadas', studded bracelets and a first of its kind; a three-in-one watch. A designer's collection, Raga is the complete wardrobe for the Indian woman's wrist.*

Source: Titan Industries Limited Promotional Literature

ROYALE

A stunning collection of alluring gold-plated cases matched
with exquisite gold-plated straps, the 'Royale' collection
has designs that suit everyday wear.

Source: Titan Industries Limited Promotional Literature

b a n d h a n

Bandhan is Titan's tribute to the everlasting bond between man and woman. A collection of diverse watches in leather, gold and steel-gold combinations. A perfect complement for any couple.

Source: Titan Industries Limited Promotional Literature

EDGE

679SL01
R811

679SL02   679YL01   679YL02   679YL03
R812   R609   R810   R861

1043SL01   1043SL02   1043SL03   1043SL04
Q560   Q561   Q562   Q563

1044SL01   1044SL02   1044YL01   1044YL03
Q564   Q565   Q566   Q609

33

Source: Titan Industries Limited Promotional Literature

165

STEEL

In combinations of all steel, steel-gold and steel braced with leather, these watches are meant for people who appreciate something out of the ordinary. Extending from simple round cases to complicated shaped cases, these watches are sure to be the cynosure of all eyes.

Source: Titan Industries Limited Promotional Literature

CLASSIQUE

The Classique collection exemplifies the elegance of time. A timeless embodiment fusing finesse and function to create the ultimate fashion accessory for formal wear.

43

Source: Titan Industries Limited Promotional Literature

Source: Titan Industries Limited Promotional Literature

Source: Titan Industries Limited Promotional Literature

The peppy, sporty, exciting collection of watches specially created for boys and girls that captures the fun and joy of childhood. With colours, characters, graphics and other interesting elements that truly make kids go 'WOW'!

Source: Titan Industries Limited Promotional Literature

Approaches to the examination

Titan industries

Overview

This case study is based in India on a reasonably large company, which is part of the giant Tata Group in India. The company is keen to use the experience gained in the Indian market to expand internationally. Titan has a very good technological base and has built considerable skills in watch manufacturing. They are quite innovative having produced the world's slimmest watch, requiring considerable technological and manufacturing skills. The range of watches offered by the company is quite breathtaking and it seems to have brought out new designs to time with festivities and particular fashion periods. As a watchmaker it is a newcomer to the International scene, which is largely dominated by the Swiss and the Japanese, with the Chinese making up the cheaper end of the market. The company is well thought of in the Indian market, but is little known in Europe. The biggest challenge for the company is to truly become international in status, befitting its strong design and technological expertise. However the watch and jewellery sector in Europe is well-established and there is little room for new entrants. At the same time, companies such as Calvin Klein, Gap and Storm augment their product range with branded watches. The case therefore illustrates an interesting marketing problem – how do companies from emerging developing countries create a market presence in the developed world? As there are many options to choose from, candidates will need to demonstrate clarity of approach within their chosen strategies. They should be able to piece together a coherent approach to the key problem facing the company.

Key Issues

a. This is a medium-sized company with a turnover of approximately £95m ($141 US)
b. The company is profitable, but the profits in relation to the turnover are low.
c. The inventory levels are quite high.
d. The company has state-of-art production facilities.
e. The Indian market is well-developed with a range of retail outlets and repair locations.
f. The company has developed locations in Europe, Asia Pacific and Dubai.
g. The Indian market is price sensitive and this has enabled the company to build up a mass-with-class appeal.
h. The company has the ability to augment the watch offering with jewellery.
i. Luxury watches are becoming an increasingly important part of the market, with celebrity backing an important element of some marketing strategies.
j. Parts of the Indian market are becoming quite sophisticated and the company is responding to this with different types of watches for different occasions.
k. The company uses an effective IT planning system (SAP) to monitor operations and supply chains.
l. The company has a range of people who are at some level into marketing the products. However there does not appear to be a clear marketing arm.
m. Key designers from Europe are used to produce 'contemporary' watches.
n. The company is under threat form all directions – similar quality watches (Timex), low quality watches (Chinese imports), high quality watches (Swiss and Japanese).
o. The company needs to be able to translate its Indian experience to the International markets.
p. A growing interest in Bollywood and Indian culture presents an interesting window of opportunity for niche marketing.
q. In the long run the company may have to incorporate more IT into its watches.

r. The company's ethical stance could prove to be a strong marketing factor in international markets, where some Asian and global manufacturers are tainted by the utilization of child slave labour.

s. The ability to develop key segments in Europe and other international markets is crucial.

Note: There will be no new brief in the SMIP Examination

The answers

This case is fairly complex and candidates need to understand the differing market sectors that the company is operating in on a geographical basis. It is important therefore, that the following issues are considered;

1. The application of theory.
2. The amount of international marketing theory/application that the students can apply to the case. The amount of communication theory that they can also apply.
3. The candidates should be thinking strategically not tactically.
4. The answers given must be realistic and practical.
5. A degree of innovation and lateral thinking should be rewarded.
6. It is important that the questions are answered within the given context.
7. The additional information exposes some of the weaknesses that the company has in its international markets. It also exposes the key threats to its local market.

Specimen Examination Questions

a. Identify and evaluate the main strategic marketing options available to Titan.

25 marks

b. Critically assess the impact of cultural issues in developing the Titan brand.

25 marks

c. Outline and elaborate some of the key factors of importance in expanding the company's products in international markets.

25 marks

Note: Additionally, 25 Marks will be allocated to analysis and application of the analyses to the questions that have been set (10 Marks for the Analyses and their quality 15, Marks for the application of the Analysis to the questions set).

Question one

a. Identify and evaluate the main strategic options available to Titan.

25 marks

This question requires students to consider the main avenues open to Titan

a. Take into account the changes within a more open market with a wide range of imports now available to the Indian market.
b. Take advantage of its strong brand presence and augmented service (service centres).
c. An understanding of how web technology can be enhanced for marketing purposes.
d. The company may need to undertake regular market research in order to understand the changing nature of consumer tastes.

e. Currently, although the company is profitable, it is very weak in terms of the commitment it can make in marketing.

f. What market positioning strategies should the company adopt *vis-a-vis* the different markets? – it appears that Tables 7.3, 4 and Appendix 4 are quite important.

g. Should the company be splitting its marketing budget according to the sub-brands in the portfolio? – How much further should the company proceed in launching luxury brands to match the Swiss and the Japanese?

h. Compared to other markets, the Indian market still has plenty of growth, both from current consumers buying more watches, to new untapped consumers.

With a high market share, the company has the ability to

a. Innovate.
b. Imitate the luxury watch manufacturers.
c. Build on the retailing strengths.

b. Critically assess the impact of cultural issues in developing the Titan brand

25 marks

This question asks for an understanding of the cultural issues involved in developing a brand. The interesting aspect of this question relies on candidates being able to understand that a branding strategy has to encompass both the Indian and the international markets. The branding strategies for the two markets may have to be slightly different. Able students will utilize the two diagrams given in the case effectively and map some of the factors against the ones proposed.

Brand structure

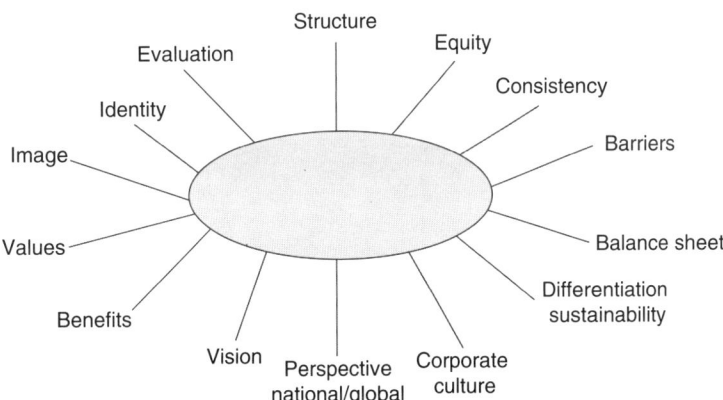

Source: Schultz and Kitchen, 2000

Later the candidates should be thinking about the detail as shown in the next diagram.

Sub-dimensions of brand-building blocks

In terms of cultural issues, candidates should be able to look at issues such as history heritage and experience, style, personality and values. The impact of Bollywood both locally and internationally should be taken into account. Aspects of postmodern marketing could also be considered.

The Indian market dimensions are:

- a. Loyalty.
- b. Mass with class.
- c. Reliability.
- d. Service efficiency and reliability.
- e. Innovation.
- f. Cultural issues, building on Bollywood.
- g. Classic styling.
- h. Innovation.
- i. Style.
- j. Price.
- k. Quality.

Note: The analyses should cover areas such as perceptual maps, brand maps, and an elaboration of the brand triangle as shown in the case.

c. Outline and elaborate some of the key factors of importance in expanding the company's products in international markets.

25 Marks

When answering this question, candidates should be able to discuss some of the key factors shown below, as well as some others they may have considered:

a. The balance of the sales between the Indian and the international markets from the sales figures.
b. The possible product mix that could be offered in international markets based on sales figures.
c. Possible enhancement of the international marketing team.
d. Buying into existing chains or developing retail outlets based on the Indian experience.
e. The relatively small international operations in Asia Pacific and Europe.
f. The possibility of buying a small well-known brand in Switzerland in order to get a headstart in the European market.
g. Developing niche products on the back of the Bollywood culture. This would be a two-pronged approach, initially within second generation Indians and then wider audiences in the Middle East, Europe and America.
h. Using Titan Edge for entering some of the more prestigious markets.
i. Building links with major retailers so that the Titan brand is offered.
j. Possibility of a shop within a shop as in some of the retail chains.
k. Using an international advertising agency in India to help to build the brands globally.
l. Analysing sales by country in order to understand buying characteristics.
m. Understanding the risks of expanding in international markets as shown in the figure below.
n. The utilization of the Internet within the international context.

Different degrees of product newness

Note: In utilizing analyses for this question, one would expect candidates to have considered the Harrel and Keifer model and aspects of Porter's diamond, taking into account the watch sector. Further elaboration and extension of the above model will also be expected.

Summary

This case is quite challenging and candidates will have to get to grips with a range of different issues. It is also set in the consumer goods market. The answers should show some links overall.

Note: In all answers, look for the usual, justification, strategic thinking, coherence and detail of information when marking the answers.

In all the answers we will be looking to assess the following.

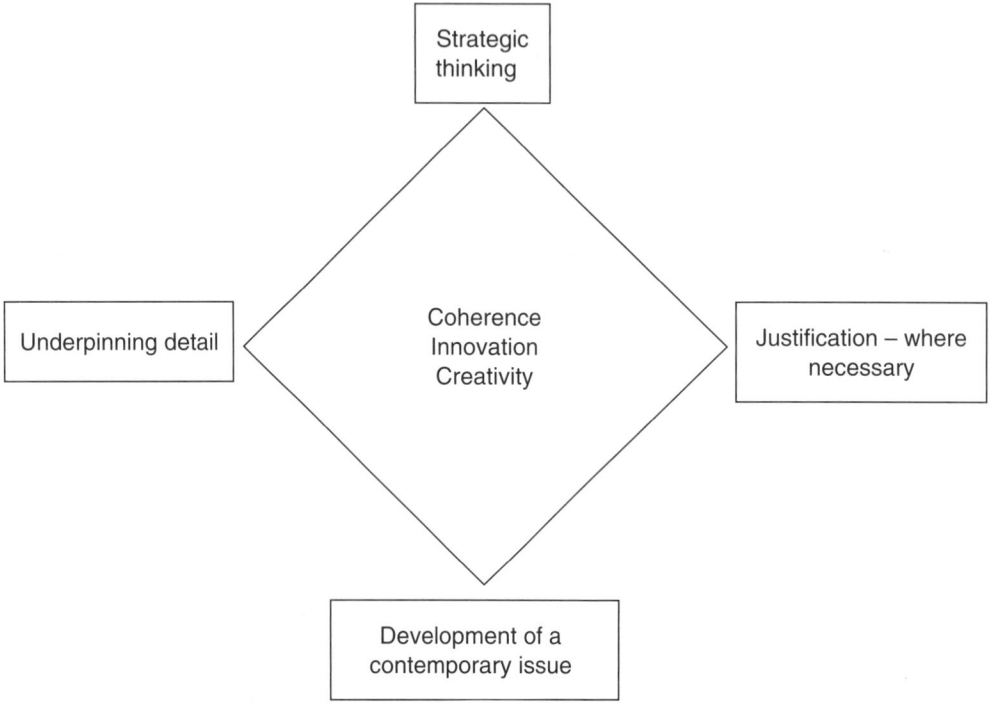

Please refer to the student analyses for this case which can be found in Appendix 1 at the back of the book.

The Chartered
Institute of Marketing

Case Study
December 2003

Strategic Marketing Management: Analysis & Decision

Reiss

Case Study – December 2003

Strategic Marketing Management: Analysis & Decision

Important Notes for Candidates

The examiners will be marking your scripts on the basis of questions put to you in the examination room. Candidates are advised to pay particular attention to the *mark allocation on the examination paper and budget their time accordingly.*

Your role is outlined in the candidates' brief and you will be required to recommend clear courses of action.

You WILL NOT be awarded marks merely for analysis. This should have been undertaken before the examination day in preparation for meeting the tasks which will be specified in the examination paper.

Candidates are advised not to waste valuable time collecting unnecessary data. The cases are based upon real world situations. No useful purpose will therefore be served by contacting companies in this industry and candidates are **strictly instructed not to do so as it may cause unnecessary confusion.**

As in real life, anomalies will be found in the information provided within this case. Please simply state your assumptions where necessary when answering questions. The CIM is not in a position to answer queries on case data. Candidates are tested on their overall understanding of the case and its key issues, not on minor details. There are no catch questions or hidden agendas.

Additional information will be introduced in the examination paper itself, which candidates must take into account when answering the questions set.

Acquaint yourself thoroughly with the case study and be prepared to follow closely the instructions given to you on the examination day. To answer examination questions effectively candidates must adopt a report format.

The copying of pre-prepared 'group' answers, including those written by consultants/tutors, is strictly forbidden and will be penalized by failure. The questions will demand analysis in the examination itself and individually composed answers are required to pass.

Candidate's Brief

You have been appointed as a Marketing Consultant to the Senior Management Team at Reiss. Reiss have recently more than doubled the size of their retail operations by entering the lucrative womenswear sector of the clothing market in September 2000. In 2002 they opened their first international store in Dublin, and they are using this operation as a test-bed for further expansion internationally. The company considers itself to have a unique place in the market being a 'bridging brand' between high-priced designer labels and lower-priced mass-market clothing brands. Fashion markets are notoriously fickle and consumers have become more demanding, expecting value for money with design-led fashion. Parents dress more like their children these days than like their own parents at their age, and lifestyle is often more important than age in targeting fashion markets. As a consequence traditional market segmentation is more difficult to apply in this market. Reiss realize that they are only just beginning to move towards their long-term goal of establishing the brand internationally as well as in the UK. Careful planning, investment in design, product development, purchasing, production and supply management, merchandising, store environments and marketing are the keys to their success. During the past six months a graduate employed by the company prepared the attached report on the fashion industry, Reiss, and its recent developments. You have been asked to prepare for detailed questions about future marketing strategies posed by the Senior Management Team at a meeting on the 5 December 2003.

Important Notice

This case material is based on an actual organization and existing market conditions.

Candidates are strictly instructed NOT TO CONTACT Reiss or any other companies in the industry. Additional information will be provided at the time of the examination. Further copies may be obtained from The Chartered Institute of Marketing, Moor Hall, Cookham, Maidenhead, Berkshire, SL6 9QH, UK or may be downloaded from the CIM student website www.cimvirtualinstitute.com.

© The Chartered Institute of Marketing

Reiss

Reiss is a retailer of 'own brand' quality fashion menswear and womenswear. It is a profitable company that established itself in London and the South East in the 1970s. During the past five years the company has grown organically and rapidly. In 2000, Reiss developed a womenswear brand to complement the long-established menswear brand. The entrepreneurial owner David Reiss is the driving force behind the business.

This report begins by explaining the company and its development and the fashion industry context before discussing the designerwear market in more detail.

Reiss the entrepreneur

David Reiss was born in London in the 1950s. He took over his father's business (wholesaling menswear) in the early 1970s and for some time owned a factory in Yorkshire where he produced his own collection. It was in 1980 that the first Reiss store opened on the King's Road, Chelsea, and it proved an immediate hit with customers. Reiss continued to open new stores in the 1980s and sold a mixture of wholesale garments and his own designed collection.

In 1987 the emphasis switched completely to retailing collections designed in-house. This was a bold move; one which David thought would guarantee the future. Establishing and developing a brand was important for Reiss. However, the final years of the decade became turbulent times for all retailers, and the recession that hit the high street hard led to a rationalization of the company and its structure. Inventory control, careful buying, and cash flow management were essential to the survival of the business and for building a solid base for the future. Today the company has a wholesale side, 25 retail stores, and owns some prime city-centre properties. In 1997 David won the Menswear/FHM Retailer of the Year Award, and Reiss received 'highly commended' from readers of Maxim in their 2001 style awards.

David's vision, energy, imagination, flair and creative abilities have driven the business forward in a determined manner. In 1998 David recognized the opportunity in the fashion market between the high street and the international designer brands and decided to target this gap. The strategy proved so successful that he decided it was time to fulfil the same niche role in the womenswear market. An external agency helped to gather market research information prior to the launch of the womenswear brand.

Reiss the stores

From its roots selling Italian suits in 1971, essentially over the next 25 years Reiss remained a small menswear business, although a number of new stores were added. With the opening of the Bond Street Store in London in 1997 the business entered a period of rapid growth and change. There were four new store openings in 1998 in Newcastle-upon-Tyne, Brighton, Trafford Park (Manchester), and Hampstead (London), and three additional stores were added in 1999 at the Bluewater Shopping Centre (just outside London), Nottingham, and Glasgow, Royal Exchange.

In 2000 Reiss made a radical departure from its roots in menswear and entered the highly competitive and lucrative womenswear market for the first time. Following significant investment in a womenswear division, womenswear was introduced into 13 of the company's 19 stores in September 2000. Womenswear accounted for 21 per cent of turnover in 2001 and increased to around 30 per cent by the end of 2002 (see Appendix 1 for financial summaries). With the successful launch of its womenswear brand, Reiss opened its Central London flagship store at Kent House, Market Place, spanning three floors with over 6,000 square feet of selling space. This was a significant step in raising the profile and perception of the Reiss brand. More store openings followed in major city locations and the first non-UK store, Dublin, was added in 2002. Three concessions were added in 2002, selling Reiss products through House of Fraser Stores at Bluewater, Glasgow and Birmingham. A fourth concession at House of Fraser (King William Street, London) was added in 2003.

During the last three years Reiss has worked with London architects Lever and Hopley to completely redesign the stores' image to project a fresh, modern style (see Appendix 4 showing Reiss stores). With all clothing and accessories designed in-house, the clothing, graphics, displays and interiors can achieve continuity and directness in design. The signature style mixes rough with smooth, creating an urban look – sandblasted walls set against smooth steel, floating oak and steel staircases, limestone floors, clear and sandblasted glass, exposed steel rafters and raw steel tables. These are combined with geometric form wall openings, counters in pebble resin, and floating wall mountings with glowing surrounds. Each store retains original features where possible to combine character with clean, modern styling. Historical stores include Glasgow, which is in a Grade 1 listed building spanning three floors, including an original Victorian staircase restored to its original shape and structure. Nottingham is also a Grade 1 listed building, formerly a dining hall for 19th-century lace workers. The original wrought-iron glazed roof and the Gothic arched frontage were fully restored. The Liverpool store, situated in the heart of the Cavern Quarter, features an impressive five-metre-high doorway, structurally cut into the building to expose both floors, and making the second floor appear to be suspended.

Table 7.15 Reiss stores, August 2003

Number	Name	Date Opened	Square Footage
001	King's Road	1977	3,680
002	Birmingham	1979	Relocated
004	Manchester King Street	1984	2,163
005	Long Acre	1985	3,612
009	Glasgow Princes Square	1988	925
007	Bond Street	1997	3,292
008	Newcastle	1998	2,052
010	Brighton	1998	1,219
011	Trafford Park	1998	1,743
012	Hampstead	1998	1,505
013	Bluewater	1999	1,722
014	Nottingham	1999	4,767
015	Glasgow Royal Exchange	1999	2,755
016	Kent House	2000	6,147
017	Liverpool	2001	1,800
018	Chester	2001	2,701
033	Lowry	2001	1,800
032	Livingston	2002	1,148
790	House of Fraser Glasgow©	2002	500
791	House of Fraser Bluewater©	2002	800
792	House of Fraser Rackhams©	2002	450
019	Cambridge	2002	2,000
020	Kingston	2002	2,000
021	Regent Street	2002	3,000
400	Dublin	2002	3,000
022	Leeds	2003	3,200
023	Manchester Shambles	2003	4,000
024	Birmingham	2003	4,000
025	Broadgate	2003	1,100
026	Canary Wharf	2003	3,000

© = concessions

Source: Company files

Thirteen stores have been opened in the past three years, together with the three concessions in House of Fraser. Guildford is the latest new store to open in 2003, bringing the total to fourteen in three years. Store development and visual marketing remain a priority in the progression of the Reiss business.

Improvements have continued in 2003 with significant increases in trade. Also the product range in both menswear and womenswear is expanding to include accessories. Turnover in 1999 was around £17 million, and is forecast to be £35 million in 2003. The company is now poised to capitalize on its market domestically and internationally.

Reiss ceased wholesaling in 2001, enabling the company to have complete control over where its clothes are sold and also to give total commitment to the expansion of the retail division.

The management structure

The rapid expansion of the business in the past three years has led the company to develop a professional management team that can take the business forward to its next stage of growth. Figure 7.12 gives details of the new management structure.

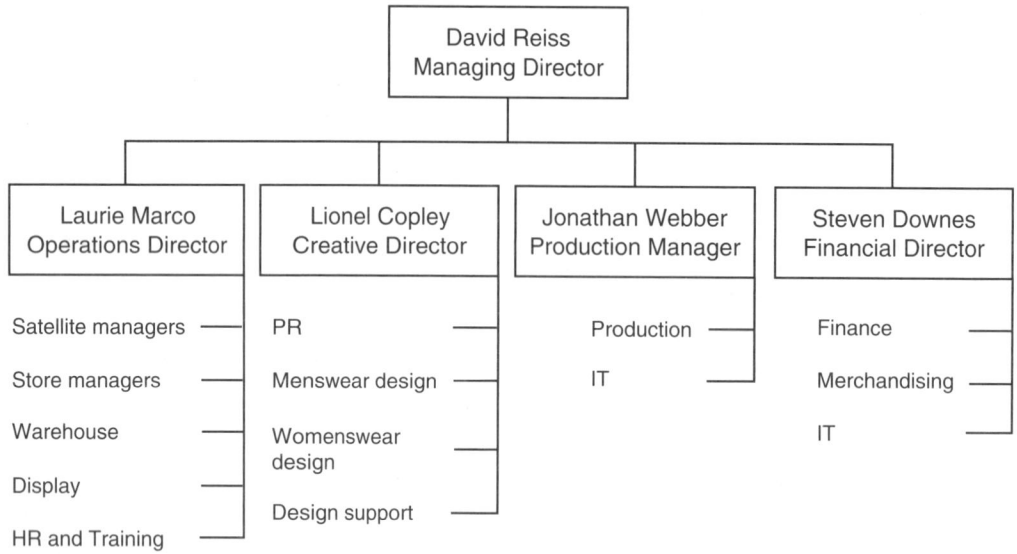

Figure 7.12
Source: Company files

Steven Downes, Financial Director (FD), has wider responsibilities than one might expect of the traditional FD. One important function that Steven manages is merchandising. Essentially this function is key to managing retail stocks and product throughput. The Merchandising Department was established in 2003 and has had a significant impact on improving the flow and management of the product in the business. Sales volumes and margins have improved and inventories have lowered substantially in the last year. In the coming year the intention is to focus management effort on reviewing stock levels at stores relative to space and store turnover.

Merchandising is a critical role for most fashion retailers. The preparation of seasonal buying plans with other key members of the team through thorough analysis of historical sales data and an understanding of future trends is key. Retailers must establish key performance indicators (KPIs) that cover sales, stock intake phasing, margins, stock-turn, mark-down and terminal stock. Monitoring trading and in-season changes requires attention if retailers are to maximize profitability and reduce risks.

The rapid growth of the management team has put a premium on office space inside Reiss, and the plan is to move to new offices at Oxford Circus, located beneath the Kent House store in January 2004. The possible synergies from the interaction of different departments are expected to bring a number of benefits. It is envisaged that the move will help the business to develop and improve its internal communications. Having staff located in one place will mean that meetings can take place on a single site and people will be available. It may also help the creative processes become more effective.

Jonathan Webber is the Production Manager and his job entails turning a designer's sketch into the finished products that are delivered to the warehouse. The product then becomes the responsibility of the Operations Director, who gets the products to the stores. Designers primarily source the fabric for a style they have in mind. However, the Production Manager often has to cross-source the fabric as designers are usually not very commercially aware. This is an important decision in developing fashion products because the price at which fabrics can be bought determines the price points retailers set in the store. Fabrics are sourced from a variety of countries, depending on the properties of the particular fabric required. China (including Hong Kong), South Korea, Japan, Romania, Italy and Turkey are regular sourcing destinations. Turkey, for example, has moved up the scale in terms of cotton fabric supply in recent months. Previously these cotton fabrics would probably have been sourced from Italian mills, who may have in turn sub-contracted the work to Turkish mills. Where possible Reiss go direct to Turkey and avoid the 'Italian middle-man'. Nevertheless, fabric is really the domain of the Italians when it comes to the special fabrics, fabrics with special treatments and finishes that Reiss requires for its 'edgy fashion'. For example, bonded fabrics would be bought from Italy. Double twisted ('doppio retorto') fabrics to accommodate and minimize perspiration would be supplied from Italy. Standard cottons can be obtained anywhere, and the Italians tend to go to Turkey or China and buy it in to supply rather than produce it themselves. It is not simply specially treated fabrics but the size of fabric order that is an important constraint on sourcing. Asia Pacific fabric suppliers only wish to supply 2,000–3,000 metres of fabric as a minimum quantity. For some lines Reiss is able to meet these minimum order quantities, but only when the fabric can be shared across men's and womenswear, covering two or three styles in two or three colours. However, this is a rarity.

Unlike many large clothing retailers, Reiss does not have many continuity lines that repeat season in and season out. As a consequence they do not tend to buy large quantities of 'greige' fabric, which is what some larger retailers tend to do with the aim of printing designs and colours when demand is known. It is easy to do this if the fabric itself is relatively less important. Reiss however does not tend to buy the same fabrics continuously because they are a fashion company trading designerwear, and pride themselves on offering the customer something new in terms of style, colour and fabrics. The fashion in fabrics changes over time. For Reiss, greige fabric would not exceed 10 per cent of its total fabric purchases.

Trims are another important aspect of purchasing for Reiss. Trims are the responsibility of one specialist inside the business who sources for both mens and womenswear. Although trims are small, they are a major part of a fashion garment. If the trim is wrong it will prevent the sale and if it is right it can help sell it. Womenswear is significantly more trim orientated than menswear. Reiss has had to develop and learn to manage this important aspect, especially since entering the womenswear market. It is another consideration when planning production.

One of the biggest influences affecting sourcing is exchange rates. If the exchange rate deteriorates between the placing of an order and the receipt of finished garments, it adversely impacts upon cost and hence the forecast profit margins. With the opening of its Dublin store Reiss will also need to monitor the effect of exchange rates on its retailing activities.

The fashion industry context

The fashion industry at retail value in 2002 was worth £26 billion in the UK, excluding footwear and leather (footwear and leather goods account for nearly £4 billion). European apparel was worth €324 billion and $314 billion in the USA in 2002. Retail supply chains span the globe in the search for the right fabrics, trims, and for the manufacturers who can deliver the right products, at the right price, at the right time. In the UK the fashion industry accounts for around 7 per cent of the gross domestic product (GDP).

The fashion industry is notoriously fickle. A glance at the daily newspapers and trade press will indicate just how fickle fashion can be. Lead times in sourcing and production inevitably create their own pressures, adding to the uncertainty of a highly risky retail environment. Time to market can be critical. Whenever sales fall retailers provide a list of reasons why they have not been as successful in selling this season's ranges. Weather is nearly always on top of this list. For example, worse than expected weather during a summer season can lead to a fall in sales of light summer clothing, or a warmer than expected autumn period can lead to a downturn in the sale of autumn and winter outerwear ranges. There are also differences in purchases by country and by region, owing to external factors other than mere fashion trends. For example, London accounts for a substantial proportion of total expenditure on formal wear, suits, overcoats, hats, gloves, ties and traditional leather shoes. A partial explanation for this might be found in the large numbers of people employed in professional offices travelling by public transport. In provincial cities, where more people tend to travel by car, the need for overcoats, hats and gloves is lower than that demanded in London. Additionally, retailers who have tried to expand their business to international locations have to be sure that they understand the market drivers behind the purchases. Southern Europe, where climates are generally warmer, may not appreciate the ranges that a retail store in Glasgow or Edinburgh would offer! Demographic trends and physical attributes also contribute to the complexity experienced by the fashion retailer. Average shirt collar sizes, waistlines, chest sizes and leg length have all become bigger in the UK since the 1960s. The UK population has grown by around 10 million since 1960, and the make-up of that population has changed over time. People live longer and the numbers over the age of fifty is set to increase to over 50 per cent by 2020. All of these factors contribute to the changing nature of fashion and retailing.

Table 7.16 Size of apparel segments in the UK 1997 (£m)

Women's outerwear	11,785	
Lingerie	1,675	
Hosiery	508	
Womenswear total	**13,968**	**56.60%**
Men's outerwear	6,036	
Men's underwear	610	
Menswear total	**6,646**	**26.93%**
Childrenswear	**4,064**	**16.47%**
Total	**24,678**	**100.00%**

Source: UK Fashion Report, EMAP/MTI 1999

Table 7.16 gives an indication of the size of particular market segments, split between women and menswear in 1997. The womenswear segment is more than double the size of menswear. This is an interesting statistic because more men are in employment and generally male-disposable income is higher.

Within the UK, clothing retailing is highly concentrated in the hands of a small number of large retail chains who dominate the market (see Tables 7.17a,b). The so-called 'middle market' in particular has been saturated in recent years, with too many retailers chasing the same customers, with very little difference in the product offer, apart from price. As a consequence some high profile 'exits' from the high street have occurred (C&A, Littlewoods), whilst some new entrants from international retailers (Zara, Mango, Hennes & Mauritz), and non-traditional retail sectors such as supermarket chains (George at Asda Wal-Mart, Tesco and Sainsbury), have developed their clothing offers. Nevertheless, other specialists, including independent retail outlets, still accounted for 26 per cent of the market. Reiss is a retailer that falls into this latter category.

Table 7.17
(a) UK Clothing Market Shares 1999

Specialist Retailers	(%)
Marks and Spencer	11.00
Arcadia	8.20
Next	4.50
C&A*	2.20
BhS	2.20
New Look	1.60
Matalan	1.30
Littlewoods*	1.10
River Island	1.10
Gap	0.90
Etam	0.80
Monsoon	0.60
Oasis	0.50
Austin Reed	0.40
Others	26.00
Total Specialists	**62.40**

Source: EMAP/E-business

(b) Total UK Clothing Market

All Retailers	(%)
Specialists	**62.40**
Grocers (Supermarkets)	4.90
Department Stores	12.30
Mail Order	12.30
Other	8.10
Total	**100.00**

Source: Verdict/E-business

* These two retailers exited from the UK High
  Street market in 2000 after many years.

The smaller independent retailers face a number of challenges. They do not generally have large selling spaces by comparison with their large counterparts, and as a consequence they find it difficult to achieve any economies of scale. In fact they may suffer from quite the reverse. These firms have to make decisions about merchandise that determine and define their market position more clearly. For example, should they offer established designer brands, and more importantly, will the brand allow them to? If they choose this route they may be constrained by the brands in terms of promotion, pricing, products, and how and what they can sell. Should they offer non-branded goods? Should they contract their own clothing ranges? Should they establish their own brand label? There are no easy answers to these questions.

The specific market sector – designerwear in the UK

Designerwear is defined as haute couture and diffusion, off-the-peg ranges, where usually the label is a designer name. The latter are often called 'bridge collections'. This report focuses on the latter category, where Reiss is competing with other bridge collections. Designerwear products are priced at a premium and consumers are more likely to buy such items when levels of discretionary income are high. In this respect a rise in the number of working women (from 12.04 million in 1997 to 12.74 million in 2001, a rise of almost 6%) has contributed significantly to the recent growth of this sector. The most fashion-conscious age group are the 15–24-year-olds. This age group is forecast to expand by 7 per cent between 2001 and 2006 (Mintel, 2002). The number of 55–64-year-olds is also set to grow, but this group has more traditional tastes that may impact negatively on the designerwear market, unless the products offered meet the needs of these customers as they experience a different lifestage.

The UK designerwear market is highly fragmented in nature, represented by a large number of small players and relatively few large suppliers. According to Mintel (2002), the ten most desirable brands are in rank order: Calvin Klein (26 per cent), Giorgio Armani (26 per cent), Gucci (25 per cent), Versace (18 per cent), Christian Dior (15 per cent), Ralph Lauren/Polo (15 per cent), Burberry (14 per cent), Hugo Boss (13 per cent), Yves St Laurent (13 per cent) and Chanel (11 per cent).

In recent years designers have been prepared to extend their market coverage by entering partnerships with retail stores. Debenhams was the first store to enter agreements with 26 designers under its 'Designers at Debenhams' initiative. Marks and Spencer (M&S) launched the 'Autograph' collection in February 2000, hoping to emulate the success of Debenhams and recapture some of its lost market with designers such as Betty Jackson (womenswear) and Timothy Everest (menswear). M&S also launched 'Per Una' in partnership with George Davis. These initiatives have broadened the appeal of designerwear and the retail partnerships have made the clothes more accessible.

A number of key factors influence the size and structure of the UK market for designerwear. Demographic, social and economic factors, as well as fashion trends, play a large part, as do availability of product, pricing and advances in retail distribution.

Demographic trends

According to the Office of National Statistics (ONS) data and Mintel, the working population is increasing whilst the number of people unemployed is falling and will remain low in the foreseeable future. Steady growth in the numbers of women in employment has led to greater financial independence, and more women are in professional employment where they need to wear smart clothing. Women, as a grouping, also tend to spend more on clothing and have a higher propensity than their male counterparts to spend on fashion. Working women are often time-poor, which leads to a boost in retail activity at the outlets most convenient to shop at. This includes supermarkets, some of which are now open 24 hours a day. Convenience and availability are paramount to women when purchasing clothes.

Table 7.18 Workforce in employment in the UK, by gender and employment Level, 1997–2006

	Men m	%	Women m	%	Total m	Index	Unemployed m	Index
1997	14.99	55	12.04	45	27.07	100	2.09	100
1998	15.19	56	12.13	45	27.32	101	1.83	88
1999	15.33	55	12.32	45	27.64	102	1.81	87
2000	15.53	55	12.47	45	27.99	103	1.70	81
2001	15.66	55	12.74	45	28.41	105	1.50	72
2003 (est)	15.62	55	12.87	45	28.49	105	1.65	79
2006 (proj)	15.85	55	13.07	45	28.92	107	1.60	77

(Data may not equal totals due to rounding.)

Source: National Statistics/Mintel

Table 7.18 indicates that the workforce is composed of 55 per cent men and 45 per cent women. Unemployment was at its lowest level for five years in 2001, and the numbers in employment rose by 5 per cent over the period, with female employment rising at a faster rate than male employment. This is good news for fashion retailers whose market is dominated by female expenditure. More women in work increases the demand for smarter, more fashionable, workwear as well as leisurewear. Consumer expenditure surveys show that women are more inclined to spend their income on designerwear than their male colleagues, although younger males spend more than their older colleagues. One consequence is that the increase in the number of women working will have a positive effect on the designerwear market. Table 7.19 shows the number of young people in the age band 15–24-year-old is set to rise by 7 per cent between 2001 and 2006, and it is widely reported that this group are more likely to spend a higher proportion of their income on branded fashionwear.

Table 7.19 Trends and projections in UK adult population, by age group, 1997–2006

	1997 000	%	2001 000	%	2006 (proj) 000	%	% change 1997-2001	% change 2001-06
15–19	3,602	8	3,727	8	3,995	8	+3	+7
20–24	3,628	8	3,635	7	3,903	8	–	+7
25–34	9,360	20	8,679	18	7,857	16	−7	−9
35–44	8,294	17	9,213	19	9,645	19	+11	+5
45–54	7,696	16	7,877	16	8,028	16	+2	+2
55–64	5,783	12	6,248	13	7,229	14	+8	+16
65+	9,272	19	9,369	19	9,585	19	+1	+2
Total	**47,635**	**100**	**48,747**	**100**	**50,239**	**100**	**+2**	**+3**

(Data may not equal totals due to rounding.)

Source: National Statistics/GAD/Mintel

Social and economic change

Consumer behaviour is constantly changing. Personal disposable income (PDI) rose by 11 per cent between 1997 and 2001, and there is a further projected increase of 13 per cent between 2001 and 2006 according to Mintel (2002). PDI is the greatest influence on people's propensity to spend. PDI generates a 'feel good factor'. For example, if mortgage payments reduce, payments on loans reduce, taxes reduce, and incomes rise, people feel happier about spending more. As Table 7.20 indicates, PDI increased by 11 per cent between 1997 and 2001 and consumer expenditure grew by 16 per cent.

Table 7.20 PDI and consumer expenditure, 1997–2006

	PDI at 1997 Prices £bn	Index	Consumer Expenditure at 1997 Prices £bn	Index	Savings Ratio %
1997	577.6	100	523.0	100	9.5
1998	575.9	100	542.6	104	5.7
1999	594.5	103	566.2	108	4.8
2000	619.5	107	587.9	112	5.0
2001	641.1	111	605.3	116	5.1
2003 (est)	672.3	116	634.1	121	6.6
2006 (proj)	722.5	125	683.5	131	5.6

Source: National Statistics/Mintel

As PDI rises there has also been a trend for people to want to spend more on themselves. This is good news for fashion retailers because they become beneficiaries of the trend. People have a tendency to want to trade up when they have more disposable income, and they spend more on branded fashionwear. Consumers are spending rather than saving, and many spend beyond their current PDI using credit cards and other loans when they 'feel good' about their current position.

People also spend more on leisure than their counterparts in earlier generations. For example, people generally spend more time and disposable income on holidays (including short-breaks), eating out, shopping, and going out generally than previous generations did.

Fashion trends

Each new collection of branded fashion garments is created to satisfy a predicted target consumer demand. Consumer demand predictions are based on target market research, past sales analysis, and input from experienced product merchandisers, designers and buyers. The collections are influenced by trends observed in fashions (e.g. textiles, shoes, accessories, home furnishings), and other fashion-related industries (e.g. automobiles, music, entertainment, sports, leisure activities), as well as wider environmental movements (e.g. political, social, cultural, ecological, technological, economic). All of these elements combine to help determine concepts and themes for a new season. Relevant textile materials, colour palettes and silhouettes are developed and selected accordingly. Trims and details are added as further embellishments to the garment. These former and latter design elements are co-ordinated and grouped into product lines that meet cost, production and delivery time requirements.

The introduction of new colours and styles by designers is critical in maintaining consumers' interest in keeping up with the latest fashion and hence encouraging spending. From spring 1996 to summer 1999 there was little change in styling, with urban and minimalist trends dominant. This together with a predominantly dark colour palette did little to stimulate the market according to Mintel (2002).

The product development process is complex. Figure 7.13 illustrates typical sources and criteria for various decisions in developing a concept. Once a concept has been developed this is only the beginning. Lines then need selection and approval before they are fully developed for ranges in the retail store.

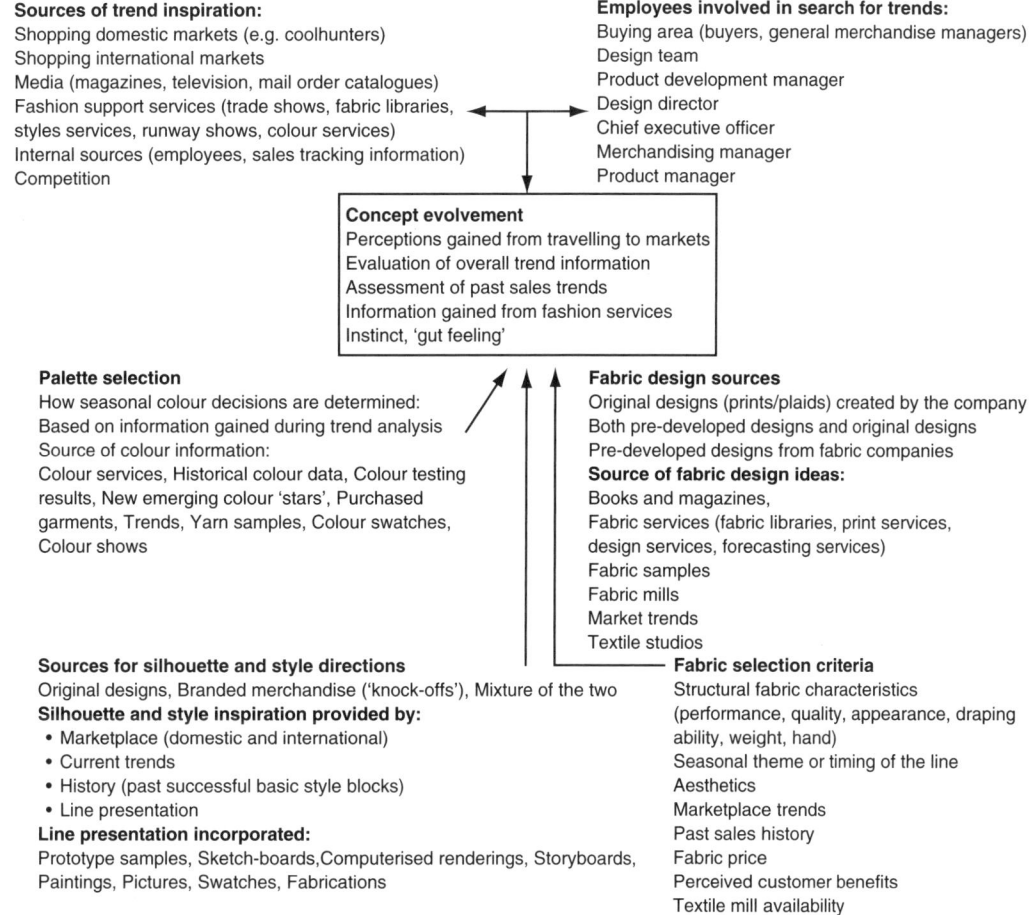

Sources of trend inspiration:
Shopping domestic markets (e.g. coolhunters)
Shopping international markets
Media (magazines, television, mail order catalogues)
Fashion support services (trade shows, fabric libraries, styles services, runway shows, colour services)
Internal sources (employees, sales tracking information)
Competition

Employees involved in search for trends:
Buying area (buyers, general merchandise managers)
Design team
Product development manager
Design director
Chief executive officer
Merchandising manager
Product manager

Concept evolvement
Perceptions gained from travelling to markets
Evaluation of overall trend information
Assessment of past sales trends
Information gained from fashion services
Instinct, 'gut feeling'

Palette selection
How seasonal colour decisions are determined:
Based on information gained during trend analysis
Source of colour information:
Colour services, Historical colour data, Colour testing results, New emerging colour 'stars', Purchased garments, Trends, Yarn samples, Colour swatches, Colour shows

Fabric design sources
Original designs (prints/plaids) created by the company
Both pre-developed designs and original designs
Pre-developed designs from fabric companies
Source of fabric design ideas:
Books and magazines,
Fabric services (fabric libraries, print services, design services, forecasting services)
Fabric samples
Fabric mills
Market trends
Textile studios

Sources for silhouette and style directions
Original designs, Branded merchandise ('knock-offs'), Mixture of the two
Silhouette and style inspiration provided by:
• Marketplace (domestic and international)
• Current trends
• History (past successful basic style blocks)
• Line presentation
Line presentation incorporated:
Prototype samples, Sketch-boards,Computerised renderings, Storyboards, Paintings, Pictures, Swatches, Fabrications

Fabric selection criteria
Structural fabric characteristics
(performance, quality, appearance, draping ability, weight, hand)
Seasonal theme or timing of the line
Aesthetics
Marketplace trends
Past sales history
Fabric price
Perceived customer benefits
Textile mill availability

Figure 7.13
Source: Hines (2003)

Final line decisions are based on:

- o Saleability judgements.
- o Testing results.
- o Perceived customer reaction.
- o Cost.
- o Selling history.
- o Co-ordination with other apparel product groups.
- o Marketplace trends.
- o Other factors such as newness, variety, lead time, quality, colour, instinct or 'gut feeling' as it is often expressed by people in the industry.

The current trend in womenswear towards 'mixing and matching' garments, means that women are buying designer items and complementing them with high street brands, to make their appearance casually formal. As a consequence, clothing accessories are experiencing a dramatic increase in sales, as women buy them to enhance and complement their outerwear.

During the latter part of the 1990s there was a noticeable move towards casual clothing. There was also a relaxation in office dress codes. Men are increasingly looking for greater flexibility and a certain amount of mixing and matching takes place similar to the womenswear market. No longer is a white shirt the only accepted office shirt. There has also been a discernable trend in the decline of formal wear. There is a wider acceptance of different and brighter-coloured shirts within the workplace. Trends in the rest of Europe have led the way, whereby a greater variety of colours have been acceptable for many years as a means of individual self-expression.

Other fashion influencers

One of the greatest influences on fashion during the last decade has been the proliferation of magazine titles, particularly in the target group aged 25–34. Male magazines such as *Loaded*, *Maxim*, *FHM* and *GQ* have led the way. It is offered as one reason why younger men have become more fashion- and brand-conscious. There have also been a number women's magazine titles launched, with fashion-oriented titles such as *Glamour* and *In Style* providing further avenues for advertising, editorial review and promotion. Fashion promotion through the media is very important for retail brands.

A further important influence, particularly in the younger age groups (apart from peer pressure) has been celebrity endorsement. Film stars, pop idols and sports stars have become fashion leaders. In some cases, for example David Beckham, the soccer star has become a fashion icon. Magazines such as *Hello!* and *OK!* run numerous stories on the personal lives of these celebrities, with accompanying pictorial imagery. These lifestyle magazines have become influential in what people wear and want to wear.

Fashion has also become more widely available. More retailers sell fashion, even in the mass-market, which was once the province of commodity clothiers. There is more square footage devoted to fashion and there are more places to buy. The rise in the number of designer factory outlets has made designerwear more accessible to the public at large. Often these designer retail outlets offer end of line or seconds stock at a discount. Discounts vary, but typically the product will be sold at 60–70 per cent of the full price. Attractive prices, ease of accessibility, and free parking make these retail outlets particularly attractive to consumers. In 2000 there were 34 factory outlet schemes operating in the UK, offering over 400,000 sq m of selling space. There are also large retail parks located on the fringe of large cities or conurbations likeTrafford Park in Manchester and Bluewater in Kent. These retail parks offer a variety of designerwear amongst a much larger clothing and non-clothing offering. Many of these retail outlets offer consumers a different shopping experience from traditional stores. Family shopping visits and even days out are planned around these venues.

Even market traders offer designerwear. Some of this may be genuine, acquired legitimately on the 'grey market' whilst some of it may be illegal, counterfeit products. The Anti-Counterfeiting Group (ACG) estimated the loss to brand owners to be in the region of £3 billion in 2000. Brand owners are not simply concerned about lost sales revenue, but also the damage that these products might do in tarnishing the brand image. Anecdotal reports from some lesser-developed countries cite incidents where a customer can enter the store, purchase an item of clothing, and be asked the question 'which brand logo would you like to have on it?'. In the UK, market Trading Standard Officers from the local authorities remain vigilant to the problem, and it is likely to be less of a problem in the UK than elsewhere.

Fabric trends also help in the development of new fashionwear. For example, Du Pont has developed fabrics with moisturising cream. There have been developments with fabrics that change colour in response to changes in body heat. Intelligent fabrics that offer health benefits are also expected to become readily available within the next five years. Transfer of technologies from space exploration, such as Teflon-coated fabrics, have been used for several years to offer people stain-resistant clothes and easy removal of difficult stains, including red wine, which was notorious for staining cloth. Men's shirts, ties and trousers have all benefited from Teflon coatings. There is also expected to be an increase in machine-washable fabrics, offering convenience to time-poor professionals who will have the opportunity to put their clothing (including suits) into domestic washing machines.

Phillips, the electronics company, amongst others has been working on intelligent garment technologies for aerospace projects for several years. Intelligent garments that offer a range of inbuilt custom electronics may also become popular with younger consumers as fashionwear. Telephones, cameras, radio, digital music and thermal controls could all be contained within intelligent garments. Radio Frequency Tags (RFT) are already being used in clothing to store product and sales data. The cost of RFTs has fallen dramatically in the past few years, making it viable to place them in everyday wear. It is possible that garments with RFTs could contain washing instructions, and combined with bluetooth technology, in an intelligent washing machine the only human intervention necessary would be to place the garment in the machine. The rest would be performed automatically.

Market size and trends

Towards the end of the 1990s, the clothing industry did not perform so well as some other market sectors, as increased discretionary expenditure was diverted to other areas of the economy. Sectors that benefited were travel and tourism, DIY, IT and mobile phone products. During this period much of the potential spend on clothing was channelled into lifestyle home products. As a consequence many clothing specialists diversified into home products, such as bed linen and other soft furnishings, in the hope of recapturing the revenue. Furthermore, middle-market shoppers looked towards added-value products on the one hand, and on the other to the discount clothing market at the value end for everyday purchases. As a result many retailers in the middle market felt the pinch, and as a consequence responded by lowering prices and having never-ending sales. The effect of this was price deflation in the sector. Customers expected more for less. Suppliers also got caught in the cross fire, and often bore the brunt of retailer discounting through lower prices for their goods to the retailer.

Table 7.21 UK Retail Sales of Men's and Women's Designerwear, 1997–2002

	£m	Index	£m at 1997 Prices	Index	€m	Index
1997	1,186	100	1,186	100	1,771	100
1998	1,230	104	1,237	104	1,831	103
1999	1,249	105	1,291	109	1,899	107
2000	1,312	111	1,410	119	2,155	122
2001	1,360	115	1,523	128	2,190	124
2002 (est)	1,417	119	1,656	140	2,168	122

Source: Mintel (2002)

Table 7.21 shows that the real increase in expenditure on designerwear between 1997 and 2002 is 40 per cent. This increase was fuelled by consumers becoming more brand-conscious and more fashion-aware. Consumers moved away from the middle market. Middle-market retailers found themselves squeezed between branded fashion and discounters.

The market split between men and women is given in Table 7.22.

Table 7.22 UK Retail Sales of Designerwear, by Type, 1997–2002

	1997 £m	%	1999 £m	%	2001 £m	%	2002 (est) £m	%	% Change 1997–2002
Women's	729	61	756	61	790	58	810	57	+11.1
Men's	457	39	493	39	570	42	607	43	+32.8
Total	**1,186**	**100**	**1,249**	**100**	**1,360**	**100**	**1,417**	**100**	**+19.5**

Source: Mintel (2002)

It is interesting to note the change in the gender mix between 1997 and 2002, and the trend towards more menswear as a proportion of total designerwear sales. The male share of this market has grown by nearly 33 per cent since 1997. Overall market growth for the period is just under 20 per cent.

Reiss the brand

Reiss established a fashion brand in the early 1970s. Today, Reiss fashion can only be purchased through Reiss stores, unlike many fashion brands who sell through other distributors. The Reiss brand has become recognised as a progressive, fashion-led retail company, designing and producing own-label ranges targeted towards style-conscious men and women aged 18–40 years. It offers an individual and aspirational look at affordable prices, successfully combining good design, quality and value.

Table 7.23 AW03 Price Points

Womenswear	
Jackets	£135-£175
Leather Jackets	£295
Trousers	£79-£110
Skirts	£69-£110
Dresses	£89-£130
Shirts	£65-£75
Cottons	£25-£79
Tops	£65-£89
Knitwear	£59-£79
Coats	£129-£195
Shoes	£95-£115
Menswear	
Shirts	£69-£89
Trousers	£79-£89
Sweaters	£59-£89
Cottons	£28-£49
Suits	£295-£495
Outerwear	£159-£450
Shoes	£89-£120
Belts	£39-£59
Ties	£39-£45

AW = Autumn/Winter

Source: Company files

Significant effort has been put into the visual imagery to support the brand. Window displays and in-store graphics have helped communicate a strong brand image for Reiss.

Reiss aims to develop an aspirational, fashion-led men's and womenswear brand, with a clear identity that can be expanded domestically and internationally. Key values underpin the brand's image and these may be summarized with words such as: creative, contemporary, essential, comfortable, affordable and directional. The brand has established a reputation for good-quality, fashion-forward and price-competitive offerings, sold in a well-considered retail environment.

The company recognizes that international expansion needs careful consideration. The Dublin store (see Appendix 2) will provide a microcosm laboratory from which the management team can learn. They already recognise that perhaps Northern European markets may be easier to serve than Southern European ones, focusing on fashionable consumers with similar tastes to UK customers, and markets with similar climatic, social and cultural environments. The company is keen to exploit the brand and new market opportunities, and has identified the USA and Japan as possibilities in the future, in addition to Europe.

Under Creative Director Lionel Copley, the design teams produce clothes that are individual, stylish and sexy. Key to the brand's success is a contemporary and directional product. Reiss fashion has a definitive look, which aims to lead rather than follow trends. Since the clothing product itself is not overtly branded, it is important that other aspects of the trading format complement and enhance the brand in four main areas: location, store design, marketing and store environment.

Location and store design

Since the product is aspirational, stores are chosen in prime, quality locations nationwide. Generally new stores are larger (in excess of 3,000 sq ft) to accommodate the combined offer of men's and womenswear. Where possible, buildings with individual architectural features are chosen, which help make the stores unique.

The actual store design is undertaken by a retained architect to enhance and complement the environment, whilst achieving the Reiss signature. Key to design is the ability to use materials, lighting, and textures conveying warmth and vibrancy.

Marketing

Following a management review in 2001 it was decided to refocus marketing resources into making sure more emphasis was placed on store windows and campaign graphics. The seasonal campaigns aim to promote menswear and womenswear, ensuring they represent the combined brand. A greater emphasis has been placed on imagery to match the brand statement: individual, stylish and sexy. Fashion shoots need to have an artistic merit that reflects and refines the brand identity, and locations can be as diverse as Blackpool and Zanzibar.

In addition, the display team has expanded and a dedicated Visual Manager creates the window displays with a team that implements plans, ensuring that the windows match the creativity of the campaigns and the product.

Public Relations (PR) is another key activity for Reiss and this is now under the control of Lionel Copley, the Creative Director, and has been developed significantly in the last three years. It was noted In 1998 that BT spent more on advertising than all the clothing retailers in the UK did (Jones, 2002, p. 242).[3] However, it is equally important to recognize that the growth of style and celebrity fashion magazines has quadrupled since the mid-1990s, and fashion editors and journalists need to fill the newly created spaces. This has presented many fashion retailers with opportunities to gain press coverage for their brands. This is an area that Reiss have been reasonably successful at exploiting in the past three years since they entered the womenswear market. Fashion, being a visual medium, allows it to gain easier press interest without spending on advertising.

Store environment

Reiss aims to communicate a consistent creative marketing message through their stores. The store environment is carefully considered with staffing, merchandising, music and seasonal graphics as key elements of the mix. Service levels, staff presentation and training are imperative to Reiss's success. All staff attend induction programmes where they learn about the brand and its history, and receive an intensive introduction to the Reiss customer service ethic.

---

[3]The Apparel Industry – Richard Jones (2002).

All the stores are individually merchandised to take account of the specific context of the store, its local market, and to ensure that each store has its own personality within the Reiss offer. The music is selected to enhance the environment and changes to reflect the mood required. During each season the internal graphics are changed, including pictures, wallpaper, and handpainting, with the intention of communicating the current season's messages. London stores now also sell a selection of books and CDs in line with the Reiss brand.

In summary, Reiss is a unique proposition being the only men's and womenswear brand that bridges the market between the high street and international designer brands. This is achieved by focus upon the design of product, complemented and reinforced through the store environment and individual store aesthetics.

Reiss customers

Table 7.24 Reiss customers

Age	Person Type	Purchase Type
18–25	Young student	Limited purchases
25–35	Professionals	Buying larger range
35+	older fashionable	Aspirational

Source: Company files

Reiss competitors

Table 7.25 Reiss Competitors

Position	Men	Women
Above	Paul Smith/Armani	Joseph
Par	BOSS/DKNY	Jigsaw/Whistles
Below	Ted Baker/FCUK	FCUK/Zara

Source: Company files

The company refers to its brand as a 'bridging brand', by this they mean it bridges the gap between higher-priced fashion from the likes of Armani and Paul Smith at one end of the spectrum, and Ted Baker and FCUK at the lower-priced end for menswear. They have established a similar position for womenswear, sitting between Joseph at the top end and FCUK and Zara at the lower end of the price ranges.

Reiss website

Reiss has established a non-transactional website (see Figure 7.14). The website provides store information, product ranges and new season collections information for customers, and information for job applicants. One recent innovation allows visitors to the site to enter and walkthrough selected store locations. The main aim of the website is to attract footfall to the 'bricks and mortar' stores. Although the management team thinks the website is important to their overall market strategy, they do not consider the website important as a transactional tool. Unlike many retail ventures, the market for fashion is one that is difficult to pursue through electronic marketing strategies. This is because fashion is a tactile business, and consumers like to try clothes for style, fit and colour before purchase.

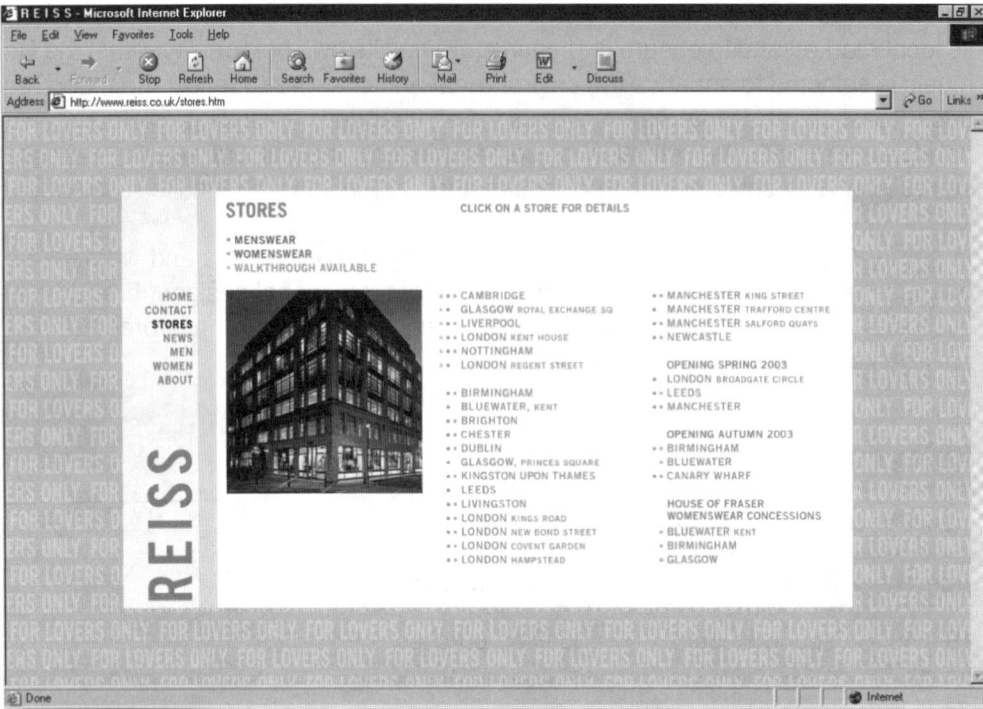

Figure 7.14
Source: Reiss website

Fashion branding

According to a report by KPMG (2002), creating customer loyalty by means of branding is becoming ever more important for companies' survival in all price ranges of the fashion business. This applies in equal measure to retailers and producers. Only strong brands are able to serve the customers as fixed points and to awake their interest in associated product features and stories. However, from time to time there are success stories such as Tommy Hilfiger, who hyped the brand and spent huge amounts on advertising. Sometimes customer satisfaction may not lead to loyalty, as the timing and the availability of goods may be more important. Customers tend to be fickle and may be willing to swap brands regardless of satisfaction levels. Better measures of loyalty are needed. Research carried out in Germany showed influences as in Figure 7.15.

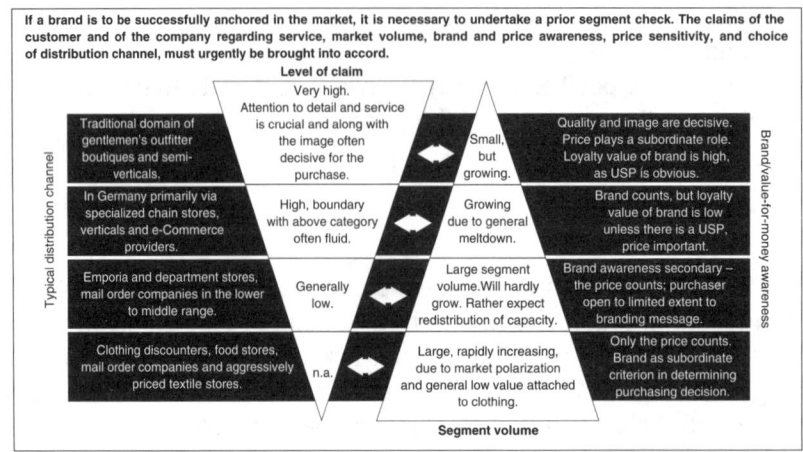

Figure 7.15
Source: From *Fashion Branding - The Power of the Brand* found at www.kpmg.de/library/surveys/pdf/fashionbranding2002_engl.pdf. Reprinted with the kind permission of the authors C/o KPMG

The brand is a very important part of a retailer's armoury and that promise needs to be sustained. However, the means of establishing a clear brand presence can vary according to the emotional values that have been established by each brand in the marketplace.

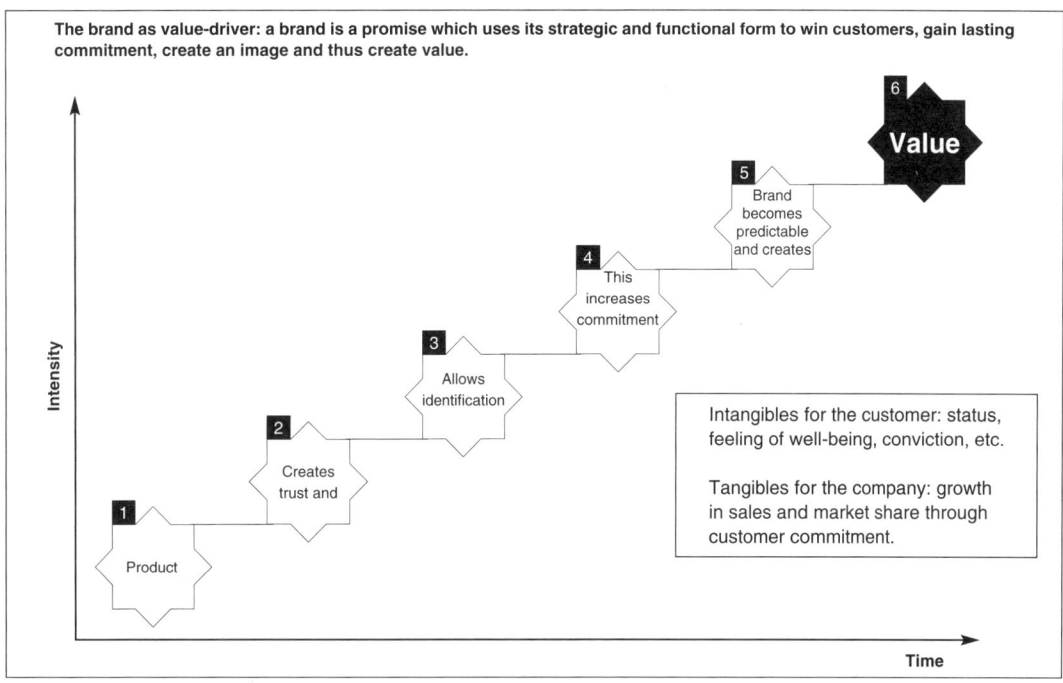

The brand as value-driver: a brand is a promise which uses its strategic and functional form to win customers, gain lasting commitment, create an image and thus create value.

Figure 7.16
Source: From *Fashion Branding - The Power of the Brand* found at www.kpmg.de/library/surveys/pdf/ fashionbranding2002_engl.pdf. Reprinted with the kind permission of the authors C/o KPMG

Summary

Fashion retailing is now one of the most challenging areas of business activity in the developed world, as there is intense competition, smaller profit margins and variable selling seasons, with delivery times getting longer in some instances. Typically a fashion season is marked by a bell-shaped curve (see Figure 7.17).

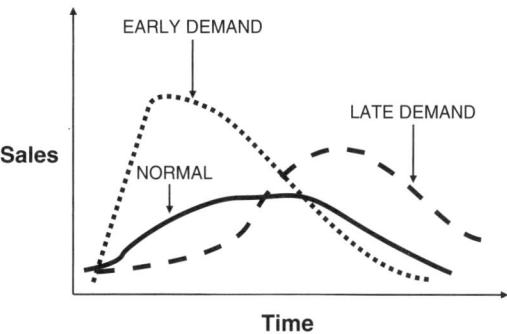

Figure 7.17 Fashion life cycles
Source: Ranchhod (2003)

The differing demand patterns need to be understood, as price points need to be established at each level. Often the demand at each price, in each period of the season, is uncertain, and price sensitivity to particular items may also vary. Goods left over at the end of the season lose their value dramatically and the demand may completely disappear! Thus companies such as Reiss need to monitor price levels and stock levels as accurately as possible. Discounting could

197

cause a heavy demand resulting in poor stock levels, or vice versa, marking-down too late or too little could also cause heavy losses. Each market is likely to react in different ways, so the company needs both localized and globalized information systems. Reiss is at an important stage in its development, with its rapid expansion programme throughout the UK and ambitious plans to become an international brand. The company needs to consider what the next stages of development might be. A number of strategic options are available to Reiss. It is a small, strong brand in a very large market, and it therefore needs to leverage this position effectively in the marketplace and establish a presence beyond the United Kingdom. It also needs to consolidate its position in its current main market. These issues are exercising the directors who are now considering the best strategies the company should pursue.

Appendix 1

Reiss Financial Statements

Profit and Loss Account

Date of Accounts Y/E	31st Jan 2003	31st Jan 2002	31st Jan 2001
Total Sales	20,883,000	18,138,000	17,653,000
Cost of Sales	6,752,000	6,658,000	6,131,000
Gross Profit	14,131,000	11,480,000	11,522,000
Operating Profit	1,977,000	1,255,000	1,201,000
Exports	N/A	129,000	252,000
Non-trading Income	119,000	119,000	125,000
Interest Payable	289,000	328,000	322,000
Pretax Profit	1,807,000	1,046,000	1,004,000
Taxation	588,000	441,000	276,000
Profit After Tax	1,219,000	605,000	728,000
Retained Profits	1,219,000	605,000	728,000
Value Added	8,509,144	6,778,768	6,070,712
Capital Employed	7,008,000	6,362,000	5,788,000
Net Worth	4,545,000	3,321,000	2,710,000
Working Capital	−2,396,000	−1,441,000	−1,497,000
Employee Remuneration	4,886,000	4,267,000	3,603,000
Director Remuneration	299,000	277,000	272,000
Audit Fees	25,000	27,000	27,000
Non-audit fees	7,000	4,000	12,000
Depreciation	1,138,000	813,000	892,000
No. of Employees	325	276	234

Balance Sheet

Assets

Date of Accounts	31st Jan 2003	31st Jan 2002	31st Jan 2001
Tangible Assets	9,356,000	7,750,000	7,226,000
Intangible Assets	48,000	53,000	59,000
Total Fixed Assets	9,404,000	7,803,000	7,285,000
Stocks	2,985,000	2,179,000	2,450,000
Debtors	70,000	55,000	162,000
Cash	41,000	860,000	692,000
Misc. Current Assets	1,376,000	1,024,000	1,167,000
Other Current Assets	1,417,000	1,884,000	1,859,000
Total Current Assets	4,472,000	4,118,000	4,471,000
Fixed Assets	9,356,000	7,750,000	7,226,000
Total Assets	**13,876,000**	**11,921,000**	**11,756,000**

Liabilities

Date of Accounts	31st Jan 2003	31st Jan 2002	31st Jan 2001
Creditors	1,310,000	1,171,000	1,867,000
Bank Overdraft	400,000	400,000	400,000
Misc. Current Liability	5,158,000	3,988,000	3,701,000
Other Short Term Finance	1,253,000	1,087,000	1,587,000
Due to Group, Current	1,000	1,000	507,000
Other Current Liabilities	3,905,000	2,901,000	2,114,000
Short-Term Loans	1,653,000	1,487,000	1,987,000
Long-Term Loans	2,320,000	2,853,000	2,857,000
Long-Term Bank Loan	0	400,000	800,000
Other Long-Term Finances	2,320,000	2,453,000	2,057,000
Due to Group, Non-current	1,539,000	1,539,000	1,161,000
Other Long-Term Liabilities	95,000	135,000	162,000
Total Current Liabilities	6,868,000	5,559,000	5,968,000
Total Long Term Liabilities	2,415,000	2,988,000	3,019,000
Total Liabilities	**9,283,000**	**8,547,000**	**8,987,000**

Liabilities	31st Jan 2003	31st Jan 2002	31st Jan 2001
Called Up Share Capital and Sundry Reserves	266,000	266,000	266,000
Profit and Loss Account Reserve	4,327,000	3,108,000	2,503,000
Shareholder Funds	4,593,000	3,374,000	2,769,000
Called Up Share Capital	266,000	266,000	266,000
Net Assets	**7,008,000**	**6,362,000**	**5,788,000**

Source: Reiss

Appendix 2

I haven't got a thing to wear! Why are so many men badly dressed? Because high-street menswear is rubbish, says Gareth McLean

The Guardian – United Kingdom; 06 June 2003

I am standing in Zara menswear, surrounded by a dizzying array of drawstring linen-ish trousers, highly patterned (and, I imagine, highly flammable) short-sleeved shirts and non-descript knitwear. There are fleets of tan sandals, knots of ties and a clot of blue sleeveless rayon grandad shirts. They are very Gala bingo. Some curious Christian country music is playing and there's that Zara smell, the odd aroma that is cold on the nostrils like an overly air-conditioned holiday apartment.

'This,' says my friend Gill, with whom I am shopping, 'is where DJ Sammy buys his clothes'. We pause to consider the Euro-disco DJ who recently murdered the 1980s' soft-rock classic Boys of Summer. Gill has a point. Even without the multitude of kaftan tops (the preponderance of which I blame entirely on David Beckham), there is something very Eurotrash about Zara menswear.

Zara womenswear isn't quite so bad, but womenswear never is. Women have the best shops. They have Topshop, feted for taking catwalk trends and translating them into high-street apparel in a matter of weeks. Men, on the other hand, have Topman. It is the preserve of 19-year-old mobile phone salesmen, thirtysomethings who think buying a T-shirt emblazoned with the words 'Doggy Style' makes them appealing to the opposite sex, and boys who consider Avril Lavigne an attractive older woman. I've always found French Connection to be a store with delusions of grandeur, and you may as well hook yourself up to Dr Nitschke's suicide machine if you're going to frequent Next.

Granted, there is Gap, but there are only so many classic T-shirts a boy needs (sometimes I get to work, realise I am dressed head to toe in Gap and feel so boring that I contemplate getting a tattoo. On my neck). There's always Marks & Spencer, but it has only made a half-hearted attempt to engage with the under-40s, doing such a good job of hiding the decent bits of its Autograph range that Indiana Jones would have trouble uncovering them. We simply shan't be mentioning its Blue Harbour brand-within-a-brand.

You wonder why so many men are so badly dressed? I'll tell you why. High-street menswear is rubbish. The best thing you can say about it is that it's consistent. And that's just another word for monotonous.

Now, I am aware that pessimism isn't exactly an attractive attribute, so I decided to give the high street the benefit of the doubt. I identified key trends in designer fashion and tried to find them in the likes of Topman, H&M, River Island and Zara. There must be at least a hint on the high street of neon as used by Helmut Lang on vests and T-shirts, Miu Miu's biker-lite, multi-buckle, many-zipped jackets, and Junya Watanabe's Jamaican-themed, logo-tastic, acid-coloured T-shirts.

In Topman, there are neon sweatbands and a not bad print of neon squares on some T-shirts, but the sweatbands are reminiscent of the aforementioned Avril and the T-shirts are as boxy and shapeless as the million other pounds 15 Topman T-shirts. There is a biker-ish denim jacket with zips and buckles priced at pounds 45, but it's just nasty, Miu Miu's idea horribly mutated. Of all that Topman has to offer – and, as the Oxford Circus store is the flagship, the choice is better than the average branch – a white suit jacket and some Marimekko-esque striped T-shirts stand out as, if not must-haves, then certainly may-buys.

H&M, conversely, was a complete wasteland. There were plenty of bad jeans, worse shirts and saggy-necked T-shirts, but no echoes of the designer trends. My lack of faith in the shop – I have always viewed it as a glorified jumble sale in which the occasional nice item is hidden, lucky dip-style – was vindicated.

Meanwhile, someone should do the world a favour and burn every branch of River Island to the ground.

Even in the posher shops – Reiss, for example – everything is terribly subdued and decidedly non-fashionable, preferring instead to be stylish. There is nothing wrong with this: Reiss has lots of lovely things. Yet most of its wares are slightly too expensive, seemingly designed to appeal to the man wealthier than I, someone who buys signature items to add to his shades-of-grey capsule wardrobe. Aspirational rather than everyday-wearable. Suave rather than fun.

And that is the fundamental problem. Shopping for men's clothes can be incredibly dull, not an adjective you could reasonably attach to the Topshop experience. For many men, shopping is a means to an end, not an end in itself. Men don't enjoy shopping and, crucially, don't think when they shop. This gives retailers the latitude to be lazier when assembling their men's collections. They go for a lower common denominator and provide less choice because they assume their male customers aren't interested in browsing; making a day of it. Men want to go into a shop, get what they want and leave quickly.

But I am not convinced that, given the choice and the right environment, modern man would not happily wander round surveying what's on offer. It is true that the majority of men aren't as fashion-conscious as women, so there isn't the demand for a male Topshop. Women spend more – and more often – on clothes, while men tend not to care about seasonal trends other than vests-in-summer, jumpers-in-winter. And, of course, men's fashion isn't as dynamic as women's. Such is the dominance of jeans, all the action tends to play itself out on our top halves (unless we're talking tracksuit trousers, which, let's face it, don't suit everyone).

Men who are interested in fashion tend to buy labels from smaller shops – your Duffers, Diesels, Boxfresh and Carhartt – and there's a lot to be said for it. A pair of Carhartt trousers will last you for years, a Duffer hooded top is a classic. But there are times when I don't want a pair of timeless trousers. Sometimes I want a pair that will be smashing for two months then distinctly not. Amid the reliable Diesel jeans and Boxfresh sweatshirts, a bit of fickle fashion would be marvellous, something that is not H&M-cheap but not Reiss-expensive. Now that choice would be a real treat.

Source: *The Guardian* – United Kingdom; 06 June 2003. © The Guardian, 2003, Reprinted with permission

Reiss finds pink is not big on Green
Financial Times Information Limited – United Kingdom; April 2003

UK designer David Reiss has brought his upmarket store to Ireland and is optimistic that our fashion fans will ensure the success of the stylish venture.

AFTER five years of trying to open in Dublin, David Reiss, founder of the upmarket British women's and men's fashion company Reiss, recently opened a store at a prime location, opposite St Stephen's Green.

He describes getting prime retail space in the city as 'close to impossible' and when the company took over the lease of the store it was reported that a new level for Dublin retail rents had been reached.

The company then spent GBP750,000 on the fit of the Irish store, which marks its first step in international expansion.

'Our end of the market is all around the Grafton Street area, and it's quite a tight space if you're quite specific about where you want to be. What we've finished up with is probably the ideal,' said Mr Reiss, who started the business in the mid-70s.

However, the shape of the premises was not ideal, even though it has about 3,500 sq ft of trading space.

'We tend to have big frontages which make a powerful statement and this is a relatively small frontage and it opens out at the back, so we've had to be very creative,' he said.

The company chose to set a precedent with its new Dublin store, with a new format which will be reflected in seven more stores opening in Britain later in the year.

The company worked with three architects to get what they wanted, using lighting specialists and an architect who has just finished working on British designer Alexander McQueen's New York store.

Explaining the investment in Dublin and his appetite to open here, Mr Reiss said: 'Dublin is a vibrant city, one of the most exciting cities in Europe. We just felt very strongly that it was an area where we would compete.'

'It lacks the normal intense competition you get in big cities. I'm quite surprised, actually, that at our level, other than Brown Thomas, there didn't seem to be an awful lot on offer.'

Reiss is at the mid to upper end of the market, with most items priced at 100-plus and the label is described as a 'bridge', covering the gap between the high street and designer stores.

The best comparison already operating in Ireland is Karen Millen, which is in a similar price range but differs in style.

Mr Reiss describes as 'phenomenal' the initial response of Irish shoppers to the store and said that within the first few minutes of the opening in November, between 60 and 70 people were inside.

'What really surprised us when we opened the store was it pretty much took off from the first day, and that may well have been because people were waiting for something new to happen,' said the designer.

'We certainly had a very strong initial reaction, which doesn't always follow through with the opening of a new store,' he added.

The shop opened during the fashion business's peak time, with November, December and January all strong months.

Mr Reiss said that business has slowed since that but should build up again into the summer.

'He will be closely watching the profitability of the shop. 'We normally look for quite a quick return from all our stores' he said.

Other store openings are possible, with the developers of the new shopping centre in Dundrum very interested in involvement from Reiss.

'They're pushing hard certainly to open in Dundrum. What I've told them is, give us a year.'

'One of the things that's becoming apparent on the men's side is that Irish men are probably more conservative than customers we get in the UK. So we're having to tweak it slightly,' he said, with pink proving not to be a very popular colour with Irish men.

'Certain things which are strong sellers in the UK are not such strong sellers here,' he said.

Despite the economic slowdown, Mr Reiss is optimistic that his label will fill a niche in the Irish market.

'What's happening (economically) in Ireland is happening all over the world,' he said.

'All I can tell you is that so far we've no complaint and we're certainly well above budgets that have been set, so we're very happy.'

Source: Financial Times Information Limited – April 2003

Commercial Property (Retail): Retail steady as outlook remains positive – Consumers are still consuming, so the retail sector is holding up in spite of the uncertain economic climate; some retailers are seeking to expand, and Zone A rents in Grafton Street and Henry Street are on the way up. Edel Morgan reports

The Irish Times – 12 February 2003

The consumer mattress-money spending spree that accompanied Euro-changeover last year – bringing with it an unrealistic buoyancy to the retail market – has proven a tough act to follow for many retailers.

However, all things considered, feedback from traders has indicated that sales over the Christmas period and January went reasonably well this year, says Fintan Tierney of Lambert Smith Hampton.

'Out-of-town shopping centres such as Liffey Valley and Blanchardstown probably fared better than Dublin city centre, with some people opting to avoid the hassle of city gridlock and the scramble for parking, although some suburban centres were also choked with traffic,' says Tierney.

There is still an appetite for expansion among existing retailers – for example Next is actively seeking suitable locations.

However, the scarcity of prime retail space continues to be a problem as vacancy rates remain negligible.

'Dundrum shopping centre and Mahon Point in Cork are among the few new shopping centres coming on stream in 2004 and they are filling up already,' he says.

Blanchardstown centre's extension will also provide much needed space, as will Stack A which is under construction on Dublin's docklands and will be aimed at high-end retailers.

Despite continuing demand for high-profile locations, retailers are not as aggressive as in previous years as caution prevails in an uncertain climate.

'There is still plenty of demand with substantial rental premiums being paid at prime locations such as Grafton Street and Henry Street. Saying that, it's a strange time; we don't know if there's going to be a war, and some retailers are taking a more short-term view.'

The continuing growth in Zone A rents will surprise many when a number of rent reviews are completed on Grafton Street in the coming months. Already, the ICS Building Society is paying a rent of E5,260 per sq m for its shop premises fronting on to both Grafton Street and Nassau Street. Another shop off the top of Grafton Street, 1 St Stephen's Green, was let to the UK fashion retailer Reiss at a Zone A level of E5,1 88 per sq m.

Marie Hunt of Gunne's commercial division says a number of European retailers have been looking to enter the Irish retail market since the Euro was introduced.

While Spanish fashion chain Zara is due to open in Roches Stores, for other operations such as French cosmetics giants Sephora and Louis Vuitton (LVHM), a division of Moet Hennessy, a high street premises has proven elusive.

UK companies Gap and Space NK have also been on the lookout for suitable premises.

'There are retailers that have been looking to gain a foothold in the Irish market for years but can't. Gap, for instance, won't go into out-of-town centres, it will only consider a prime shopping street,' says Hunt.

While Christmas trading was generally positive for retailers – with an estimated maximum of 10-15 per cent drop in footfall in the city centre – it did not take off until the second week in December – with November being a quiet month.

John Reynolds, CEO of the Henry Street/Mary Street partnership, says this is accounted for by more cautious spending patterns, given the downturn in the economy.

A survey on consumer spending conducted by the IIB Banks and the ESRI found that consumer confidence picked up in January, but pointed out the significance of this should not be overestimated.

The outlook for the rest of 2003 is quite positive, says Marie Hunt, with 'demand continuing to outstrip supply. Even in a slower economic environment, the outlook for retail consumption is positive.'

Source: The Irish Times – 12 February 2003

Appendix 3

Fashion retailing at a crossroads
Published: 3 May 2000

The UK high street in the year 2000 is a microcosm of trends that will impact retailing worldwide. Middle market retailers are being squeezed at both ends by designer labels from above and value-for-money operators from below. Retail is changing painfully because of the increasing sophistication of the consumer; the self-created problems of retail space and profitability; and the globalisation of retailers and their suppliers.

Although this could lead to more merchandise variety in the high street, the variety will be supplied through fewer and fewer mega-big retail conglomerates and major groups striving to operate worldwide. The evidence is that we are entering a 'buy or be bought' retail era. Malcolm Newbery reports.

UK fashion retailers in turmoil
Although there always has been change in fashion retailing, the pace of that change has undoubtedly been accelerating. The established and secure major players are no longer that. Marks and Spencer has undergone an 'annus horribilis' in 1999, and staff are still bailing out. The women's wear brands of Sears fell into the hands of Philip Green, who promptly sold them on to Arcadia. Arcadia, having just managed to avoid insolvency by doing a new financing deal with its banks, has now announced the disposal of 350 stores and the axing of three brands, SU214, Principles for Men, and Wade Smith Jnr. The last was only bought in 1998 for £17.3 million. And BhS has been bought by the same asset-stripper Philip Green, who says he intends to keep and run the retail fascia, but will either drive it upmarket or down!

To add to the confusion in the high street, the middle ground (variety stores, multiple chains, and mass market brands) is being attacked from above and below. Label conscious consumers are deserting St Michael for designer names with 'street cred' such as Calvin Klein. 'Value for money' shoppers are heading the opposite way to buy George at Asda. As a recent trade press article put it: 'cheap and nasty has become cheap and clever'.

The reason this has happened now is because of the confluence of three factors:

1. The increasing sophistication of the consumer.
2. The self-created problems of retail space and profitability.
3. The globalisation of retailers and their suppliers.

The consumer
Retailers used to sell on a good gross margin at full price for 46 weeks of the year, and discount to move old stock twice a year. Now there are sales and offers in store at least six times a year: January and July, mid-season and special events. The consumer has learnt to wait for these, and has become adept at buying at discounted prices.

Moreover, the growth of factory outlets and off-price shopping centres has sharpened consumers' desire for a bargain. Many brands now deliberately make products obsolete in order to make them available to outlet stores.

Space and profitability
Across the same period, in almost all developed countries, 'organised retail' (the chains) built square meters of space faster than they grew sales. The combination of this and the squeeze on gross margins as a result of consumer opportunism has cut profits to the bone.

Globalization

The third factor impacting on the retail scene in all developed countries is globalisation. Retail was presumed in the past to be national, with national preferences restricting cross-border activities. That is no longer the case. In food, electricals and fashion, multi-national retailers are growing at the expense of those with a purely domestic franchise. Very recent examples from the fashion sector are: Zara with more than 900 stores in over 30 countries; Hennes & Mauritz, whose stock is currently valued at £12 billion, and is stepping up its store expansion plans in Europe and the USA; and Gap, which will roll out the Old Navy format in the UK later this year, with Banana Republic to follow. J Crew, the USA mid-market chain with 120 stores, has announced a start-up in the UK next year.

Brands are also becoming international, whether they are part of a massive luxury stable such as LVMH (Louis Vuitton Moet Henessey), or a quick-on-their-toes minnow like Ted Baker. The perceived wisdom is that a brand cannot survive in one market, not even in one as big as the USA.

And to complete the story, although it is primarily in food, the takeover by Wal-Mart of Asda looks likely to lead to the sale of value-for-money George clothing in the States. These global retailers and brands will sell globally and source globally.

Where will it end?

The shopping mall is looking more and more like a shopping 'maul', with the global retail giants struggling for domination of the high streets around the world. As events prove that there is no effective domestic defence against the aspirations of the multi-nationals, lessons can and should be learned from other industries such as chemicals and automobiles.

In the chemicals business, the major players bought and sold (in some cases swapped) their investments in different types of chemical, in order to become the market leader worldwide in a particular sector. In cars, the famous Boston Consulting theory of the 1960s has been proved right over the last three decades. You use your investment muscle to become the biggest. You use that to drive down costs and kill the competitors. You then either buy the weakened competitor or leave it to die, and then, like a vulture, pick over its corpse (collect its market share). This inevitably has meant fewer and fewer car manufacturers. In the UK in the month of April alone, we have seen BMW retreating from Rover, and Ford announcing the end of car assembly at Dagenham.

Buy or be bought

If the analogy with automobiles is sound, and it would appear to be so, then the reaction of food and fashion companies with genuinely global aspirations is clear. It's 'buy or be bought!' Certainly Kingfisher thought that way, when in April 1999, it tried to merge with Asda. But the party was spoilt by the speed with which Wal-Mart moved to secure Asda and provide itself with a launchpad for Europe.

More recently, the French merger of Promodes and Carrefour has created a genuine European food and fashion giant, capable of playing in the same league as Wal-Mart.

Such is the confusion amongst food and fashion retailers in the UK at the moment that absolutely anyone, including blue-chips like M&S, is deemed to be 'in play'. One thing is certain; in today's edgy environment, there will be some more surprising mergers and acquisitions in retail before long.

Accreditation

just-style.com is the leading global textile, apparel and footwear web site, giving industry professionals easy access to the latest industry news, hundreds of valuable feature articles, and over three years of archive material. The site's unique content is researched and produced via our dedicated editorial team and a worldwide network of correspondents. In addition, the new just-style.com research store provides you with instant access to over 300 reports, books and research products from leading market information providers.

To browse just-style.com and discover how you could benefit, go to: www.just-style.com

Source: just-style.com

European apparel retailers face rocky road
Published: 25 March 2003

Continued sluggish retail sales growth in 2003 across much of Western Europe will exacerbate the already tough competitive environment for apparel retailers, according to a new study of the region's clothing and footwear retail industry.

Total consumer spending on apparel, footwear and accessories in Western Europe in 2002 was around 324 billion euros, roughly the same as the entire US market at $314 billion. However, new Retail Forward research shows the growing trend for ageing consumers to spend cash on homes, personal care, savings or leisure time, means apparel retailing in Europe is going through major structural change.

The study, entitled Apparel Retailing in Western Europe, says several factors are transforming apparel retailing in major countries such as Spain, France, Germany, Italy, Sweden, Portugal, the UK and the Netherlands, like never before.

But despite the difficult environment, it says major European clothing chains, and particularly multi-national specialty operators, are succeeding by taking market share through innovative, fast-changing product offers and lower cost, more efficient business models.

'The ability of these specialty chains to implement faster and more flexible supply chains is giving them a real competitive advantage,' said Ira Kalish, director of Retail Forward's Global Intelligence Program.

Changing face
Kalish said the factors seen as transforming fashion retailing in Western Europe over the next few years and early part of this century are:

- o Weakening demand – while apparel spending in Western Europe grew at an annual rate of 3.8 per cent from 1997 to 2000, the industry's share of total consumer spending is declining as the economy decelerates and consumer confidence slips.
- o Rapid consolidation – although apparel distribution channels and the concentration of apparel sales are still quite different across Europe, rapid consolidation reflects growing market maturity.
- o Greater internationalisation of styles – multi-national retailers like H&M, Zara, and Mango, have moved toward greater internationalisation of styles and more disposable fashion through low prices and fast rotation of inventory.
- o Supply chain flexibility and speed to market – faster and more flexible supply chains are the principal drivers of the retail apparel industry in Europe, and are key to the success of these specialty apparel chains.

'Consolidation, internationalisation, and the speed of the fashion cycle will continue to drive change in the structure of European apparel retailing,' Kalish explained.

Size and Growth of Western European Apparel Market, Total Apparel Spending by Country (€ billions, ranked by 2000 Spending).

Country	1997	1998	1999	2000	2001	1997 to 2000 CAGR[1]
Germany	69.5	69.6	70.7	71.6	72.0	0.9%
Italy	58.0	62.2	63.9	64.4	68.3	4.2%
UK	44.8	47.4	50.9	56.3	58.2	6.8%
France	37.2	37.7	38.2	39.0	NA	1.6%
Spain	20.6	21.8	23.5	24.9	NA	6.6%
Netherlands	10.1	10.9	11.5	12.0	NA	6.0%
Greece	8.9	9.0	9.7	10.0	NA	4.0%
Austria	7.2	7.5	7.7	7.7	NA	2.5%
Belgium	6.5	6.7	6.7	7.0	NA	2.1%
Switzerland	6.1	6.2	6.4	6.6	NA	2.8%
Portugal	4.7	5.1	5.4	5.8	NA	7.0%
Norway	3.8	3.7	3.9	4.2	4.4	4.0%
Denmark	3.8	3.9	4.0	4.0	4.1	1.8%
Sweden	3.2	3.2	3.5	3.8	3.6	3.5%
Ireland	2.4	2.7	2.9	3.4	NA	12.1%
Finland	2.5	2.6	2.7	2.8	NA	4.5%
Luxembourg	0.4	0.5	0.5	0.5	0.5	2.3%
Total	**289.5**	**300.6**	**312.0**	**324.0**	**NA**	**3.8%**

Source: Retail Intelligence and Retail Forward, Inc.

Note: [1]Germany, Italy, UK, Norway, Denmark, Sweden and Luxembourg growth is from 1997 to 2001.

According to Kalish, the most significant issue transforming the retail apparel industry in Europe is fast response. 'Speed and integration of the supply chain will continue to shape the future of the retail apparel industry in Europe by enabling more flexible, demand-driven fulfillment,' he said. 'The hallmark of successful apparel retailers is an ability to create distinctive product ranges that are responsive to quickly changing consumer expectations.'

Under pressure

The ability of specialty chains to implement fast response is placing pressure on traditional retailers, including independents and department stores. Their explosive growth is shifting apparel market share and is changing the structure of apparel distribution across Europe, argue the report's authors.

Recent tough market conditions have favoured those retailers who can respond to consumer demand more quickly and at lower cost. A handful of specialty retailers such as Sweden's Hennes & Mauritz (H&M) and Spain's Zara (part of the Inditex fashion empire), continue to defy the global economic downturn. 'These companies are particularly adept at understanding what consumers buy – and want to buy – in real time and responding quickly to sales trends and customer feedback,' Kalish added.

The explosive growth of these chains also is driven by diversification and international expansion. As a growth strategy, they are capitalising on the heightened interest in their brands by extending them into new product areas, new customer segments, and new formats.

UK: Apparel Retail Concentration, Sales of Top 10 Apparel Specialty Retailers, 2001/2002

Rank	Retailer	2001/2002 Sales (£m)	1996/1997 Sales (£m)	1996/1997 to 2001/2002 CAGR	2001/2002 # Outlets	Operation(s)
1	Arcadia	1,925	1,102	11.8%	2,750	Menswear/ womenswear
2	Next Retail	1,359	730	13.2%	331	General Clothing
3	Matalan	847	185	35.6%	143	General Clothing
4	New Look (UK)	527	218	19.3%	487	Womenswear
5	Primark Stores	376	111	27.6%	67	General Clothing
6	Mothercare UK	375	395	−1.0%	252	Womenswear and Childrenswear
7	Gap UK	368	112	26.9%	184	General Clothing
8	Alexon Group	341	108	25.9%	1,242	Clothing and Footwear
9	River Island Clothing Co.	301	285	1.1%	195	Menswear/ womenswear
10	TK Maxx (USA)	254	48	39.6%	69	General Clothing
	Total sales of Top 10	6,673	3,294	15.2%		
	Total Apparel Specialty Retail Sales	16,984	13,289	5.0%		
	Top 10 Retailers % of Total	39%				

Source: Retail Intelligence and Retail Forward, Inc.

Flexibility the key

The report says the secret to the rapid rise of these vertically integrated, multinational corporate chains is flexibility – flexible supply chains, the flexibility to price aggressively, flexible product ranges, and flexible retail formats. The winners are taking market share through a combination of innovative, fast-changing product offers and lower cost, more efficient business models. Supply chain advantages are giving these retailers a price advantage, which leads to market share gains, as well as the opportunity to improve gross margins, both of which support further expansion of the concept.

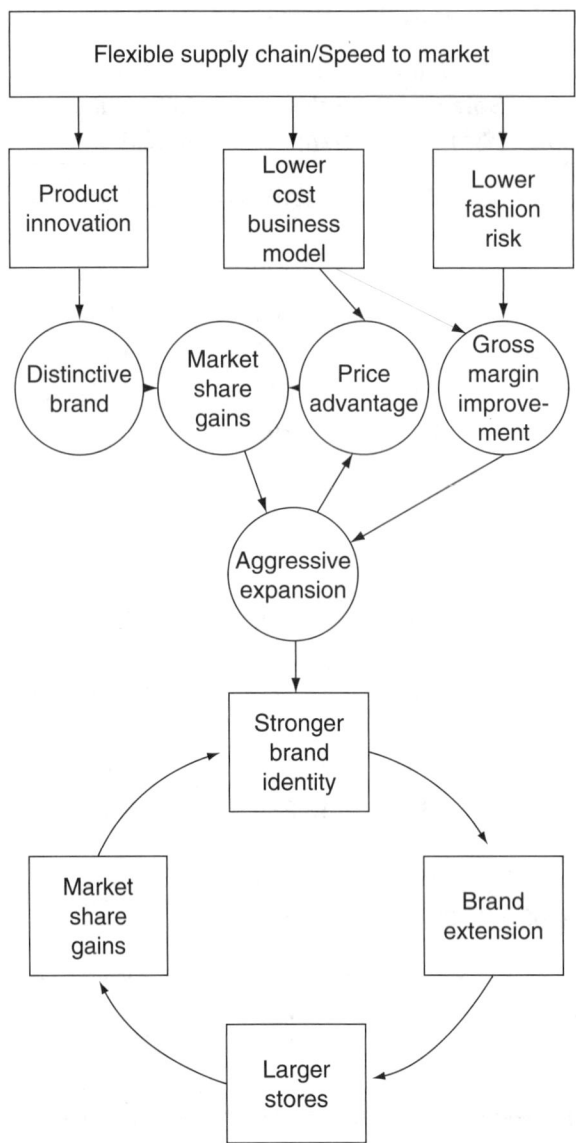

Source: Retail Forward, Inc.

It cites H&M and Zara as great examples of the competitive advantages and benefits of greater speed to market. The secret to their success is the ability to provide the latest fashion trends to their customers. Zara, seen to be more at the cutting edge of fashion than H&M, has maintained a lead in its ability to respond rapidly to fashion trends. It puts fashion ranges together in 7–30 days and can replenish bestsellers in the stores in five days. H&M can respond in 30–60 days. This compares to as much as 40–50 weeks from design to delivery for a typical clothing retailer.

The explosive growth of these chains also is driven by diversification and international expansion. As a growth strategy, they are capitalising on the heightened interest in their brands by extending them into new product areas, new customer segments, and new formats.

Product offers are being broadened to include categories such as childrenswear, lingerie, fragrance and personal care products, and homewares. Many have launched petite, large size, and maternity ranges. Bigger stores are then justified to accommodate the expanded product ranges. To further appeal to different customer groups, some chains adopt a portfolio strategy to extend their reach through the development or acquisition of multiple branded concepts.

With either approach, the impact of these retailers on the competitive landscape is becoming more pervasive. International expansion is slowly but surely leading to the homogenisation of European high streets.

Rosy retail future?

Economic and retail sales growth has slowed across much of Western Europe since the turn of the millennium, with the softness in the economy driven in large part by cyclical factors such as reduced exports amid global weakness. However, in countries such as Germany and Italy, the economy also suffers from structural barriers to growth, such as a rigid labour market and a strict regulatory environment. Among Europe's five largest economies, the outlook for retail sales growth is mixed.

Retail Forward forecasts that retail sales in Germany will continue to fall this year following a 2.3 per cent slide in 2002. In France, retail sales growth has been on a slowing trend since 1999 and sales are forecast to grow at a moderate 2.4 per cent pace in 2003 as the economy recovers from the recent slowdown.

Following several years of rapid growth in the UK, sales are expected to slow, registering about a three per cent increase. Despite the slowdown in the Italian economy, the retail sector grew nearly two per cent in 2002, the strongest increase in more than 10 years. However, growth is expected to ease below one per cent in 2003. Retail sales grew an estimated 2.9 per cent in Spain last year and that growth is expected to improve slightly in 2003 to more than three per cent.

Accreditation

just-style.com is the leading global textile, apparel and footwear web site, giving industry professionals easy access to the latest industry news, hundreds of valuable feature articles, and over three years of archive material. The site's unique content is researched and produced via our dedicated editorial team and a worldwide network of correspondents. In addition, the new just-style.com research store provides you with instant access to over 300 reports, books and research products from leading market information providers.

To browse just-style.com and discover how you could benefit, go to: www.just-style.com

Source: just-style.com

Aroq Limited
Registered in England no: 4307068
Seneca House, Buntsford Hill Business Park, Bromsgrove, Worcs, B60 3DX, UK.
Tel: +44 (0)1527 573 600 Fax: +44 (0)1527 577 423 Web: www.aroq.com

Appendix 4

Cambridge Store

Source: Lever and Hopley

King's Road, London Store

Source: Lever and Hopley

Leeds Store

Source: Lever and Hopley

Newcastle Store

Source: Lever and Hopley

Approaches to the Examination

Reiss

Overview

This case represents an important departure from the more conventional marketing dilemmas and offers an insight into the challenges faced by retailers. The case is based on an SME that is becoming well established in the designer clothing niche within the UK. The company finds that it has been quite successful in the UK and that it would seem reasonable to emulate this elsewhere in Europe. The company has a loyal following and the Reiss brand is often featured in the clothing sections of the major magazines (male and female) and the Saturday and Sunday magazines of the major papers such as the *Guardian* and the *Sunday Times*. Its organic growth is a testimony to its success. The reasons for its success are complex and manifold. Part of this is design, part niche marketing and part store design. The company has a good eye for new trends and designs and the move to retailing has meant that it has had to give up its wholesale arm. In recent years the company has grown very rapidly and has reflected the general trend of prosperity within the UK. This is a very positive outcome as it competes in a messy and fickle market. The clothing market in the UK is huge – around £25bn. Reiss with a £35m turnover is a tiny but significant niche player in a market dominated by major players such as M&S, Debenhams and medium sized concerns with fashionable but medium priced clothing such as Zara and Mango. At the same time unconventional players such as Asda (George) and Sainsburys are becoming entrenched in the market. Given the range of issues such as supply chain management, marketing and competition the company now has to position itself to take advantage of the opportunities and to minimize the risks associated with international expansion.

Key issues

a. This is a medium-sized company with a turnover of approximately £21m.
b. The company is profitable, but the profits in relation to the turnover are low but indicating an upward trend (around 4 per cent net profit in 2001 to 5.8 per cent in 2003).
c. The stock levels are quite low indicating good operations management.
d. The assets of the company are 50 per cent more than the liabilities, largely because of the fixed assets (the retail premises).
e. The UK market is intensely competitive offering a range of options to the consumer who wishes to purchase clothes.
f. The company has just launched its first shop outside the UK in Dublin.
g. The UK clothing market is quite fragmented and the niche that Reiss operates in needs to be monitored continuously in order to meet challenges from the likes of Zara and the highly regarded marques such as Christian Dior.
h. The company faces the biggest threats from more moderately priced shops as indicated in the *Guardian* article.
i. The shop in Ireland appears to be a success, but it is of high cost and will need to be monitored effectively.
j. As disposable incomes increase, more people could be drawn into purchasing clothing from Reiss.
k. The company is still very much a niche operator and is not really very well known as a brand.
l. Store management and design are great assets and the importance of this is highlighted in Figure 7.15, when building brands.
m. The company now has many opportunities in the large womenswear market.
n. The company has begun to diversify into other merchandise in the London stores (books, CDs, etc).
o. The company needs to consider the mix of its communication strategies.
p. The company needs to be continuously creative and lead trends.

The answers

This case is fairly complex and candidates need to understand the market sector that the company is operating in. It is important, therefore, that the following issues are considered:

1. The application of theory
2. The amount of international and communications marketing theory/application that the students can apply to the case. The amount of communication theory that they can also apply.
3. The candidates should be thinking strategically not tactically.
4. The answers given must be realistic and practical.
5. A degree of innovation and lateral thinking will be rewarded.
6. It is important that the questions are answered within the given context.
7. The additional information offers some insights into managing customer relations.

Possible examination questions

a. Critically assess the main factors affecting Reiss's market position in fashion retailing.

25 Marks

b. Evaluate the current web strategy and propose a customer relationship management (CRM) strategy for the company.

25 Marks

c. Assess and evaluate how Reiss could develop its brand equity within Europe.

25 Marks

25 Marks will be allocated to the pre-prepared analyses and their application to the questions set

Question one

a. Critically assess the main factors affecting Reiss's market position in fashion retailing

25 Marks

There are many factors that need to be taken into account:

a. The company's niche position and tiny market share, making it difficult to establish a strong brand image. However it has a strong cult following, brand and store design.
b. The company's net profitability is not particularly exciting, but it has enough reserves to push for expansion.
c. The company may need to undertake regular market research in order to understand the changing nature of consumer tastes and develop its web presence.
d. The importance of operations and inventory management.
e. The possibilities of diversification into other product areas.
f. The company's strong asset base.
g. The company's ability to innovate.
h. The strong bases established by retailers such as Mango, Zara, Monsoon and Next.
i. The problems associated with expansion into international markets.

Candidates should be able to discuss these more fully utilizing analyses. For instance, financial analyses could be used as well as analyses of the European market. Models such as Porter and the GE matrix could also be used to indicate positioning. In all cases candidates are expected to be critical in their assessment of the issues.

b. Evaluate the current web strategy and propose a Customer Relationship Management (CRM) strategy for the company

25 marks

It is clear that the company is using the website for informational and not transactional purposes. The issues surrounding this are important to discuss, especially in the light of the 'bricks n' clicks' debate. The company has got rid of its wholesaling arm and is very tight on stock control as this may not be very helpful if transactions are carried out via the Web.

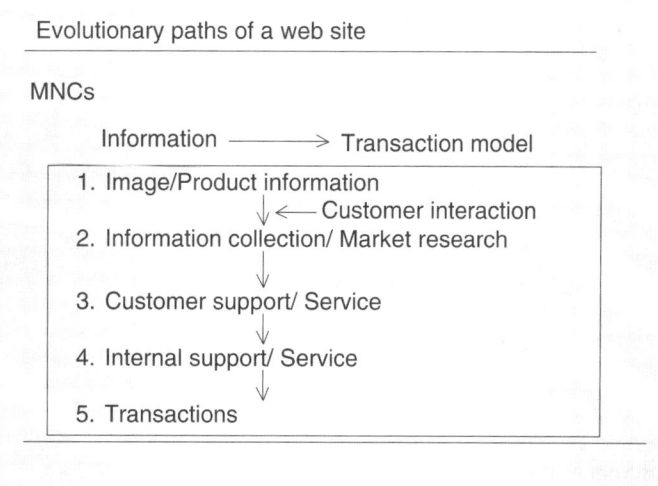

Figure 7.18
Source: Adapted from Quelch and Klein, (1996)

For many companies the Web is an important part of building a CRM strategy. This is because many of the functions can be automated and companies can manage to track customer preferences and needs. The diagram above shows the path that Reiss could follow in the way it can develop its web site in the future.

At the same time classic relationship marketing requires the company to attract and retain customers. For this to happen customer information needs to be captured. This is not easy unless a database is involved. The best way to do this is through direct and web-based marketing. A purely transactional site is limiting. The figure below highlights the key strategies for developing a CRM strategy. At same time the benefits of such a strategy will allow the company to build brand equity as shown in Figure 7.20.

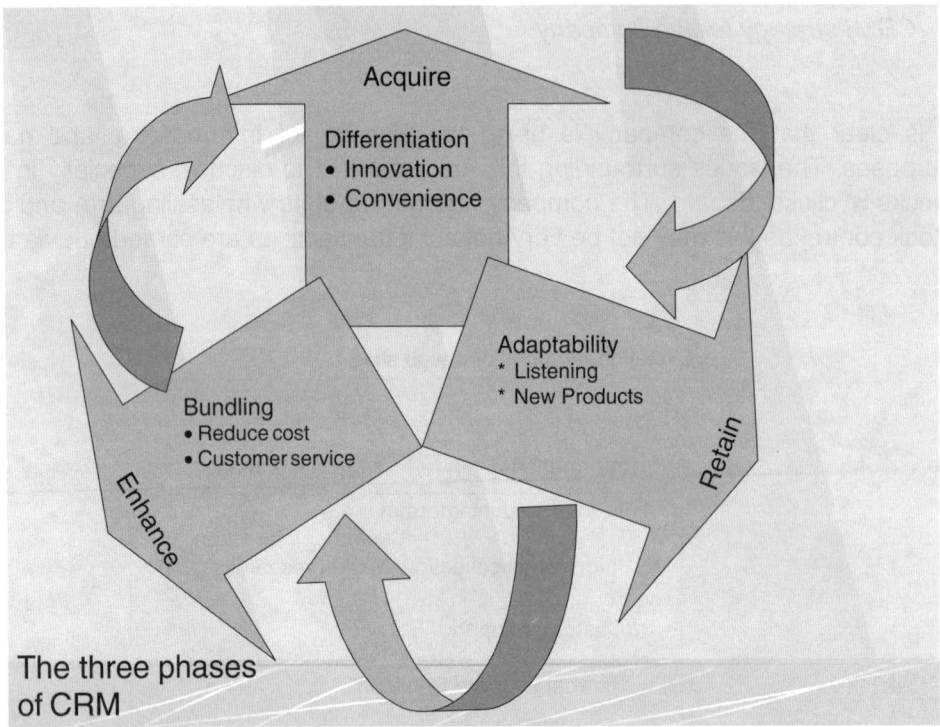

Figure 7.19
Source: Adapted from Kalakota and Robinson (1999)

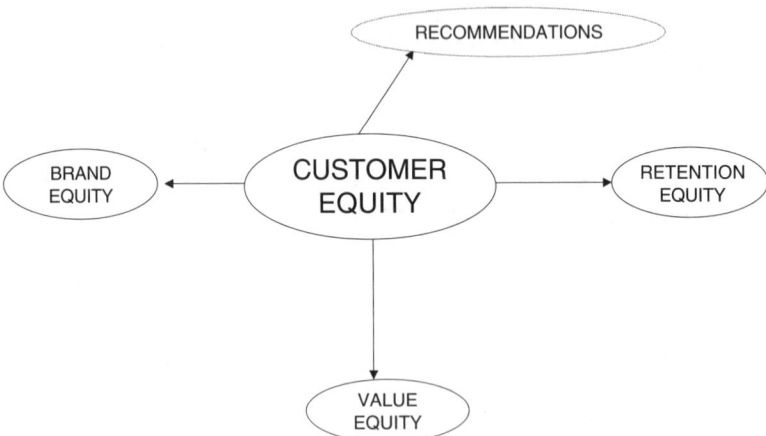

Figure 7.20 Factors driving customer equity

A good CRM strategy will help the company to build its customer profitability profiles and retention levels.

Note: The types of analyses that students could utilize in this answer would be those related to understanding the customer focus required in developing CRM. The development of Internet models. Demographic and trend analysis as given in the case.

e.g.

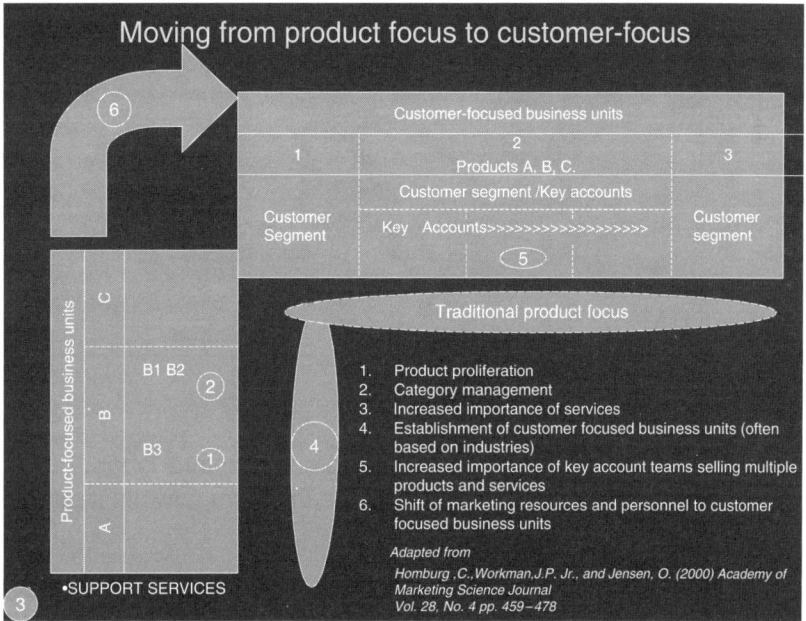

25 Marks

c. Assess and evaluate how Reiss could develop its brand equity within Europe.

25 Marks

When answering this question, candidates should draw on the brand models already given within the case study.

According to the article in the appendix,

> *Speed and integration of the supply chain will continue to shape the future of the retail apparel industry in Europe by enabling more flexible, demand driven fulfillment. . . . The hallmark of successful apparel retailers is an ability to create distinctive product ranges that are responsive to quickly changing consumer expectations.*

Students need to bring this out in their answers as well as the models contained within the case regarding brands.

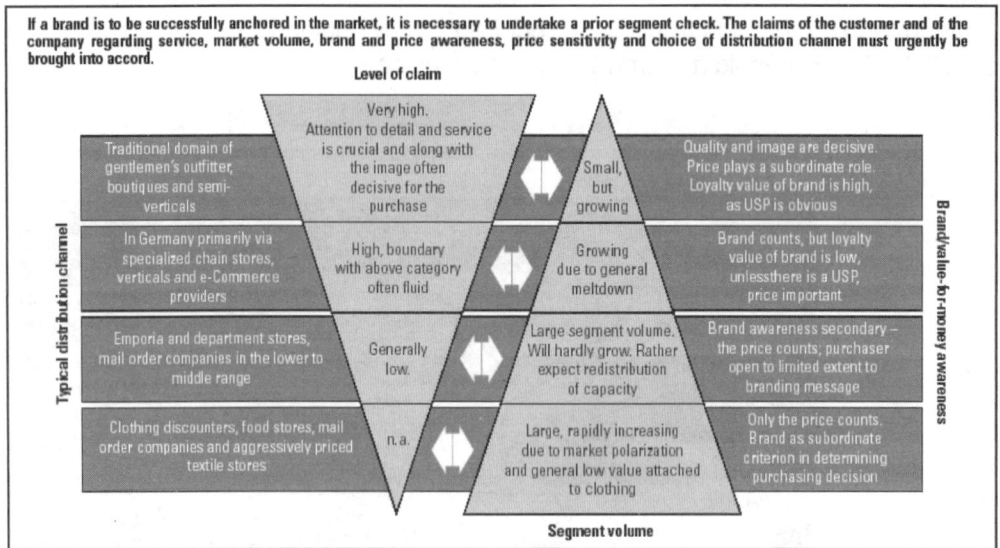

The brand will have to convey a strong coherent image throughout Europe in order to develop recognition and trust. It is also important for the company to segment and target specific markets.

Brand equity is based on the following:

1. *Brand loyalty*:   Encourages customers to buy a particular brand time after time and remain insensitive to competitors' offerings.
2. *Brand awareness*:   Brand names attract attention and convey images of familiarity. This can be translated into how large a percentage of the customers know the brand name.
3. *Perceived quality*:   'perceived' means that the customers decide upon the level of quality, not the company.
4. *Brand association*:   the values and the personality linked to the brand.
5. *Other proprietary brand asset*:   including trademarks, patents and market channel relationships. (Aaker, 1991)

> *The strength, depth and character of the customer-brand relationship is referred to as the brand relationship quality (BRQ). (Marketing Science Institute, 1995)*

Candidates should be able to use these ideas to establish the quality of their answers and some of this should be reflected in their analyses. They can then use the analyses as a base to build their answers.

Note: Examples of indicative analyses are provided in the appendix.

Summary

This case allows for a range of innovative and creative answers. The fashion market is fickle and difficult. Candidates need to understand this as well as the need for Reiss to build a convincing brand. Candidates should also give convincing strategies for CRM development. They should also utilize the growth figures within the European market. The financial results are simply represented and these should be used in the answers.

Note: In all answers, look for the usual, justification, strategic thinking, coherence and detail of information when marking the answers.

In all the answers we will be looking to assess the following.

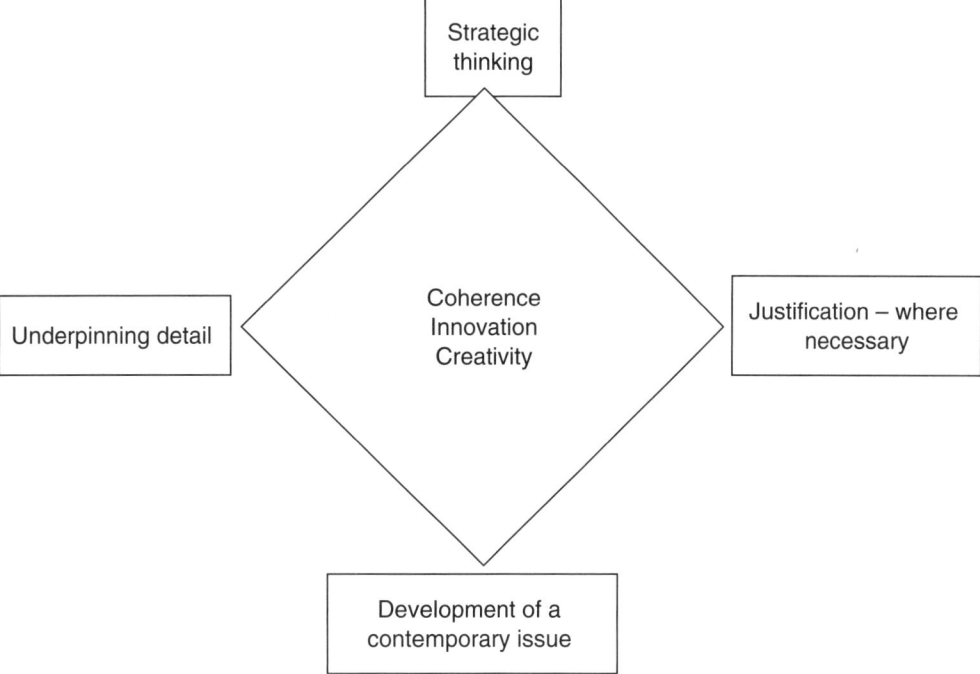

Figure 7.21

Please refer to the student analyses for this case which can be found in Appendix 1 at the back of the book.

appendix 1 student analyses

Titan Industries Ltd

Fig 1 Value Chain

Source: Porter

Firm infrastructure: Hierarchical and autocratic. Not market focused. Lack international structure

HR Management: Ethically & socially positive. Pay high with excellent training
HR does not feature in company structure

Technology: Good core watch tech. R & D good but product focussed.

Procurement: SAP systems. Short supply chain

Inbound	Operations	Outbound	Sales & Marketing	Service
Stock level problems	State of art production facilities	Complex domestic	Large domestic sales force thru distribution system	Good after sales as differentiator domestic
? Parent Co advantages	Use lot manual labour Not suited to manufacture of budget brand	No international structure	No evidence international structure	
			High product/ brand recall	

Falling Operational Margins

Fig 3 Balanced Score Card

Source: Kaplan

Financial	Customer
Low ROCE	100% Brand recall
Liquidity falling/debtors days increasing	Excellent after sales service
Falling operating margins	Strong Ethical stance
Gearing high and increasing	Competitive price – mass market
	Missing out on youth market

Internal Business Process	Innovation & Learning
Product/technology Led	No measure of NPD Sales
International Market research poor despite good MkIS	Time to market too long
Low brand spend compared to competition	Highly trained – satisfied & motivated workforce
Cost structure not suited to budget brands	High % disabled employees
SAP System	No internal Marketing
Large sub brand & product brand portfolio	Good continuous improvement in manufacturing facilities
Multi distribution channels	

Analysis

IMPLEMENTATION

Fig 2 McKinsey's 7S's

Structure
Flat management structure - Strong central figurehead
Lack departmental integration & core support functions
Weak financial management

Staff
Good calibre marketing personnel
Trained, motivated workforce
High percentage disabled
High salary structure for region

Skills
Good IT skills
Strong design & R&D
Trained workforce

Strategy
Mass with Class/Product Led
Not clear if in manufacturing or retailing
Long term plan for global growth

Systems
Automated state art manufacturing (but high unit costs)
Excellent IT systems/MkIS

Style
Quality & reliability
Product Innovation
True to Indian culture

Shared values
Innovation, design, quality & reliability
Ethical beliefs

Fig 4 Financial Chart

	2001/2	2000/1
ROCE	2.78%	2.52%
Liquidity Ratio	4.33	5.28
Gearing	68%	67%
Nett Profit Margin	2.5%	2.28%
Gross Profit Margin	9.27%	13.3%
Debtors (days)	28.6% (104)	22.8% (83)
Creditors (days)	17.4% (64)	13% (48)
Inventory Stock (days)	21% (77)	17% (63)

Fig 5 Pricing in 'mass' watch market

ASP Scnata (450)
ASP Titan (1050)
Edge (4,500 - 5000)
Top priced Steel (6000)

1,000   5,000   10,000   Rupees

Chinese Imports   Japanese Imports   Luxury Swiss watches

positioning strategies of case studies to see who are main competitors are

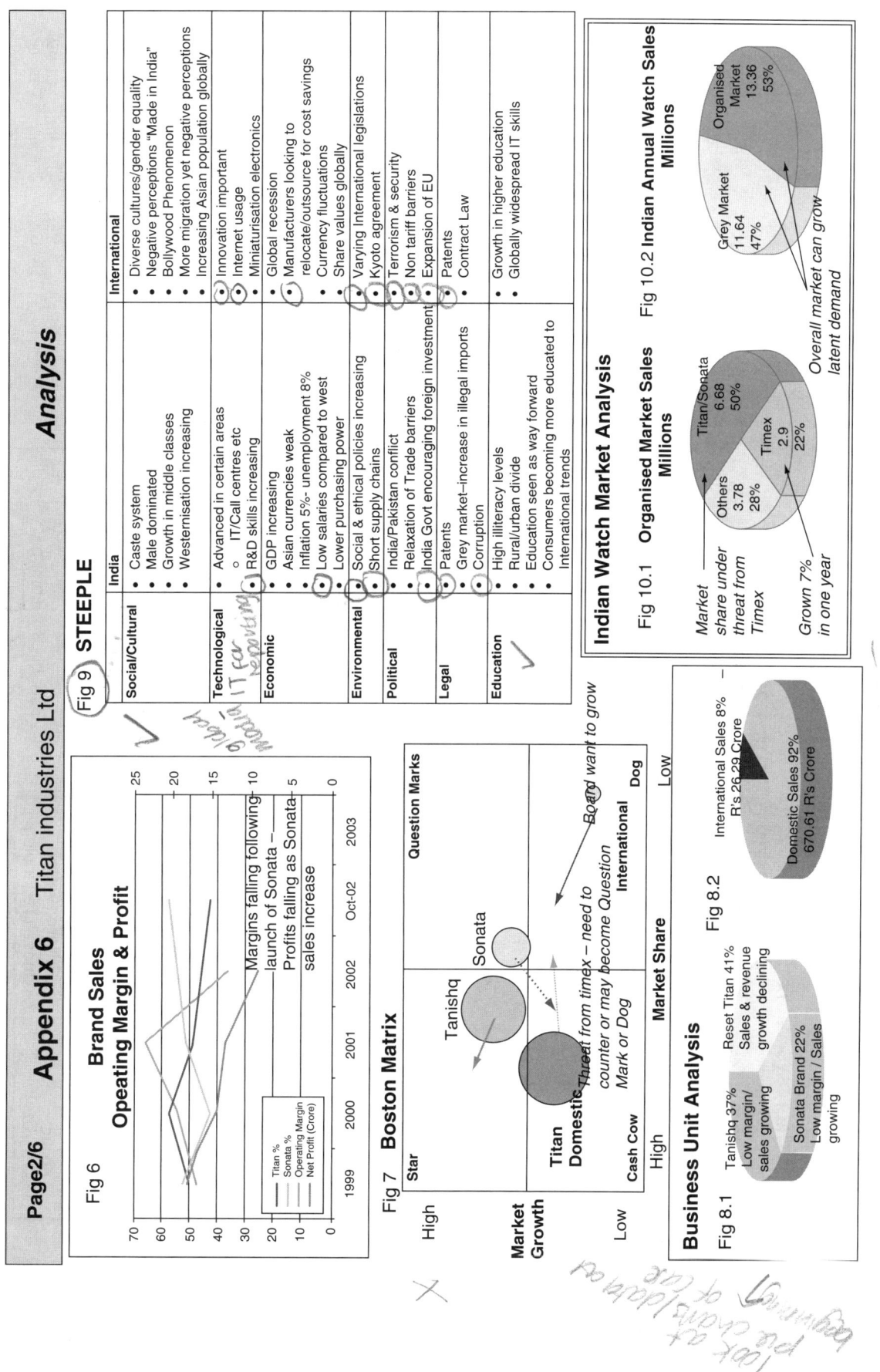

Page2/6   Appendix 6   Titan industries Ltd   Analysis

Fig 6   Brand Sales
Opeating Margin & Profit

Margins falling following —
launch of Sonata —
Profits falling as Sonata-
sales increase

Legend: Titan %; Sonata %; Operating Margin; Net Profit (Crore)
Years: 1999 2000 2001 Oct-02 2003

Fig 7   Boston Matrix

	Star	Question Marks
High	Tanishq	Sonata
Market Growth	Titan	
	Cash Cow Domestic	International Dog
Low		

Market Share: High   Low

Threat from timex – need to counter or may become Question Mark or Dog
Board want to grow

Business Unit Analysis

Fig 8.1   Tanishq 37% Low margin/ sales growing
Sonata Brand 22% Low margin / Sales growing
Reset Titan 41% Sales & revenue growth declining

Fig 8.2   International Sales 8% R's 26.29 Crore
Domestic Sales 92% 670.61 R's Crore

Fig 9   STEEPLE

	India	International
Social/Cultural	• Caste system • Male dominated • Growth in middle classes • Westernisation increasing	• Diverse cultures/gender equality • Negative perceptions "Made in India" • Bollywood Phenomenon • More migration yet negative perceptions • Increasing Asian population globally
Technological	• Advanced in certain areas ○ IT/Call centres etc • R&D skills increasing	• Innovation important • Internet usage • Miniaturisation electronics
Economic	• GDP increasing • Asian currencies weak • Inflation 5%- unemployment 8% • Low salaries compared to west • Lower purchasing power	• Global recession • Manufacturers looking to relocate/outsource for cost savings • Currency fluctuations • Share values globally
Environmental	• Social & ethical policies increasing • Short supply chains	• Varying International legislations • Kyoto agreement
Political	• India/Pakistan conflict • Relaxation of Trade barriers • India Govt encouraging foreign investment	• Terrorism & security • Non tariff barriers • Expansion of EU
Legal	• Patents • Grey market–increase in illegal imports • Corruption	• Patents • Contract Law
Education	• High illiteracy levels • Rural/urban divide • Education seen as way forward • Consumers becoming more educated to International trends	• Growth in higher education • Globally widespread IT skills

Indian Watch Market Analysis

Fig 10.1   Organised Market Sales
Millions
Others 3.78 28%
Titan/Sonata 6.68 50%
Timex 2.9 22%

Market share under threat from Timex
Grown 7% in one year

Fig 10.2 Indian Annual Watch Sales
Millions
Grey Market 11.64 47%
Organised Market 13.36 53%

Overall market can grow latent demand

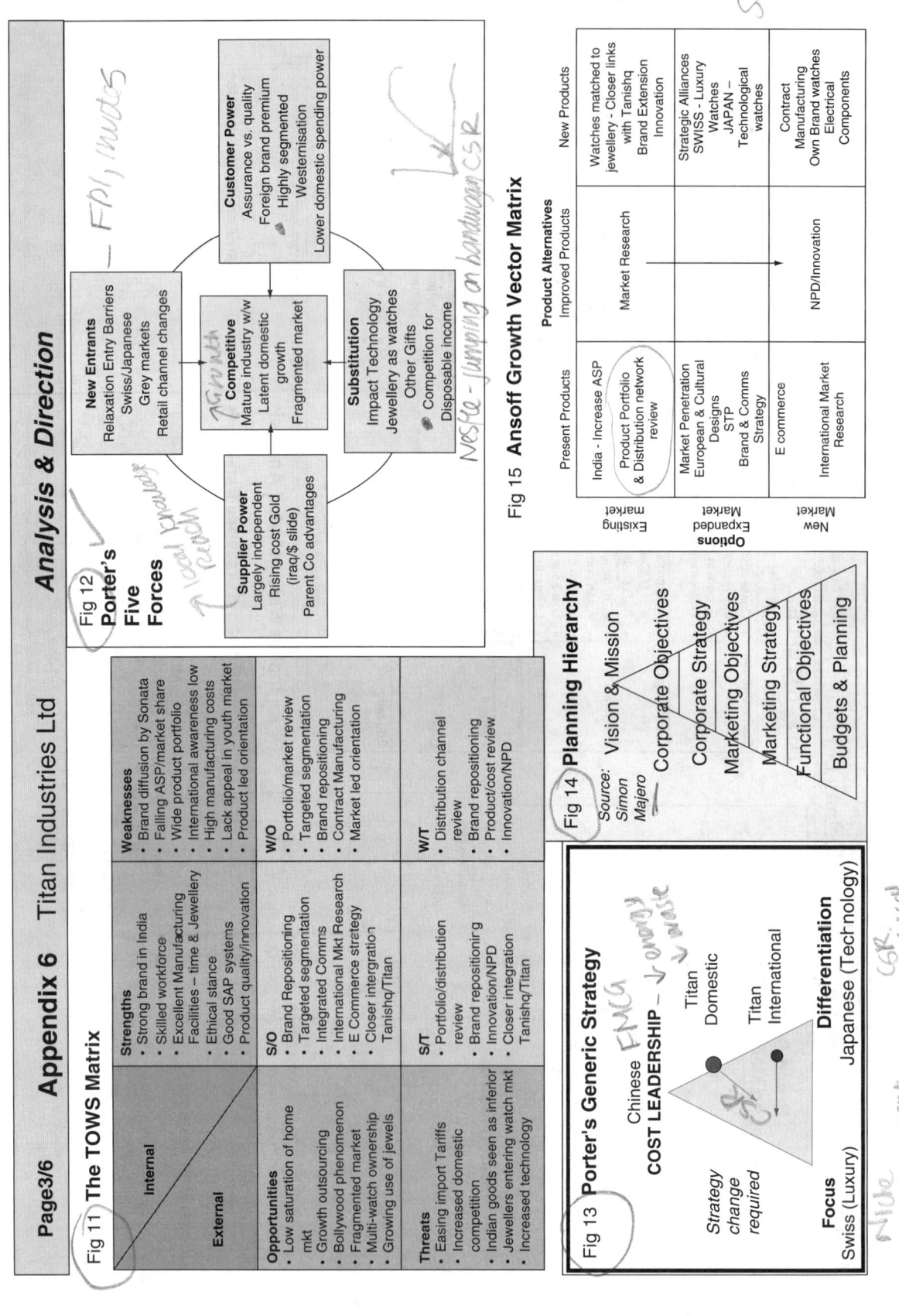

Page3/6 **Appendix 6** **Titan Industries Ltd** **Analysis & Direction**

Fig 11 **The TOWS Matrix**

	Strengths	Weaknesses
Internal	• Strong brand in India • Skilled workforce • Excellent Manufacturing • Facilities – time & Jewellery • Ethical stance • Good SAP systems • Product quality/innovation	• Brand diffusion by Sonata • Falling ASP/market share • Wide product portfolio • International awareness low • High manufacturing costs • Lack appeal in youth market • Product led orientation
External	S/O	W/O
Opportunities • Low saturation of home mkt • Growth outsourcing • Bollywood phenomenon • Fragmented market • Multi-watch ownership • Growing use of jewels	• Brand Repositioning • Targeted segmentation • Integrated Comms • International Mkt Research • E Commerce strategy • Closer intergration Tanishq/Titan	• Portfolio/market review • Targeted segmentation • Brand repositioning • Contract Manufacturing • Market led orientation
	S/T	W/T

Threats
• Easing import Tariffs
• Increased domestic
  competition
• Indian goods seen as inferior
• Jewellers entering watch mkt
• Increased technology
	• Portfolio/distribution
	  review
	• Brand repositioning
	• Innovation/NPD
	• Closer integration
	  Tanishq/Titan
		• Distribution channel
		  review
		• Brand repositioning
		• Product/cost review
		• Innovation/NPD

Fig 12 **Porter's Five Forces**

- **New Entrants** — Relaxation Entry Barriers, Swiss/Japanese, Grey markets, Retail channel changes
- **Customer Power** — Assurance vs. quality, Foreign brand premium, Highly segmented, Westernisation, Lower domestic spending power
- **Competitive** — Mature industry w/w, Latent domestic growth, Fragmented market
- **Substitution** — Impact Technology, Jewellery as watches, Other Gifts, Competition for Disposable income
- **Supplier Power** — Largely independent, Rising cost Gold (iraq/$ slide), Parent Co advantages

Fig 15 **Ansoff Growth Vector Matrix**

Product Alternatives

Options		Present Products	Improved Products	New Products
	Existing market	India - Increase ASP Product Portfolio & Distribution network review	Market Research	Watches matched to jewellery - Closer links with Tanishq Brand Extension Innovation
	Expanded Market	Market Penetration European & Cultural Designs STP Brand & Comms Strategy		Strategic Alliances SWISS - Luxury Watches JAPAN – Technological watches
	New Market	E commerce International Market Research	NPD/Innovation	Contract Manufacturing Own Brand watches Electrical Components

Fig 14 **Planning Hierarchy**

Source: Simon Majero

- Vision & Mission
- Corporate Objectives
- Corporate Strategy
- Marketing Objectives
- Marketing Strategy
- Functional Objectives
- Budgets & Planning

Fig 13 **Porter's Generic Strategy**

- **COST LEADERSHIP** — Chinese
- **Differentiation** — Japanese (Technology)
- **Focus** — Swiss (Luxury)
- Titan Domestic
- Titan International
- *Strategy change required*

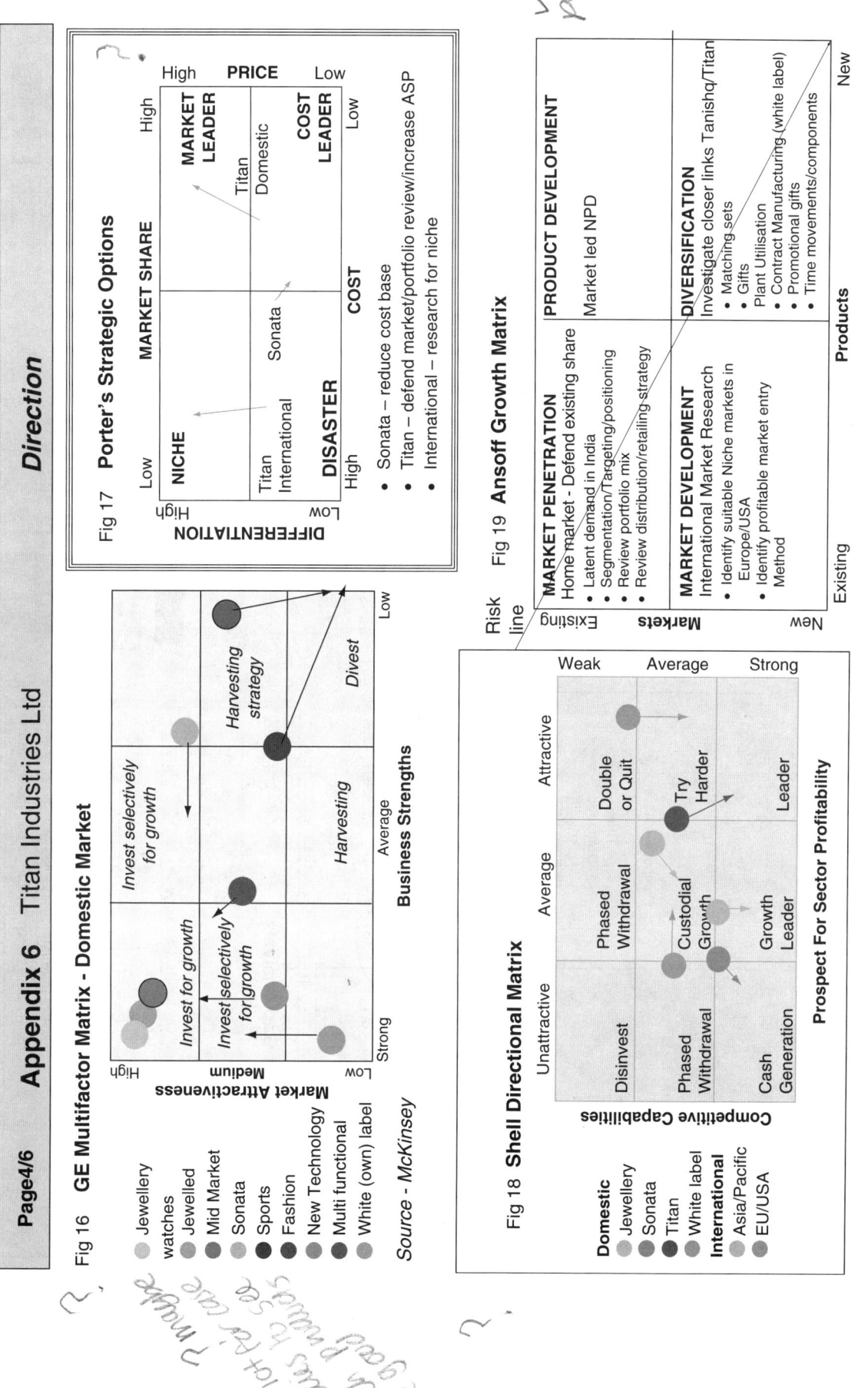

Page4/6 **Appendix 6** Titan Industries Ltd

Direction

Fig 16 **GE Multifactor Matrix - Domestic Market**

Market Attractiveness (High / Medium / Low)
Business Strengths (Strong / Average / Weak)

- Invest for growth
- Invest selectively for growth
- Invest selectively for growth
- Harvesting strategy
- Harvesting
- Divest

Jewellery watches
Jewelled
Mid Market
Sonata
Sports
Fashion
New Technology
Multi functional
White (own) label

Source – McKinsey

Fig 17 **Porter's Strategic Options**

PRICE (High / Low)
MARKET SHARE (High / Low)
DIFFERENTIATION (High / Low)

NICHE
MARKET LEADER
COST LEADER
DISASTER
COST

Titan
Domestic
Sonata
Titan
International

- Sonata – reduce cost base
- Titan – defend market/portfolio review/increase ASP
- International – research for niche

Fig 18 **Shell Directional Matrix**

Prospect For Sector Profitability (Unattractive / Average / Attractive)
Competitive Capabilities (Weak / Average / Strong)

Disinvest
Phased Withdrawal
Cash Generation
Phased Withdrawal
Custodial Growth
Growth Leader
Double or Quit
Try Harder
Leader

Domestic
Jewellery
Sonata
Titan
White label
International
Asia/Pacific
EU/USA

Fig 19 **Ansoff Growth Matrix**

Risk line
Markets (Existing / New)
Products (Existing / New)

MARKET PENETRATION
Home market - Defend existing share
- Latent demand in India
- Segmentation/Targeting/positioning
- Review portfolio mix
- Review distribution/retailing strategy

PRODUCT DEVELOPMENT
Market led NPD

MARKET DEVELOPMENT
International Market Research
- Identify suitable Niche markets in Europe/USA
- Identify profitable market entry Method

DIVERSIFICATION
Investigate closer links Tanishq/Titan (white label)
- Matching sets
- Gifts
- Plant Utilisation
- Contract Manufacturing (white label)
- Promotional gifts
- Time movements/components

225

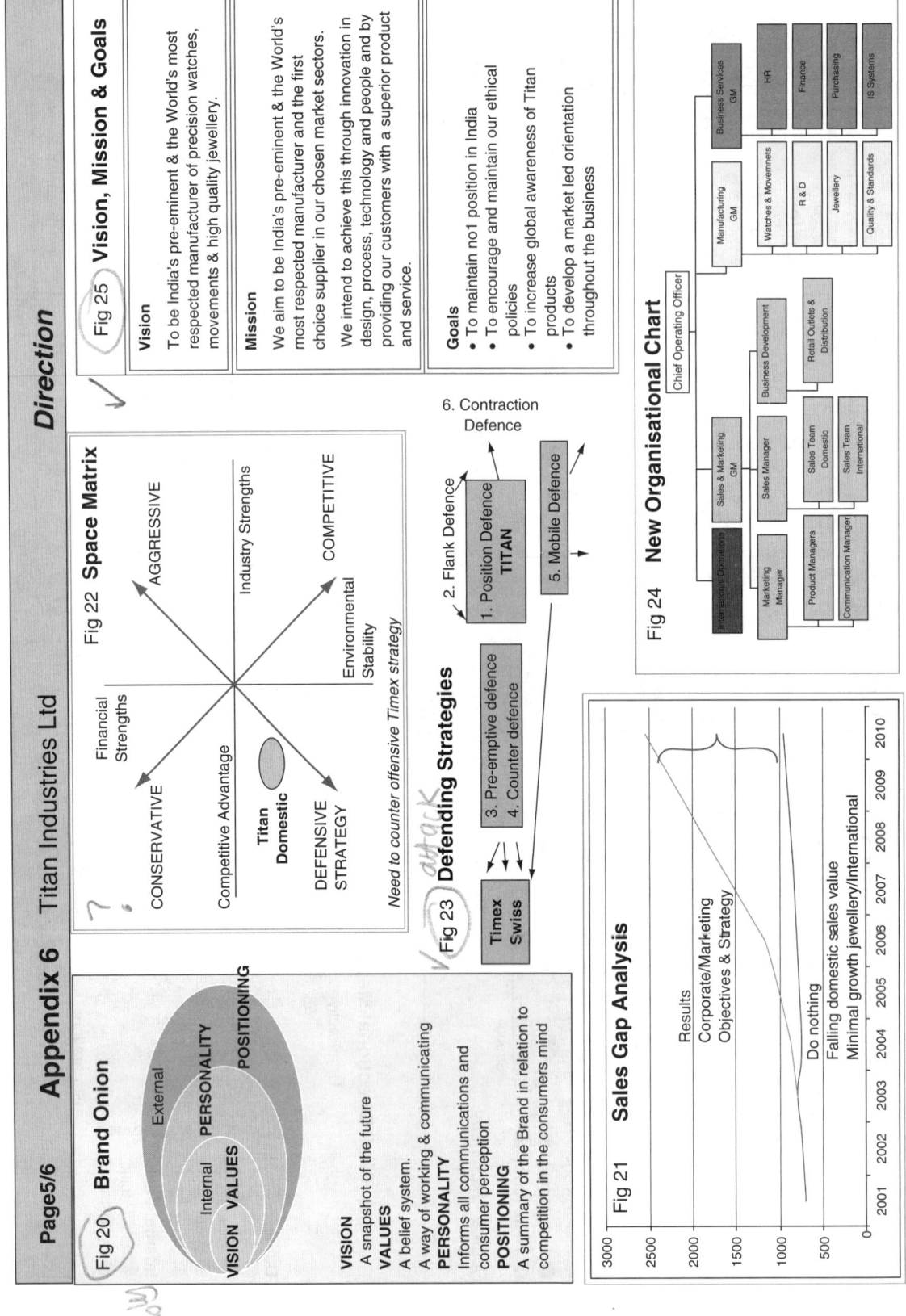

Page5/6 **Appendix 6** Titan Industries Ltd **Direction**

Fig 20 **Brand Onion**

External **PERSONALITY** **POSITIONING**
Internal **VALUES**
VISION

VISION
A snapshot of the future
VALUES
A belief system.
A way of working & communicating
PERSONALITY
Informs all communications and consumer perception
POSITIONING
A summary of the Brand in relation to competition in the consumers mind

Fig 22 **Space Matrix**

AGGRESSIVE
Industry Strengths
COMPETITIVE
Financial Strengths
Environmental Stability
CONSERVATIVE
Competitive Advantage
Titan Domestic
DEFENSIVE STRATEGY

Need to counter offensive Timex strategy

Fig 23 **Defending Strategies**

6. Contraction Defence
2. Flank Defence
1. Position Defence **TITAN**
5. Mobile Defence
3. Pre-emptive defence
4. Counter defence
Timex Swiss

Fig 25 **Vision, Mission & Goals**

Vision
To be India's pre-eminent & the World's most respected manufacturer of precision watches, movements & high quality jewellery.

Mission
We aim to be India's pre-eminent & the World's most respected manufacturer and the first choice supplier in our chosen market sectors.
We intend to achieve this through innovation in design, process, technology and people and by providing our customers with a superior product and service.

Goals
- To maintain no1 position in India
- To encourage and maintain our ethical policies
- To increase global awareness of Titan products
- To develop a market led orientation throughout the business

Fig 24 **New Organisational Chart**

Chief Operating Officer
International Operations
Sales & Marketing GM
Manufacturing GM
Business Services GM
HR
Finance
Purchasing
IS Systems
Marketing Manager
Sales Manager
Business Development
Watches & Movemnets
R & D
Jewellery
Quality & Standards
Product Managers
Sales Team Domestic
Sales Team International
Retail Outlets & Distribution
Communication Manager

Fig 21 **Sales Gap Analysis**

3000
2500
2000
1500
1000
500
0
2001 2002 2003 2004 2005 2006 2007 2008 2009 2010

Results
Corporate/Marketing
Objectives & Strategy
Do nothing
Falling domestic sales value
Minimal growth jewellery/International

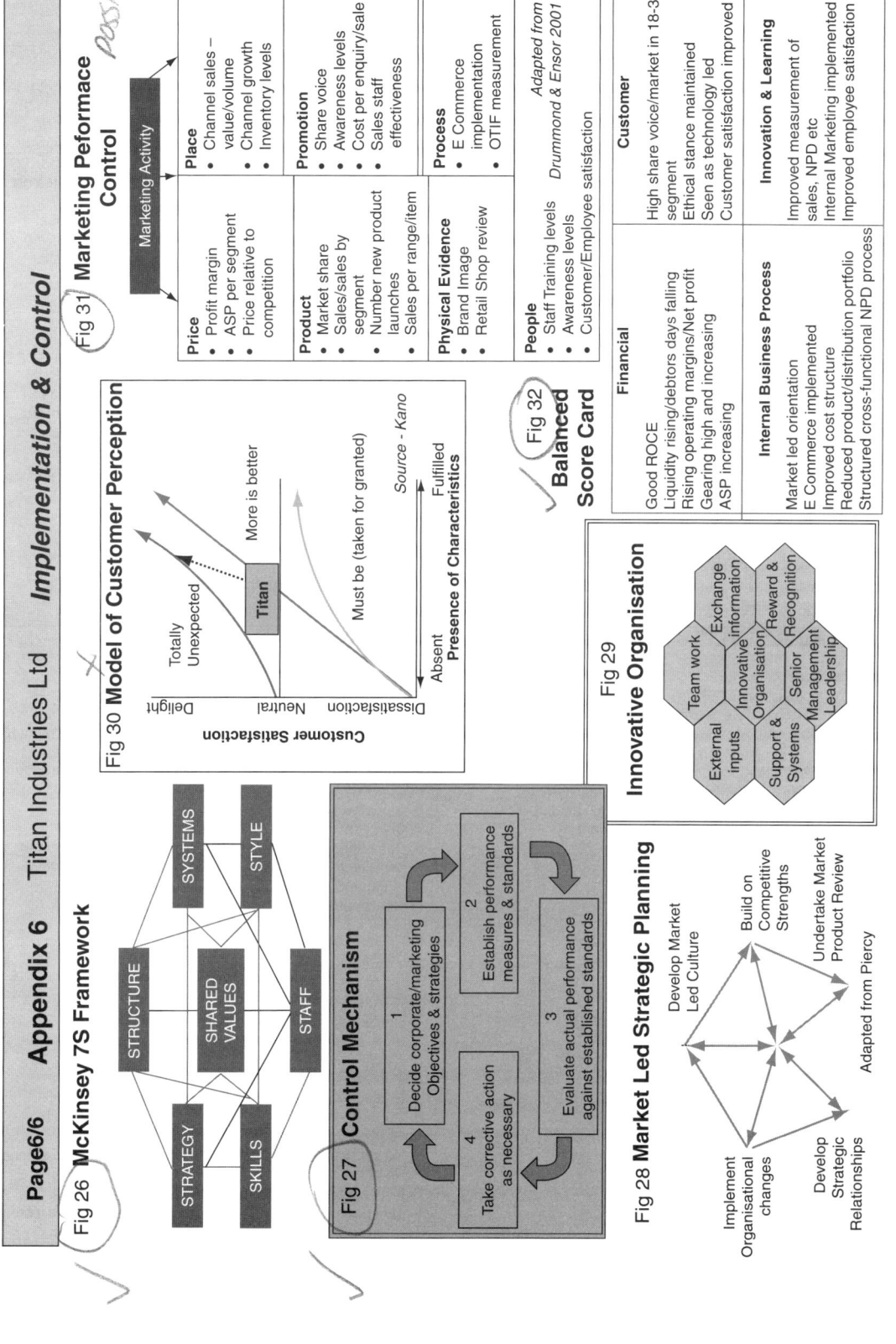

Page6/6   Appendix 6   Titan Industries Ltd   Implementation & Control

Fig 26 **McKinsey 7S Framework**

Fig 27 **Control Mechanism**

Fig 28 **Market Led Strategic Planning**

Fig 29 **Innovative Organisation**

Fig 30 **Model of Customer Perception**

Fig 31 **Marketing Peformace Control**

Fig 32 **Balanced Score Card**

To: The Titan Industries Board **SITUATIONAL ANALYSIS** *(Report 2)*   Date: 13th June 2003
From: Jane Marandi   The report prepared prior to this will be referred to as *Report 1.*

1. PEST Analysis: Ranked by importance from 1 (high) to 10 (low).

1.1. Political & Legal factors
1. India's domestic watch market under threat from foreign imports because import restrictions abolished means increased competition.
2. Increased foreign confidence in India facilitates competition.
3. Legislation over foreign companies entering new geographical markets needs further investigation.
4. Protecting any patents & trademarks may be an issue in overseas markets.
5. India is politically stable.
6. Political unrest in Middle East – may affect demand for luxury goods.
7. Global environmental agreements facilitate international expansion.

1.2. Technological Factors
1. Competitors in watch market are producing watches with added features that are technology based (Report 1 pp21-2) achieving competitive advantage.
2. Distribution – new technology e.g. Internet, interactive digital TV offers new channels to market.
3. Internet developments provide a further platform to promote products & services.
4. Intranets on a global scale provide fast & efficient global communication to supply chain networks.
5. Globalisation of technology means new watch production techniques are easily copied – no longer a base for sustainable competitive advantage.

1.3. Social Factors
1. Significant globalisation of trends, styles & cultures with increased & wider acceptance of foreign cultures in all domestic markets
2. Horizontal segmentation now possible with the identification of similarities among consumers around the globe. Hybridisation in preconceptions & perceptions of India.
3. Changing buying patterns. Demanding different watch attributes for different occasions.
4. TI has strong ethical stance.
5. Watches becoming items of jewellery.
6. Indian culture - jewellery sets are meaningful gifts.
7. Consumers demanding more augmented product features.

1.4. Economic factors
1. Since 1997, situation in Asia & weakness of currencies has increased the buying power of Western brands globally.
2. US economic climate falling since March 2001 – consumer confidence may be hit.
3. UK economic climate favourable to increase spending by consumers.
4. Currency fluctuations paramount when looking internationally. Huge financial investment involved & currency fluctuations dangerous.
5. Interest rate problems in India.
6. Ex-pat Asian Indians - high average per capita income.
7. Generally slowing global economy.

2. Ranked SWOT Analysis: Ranked by importance from 1 (high) to 10 (low).

Opportunities:
1. Use technological innovations - develop new designs & features to be competitive & exploit niche markets.
2. Strong global cultural support for Indian-made products.
3. Increasing Asian American market to exploit – globalisation/self-reference criterion used.
4. Target youth - increase lifetime value of customers.
5. UK - luxury watches driving growth in watch market with a shift towards upmarket & premium priced goods.
6. Global luxury watch market growing – reflects economic prosperity in individual countries.
7. Report 1 shows US importing more of all watch types (increase average +8% 1999-2000).
8. Potential to expand existing retail outlets.
9. Acquisition of Swiss watch manufacturer.
10. Build experience stores as flagships in new markets.

Threats:
1. Removal of import barriers into India - cheaper watches in domestic market.
2. New global substitutes due to technological developments.
3. Japanese/Swiss imports influencing domestic market.
4. European competitors exercising control over their distributors.
5. Currency fluctuations.
6. Globally competition in all price bands is increasing.
7. Changes in European tastes & styles.
8. Competition in customer service or after-sales support.
9. Legislation from regional trading areas on 'outsider' imports.
10. Future ISO certifications required for goods sold internationally - may require further investment.

Strengths:
1. Marketing orientation throughout company.
2. Leaders in innovation & design with global appeal.
3. 100% brand awareness & strong brand equity in India.
4. Cover many market segments with different sub-brands.
5. Developed a global retail chain controlled by them - exclusive distribution key to their brand equity.
6. Extensive customer service network & SAP Supply chain management system – strong IT focus.
7. Good MkIS developed.
8. Positive country of origin effect.
9. Well-perceived & established ethical stances.
10. Fully integrated manufacturing facilities close together.

Weaknesses:
1. Limited brand awareness outside domestic market.
2. Product portfolio too big for entering unprotected markets.
3. Relative newcomer to the watch industry - difficult to be perceived as luxury brand without 'heritage'.
4. Limited research done on new international markets.
5. Success of 'Sonata' - impacting on overall cost structure - not getting the returns they need.
6. No strong relationships established with European distributors.
7. Negative country of origin effects.
8. Poor past experiences of European markets.
9. TI experiencing cash flow problems as debtors' days increase.
10. Current international exploits are making a loss.

3. Porter's Five Forces *(Model adapted from Porter 1980)*

Potential Entrants
- Low barriers to entry to the luxury watch market means TI needs to protect its position.
- Leading designer clothes companies producing timepieces (e.g. Gucci, DKNY) – easier for established brands.
- China entering market with relatively cheap watch products - threat from other NICs doing the same (advantage of established technology & skills base in Asia).

Suppliers
- Currently supplier power is low.
- TI has international suppliers: opened up their supply chains but need to take care over contract terms & conditions. Make sure that they can withdraw from any contract easily.
- Advantageous to source components from NICs or other developing countries where cheap to purchase & suppliers have less bargaining power (to be traded off against purchasing higher quality, more expensive components from European countries where supplier bargaining power may not be so low).

Intra-industry Rivalry
- Watch market is highly competitive
- Market has not reached maturity.
- Increased presence from non-watch specialist competitors.
- Increased variety of watches and variations.
- Changing retail sector & growth of department stores means head-on competition with other market players with similar distribution options.

Buyers
- Consumers have more choice than ever. Advances in technology, e.g. the Internet, means purchase watches from anywhere. Imperative that TI determine target markets' perceived important factors when buying a watch (specifically purchase context). Need for extensive research.
- International luxury goods market is growing as consumer wealth & sophistication increases – more consumer choice.
- Market is highly fragmented & highly competitive.
- Need to research different buying motivations of consumers.

Threat of Indirect Substitutes
- Consumers can use other items as a timepiece that isn't a watch e.g. mobile phones, PalmPilots, PDAs etc.
- Consumers may choose to buy other personal adornment items if horological function not required.
- If an investment being made – stocks, shares & antiques are potential substitutes.
- Consider purchasing context – e.g. as a gift purchasers may choose elaborate jewellery over a watch.

4. Financial Overview

Since there is limited financial data available on Titan Industries, the performance of sub-brands (with the exception of the Sonata range) and international operations only a brief analysis of the figures provided in Report 1 could be undertaken. The following observations can be noted for Titan Industries (TI) between 2001 & 2002:

Key ratio	Value	Comment
Gross Profit Net Profit	decreased by 3% decreased by 0.2%	reflects the slowing down of the global economy & decrease in profitability
ROCE	12.6% in 2002	reasonable but need to improve to increase profitability.
Liquidity ratio	0.82 in 2002	Insolvency? Could raise current assets, increase equity, and pay back debt.
Stock turnover	improved from 3.56 to 4.89	too high as cash is being tied up in capital assets
Stock days	decreased (from 102.5 to 74.6)	See above.
Debtor days	increased from 83 to 104	reflects bad debts – could review distribution methods
Gearing	67.9% for 2002	Slight decrease but still high. Aim for 50% of debt + equity.
Share Price against BSE Sensex	Stable	Offers shareholders (potential/existing) a low risk, low return investment. Will not attract venture capitalists.
With regard to the Asia Pacific arm of the organisation it would be advisable to investigate further before drawing any conclusions about a strategic way forward.		

5. Strategic Options *(Model adapted from Ansoff)*

	Existing Products	Related Products	New Products
Existing Markets	**Market Penetration:** 1. *Create More Users* (currently only 25 per '000 watch owners) 1.1. Continue to promote Sonata range 1.2. Maintain high customer service levels 1.3. Promote all brands cost-effectively 2. *Increase Usage from Existing Customers* (domestic market only) 2.1. Change positioning of sub-brands 2.2. Marketing alliance with Tanishq jewellery.	1. Improve on existing sub-brands 2. Design & manufacture a 'private label' watch. 3. Develop a watch to supply to retailers as 'own label'.	**Product Development:** 1. Create new sub-brands focused on niche markets i.e. "more than just a watch". 2. Create sub-brands with added features using technological advances. 3. Create a more fashion-led sub-brand for younger market to increase brand loyalty over time. 4. Develop sub-brand with interchangeable straps/faces.
Related Markets	3. *Attract Competitors' Customers* 3.1. Promote 'Indian-made' values (to devalue foreign imports) 3.2. Maintain 'youth' image to compete with Japanese imports. 3.3. Promote Sonata quality to compete against cheap Chinese imports. 3.4. Push differentiation based on service levels. 3.5. Create barriers to entry – reward distribution channels.		
New Markets	**Market Development:** 1. *Target New Segments* 1.1. Technology-aware Third Age consumers. 1.2. Fashion-conscious youth market (<21 yrs old) - complement Sonata range. 2. *Enter new Geographical Markets* 2.1. Horizontal segments for sub-brands. 2.2. Ex-pat. Asian Indian consumers. 2.3. International niche markets based on consumers' perceived differentiation. 2.4. New markets with similar cultural profile of users e.g. UK, USA, South Africa & Australia.	4. Use new distribution channels 5. Expand offering into broader market of personal adornment using existing skills/technology e.g. complementary hair accessories, earrings, spectacles (sun/prescription).	**Diversification:** Use strategic partnerships or acquisitions (to minimise risk) 1. *Clothing* 1.1. Sportswear. 1.2. 'High Street' or 'Designer' fashion. 2. *Home ware* - e.g. ornaments, picture frames, vases. 3. *Leather accessories* e.g. handbags, gloves, wallets. 4. *Designer executive accessories* e.g. engraved pens, money clips, business card holders. 5. *Component Manufacture* for other industries requiring quality engineering.

6. Multi-directional Policy Matrix Model *(adapted from the GE Model)*

(using criteria from Report 1 p.19)	Domestic Market	International Market
Luxury	Insignia, Nebula, Regalia & Royale, Raga	Insignia, Nebula, Regalia & Royale, Raga, Ovations 2000, Euro Watches
Medium range	Titan Steel, Fastrack, Classique	Titan Steel, Fastrack, Classique
Mass market	Sonata	Sonata

Market Attractiveness: • market growth rate • strength of competition • social factors • profit opportunity	**Business Strengths:** • 100% brand awareness & strong brand equity in India • controlled distribution network • leaders in design & technology • extensive customer service network

Relative Business Strengths

This model shows different brands can be leveraged to achieve goals on both an international & domestic level.
• different products have different roles e.g. Luxury sub-brands could be invested in for growth while Sonata can be maintained.
• need to establish different reward systems & types of managers for the sub-brands to succeed.

7. Porter's Generic Strategies *(Model Adapted from Porter '1980)*

Report 1 on TI suggests current strategy is '**stuck in the middle'.** They have broad product portfolio but are unable to maximise revenue and market potential on all of them at the same time. Whilst the Tanishq jewellery range is prospering, the success of the Sonata range is impacting TI's overall profitability. International strategies are failing.

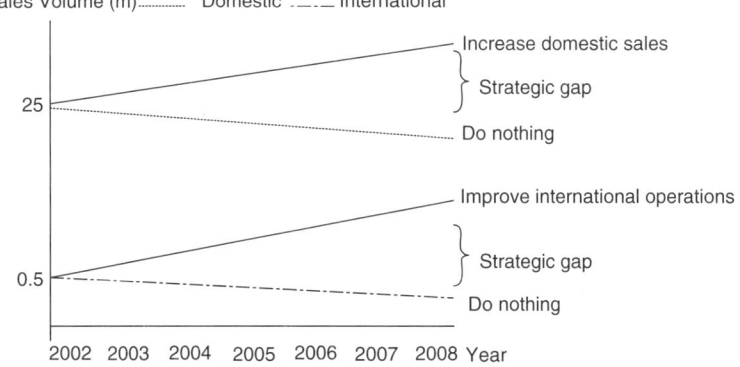

Cost Leadership

Focus   Differentiation

8. Gap Analysis

Sales Volume (m) ——— Domestic ‒·‒·‒ International

Increase domestic sales

} Strategic gap

Do nothing

Improve international operations

} Strategic gap

Do nothing

25

0.5

2002 2003 2004 2005 2006 2007 2008 Year

Report 1 indicates there are several corporate goals for TI:
6.1. Maintain domestic market position as market leader in watch manufacturing
6.2. Improve profitability of international operations (new strategy needed?)
6.3. Develop niche markets internationally

The options available to reduce these strategic gaps are discussed in section 6 using an adapted directional policy matrix.

KEY EXTERNAL ISSUES:
- Global watch market growing
- Enjoying extreme success in domestic market
- Increased competition in the domestic market
- Strong potential for niche international markets
- Highly fragmented industry (watches)
- Currency fluctuations paramount

KEY INTERNAL ISSUES:
- Low brand awareness internationally – review branding (country of origin effect) & distribution
- Strong domestic brand awareness
- Making losses in international markets
- Need to improve financial situation
- Good after-sales/customer service networks established
- Large product portfolio

9. Other Organisational Assets *(adapted from Hooley et al., 1998)*

Marketing Assets	Comment
Customer based	Image & reputation – strong in domestic market. Low in international markets.
	Brand franchises – assume relatively high brand loyalty in domestic market with competitive advantage established. This needs to be made sustainable over time.
	Unique products & services – exist in domestic market. Potential in international markets.
Distribution based	Level of control – high in domestic market. Weak in international markets creating bad debts and poor cash flow.
	Geographical coverage & quality of network – good in domestic market, need to maintain. Internationally have physical presence in several countries (report 1 p25) e.g. UK, Middle East & Asia Pacific but operating at a loss for Titan overall. Opportunity to improve quality of network or withdraw and start afresh because links already established.
Internally based	Cost structure – assume that since manufacturing facilities close together this means a favourable cost structure for TI. This could be used to achieve higher margins domestically & internationally.
	Information systems – see section 2 Strengths points 6 & 7. Good customer and retailer data available.
External Relationships	Access to markets – strong reputation in domestic market means possibility of forging alliances with more distributors or negotiate better terms with current distributors. Internationally a well respected company especially in Far East, TI could develop partnerships in new countries e.g. as with Samson Enterprises in Malaysia.
	Access to technological developments & processes – strong in-house R&D and design facility. Already developed a proven success in domestic market with Titan Edge.
	Exclusive agreements – opportunity for international markets to build barriers to entry for competitors.

10. Value Chain Analysis

needed

Support Activities

Firm's infrastructure:
• strong organisational structure to support new development strategies domestically & internationally.
• marketing focused management style gives strength to new initiatives being rolled out effectively.
• marketing orientated culture with positive attitude and strong belief in the Titan brand.
• well established systems in domestic market need to be used effectively on international level.

HR management:
• recruitment – need staff that understand targets & requirements of any strategic plans, not necessarily of Indian origin.
• training – need to provide initial and on-going training both domestically & internationally.
• rewards – domestic market rewards related to customer retention & development, international markets reward relating to new customers won.

Technology development:
• domestic market needs to exploit strength in this area for customers and intermediaries.
• not an immediate area of concern for the international market.

fair trade?

Procurement:
• need to ensure inputs are purchased at competitive rates without comprosing quality. Can look to international supply chains.

Inbound Logistics:	Operations:	Outbound Logistics:	Marketing & Sales:	Service:
• keep stock levels to a minimum to free up capital. • have suppliers on quick response delivery arrangement.	• maintain manufacturing facilities in India. • could look to overseas manufacture in the future.	• avoid accumulation of stock. • distribute product in line with demand.	• new focus for international markets – promotional mix paramount.	• well-established in domestic market • need to develop service/repaire network for international markets. • provide training for distributors & retailers.

margin

Primary Activities

Marketing VCA

10. Customer Buying Behaviour *(model adapted from Assael 1987)*

Customer's degree of involvement with the product

		Low	High
Degree & significance of differences between brand alternatives	Low	Repetitive buying behaviour	Behaviour designed to reduce buyer dissonance (International Titan brand)
	High	A search for variety (Domestic Titan brand)	Complex buying behaviour

This indicates that Titan's approach in the domestic market of different brands for different occasions works well with the consumer buying behaviour there. Internationally, Titan has less presence and this is reflected by their position where buyers will reduce dissonance and go with a more prevalent brand e.g. Swiss or Japanese that they have more knowledge/awareness of.

11. Competitor Analysis
(adapted model from Report 1 p20)

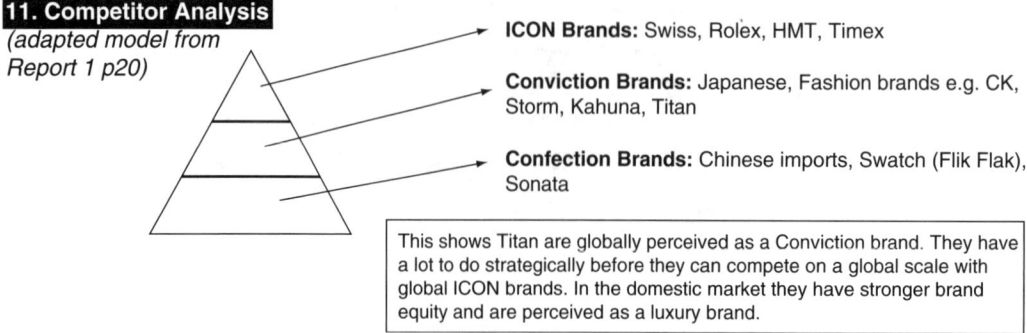

ICON Brands: Swiss, Rolex, HMT, Timex

Conviction Brands: Japanese, Fashion brands e.g. CK, Storm, Kahuna, Titan

Confection Brands: Chinese imports, Swatch (Flik Flak), Sonata

This shows Titan are globally perceived as a Conviction brand. They have a lot to do strategically before they can compete on a global scale with global ICON brands. In the domestic market they have stronger brand equity and are perceived as a luxury brand.

12. Sales Trends Using data from Report 1 p48 the following graphs were plotted:

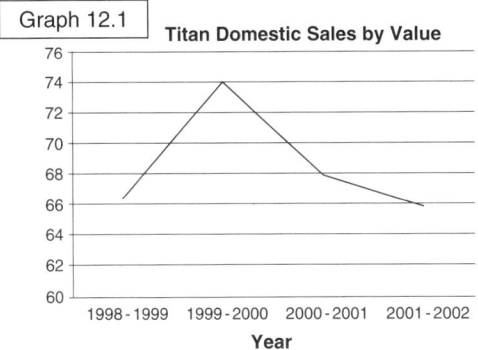

Graph 12.1

Titan Domestic Sales by Value

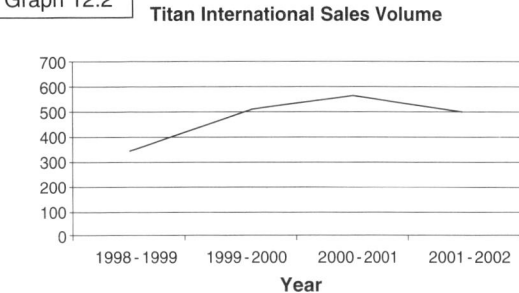

Graph 12.2

Titan International Sales Volume

Graph 12.1 shows that in the domestic market the Titan brand sales as a % of total sales has reached 74% but has since declined. It is possible that this figure can be reached again and even be exceeded since the volume of watch sales in India is reported as being only 25 sales per '000 consumers (report 1 p13). There is huge potential in the domestic market.

Graph 12.2 shows how Titan's international sales have progressed over the last 4 years. Sales volume exceed 500 000 from 1999-2001 and there is potential for this to be achieved again. Yet, at a broader perspective report 1 p19 states that total watch units (assume this is recent data) were at 500 million, demonstrating a huge volume Titan can 'gain' on the global market.

13. Customer Analysis Segmentation – it is best to segment consumers of Titan's products as follows:

	Domestic	International
Luxury	Affluent adults (30-65yrs) with high disposable income used for maintaining a high standard of living & investment. Mid to upper class professionals that work hard & play hard. Take luxury holidays, read a quality daily newspaper, don't watch much TV except for daily news programmes & documentaries. May subscribe to special interest magazines e.g. golf, sailing, gardening. May commute to work & travel at weekends so exposed to outdoor media. Strong Indian culture, seeking to demonstrate wealth & status. May view timepieces as an investment. Located in high-density cities and surrounding suburban areas. Shop in exclusive (own brand or multi-brand) outlets. Can afford different watches for different occasions. See exclusive watches as significant symbol &/or gift for loved ones and as key lifetime milestone gifts e.g. retirement, child's 21st birthday.	As 'domestic' profile but culture is more Westernised (in developed countries especially) therefore may have preconceptions of Indian-made products. Seek established brands. If making an investment will conduct a wider information search on product options. Exposed to and used to established international watch brands. Ex-pat Asian Indians of this profile will view Titan as a luxury brand.
Medium Range	Young adults (18-30yrs) & less affluent older adults (30-65yrs). Blue-collar workers, skilled manual workers and junior management employment status. Proud of their Indian culture but influenced by Western culture. Watch a fair amount of TV and younger adults read entertainment & popular culture magazines. Use public transport a lot. Younger adults seek heightened image, quite fashion conscious. Urban & suburban dwellers with income to spend cautiously. Look for value for money from known brands (i.e. mass with class). Majority only able to afford one watch but aspire to having more than one for different occasions. Watches viewed as being more practical than item of personal adornment.	As 'domestic' profile but include ex-pat. Asian Indian customers who will use self-reference criteria and go with a brand they know. Other cultures will be tied to their country. They seek value for money but also added features on watches. Open to owning more than one watch if the design & function meets their requirements.
Mass Market	Low wage/unemployed adults (18-65yrs). Seeking good value for money and function from a timepiece. Not influenced by branding unless the price is right. Seek a quality item with importance placed on intrinsic values. Don't consider having more than one watch because all watches tell the time.	As 'domestic' profile. Differences in culture will be tied to their country of origin/upbringing.

Reiss

Analysis

Page1/6   Appendix 5 Reiss

Fig 1 - Porter Value Chain Analysis

Infrastructure:- 26 Retail stores in UK, plans to provide central merged location. Doesn't support customer orientation.

Management:- Staff presentation & training key to Reiss Success. Current orgnisation informal staff located across multiple locations. HR may be subcontracted. Staff training in-house?

Technology:- Limited IT & internet strategy –No evidence of MKiS or CRM / SCM or Inventory Management. No Localised Info Systems N> E-Business

Procurement:- Major challenges from lack of economies of scales to no recognition of Supply chain management. Sell own brand only. Conflict between buyers & designers.

Inbound Logistics	Operations	Outbound Logistics	Sales Marketing	Service
Merchandising reports from FD? Inefficient Stock Management. Relationship with suppliers? Distribution work? How efficient is the supply chain?	No evidence of Key Performance Indicators (KPIs) Where is their manufacturing done? How efficient is it?	26 Stores in UK. Ceased Wholesaling in 2001. Use own carrier or subcontract?	No marketing. Activities focus on PR & store design. Why sell Books & CDs? Use PR & WOM as promotional tools.	Shopping experience not complete – Need Analysis of Relationships / CRM Is training ongoing?

Primary Activities

Margin — Excellent by any terms

Fig 2. Balanced Score card   Source – Kapplan & Norton 1996

Customer
Women in work increasing – more tailored clothing
Increase in designer-wear purchased
Bored with shopping experience
Cautious spending patterns

Financial
Good ROI/ROCE
Poor cash flow
Poor stock turnover
Debtors days are good
Creditors days good - maybe pay too quickly.

Innovation / Learning
lack or KPIs
Fragmented NPD process
FD involved in merchandis ng?
Good employee training
Improving management communication

Business Process
Supply chain – time to market
Lack of clear IT strategy
Lack of communication in management team

Fig 3 - McKinseys 7 S's

Strategy	Clothes only bought through the stores – more control (over the counter sales) No advertising, just PR Bridges market between high st. and international designer brands. Design complemented through the store environment & individual store aesthetics. Moved into women's wear in 2000. Expanded to include accessories Ceased wholesaling in 2001
Skills	Entrepreneur Designers –competitive advantage. Innovation & Creativity Good merchandising dept
Staff	Service levels are important Training for induction but no CPD Lack of departmental interaction.
Structure	No marketing department Disjointed management team Lacking a strategy team that can plot future
Systems	All the stores individually merchandised Merchandising under finance – improved flow and management of product Long stock turnover period No evidence of CRM, MKIS or E-POS
Style	Family business David Reiss: Entrepreneur & dictatorship, he makes all decisions "small family business" culture Current communicatons is disjointed.
Shared Values	Staff should share good customer service values & ethics This should be invoked from top down. There should be a common vision Offering the customer something new.

Page2/6 Appendix 5 Reiss

Analysis

Fig 4 Financials

Profitability Ratios	Reiss		
	2003	2002	2001
Net Profit Margin	6%	3%	4%
Asset Turnover	150%	152%	150%
ROCE / ROI	17%	10%	13%
Operational Ratios			
Debtors Turnover Period	0.00	0.00	0.01
Debtor Days	1.22	1.11	3.35
Stock Turnover	0.14	0.12	0.14
Stock Turnover Period	52.17	43.85	50.66
Creditor Turnover	0.06	0.06	0.11
Creditor Turnover Period	22.90	23.56	38.60
Liquidity Ratios			
Current Ratio: 1	0.65	0.74	0.75
Quick Ratio: 1	0.22	0.35	0.34
Gearing	34%	47%	52%
Sales / Ft Sq'd	£298.33	£329.78	£420.31

(approx 70k ft Sq 2003)
(approx 55k ft Sq 2002)
(approx 42k ft Sq 2001)

Callouts:
- Asset Turnover good (for every £1 invested, Reiss grows 50%)
- ROCE is much better than most other businesses
- Stock turnover days too long for fashion industry
- Low liquidity which is decreasing Gearing compounded by this.
- Sales per Sq/Ft is dropping – loss of focus ?

Fig 5 - STEEPLE Analysis

Socio / cultural	Economical
Increasing population 55yrs+	Economic indicators (exch rates)
Increasing population 15-24yrs	Impact of Credit Card Fraud
Increasing size requirement	Impact Purchasing and Retailing
Internationalisation of fashion	Emergence from Recession
New shopping experiences	Working Women / PDI Growing
Brand consciousness	Retail Price Deflation
Growth of women in work	Globalisation / Cheap Labour
Men becoming fashion conscious	Expansion of WTO / EU
Cash rich, time poor	Retail Industry Consolidation
Fair trade – 'sweat shops'	Relocation Outsourcing

Technological	Political / Legal
Fabric & Electronic Technology (smart fabrics)	Grey / Counterfeit Markets
Product Development,	War Against Terror
Fickle Industry – Shorter PLCs	Design Copyrights
Growth of The Internet & E-Business	EU Expansion / Euro
24/7 shopping	Ethics Impact (Post Enron)
Shortening of Supply Chains	Patent Handing (Or Lack Of)
Impact of RFID (Radio Frequency Identification)	Consumer law
	Retail law

Education	Environmental
Increasing Higher Education	Impact of Climate on Sales
Better Consumer Education	More casual leisurewear
Intelligent consumers	Seasonal variation
HR issues (over qualified staff)	Urban vs rural
Global Communications	Recycling issues
	Corporate Responsibility
	Waste Processing
	Kyoto Protocol / Climate Change

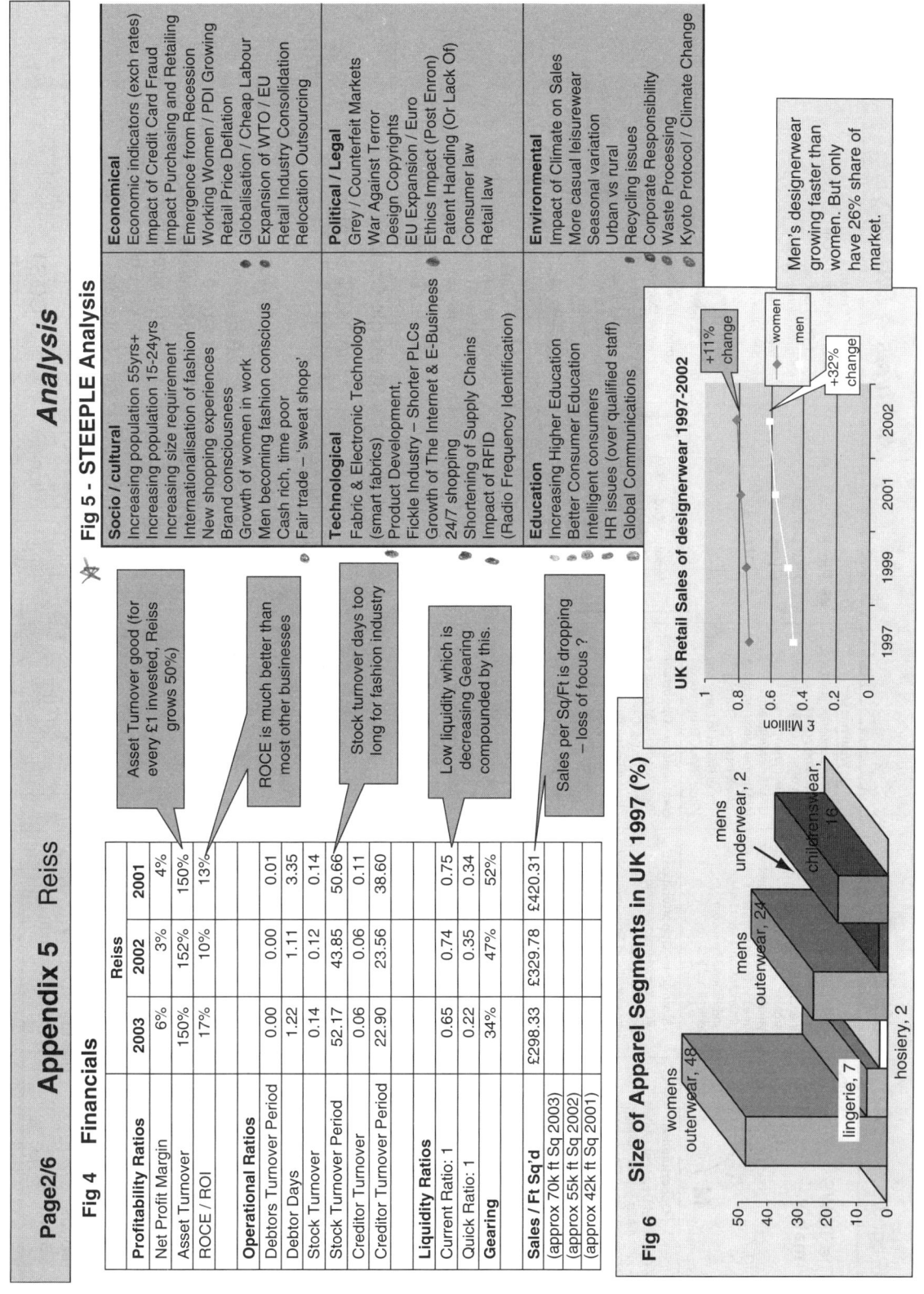

Fig 6 Size of Apparel Segments in UK 1997 (%)

womens outerwear, 48; mens outerwear, 24; mens underwear, 2; childrenswear, 16; hosiery, 2; lingerie, 7

UK Retail Sales of designerwear 1997-2002

women +11% change; men +32% change

Men's designerwear growing faster than women. But only have 26% share of market.

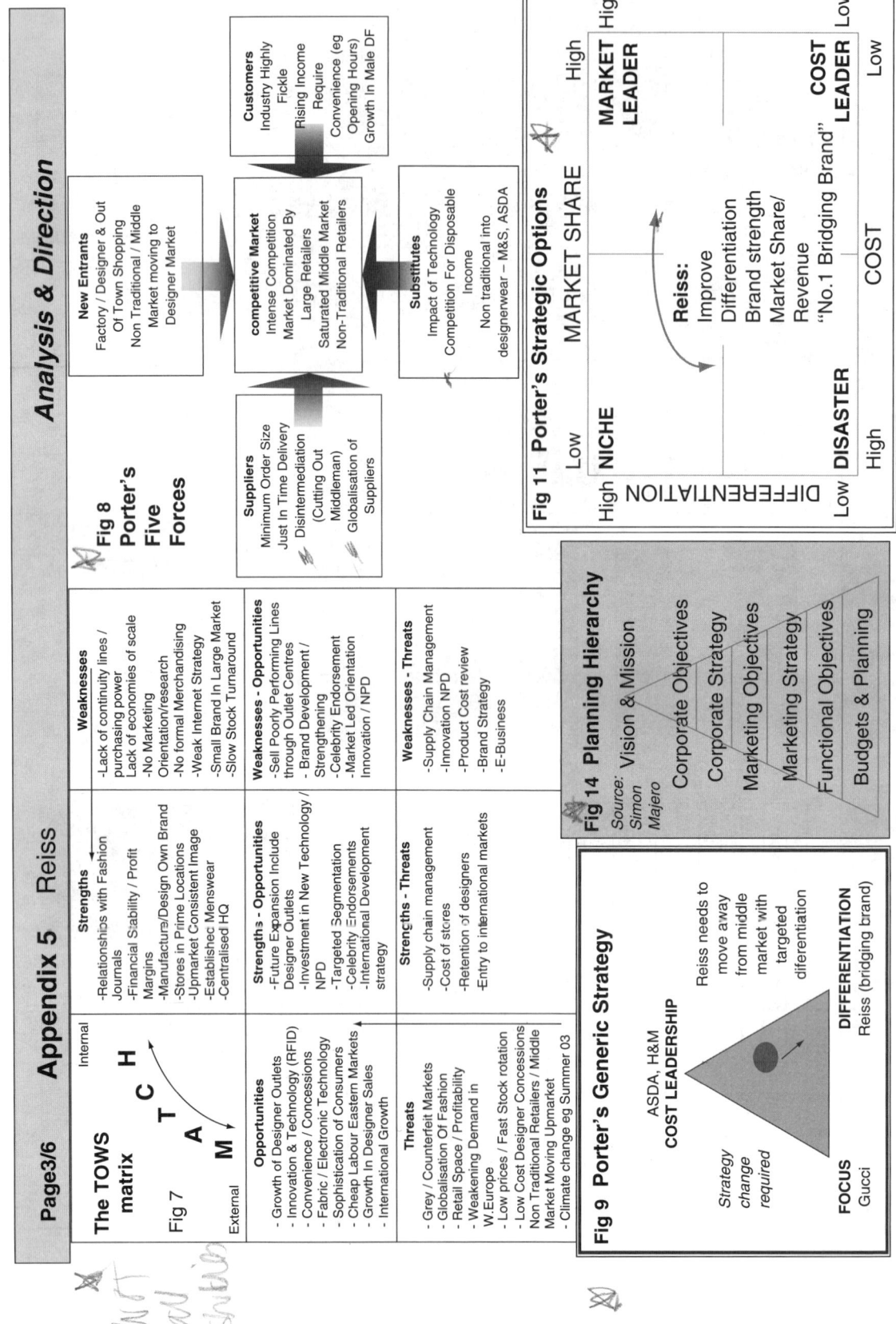

Page 3/6

Appendix 5 Reiss

Analysis & Direction

The TOWS matrix

Fig 7

Internal

T O W S
C H
A
M

External

Strengths
- Relationships with Fashion Journals
- Financial Stability / Profit Margins
- Manufacture/Design Own Brand
- Stores in Prime Locations
- Upmarket Consistent Image
- Establishec Menswear
- Centralised HQ

Weaknesses
- Lack of continuity lines / purchasing power
- Lack of economies of scale
- No Marketing Orientation/research
- No formal Merchandising
- Weak Internet Strategy
- Small Brand In Large Market
- Slow Stock Turnaround

Opportunities
- Growth of Designer Outlets
- Innovation & Technology (RFID)
- Convenience / Concessions
- Fabric / Electronic Technology
- Sophistication of Consumers
- Cheap Labour Eastern Markets
- Growth In Designer Sales
- International Growth

Threats
- Grey / Counterfeit Markets
- Globalisation Of Fashion
- Retail Space / Profitability
- Weakening Demand in W.Europe
- Low prices / Fast Stock rotation
- Low Cost Designer Concessions Non Traditional Retailers / Middle Market Moving Upmarket
- Climate change eg Summer 03

Strengths - Opportunities
- Future Expansion Include Designer Outlets
- Investment in New Technology / NPD
- Targeted Segmentation
- Celebrity Endorsements
- International Development strategy

Strengths - Threats
- Supply chain management
- Cost of stores
- Retention of designers
- Entry to international markets

Weaknesses - Opportunities
- Sell Poorly Performing Lines through Outlet Centres
- Brand Development / Strengthening
- Celebrity Endorsement
- Market Led Orientation Innovation / NPD

Weaknesses - Threats
- Supply Chain Management
- Innovation NPD
- Product Cost review
- Brand Strategy
- E-Business

New Entrants
Factory / Designer & Out Of Town Shopping Non Traditional / Middle Market moving to Designer Market

Suppliers
Minimum Order Size
Just In Time Delivery
Disintermediation (Cutting Out Middleman)
Globalisation of Suppliers

competitive Market
Intense Competition
Market Dominated By Large Retailers
Saturated Middle Market
Non-Traditional Retailers

Customers
Industry Highly Fickle
Rising Income
Require Convenience (eg Opening Hours)
Growth In Male DF

Substitutes
Impact of Technology
Competition For Disposable Income
Non traditional into designerwear – M&S, ASDA

Fig 8 Porter's Five Forces

Fig 11 Porter's Strategic Options

MARKET SHARE
Low   High

DIFFERENTIATION
High   Low

NICHE

MARKET LEADER   High

COST LEADER   Low

DISASTER   High

COST

Reiss:
Improve
Differentiation
Brand strength
Market Share/ Revenue
"No.1 Bridging Brand"

Fig 14 Planning Hierarchy

Source: Simon Majero

Vision & Mission
Corporate Objectives
Corporate Strategy
Marketing Objectives
Marketing Strategy
Functional Objectives
Budgets & Planning

Fig 9 Porter's Generic Strategy

Strategy change required

COST LEADERSHIP
ASDA, H&M

DIFFERENTIATION
Reiss (bridging brand)

FOCUS
Gucci

Reiss needs to move away from middle market with targeted differentiation

Direction

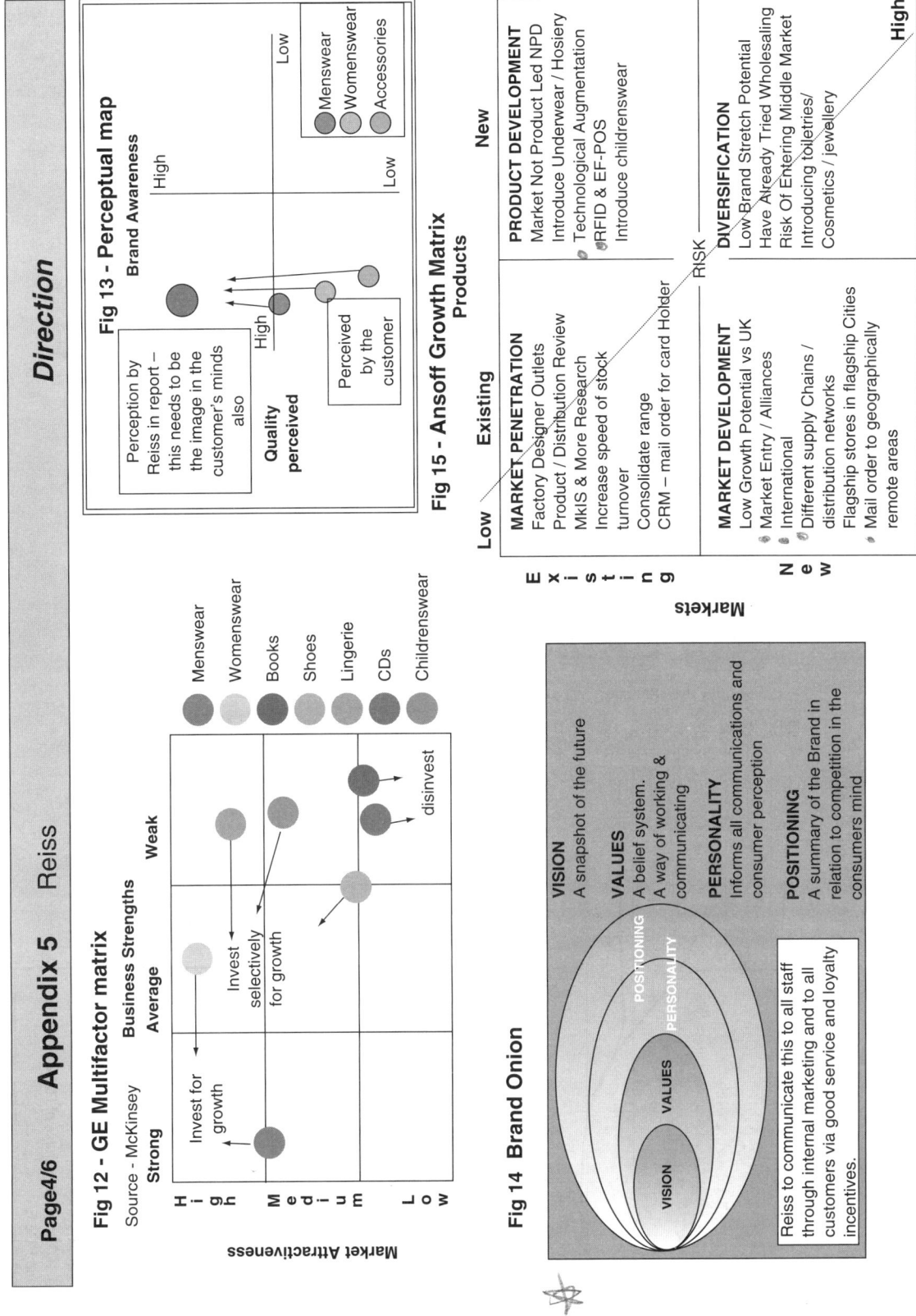

Fig 12 - GE Multifactor matrix

Source - McKinsey

Business Strengths

Strong   Average   Weak

Invest for growth

Invest selectively for growth

disinvest

Market Attractiveness

High / Medium / Low

Menswear
Womenswear
Books
Shoes
Lingerie
CDs
Childrenswear

Fig 13 - Perceptual map

Brand Awareness

High   Low

Perception by Reiss in report – this needs to be the image in the customer's minds also

Quality perceived

High   Low

Perceived by the customer

Menswear
Womenswear
Accessories

Fig 15 - Ansoff Growth Matrix

Products

Existing   New

MARKET PENETRATION
Factory Designer Outlets
Product / Distribution Review
MkIS & More Research
Increase speed of stock turnover
Consolidate range
CRM – mail order for card Holder

PRODUCT DEVELOPMENT
Market Not Product Led NPD
Introduce Underwear / Hosiery
Technological Augmentation
RFID & EF-POS
Introduce childrenswear

MARKET DEVELOPMENT
Low Growth Potential vs UK
Market Entry / Alliances
International
Different supply Chains / distribution networks
Flagship stores in flagship Cities
Mail order to geographically remote areas

DIVERSIFICATION
Low-Brand Stretch Potential
Have Already Tried Wholesaling
Risk Of Entering Middle Market
Introducing toiletries/
Cosmetics / jewellery

RISK   Low   High

Existing / New

Markets

Fig 14 Brand Onion

POSITIONING
PERSONALITY
VALUES
VISION

VISION
A snapshot of the future

VALUES
A belief system.
A way of working & communicating

PERSONALITY
Informs all communications and consumer perception

POSITIONING
A summary of the Brand in relation to competition in the consumers mind

Reiss to communicate this to all staff through internal marketing and to all customers via good service and loyalty incentives.

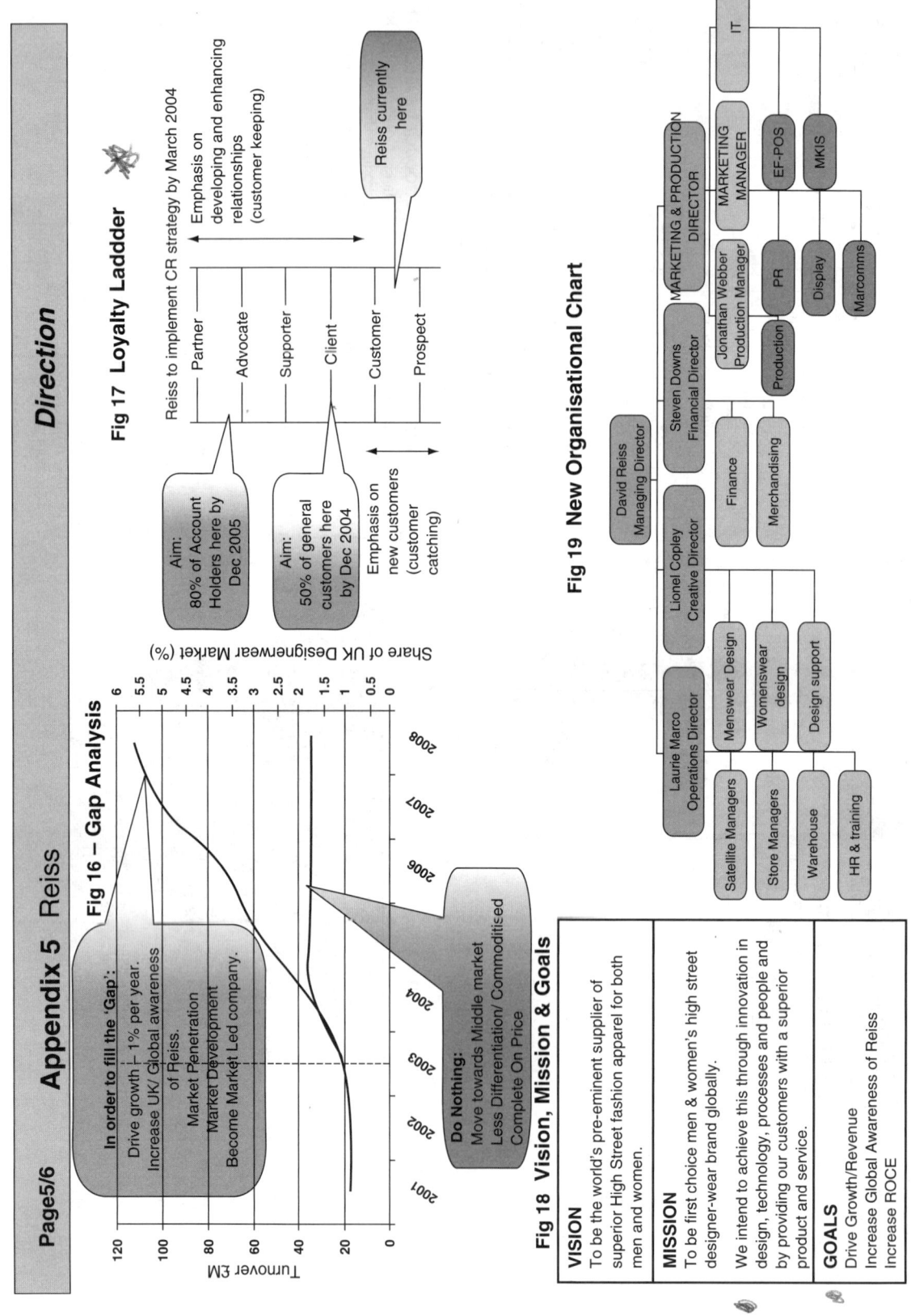

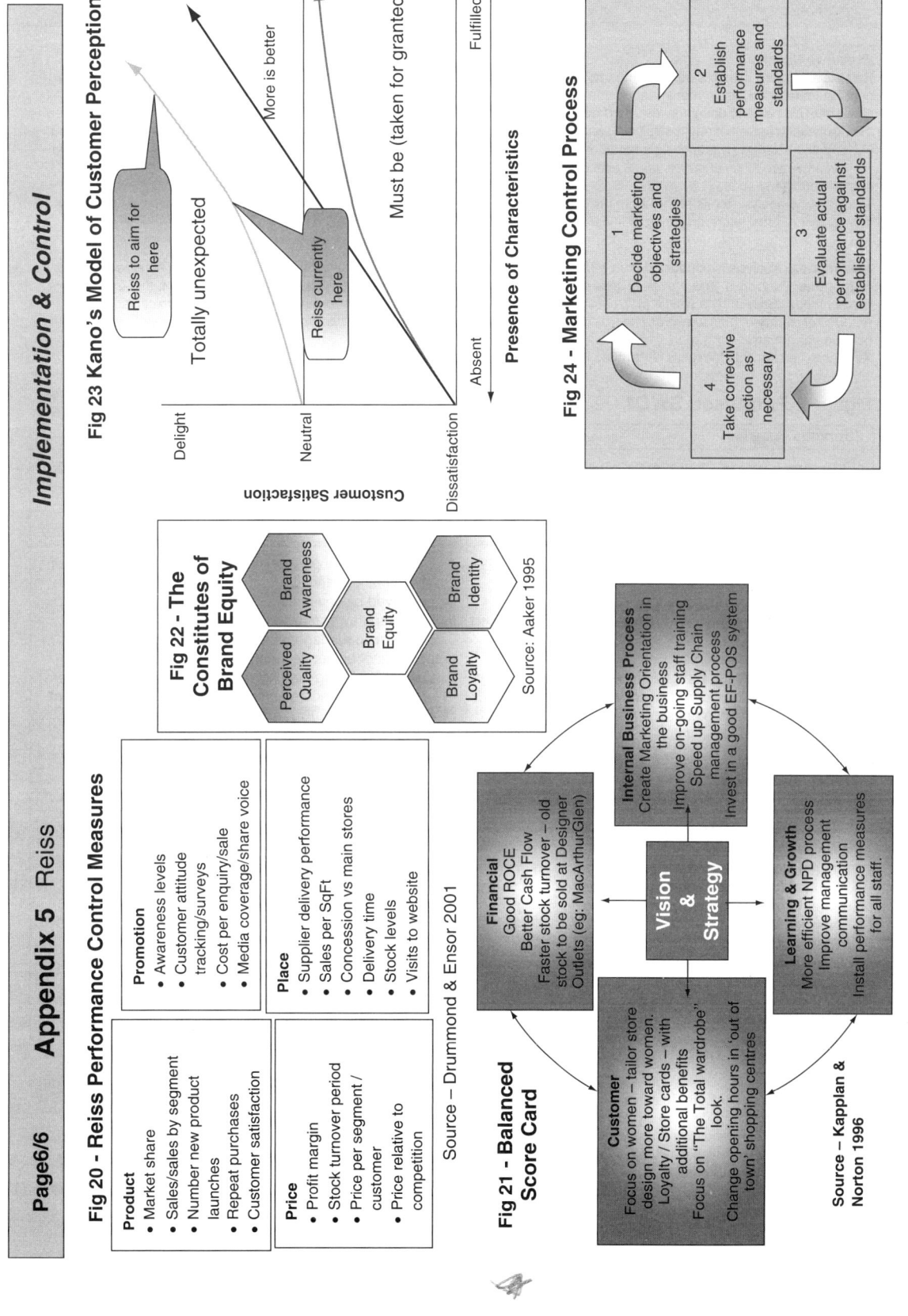

Page6/6 **Appendix 5** Reiss

Implementation & Control

Fig 20 - Reiss Performance Control Measures

Product
- Market share
- Sales/sales by segment
- Number new product launches
- Repeat purchases
- Customer satisfaction

Promotion
- Awareness levels
- Customer attitude tracking/surveys
- Cost per enquiry/sale
- Media coverage/share voice

Price
- Profit margin
- Stock turnover period
- Price per segment / customer
- Price relative to competition

Place
- Supplier delivery performance
- Sales per SqFt
- Concession vs main stores
- Delivery time
- Stock levels
- Visits to website

Source – Drummond & Ensor 2001

Fig 22 - The Constitutes of Brand Equity

Brand Awareness

Perceived Quality

Brand Equity

Brand Identity

Brand Loyalty

Source: Aaker 1995

Fig 23 Kano's Model of Customer Perception

Reiss to aim for here

Reiss currently here

Totally unexpected

More is better

Must be (taken for granted)

Delight

Neutral

Dissatisfaction

Customer Satisfaction

Absent — Fulfilled

Presence of Characteristics

Fig 24 - Marketing Control Process

1 Decide marketing objectives and strategies

2 Establish performance measures and standards

3 Evaluate actual performance against established standards

4 Take corrective action as necessary

Fig 21 - Balanced Score Card

Financial
Good ROCE
Better Cash Flow
Faster stock turnover – old stock to be sold at Designer Outlets (eg: MacArthurGlen)

Internal Business Process
Create Marketing Orientation in the business
Improve on-going staff training
Speed up Supply Chain management process
Invest in a good EF-POS system

Vision & Strategy

Customer
Focus on women – tailor store design more toward women.
Loyalty / Store cards – with additional benefits
Focus on "The Total wardrobe" look.
Change opening hours in 'out of town' shopping centres

Learning & Growth
More efficient NPD process
Improve management communication
Install performance measures for all staff.

Source – Kapplan & Norton 1996

239

Page 1

Executive Summary

Reiss is a privately owned clothing company, designing and retailing its own label range of mens and womens wear. After taking over his father's wholesale menswear business, David Reiss identified an opportunity to 'bridge' the gap between mass market high street clothes and designerwear, by providing good quality, stylish clothes at affordable prices. In 1987, David Reiss switched the business to focus entirely to designing and retailing Reiss own brand menswear. Following its success, David Reiss extended his 'bridging' strategy by launching a range of womenswear and expanding 'internationally' into Dublin, Ireland. Reiss have grown rapidly, and have 27 retail outlets and 3 concessions in the UK today. David Reiss continues to have a strong guiding influence over the company.

The following analysis looks at the strengths and weaknesses of Reiss in detail, as well as identifying the opportunities that Reiss can consider to fuel future growth as well as some of the threats that need consideration.

Assumption: Analysis is conducted from a UK consumer viewpoint that has experience shopping in Reiss and other retail stores
Definitions: Fashion is *'The prevailing style or custom, as in dress or behaviour. Something, such as a garment, that is in the current mode'*. Style is *'The way in which something is said, done, expressed, or performed'* or *'The combination of distinctive features of literary or artistic expression, execution, or performance characterising a particular person, group, school, or era'* (source - dictionary)
Key: positive elements for Reiss highlighted in blue. Negative elements highlighted in red

Figure 1: Prioritised SWOT

Match strengths with opportunities
Convert weaknesses into strengths

Strengths (high to low)	**Weaknesses** (high to low)
1. Growing business – sales, profit, retail outlets 2. David Reiss – entrepreneurial drive and industry-recognised designer 3. Total control over brand equity. Each element reflects Reiss brand – prime store location, instore enviroment, visual merchandising, product quality 4. Successful line extension into womenswear, largest market segment 5. Concessions in House of Fraser – growth with reduced risk and cost 6. Successful expansion beyond UK into Dublin - gain experience working within 'European' market 7. Excellent creative / design team in house 8. Editorial coverage in consumer magazines	1. Organic growth - no strategy driving the business forward and infrastructure insufficient to support future growth 2. David Reiss – owner/manager potential barrier to change. Lack of international experience 3. No marketing strategy 4. Confused brand positioning – 'Bridging' position between 'Mass market' and 'Designer' identified internally, but not perceived by consumers 5. Low brand awareness amongst consumers 6. No portfolio management - future funding for growth or new launches not defined 7. Lack of market research or marketing information system – no qualified understanding of the external environment, or of consumers. Product not market orientated 8. Liquidity problems from poor stock turnover 9. Lack of economies of scale
Opportunities (short - long term)	**Threats** (high to low)
1. Increase penetration into existing stores 2. Increase number of retail outlets in UK 3. Womens only stores 4. Increase use of Concessions to test new markets 5. Expand into new categories – accessories, personal care, babywear, home furnishings. 6. New fabric technology 7. Extend success of Dublin store and embrace Internationalisation of style – new markets across European cities 8. Franchises 9. Mergers / Acquisitions	1. Intensity of competition for share of disposable income 2. Fickle fashion industry 3. 'Bridging' position being squeezed from above by Designers and from below by Middle market retailers 4. Massively saturated market 5. Change in buyer behaviour towards discounters and designer factory outlets devaluing the market 6. Change in buyer behaviour when shopping – internet, supermarkets, mail order - 24/7 demand 7. Foreign competitors entering UK 8. Extreme weather conditions potential to harm supply of raw materials, increasing cost of goods.

Reiss is a growing, successful small design and retail business in the UK with a number of key strengths: Growing and profitable business. Excellent inhouse design team. Industry recognition for design. Prime retail outlets. Control over brand equity. Successful expansion into new categories (womenswear) and new cities (Dublin). Reiss also have a number of key weaknesses: No corporate strategy guiding the organisation. No marketing strategy. Actual brand positioning is not the desired position as a bridging brand. Low brand awareness. Liquidity issues. Lack of understanding of external environment. Looking outside the business, the market is highly saturated, and the 'Bridging' position is being squeezed. However, significant growth opportunities lie within the existing business as well as further expansion across the UK and into Europe.

Figure 2: Prioritised PEST and implications for Reiss

	Issue	Implications for Reiss (Positive Negative Positive & Negative)
Political/Legal	• European Union • UK Government attitude towards joining Euro • World Trade Organisation abolition of country quotes for textile manufacturing • Bank of England control over interest rates • UK Government international relations • Trading legislation • Town and planning legislation • Germany & Italy barriers to entry e.g. labour costs	• Opening up markets to consumers & competitors. New trading conditions / laws • Impact on financial accounting and cost structure • Increase number of international suppliers • Impact on disposable income available • Trading relations with international fabric & finished product suppliers e.g. Taiwan • Eg opening hours, trading standards, minimum wage, product labeling, taxation • Eg listed buildings available for retail sites, congestion charging • Potential barriers to international expansion
Economic	• Exchange rates • Rising disposable income in UK • Substitutes fighting for share of disposable income • Raw materials & finished goods supplies from international manufacturers (UK textile manufacturing uncompetitive) • Cost of prime locations & buildings rising • Price deflation of Designerwear in favour of discounters • Western Europe economies slowing	• Cost of supplies change between placing order and receiving goods • More money to spend on clothing • Less money to spend on clothing • Open to exchange rate fluctuations. Less control over quality. Less flexibility. Reliant on Italians for specialist fabrics • Increased fixed costs • Devaluing market. Stealing share form 'Bridging' segment • Less disposable income in potential new markets
Social	• Changing working behaviours • Changing profile of UK population - ageing population • Lifestyle more important than age in fashion • Womenswear >50% apparel market and inclined to spend more • Huge number of influences over fashion • Changing attitudes of men towards fashion • Variations in style/product/sizing between regions and countries • Consumers brand conscious – statement of social status • Ethics – pressure groups e.g. anti-fur, anti-sweatshops	• Increasing demand for womenswear, internet & mail order shopping, smart/casual styling • 25-34 target segment in decline. Older segment opportunity growing • New segmentation • Opportunity to grow womenswear and charge premium • Demand difficult to forecast • Core segment demand growing • Complexity in expansion • Need brand to be socially desirable • Social responsibility required in product design & manufacturing
Technological	• Direct to manufacturer relationships via Internet • Increase in use of Internet as media for reaching consumers • New fabrics – non-creasing, non-staining, easy washing, gadgets • Speed to market via EPOs systems, ordering systems etc	• Cut out 'middleman' in supply chain. Increase suppliers world-wide • Communications media • Product line extension • Decreased time to market. Improved product offering. Reduced wastage if retail in sync with manufacturing

Reiss operate in an industry influenced by a huge variety of factors. Both supply and demand markets are ever changing, presenting issues and opportunities. Reiss must develop a Marketing Information System to capture the key influences on the business as well as the challenges and opportunities in the UK and across Europe. Reiss should use this information in developing a strategy by seizing opportunities and avoiding the pitfalls of operating in such a complex industry.

Figure 3: Competitor Analysis
-Porters Five Forces

Level of importance
-high, medium, low

Potential Entrants - HIGH
• Non traditional retailers e.g. supermarkets selling 'premium' brands
• International players
• Middle market retailers launching premium ranges

Supplier Power - LOW
• Manufacturing outsourced - large number of suppliers across the world
• WTO abolition of quotas opens up more suppliers competing on open market
• Specialist fabric/trim suppliers have increased power due to the limited supply

Rivalry - HIGH
• Total retail market concentrated - small number of large chains dominate middle market
• Bridging market highly fragmented - represented by a large number of small players
• Designers partnering with retail stores
• Mergers & acquisitions prevalent - Globalisation of retail

Buyer Power - HIGH
• Very easy to switch between 'bridging' brands
• Easy to trade up to 'designer' brands or down to 'middle market' brands
• Discount/sale savvy

Substitutes - HIGH
• Massive competition for share of disposable income e.g. mobile phones, IT, leisure activities, DIY, travel, entertainment

Reiss operate in an extremely competitive industry. It is easy for new players to enter the market, and for existing retailers to add clothing to their portfolio. The 'bridging' position is highly fragmented - it is intensely competitive to become part of a customers consideration set. Customers switch easily between different categories (few switching costs of trading up or down), and between brands, plus they are increasingly seeking discount outlets or waiting for sales. There are many substitute products fighting for share of disposable income. The positive element is that suppliers have limited power as there are so many across the world.

Figure 4: Porter's Value Chain for Reiss

✓ Strength ✗ Weakness

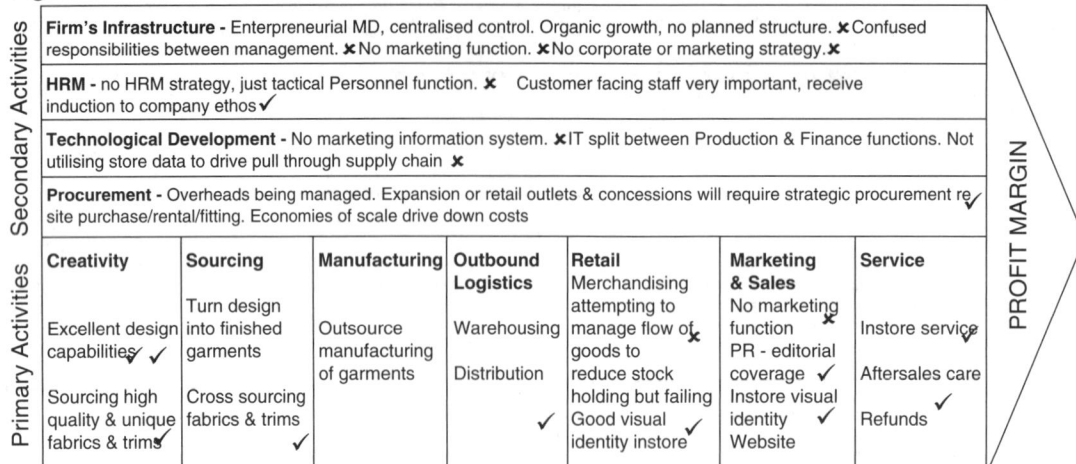

Firm's Infrastructure - Enterpreneurial MD, centralised control. Organic growth, no planned structure. ✗Confused responsibilities between management. ✗No marketing function. ✗No corporate or marketing strategy.✗							
HRM - no HRM strategy, just tactical Personnel function. ✗ Customer facing staff very important, receive induction to company ethos✓							
Technological Development - No marketing information system. ✗IT split between Production & Finance functions. Not utilising store data to drive pull through supply chain ✗							
Procurement - Overheads being managed. Expansion or retail outlets & concessions will require strategic procurement re✓ site purchase/rental/fitting. Economies of scale drive down costs							

(Secondary Activities)

(Primary Activities)

PROFIT MARGIN

Creativity	Sourcing	Manufacturing	Outbound Logistics	Retail	Marketing & Sales	Service
Excellent design capabilities ✓ Sourcing high quality & unique fabrics & trims✓	Turn design into finished garments Cross sourcing fabrics & trims ✓	Outsource manufacturing of garments	Warehousing Distribution ✓	Merchandising attempting to manage flow of goods to ✗ reduce stock holding but failing Good visual ✓ identity instore	No marketing function ✗ PR - editorial coverage ✓ Instore visual identity ✓ Website	Instore service ✓ Aftersales care ✓ Refunds

Reiss' Competitive Advantage is in Design. Reiss recognise the importance of the total brand experience demonstrated through the visual merchandising and store environment. However, Reiss' strengths are not in retailing, shown through their poor stock turnover rates and liquidity issues. Reiss are not a marketing or sales organisation as they have no marking function or strategy and are rightly not manufacturers. Strategic Choice implication for Reiss - Differentiation through Design, not Low Cost operator.

Assumption: Reiss outsource manufacturing operations. Design is inhouse. Note: Porter's Value Chain is modified from its original form as a manufacturing model.

Figure 5: Financial Analysis

Positive   Negative change on previous year↑ ↓

Trends	2001	2002		2003	
Turnover % change on previous year	N/a	+2.75%	↑	+15.13%	↑
Gross Profit % change on previous year	N/a	-0.36%		+23.09%	↑
Operating Profit % change on previous year	N/a	+4.5%	↑	+57.53%	↑
Ratios					
Gross Profit Margin	65.27%	63.29%	↓	67.67%	↑
Operating Profit Margin	6.8%	6.92%	↑	9.47%	↑
ROCE	20.7%	19.73%	↓	28.21%	↑
Current Ratio	0.75:1	0.74:1		0.65:1	↓
Quick Ratio (excluding 'misc' and 'other' current assets)	0.14:1	0.16:1		0.016:1	↓
Stock Turnover	145.9 days	119.5 days	↑	161.4 days	↓
Debtor Days	3.3 days	1.1 day	↑	1.2 days	
Creditor Days	111 days	64.2 days	↑	70.8 days	↓
Gearing	109%	89%		53%	
Turnover per square foot retail space % change on previous year	N/a	-21.44%	↓	-10%	↓
Retained Profits / Value Added	+11.99%	+8.92%	↑	+14.33%	↑

Overall financial **PERFORMANCE,** Reiss are in a fairly health position. Turnover is increasing and profitability is improving due to expansion and apparent lower cost of sales and better control of overheads. ROCE indicates an excellent return on capital and far outweighs interest rates of 4-6% during these years. However, Reiss have serious **LIQUIDITY** problems. There are insufficient assets to cover short-term liabilities. Reiss should at least be able to cover short term debt. Liquidity problems are a result of high stock holding - a risk in case it never sells and looking at **EFFICIENCY,** stock turnover indicates holding of around 3 season's stock at one time. This is slow for a fast moving industry driven by fashion. Debtor days are good, receiving payment almost immediately. Creditor days are a problem, taking over 2 months to pay, indicating Reiss may not be receiving best prices from suppliers. Turnover per retail space is declining indicating growth in retail space is costing Reiss but not generating the same or better £ sales than the smaller stores. In terms of **GEARING,** Reiss are reducing investment from external sources in favour of investment by shareholders. This reduces interest payments but increases risk if shareholders demand repayment. Indicates relative aversion to risk. Could restrict future growth unless mergers or franchises are considered to fund expansion. Finally, Reiss consider the value they add to the supply chain a significant part of their business as the **ADDED VALUE** is increasing each year.

Figure 6: **Porter's Generic Strategies**

		STRATEGIC ADVANTAGE	
		OVERALL COST LEADERSHIP	UNIQUENESS PERCEIVED
STRATEGIC MARKETS	BRAND INDUSTRY WIDE	**Overall Cost Leadership** Mass market clothing retailers e.g. Marks & Spencer, Next, BhS,Tesco, Asda	**Differentiation** Small 'labels' e.g FCUK, Ted Baker
	NARROW SPECIFIC SEGEMENT	**Focused Cost Leadership** Focused clothing retailers ?REISS? e.g. Arcadia (Wallis, TopShop, Topman, Evans, Dorothy Perkins, Burton, Miss Selfridge, Outfit), River Island, Zara, H&M	**Focused Differentiation** Bridging e.g. Duffer, Boxfresh, Carhartt Boss, DKNY, Jigsaw, Whistles Karen Millen Designer e.g. Armani, Paul Smith, Joseph, Miu Miu, Helmut Lang

Reiss do not have a clear strategy - they want to offer 'an individual and aspirational look (a potential differentiator) at affordable prices' (a potential cost advantage)

Reiss are attempting to be part of the 'Bridge' between the Mass market high street retailers focusing on a specific target market who have cost advantages and the Designer market who have differentiation advantages based on a unique design or style. However, although Reiss position themselves against Boss, DKNY, Jigsaw and Whistles, consumers do not perceive the Reiss brand as significantly differentiated enough like the other players in the 'Bridging' or 'Designer' segments, who have a distinctive style which demands a premium price.

It is worth nothing here, the value chain is not set up to be a low cost operator, but for differentiation as the organization's strengths lay in Design.

Figure 7: **Boston Consulting Group Matrix**

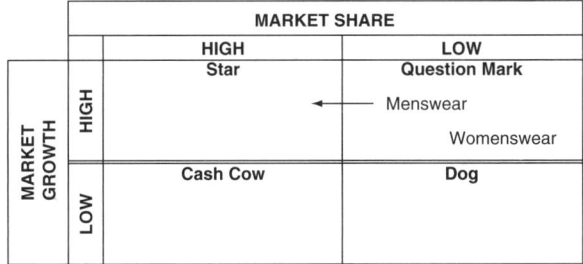

		MARKET SHARE	
		HIGH	LOW
MARKET GROWTH	HIGH	Star	Question Mark Menswear Womenswear
	LOW	Cash Cow	Dog

Assumption: Market definition includes all apparel retailers, not solely 'bridging' brands

Reiss have a portfolio problem as have only one major product line, menswear, that is a 'problem child' requiring significant investment in order to grow. Reiss need to increase market share in this growing market segment in order to sustain investment for future growth and to fund new line extensions like womenswear, lingerie or toiletries.

Figure 8: **Product Lifecycle**

Figure 9: **Brand Lifecycle**

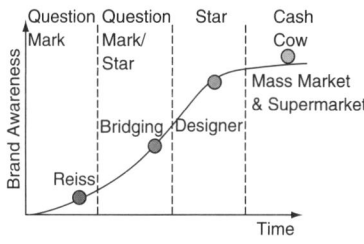

There is no standard Product Lifecycle. Fads enter and exit the market very quickly only lasting a few months. Fashions last for a 'season' (3-6 months). Style is more enduring, fluctuating less and outlasting Fashion. In Fashion, demand changes quickly requiring short lead times to get to market fast. The Style industry have longer lead times as the basic style stays in demand, with added seasonal variations. Assuming industry average applies to Reiss and the fact they have no continuation lines, it takes 40-50 weeks to bring a design to market. This is not optimal for a retailer where fashions come and go in 3-6 months, thus accounts for Reiss's high stock holding. Reiss must address the time it takes to bring designs to market via a more flexible supply chain.

Reiss are relative new entrants into a mature and very saturated market. They have low brand awareness in a cluttered market. Designer and Mass market players have invested significant resources over a long period of time in order to build brand awareness and market share.

Based on Guardian article and my perceptions as a UK consumer

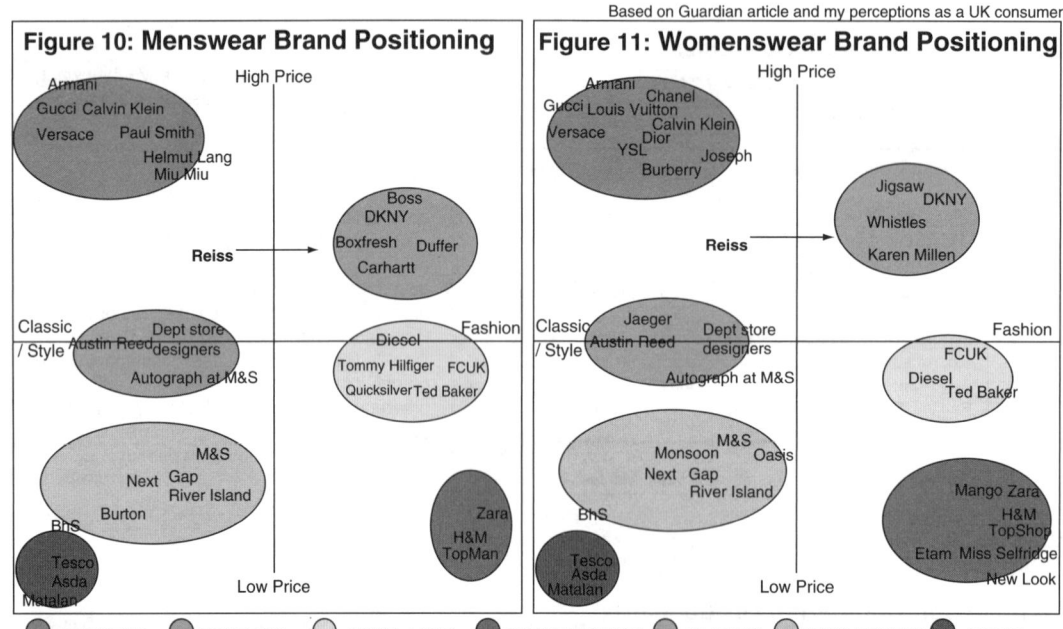

Figure 10: Menswear Brand Positioning

Figure 11: Womenswear Brand Positioning

● DESIGNER ● BRIDGING ○ SMALL LABEL ● CHEAP FASHION ● CLASSIC ○ MASS MARKET ● VALUE

Reiss's desired positioning is not the actual position consumers have in their minds. This is a massive issue for Reiss as a brand's positioning in the market is only ever as defined by consumer perception, and Reiss are failing to recognise the problem, assuming the understanding of the brand is the same understanding customers have. **Reiss's actual positioning** in the market is overpriced versus the 'Small labels' i.e. FCUK and Ted Baker, not 'fashion leading' like 'Bridging' brands like Boss, DKNY and Karen Millen, and not a 'Designer' brand. Reiss are stuck in the middle - a dangerous place, as consumers do not understand what they are buying or why they are being asked to pay a premium.

Figure 12: Value of Reiss brand as a retailer (Aaker 1991:1994)

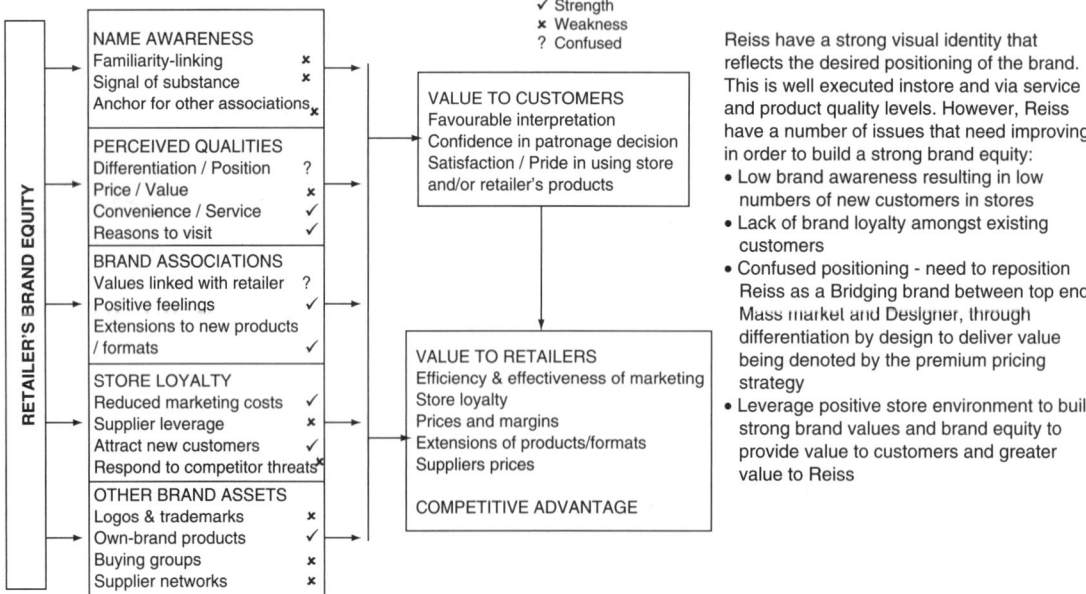

✓ Strength
✗ Weakness
? Confused

Reiss have a strong visual identity that reflects the desired positioning of the brand. This is well executed instore and via service and product quality levels. However, Reiss have a number of issues that need improving in order to build a strong brand equity:

• Low brand awareness resulting in low numbers of new customers in stores
• Lack of brand loyalty amongst existing customers
• Confused positioning - need to reposition Reiss as a Bridging brand between top end Mass market and Designer, through differentiation by design to deliver value being denoted by the premium pricing strategy
• Leverage positive store environment to build strong brand values and brand equity to provide value to customers and greater value to Reiss

Figure 13: Ansoff Matrix

		PRODUCTS	
		EXISTING	NEW
MARKETS	EXISTING	**Market Penetration** • Menswear • Womenswear • Accessories & Shoes • Books & CDs	**Product Development** • Lingerie / Underwear • Fragrances • Toiletries • Home furnishings • Luggage • Sunglasses
	NEW	**Market Development** • New UK cities • Women's only stores • Northern European cities Via internal expansion, merger, joint venture or franchise agreements	**Diversification** • Childrenswear • Babywear • Maternity wear • Larger sizes • Petite sizes • Sports wear

Figure 14: Retail growth vectors (McGoldrick 2002)

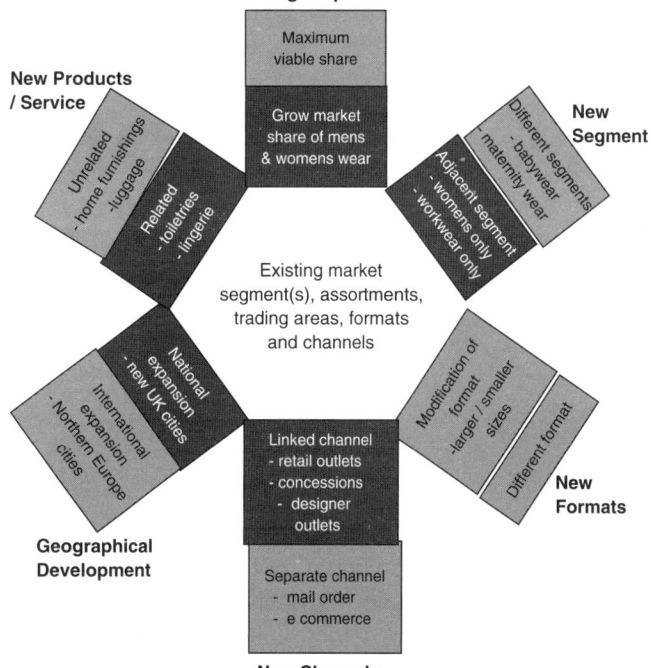

Short / medium term growth opportunities
(2004 - 2006)
- Increase market penetration, sell more volume of existing products in existing stores to both existing and new customers in target market segment
- Open new stores across new UK main urban areas e.g. Bristol, Oxford, Cardiff
- Launch women's only stores
- New product development, increasing basket spend through related added value items such as lingerie/underwear, fragrances & toiletries.
- Tactical use of designer outlets to sell through last season's designs
- Increase House of Fraser concessions

Longer term growth opportunities (2007 - 2010)
- International expansion into Northern European cities e.g. Copenhagen, Prague, Brussels, Amsterdam
- Merger, joint venture or franchise agreements
- E-commerce / Mail order
- New market segments e.g. babywear or sportswear
- Unrelated product segments e.g. home furnishings or luggage

Growth options are based on building a 'Holistic Reiss Experience' that customers use as part of their 'urban, contemporary and individual style' lifestyle. There is significant potential within current markets and product lines to increase sales as well as in new stores across the UK. Reiss add value through Design, which could be leveraged into closely related categories to build this 'lifestyle' such as toiletries and fragrances. Reiss are not yet established enough as a brand to stretch beyond clothing and closely related personal items, and stretching the brand too far before it is clearly defined would risk confusing consumers as to what the Reiss brand means to them.

Conclusions

Reiss have an excellent base business on which to improve significantly and grow. Reiss is a growing and profitable business with an excellent in house team of designers. They have a number of prime retail outlets and have successfully expanded into new categories and cities across the UK. Reiss must recognize the significant weaknesses apparent in the organisation such as a lack of strategic focus, no corporate or marketing strategy, liquidity issues, lack of understanding of the external environment, low brand awareness and a confused brand positioning. Reiss must prepare for the challenges that face the business if it is to continue to succeed in the UK and seriously consider international expansion.

appendix 2
curriculum information and reading list

Aim

Marketing has to be firmly rooted in both theory and practice. Practice informs theory and vice versa. The Strategic Marketing in Practice module is designed to allow participants to put strategic marketing into practice. As the final module at Stage 3, it not only builds on the knowledge and skills developed in all the preceding modules, but also looks for an overall competence in marketing that encompasses all the various subject areas covered in Stages 1 and 2. As marketing is constantly evolving, continuously informed by both academic and business research, one of the aims of this module is to explore the latest trends and innovations relevant to marketers who are operating at a strategic level within organizations. One of the other aims is to understand marketing as an activity, which is important in all contexts (profit, not-for-profit, societal, global). It is expected that participants undertaking this module will be able to add value to both their marketing experience and marketing knowledge. This module therefore does not have a specific syllabus and draws from all the preceding modules and syllabi.

Related statements of practice

Ad.1 Define intelligence requirements and lead the intelligence gathering process.
Ad.2 Develop a detailed understanding of the organization and its environment.
Bd.1 Promote a strong market orientation and influence/contribute to strategy formulation and investment decisions.
Bd.2 Specify and direct the marketing planning process.
Cd.1 Promote organization-wide innovation and cooperation in the development of brands.
Cd.2 Distil the essence of brands and direct/coordinate a portfolio of brands.
Dd.1 Develop and direct an integrated marketing communications strategy.
Dd.2 Lead the implementation of the integrated marketing communications strategy.
Ed.1 Promote corporate-wide innovation and cooperation in the development of products and services.
Ed.2 Direct and maintain competitive product/service portfolios.

Fd.1   Promote the strategic and creative use of pricing.

Fd.2   Lead the implementation of the strategic and creative use of pricing.

Gd.1   Select and monitor channel criteria to meet the organization's need in a changing environment.

Gd.2   Direct and control support to channel members.

Hd.1   Promote and create a customer orientation and infrastructure for customer relationships.

Hd.2   Direct and control information and activities that deliver customer relationships and service.

Jd.1   Establish and maintain a project management framework in line with strategic objectives.

Jd.2   Direct and control the delivery of programmes and projects.

Kd.1   Establish and promote the use of metrics to improve marketing effectiveness.

Kd.2   Create a system of critical review and appraisal to inform future marketing activity.

Ld.1   Provide professional leadership and develop a cooperative environment to enhance performance.

Ld.2   Promote effective cross-functional working linked to brands and the integration of marketing activities.

Ld.3   Promote and create an environment for career and self-development.

Ld.4   Contribute to organizational change and define and communicate the need for change within the department.

Learning outcomes

Participants will be able to:

9.64.1   Identify and critically evaluate marketing issues within various environments, utilizing a wide variety of marketing techniques, concepts and models.

9.64.2   Assess the relevance of, and opportunities presented by, contemporary marketing issues within any given scenario including innovations in marketing.

9.64.3   Identify and critically evaluate various options available within given constraints and apply competitive positioning strategies, justifying any decisions taken.

9.64.4   Formulate and present a creative, customer-focused and innovative competitive strategy for any given context, incorporating relevant investment decisions, appropriate control aspects and contingency plans.

9.64.5   Demonstrate an understanding of the direction and management of marketing activities as part of the implementation of strategic direction, taking into account business intelligence requirements, marketing processes, resources, markets and the company vision.

9.64.6   Promote and facilitate the adoption and maintenance of a strong market and customer orientation with measurable marketing metrics.

9.64.7   Synthesize various strands of knowledge and skills from the different syllabus modules effectively in developing an effective solution for any given context.

Knowledge and skill requirements

There is no formal specification of knowledge and skills requirements for this module. Participants are required to demonstrate a full understanding of, and to satisfy the knowledge and skills requirements specified in, the syllabus modules at Diploma, Advanced Certificate and

Certificate level. The emphasis in this module is more on applying the knowledge and practical skills acquired in the previous modules. The essential skills assessed as part of this module are:

o Analysis, interpretation, evaluation and synthesis of information, including the ability to draw conclusions.
o Identification, exploration and evaluation of strategic options.
o Selection and justification of an appropriate option using decision criteria.
o Establishing the activities, resources and schedule needed to implement the chosen strategy.
o Working with others to implement and control the strategy.

Participants will be expected to demonstrate their awareness of current issues and an ability to make recommendations for a given context. From time to time CIM will publish a list of trends and innovations to guide tutors and participants in their preparation for assessment. Participants will be expected to read widely in the area of strategic marketing as part of their studies at this level.

Assessment

CIM will offer a single form of assessment based on the learning outcomes for this module. It will take the form of an invigilated, time-constrained assessment throughout the delivery network. Candidates' assessments will be marked centrally by CIM.

The format of the assessment will be advised to the delivery network when it is finalized in December 2003.

Recommended support materials

Core texts

Doyle, P. (2000) *Value Based Marketing: Marketing Strategies for Corporate Growth and Shareholder Value*, Wiley.

Little, E. and Marandi, E. (2003) *Relationship Marketing Management*, London: Thomson Learning.

Ranchhod, A. (2004) *Marketing Strategies: A 21st Century Approach*, FT Knowledge.

Workbooks

CIM (2004) *Strategic Marketing in Practice*, Cookham, Chartered Institute of Marketing.

BPP (2004) *Strategic Marketing in Practice*, London, BPP Publishing.

Ranchhod, A. (2004) *Strategic Marketing in Practice*, Oxford, Butterworth-Heinemann.

Supplementary readings

Aaker, D.A. (2000) *Strategic Marketing Management*, 6th Edition, J.Wiley & Sons.

Doole, I. and Lowe, R. (2002) *International Marketing Strategy: Analysis, Development & Implementation*, 3rd Edition, Thomsonlearning.

Doyle, P. (2000) *Value Based Marketing: Marketing Strategies for Corporate Growth and Shareholder Value*, Wiley.

Gilligan, C. and Wilson, R. (2003) *Strategic Marketing Management*, 3rd Edition. Butterworth-Heinemann.

Hooley, G.J., Saunders, J.A. and Piercy, N.F. (1998) *Marketing Strategy and Competitive Positioning*, 2nd Edition, Prentice Hall.

Johansson, J.K, (2000) *Global Marketing: Foreign Entry, Local Marketing and global Management*, 2nd Edition, Irwin McGraw Hill.

Mathur, S.S. (2001) *Creating value: Successful business strategies*, 2nd Edition, Butterworth-Heinemann.

Walker, O.C., Harper, B.B., Mullins, J. and Larreche, J.C. (2003) *Marketing Strategy: A Decision Focussed Approach*, McGraw Hill.

Overview and rationale

Approach

This new module has been introduced to practise the knowledge and skills on formulating a strategy and dealing with implementation issues learned about during Stage 3 and, as such, to provide a vehicle for summative assessment. For those participants who undertake the work-based project, it is intended to add value both for employer as well as participants in applying generic marketing principles at the strategic and global level to their own organization.

The emphasis on trends and innovations in marketing is a mechanism to keep the topics current. These trends, which may be highlighted by CIM from time to time, will be drawn from the marketing literature and other business and marketing publications. It will be the responsibility of participants and their tutors to ensure they are prepared for assessment in this area. They are expected to read widely in the area of strategic marketing as part of their studies at this level.

Syllabus content

The syllabus focuses on strategic marketing practice in organizations and how the trends and innovations in marketing affect it. It is important that participants understand that marketing is not fixed in time and that new developments within academia and business have a profound impact in the way business is conducted. Apart from the guidance given by the Senior Examiner and the CIM, it is up to the participants to keep themselves abreast of current trends and innovations in marketing. The learning outcomes specify the analytical and creative steps involved in identifying challenges, evaluating potential solutions and making decisions that will resolve challenges faced by an organization and take advantage of innovations.

This syllabus is based on the syllabus for the other three modules at this level, to which tutors and participants should refer for additional guidance.

Delivery approach

The delivery approach for this module can be flexible. However it is likely to follow through the key issues considered within a particular organizational problem or case study. Tutors will need to demonstrate a clear ability to impart knowledge on trends and innovations in marketing. It is likely that three hour sessions will be used to cover some of the key areas in marketing. At a later stage, once the case study is distributed as well as the assignment tasks, more detailed consideration of various aspects of the elements as they relate to the problem in question (case or organizational problem) can be debated within the class.

© CIM 2004